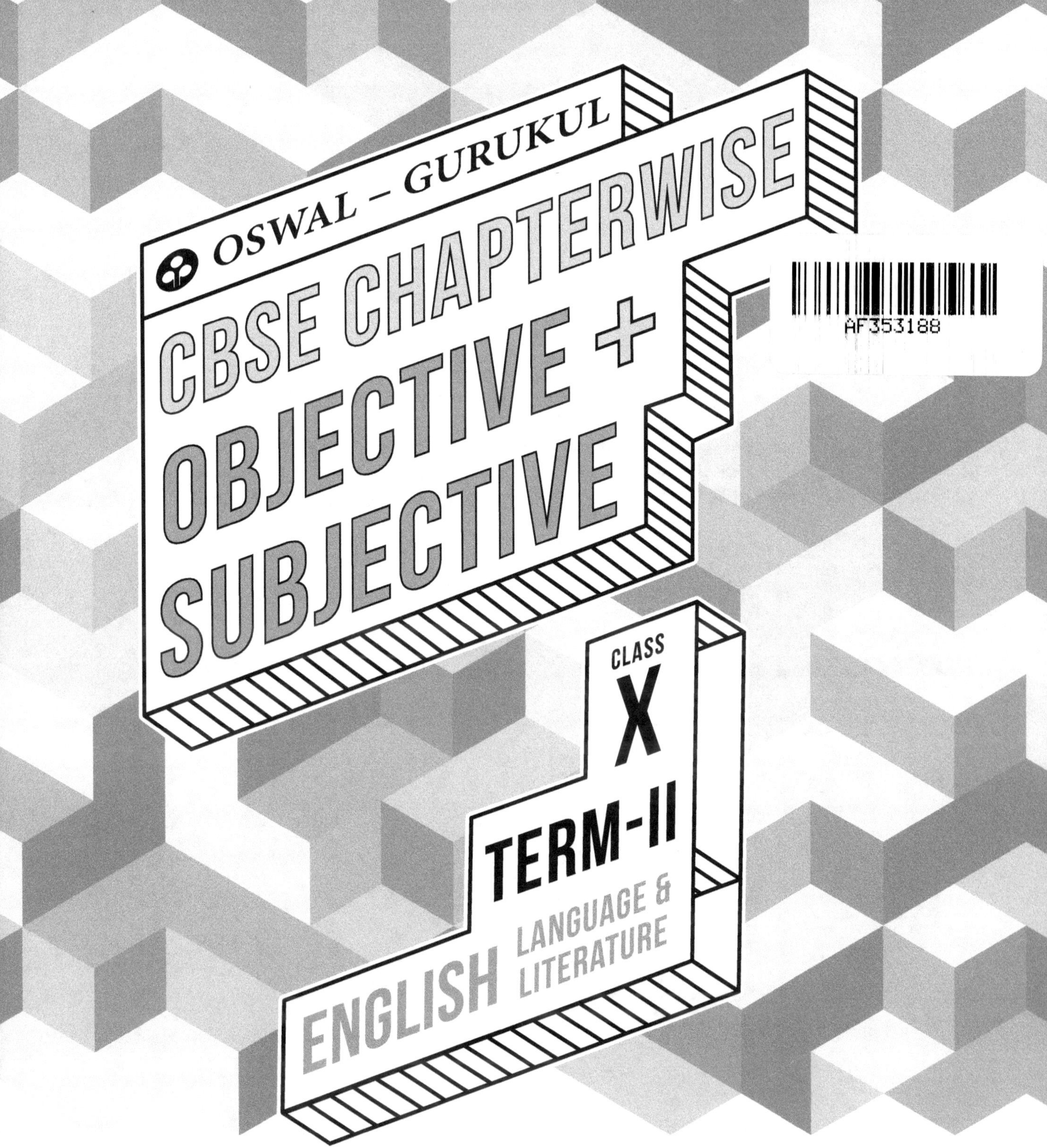

By

PANEL OF AUTHORS

EDITION : 2022

ISBN : 978-93-9256-30-34

PRICE : ₹ 280.00

PUBLISHED BY

OSWAL PUBLISHERS

Head Office : 1/12, Sahitya Kunj, M.G. Road, Agra - 282 002

Phone : (0562) 2527771-4

Whatsapp : +91 74550 77222

E-mail : info@oswalpublishers.in

Website : www.oswalpublishers.com

The cover of this book has been designed using resources from Freepik.com

PREFACE

Board exams are a crucial milestone for every student. For students to perform well in this exam, we have introduced CBSE Chapterwise Objective and Subjective book for the TERM II Examinations for class X. We have designed this book, keeping in mind all the changing scenarios and exam patterns. The content of the book is strictly based on the latest circular (Acad- 51 and 53) issued by the board in July, 2021 for TERM II examinations. This book will help the learners achieve the learning objectives in an easy to grasp manner.

This book contains matter compiled by highly proficient teachers and subject matter experts from across the country. Questions are segregated as per their respective chapters to facilitate easy navigation between them. Every attempt has been made to keep the language of the book crisp and accessible.

We hope you will find this book helpful in your preparations for Std. X board examinations. We would advise you to stay calm and manage your time wisely. Don't be overwhelmed with the amount of resources and study guides available; be selective and efficient in your preparation.

—Publisher

⊕oswal.io

create your own exam sample papers in 2 mins

Prepare a chapter, take practice test & get —— evaluated to perform better ——

Create unlimited tests based on the latest board paper pattern once you are done practicing the book questions

Scan the **QR code** and get instant access to **oswal.io** for **free**. Just register & get started!

Easy steps to follow :

Step 1 - In a few clicks, you can completely customize your test

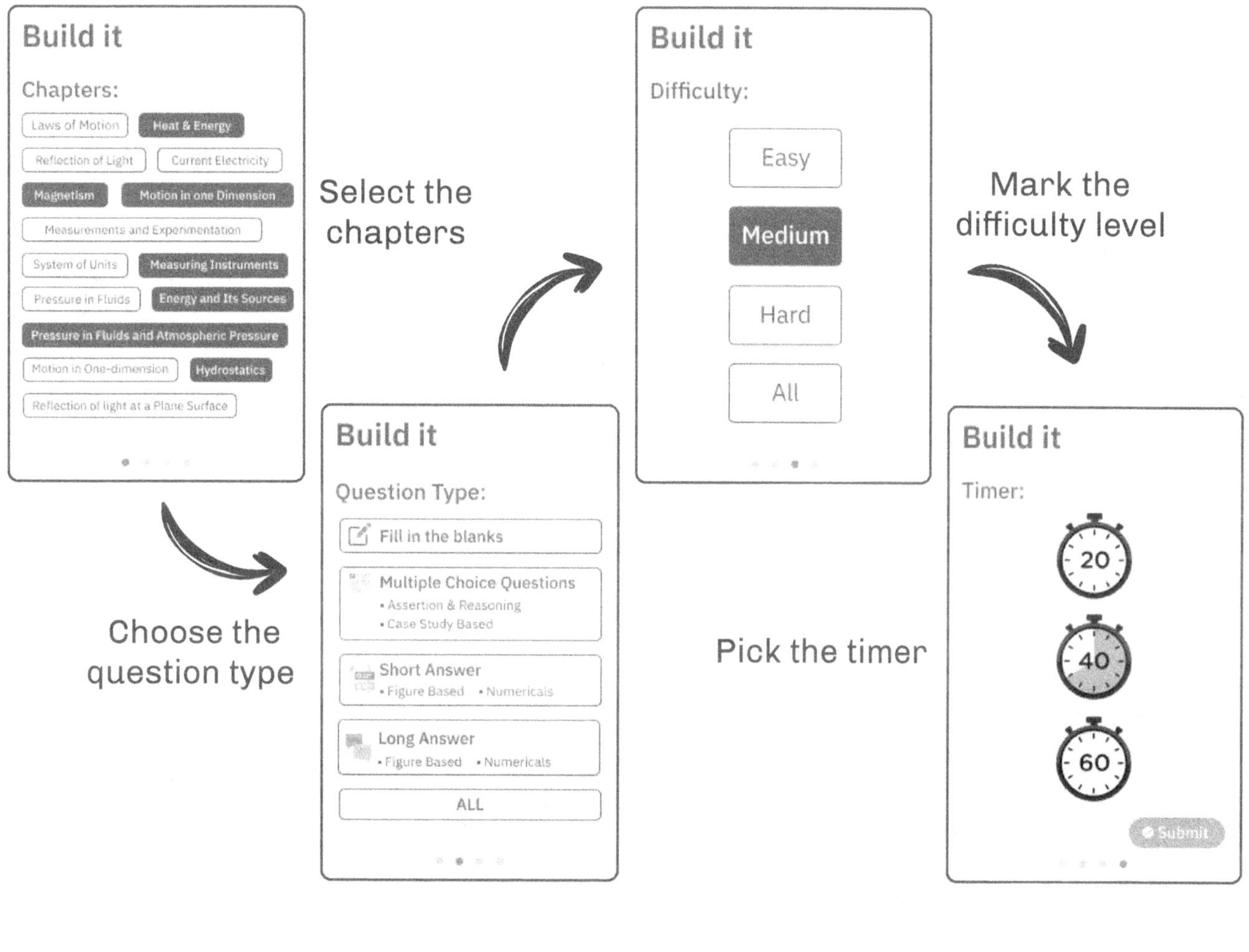

Select the chapters

Choose the question type

Mark the difficulty level

Pick the timer

Access on desktop for best experience

www.oswal.io

Step 2 - Test is based on the selected question type, chapters, difficulty, time

Step 3 - Click on start and type your answers in the given space

Step 4 - Use insert $\TeX$ equation editor to quickly & accurately insert the difficult math/physics/chem formulas

Step 5 - Skip any question if not sure, proceed to next & submit

Step 6 - You will get your result emailed right away

SPECIAL HIGHLIGHTS

SYLLABUS

COURSE STRUCTURE CLASS X
TERM - II

Section	Weightage (in Marks)
Reading	10
Writing & Grammar	10
Literature	20
Total	**40**
Internal Assessment	10
GRAND TOTAL	**50**

Reading

Question based on the following kinds of unseen passages to assess inference, evaluation, vocabulary, analysis and interpretation:

1. Discursive passage (400-450 words)

2. Case based Factual passage (with visual input/ statistical data/ chart etc. 300-350 words)

Writing Skill

Questions focused on the New Paper Pattern, according to the latest circular issued by the Board (Acad-51 and 53) in July 2021.

Study material strictly based on the reduced syllabus issued by the Board in July 2021 for TERM-II examination.

Based on the board's most recent typologies of Objective Type Questions:

Reading

Writing

Grammar

1500+ New Chapter-wise Questions Included

Stand-Alone MCQs Included

Extract Based Questions Included

Short Answer Type Questions

20-30 Words

68. What was Gautam Buddha's life before he became Buddha?

Ans. Buddha was a prince named Siddhartha Gautama, in northern India. At twelve, he was sent away for schooling in the Hindu sacred scriptures and four years later, he returned home to marry a princess. They had a son and lived for ten years as befitted royalty.

69. Why did the Buddha choose Benares to preach his first sermon? ⋆

saw a monk, begging for alms. These sights of suffering, sickness and decay, shocked the prince. He wanted to seek the final solution of all these sorrows and sufferings. He wandered for seven years in search of enlightenment. Finally, he sat down under a fig tree. He meditated there until he was enlightened after seven days. He renamed the tree as the Bodhi Tree or the Tree of Wisdom. He then finally came to be known as the 'Buddha', the 'Awakened' or the Enlightened one. The Buddha gave his first sermon at Benares on the River Ganges.

73. How did the Prince come to be known as Buddha?

Ans. At about the age of twenty-five, the Prince saw

Short Questions Included

Recent Years Board Questions Included

---

to ripe fruits that eventually decay or as earthen vessels that will break someday. Neither a father nor his kinsmen can save anyone. Weeping or grieving cannot bring back the dead to life nor bring peace of mind but can only cause pain and suffering to the grieving body. One should accept death without lamentation, complaint and overcome sorrow and grief thus bringing peace of mind, which is a blessing.

77. Through 'The Sermon at Benares', the Buddha preached that death is inevitable and we need to overcome the suffering and pain that follows. Based on your reading of the lesson, points how you would like to act in the midst of adverse circumstances. ⋆

Ans. Kisa Gotami's only son had died. Grief-stricken, she went about asking people for medicine to revive her dead son. At the behest of a man, she went to the Buddha who said he would cure her son only if she could gather some mustard seeds from a house where no death had ever occurred. After knocking several doors and being unsuccessful, she realised that death was common to all and it could not be avoided. No one can save anyone, so, weeping over a dead soul was fruitless. It was wise to stop grieving and accept the truth.

⋆ are board exam questions from previous years

Summary :

'Madam Rides the Bus' is a sensitive story about an eight year old village girl Valliammai whose way to have fun and pass time is to stand at her door and watch the passersby. Valli, as everybody calls her, loves to watch the city bus stop in front of her house every hour. As days go by, she starts to crave to take the bus ride to the city. She discreetly gets all the information about the fare and the time of journey and after saving enough money, sets out one day in the bus. She pays the full fare and much to the amusement of the conductor, expects to be treated as a grown up. She loves every bit of her onward journey and enjoys looking out of the window at the sights. She is amused by a cow running right in front of the bus. She does not get off at the city but pays the fare again to go back to her village. She is wide eyed at the shops and sights of the city. Her travel back is equally

(a) Elaborate   (b) Fascinating

(c) Unusual   (d) Habitual

Ans. (c) Unusual

3. What did Valli get from watching the stre

Choose one from the following to answer:

(a) Boredom

(b) Fascination

(c) Unusual Experience

(d) apathetic

Ans. (c) Unusual Experience

4. What fascinated Valli the most?

1. The bus conductor.
2. The colour of the bus.
3. The bus driver.
4. The sight of the bus.
5. The bus travelling between her villag the town.

Chapter Summary for Easy & Quick Revision

Prose

Reference to Context Questions

Read the extract given below and answer the questions that follow :

80. *At twelve, he was sent away for schooling in the Hindu sacred scriptures and years later he returned home to marry a princess. They had a son and lived for ten years as befitted royalty. At about the age of twenty-five, the prince heretofore shielded from the sufferings of the world, while going out on hunting, chanced upon a sick man, then an aged man, then a funeral procession, and finally a monk begging for alms. These sights so moved him that he at once became a beggar and went out into the world to seek enlightenment concerning the sorrows he had witnessed.*

(a) Who was 'he' in the passage ? When and where was 'he' born ?

and brief and combined with pain. For there is not any means by which those that have been born can avoid dying; after reaching old age there is death; of such a nature are living beings.

(a) Why was Kisa Gotami sad ? What did she do in her hour of grief ?

(b) What did the Buddha want Kisa Gotami to understand ?

Ans. (a) Kisa Gotami was sad because her only son had died. In her hour of grief, she went from house to house in search of a medicine to cure him. She had become selfish in wanting her son back.

(b) Buddha wanted Kisa Gotami to understand that death is common to all and no one could avoid dying. No one can save their relatives. So wise do not grieve after accepting this truth of dead.

82. *Mark! While relatives are looking on and lamenting*

Poetry

I. *(There is a languid, emerald sea,*
where the sole inhabitant is me—
a mermaid, drifting blissfully.)

1. There is a languid, emerald sea....
Why is the sea called languid?

(a) To create a relaxed and carefree atmosphere.

(b) To give a human attribution to the sea.

(c) To express that Amanda is lazy.

(d) To express Amanda's yearning for freedom and silence.

Ans. (d) To express Amanda's yearning for freedom and silence.

2. What does the word languid not mean in the extract?

(a) Relaxed   (b) Active

(c) Lazy   (d) Slow

Ans. (b) Active

3. How does Amanda describe the sea?

like a mermaid.

II. *Did you finish your homework, Amanda?*
Did you tidy your room, Amanda?
I thought I told you to clean your shoes,
Amanda!

1. For what do you think the speaker is constantly nagging Amanda?

(a) To make Amanda be at her best behaviour.

(b) To teach Amanda refined manners.

(c) It is the speaker's nature.

(d) To deliberately restrict Amanda's freedom.

Ans. (b) To teach Amanda refined manners.

2. Does Amanda listen to the speaker? What does she do?

(a) Yes, she becomes obedient.

(b) No, she doesn't care and continues with her work.

(c) No, she is immersed in her own thoughts.

Footprints Without Feet

---

37. Write a character sketch of the hack driver. ⋆

Ans. The hack driver seemed to be a simple countryman at his first appearance who was ready to help the narrator. The lawyer was in search of Lutkins and hence, the hack driver took him to various places where he might find Lutkins. The next day, the case came up in court. As he was unable to find Lutkins, the lawyer was asked to go back to New Mullion with a man who had worked with Lutkins. The lawyer was shocked to find that the hack driver himself was Lutkins. He felt humiliated and learned not to be hasty in judging a person.

Bill told the lawyer that Lutkins was a hard fellow to catch. He was always up to something or the other. He owed money to many people, including Bill, and had never even paid anybody a cent. He also said that Lutkins played a lot of poker and was good at deceiving people.

⋆ are board exam questions from previous years

to inform him about her son. The lady said she did not know about him. Bill then told that the narrator was a lawyer and came to search her property. Lutkins, mother invited them both in the kitchen and then took out an iron rod from the stove and threatened them to burn them with it. She chased them out and laughed at them.

40. Appearances can be deceptive. Discuss on the basis of the story 'The Hack Driver'?

Ans. When the lawyer arrives at the station of New Mullion, he doesn't like the look of the village. The only thing he finds agreeable is the delivery man at the entrance who looks very cheerful and helpful. He starts liking the village and its villagers after spending the day with the hack driver. However, it is only the next day that he realises that the very same hack driver and the seemingly simple people of the village have made a fool of him. The village that seemed boring and uninteresting to him, suddenly

CONTENTS

SYLLABUS

COURSE STRUCTURE CLASS X
TERM - II

Section	Weightage (in Marks)
Reading	10
Writing & Grammar	10
Literature	20
Total	**40**
Internal Assessment	**10**
GRAND TOTAL	**50**

Reading

Question based on the following kinds of unseen passages to assess inference, evaluation, vocabulary, analysis and interpretation:

1. Discursive passage (400-450 words)

2. Case based Factual passage (with visual input/ statistical data/ chart etc. 300-350 words)

Writing Skill

1. Formal letter based on a given situation.

   • Letter of Order

   • Letter of Enquiry

2. Analytical Paragraph (based on outline/chart/cue/map/report etc.)

Grammar

1. Tenses

2. Modals

3. Subject-Verb Concord

4. Determiner

5. Reported Speech

6. Commands and Requests

7. Statements

8. Questions

Literature

Questions based on extracts / texts to assess interpretation, inference, extrapolation beyond the text and across the texts.

First Flight

1. Glimpses of India

2. Madam Rides the Bus

3. The Sermon at Benares

4. The Proposal (Play)

Poems

1. Amanda

2. Animals

3. The Tale of Custard the Dragon

Footprints Without Feet

1. The Making of a Scientist

2. The Necklace

3. The Hack Driver

4. Bholi

READING

Discursive Passages

1. Read the passage and answer the questions that follow:

1. Have you ever failed at something so miserably that the thought of attempting to do it again was the last thing on your mind?

2. If your answer is yes, then you should understand that you are not a robot. Unlike robots, we human beings have feelings, emotions, and dreams. We are all meant to grow despite our circumstances and limitations. Flourishing and trying to make our dreams come true feels great when life goes our way. But what happens when it does not? What happens when you fail despite all your hard work? Do you stay down and accept defeat or do you get up again? If you tend to persevere and keep going, you have what experts call 'grit'.

3. Falling down or failing is one of the most agonising, embarrassing, and scary human experiences. But it is also one of the most educational, empowering, and essential parts of living a successful and fulfilling life. Did you know that perseverance (grit) is one of the seven qualities that has been described as the key to personal success and betterment in society? The other six are curiosity, gratitude, optimism, self-control, social intelligence, and zest. Thomas 44 is an example of grit for trying more than 1,000 times to invent the light bulb. If you are reading this with the lights on in your room, you will realise the importance of his success. When asked why he kept going despite hundreds of failures, he merely stated that they had not been failures, they were hundreds of attempts towards creating the light bulb. This statement not only revealed his grit but also his optimism for looking at the bright side.

4. Grit can be learnt to help you become more successful. One of the techniques that help is mindfulness. Mindfulness is a practice that makes an individual stay at the moment by bringing awareness of his or her experience without judgement. This practice has been used to quieten the noise of fears and doubts. Through this simple practice of mindfulness, individuals have the ability to stop the self-sabotaging downward spiral of hopelessness, despair, and frustration.

5. What did you do to overcome the negative and self-sabotaging feelings of failure? Reflect on what you did, and try to use those same powerful resources to help you today.

(a) According to the passage, what, from the following, is the greatest human quality to hold on to?

(i) healthy diet and good nutrition.

(ii) perseverance and learning from failure.

(iii) being inquisitive and not giving up on studies.

(iv) self-sabotaging feelings of failure.

Ans. (ii) perseverance and learning from failure.

(b) Select the option that suitably completes the dialogue with reference to paragraph 3.

Simran: I can't seem to be good at anything I try, why is it always me who has to fail and be a disappointment all the time?

Vivekni: Don't sell yourself short! You have ___________

(i) to understand that human beings have their limitations and move on.

(ii) to be realistic in your approach and give up if it doesn't work out.

(iii) all the money in the world to never worry a day about your future.

(iv) shown the will to try something new even after all you've gone through.

Ans. (iv) shown the will to try something new even after all you've gone through.

(c) Choose the option that best conveys the message in - 'quieten the noise of fears and doubts.'

(i) shun all the anxiety and be mindful of your capabilities

(ii) hear the sound of chaos and confusion in your mind

(iii) focus on what's wrong with you all the time

(iv) lower down the volume of all the noises in the surroundings

Ans. (i) shun all the anxiety and be mindful of your capabilities

(d) **What qualities are the key to personal success and betterment in society? Choose one option from the following:**

(i) Pessimism, self-control and social intelligence.

(ii) Guilt, gratitude and optimism.

(iii) Curiosity, perseverance and zest.

(iv) Determination, procrastination and grit.

Ans. (iii) Curiosity, perseverance and zest.

(e) **Select the option with the underlined words that can suitably replace the word *despair* (paragraph 4).**

(i) My car has been in a state of disrepair for a while now so I must get it checked.

(ii) The little kid was in **distress** to find out that all the chocolates have already been eaten.

(iii) Those who were not present at the meeting will be **demanded** an apology to the panel.

(iv) It is hard to believe sometimes that he can have such **disregard** for his family.

Ans. (ii) The little kid was in **distress** to find out that all the chocolates have already been eaten.

(f) **A metaphor is a figure of speech that indirectly refers to one thing by mentioning another, which is not meant to be taken literally.**
From the options given below, select a Metaphor for optimism that appears in the para 3.

(i) spiral of hopelessness

(ii) fulfilling life

(iii) looking at the bright side

(iv) stay at the moment

Ans. (iii) looking at the bright side

(g) **Select the qualities from paragraph 3, that the author wants us to imbibe.**

Being:

(1) grateful (2) pacifistic

(3) optimistic (4) determinate

(5) sarcastic

(i) (1), (3) and (4) (ii) (3), (4) and (5)

(iii) (1), (2) and (4) (iv) (2), (4) and (5)

Ans. (i) (1), (3) and (4)

(h) **Which of the following is meant by the downward spiral of hopelessness?**

(i) disturbing the natural course of events.

(ii) plummeting into depression.

(iii) circling around one thought.

(iv) deliberately trying again.

Ans. (ii) plummeting into depression.

(i) **What does the author advise, in paragraph 5?**

(i) To be socially intelligent and knowledgeable.

(ii) Introspecting failure and moving on.

(iii) Relaxing after a day of hard work.

(iv) Sharing life lessons with one another.

Ans. (ii) Introspecting failure and moving on.

(j) **Choose the option that lists the quote best expressing the central idea of the passage.**

(i) "I think I am going to have to supercharge my optimism to arm myself for the battle ahead." —Rebecca Bloom

(ii) "Develop your character so that you are a person of integrity." —Peter Cain

(iii) "Failure is only the opportunity to begin again, this time more intelligently."

—Henry Ford

(iv) "Our deeds determine us, as much as we determine our deeds." —George Eliot

Ans. (iii) "Failure is only the opportunity to begin again, this time more intelligently."

—Henry Ford

2. **Read the passage and answer the questions that follow:**

1. In the second week of August 1998, just a few days after the incidents of bombing the US embassies in Nairobi and Dar es Salaam, a high-powered, brain-storming session was held near Washington D.C., to discuss various aspects of terrorism. The meeting was attended by ten of America's leading experts in various fields such as germ and chemical warfare, public health, disease control and also by the doctors and the law enforcing officers.

2. Being asked to describe the horror of possible bio-attack, one of the experts narrated the following gloomy scenario. A culprit in a crowded business centre or in a busy shopping mall of a town empties a test tube containing some fluid, which in turn creates an unseen cloud of germ of a dreaded disease like anthrax capable of inflicting a horrible death within 5 days on any one who inhales it. At first 500, or so victims feel that they have mild influenza which may recede after a day or two. Then the symptoms return again and their lungs start filling with fluid. They rush to local hospitals for treatment, but the panic-stricken people may find that the medicare services run quickly out of drugs due to excessive demand. But no one would be able to realize that a terrorist attack has occurred.

3. One cannot deny the possibility that the germ involved would be of contagious variety capable of causing an epidemic. The meeting concluded that such attacks, apart from causing immediate human tragedy, would have dire long-term effects on the political and social fabric of a country by way of ending people's trust on the competence of the government. The experts also said that the bombs used in Kenya and Tanzania were of the old-fashion variety and involved quantities of high explosives, but new terrorism will prove to be more deadly and probably more elusive than hijacking an aeroplane or a gelignite of previous decades.

4. According to Bruce Hoffman, an American specialist on political violence, old terrorism generally had a specific manifesto to overthrow a colonial power or the capitalist system and so on. These terrorists were not shy about planting a bomb or hijacking an aircraft and they set some limit to their brutality. Killing so many innocent people might turn their natural supporters off. Political terrorists want a lot of people watching but not a lot of people dead.

5. Old terrorism sought to change the world while the new sort is often practised by those who believe that the world has gone beyond redemption, he added. Hoffman says, New terrorism has no long term agenda but is ruthless in its short-term intentions. It is often just a cacophonous cry of protest or an outburst of religious intolerance or a protest against the West in general and the US in particular. Its perpetrators may be religious fanatics or diehard opponent of a government and see no reason to show restraint. They are simply intent on inflicting the maximum amount of pain on the victim.   (words 489)

(a) **According to Hoffman, what, from the following, is the greatest threat from new terrorism?**
   (i) political display for public support.
   (ii) ruthlessness and their disregard to long-term implications.
   (iii) inconvenience to the economy.
   (iv) taking many human lives.

Ans. (ii) ruthlessness and their disregard to long-term implications.

(b) **Select the option that suitably completes the dialogue with reference to paragraph 2.**
   Raj: With all the advancement and awareness in science, I fear there's a good chance someone might misuse it with major implications.

   Rahul: That's a possibility of biological warfare which can be _______________________
   (i) deadlier and have prolonged effects than usual terrorism.
   (ii) not as grave and dangerous than usual terrorism.
   (iii) controllable and containable to a confined space.
   (iv) studied as a case for understanding terrorist ideology.

Ans. (i) deadlier and have prolonged effects than usual terrorism.

(c) **Choose the option that best conveys the message in - 'cacophonous cry of protest'.**
   (i) Protesting by crying with tears
   (ii) Demand for seeking attention at a political motive
   (iii) Hushed and harmonious opposition
   (iv) Harsh and loud display of dissent and objection

Ans. (iv) Harsh and loud display of dissent and objection

(d) **What qualities does the germ in a possible bio-attack can have? Choose one option from the following:**
   (i) Controlled form of infection.
   (ii) Targeting certain age group of people only.
   (iii) Contagious and capable of causing an epidemic.
   (d) Short-lived with not much lethality.

Ans. (iii) Contagious and capable of causing an epidemic.

(e) **Select the option with the underlined words that can suitably replace the word** *redemption* **(paragraph 5).**
   (i) It is publicly known that his policies are beyond <u>stupid</u> and counter-productive.
   (ii) The doctors refused to operate further because his body was damaged beyond <u>saving</u>.
   (iii) She always told me to stop looking for <u>answers</u> at wrong places.
   (iv) They were all disappointed that they were getting <u>detention</u> for something so insignificant.

Ans. (ii) The doctors refused to operate further because his body was damaged beyond <u>saving</u>.

(f) **An alliteration is when two or more words that start with the same sounding alphabets are used repeatedly in a sentence or a phrase.**

From the options given below, select an Alliteration that appears in the para 5.

(i) short-term intentions

(ii) panic-stricken people

(iii) cacophonous cry

(iv) religious intolerance

Ans. (iii) cacophonous cry

(g) Select the qualities from paragraph 4, that the old terrorism portrays.

Being:

(1) revolutionary motive

(2) limited brutality

(3) empathetic humans

(4) lacking restraint

(5) politically driven

(i) (2), (3) and (5)   (ii) (1), (2) and (5)

(iii) (1), (3) and (4)   (iv) (3), (4) and (5)

Ans. (ii) (1), (2) and (5)

(h) Which of the following is possible in a bio-attack?

(i) panic-stricken chaos in people.

(ii) organised control of disease spread.

(iii) people uniting to fight terrorism.

(iv) crowded places being the safest.

Ans. (i) panic-stricken chaos in people.

(i) What do the experts conclude, in paragraph 3?

(i) Terrorist acts can be controlled with proper awareness and military control.

(ii) The political and social fabric of a country remains largely unaffected by terrorism.

(iii) Terrorist acts make people lose trust on the competence of the government.

(iv) New terrorism will likely be hijacking of an aeroplane or a gelignite of previous decades.

Ans. (iii) Terrorist acts make people lose trust on the competence of the government.

(j) Choose the option that lists the quote best expressing the central idea of the passage.

(i) How can you have a war on terrorism when war itself is terrorism?

—Howard Zinn

(ii) If we destroy human rights and rule of law in the response to terrorism, they have won.   —Joichi Ito

(iii) New terrorism is the anti-order of the new world order of the 21st century.

—Mark Juergensmeyer

(iv) Do not let the behavior of others destroy your inner peace.   —Dalai Lama

Ans. (iii) New terrorism is the anti-order of the new world order of the 21st century.

—Mark Juergensmeyer

3. **Read the passage and answer the questions that follow:**

1. "Cured yesterday of my disease, I died last night of my physician", says Matthew Prior, a celebrated pharmacologist, while talking about the deleterious effects of drugs in his book, "The Remedy Worse than the Disease". There is no dearth of patients dying of misguided treatment.

2. In this era of drugs we must familiarise ourselves with the term 'iatrogenic disease (physician caused ailment)'. When a physician administers medicines without a complete understanding of the patient's condition, drugs play havoc. A person may become the victim of a worse disease or even lose his life.

3. With Analgin, for instance, special precautions should be taken in case of pregnancy, bronchial asthma, renal and hepatitic dysfunctions and blood-related disorders. It has been banned in several countries, including the USA and Sweden, because of its unexpected and negative effects that lead one even to death through an anaphylactic shock. An anaphylactic shock is a process that leads to a severe fall in the blood pressure, bronchoconstriction, the swelling of blood and lymph vessels and sometimes death because of the loss of fluid in these vessels. Anaphylaxis usually occurs suddenly, in minutes after the administration of a drug. The well-known drug, penicillin, and many other drugs, may cause anaphylaxis.

4. The term "side-effects" is a part of an ailing layman's vocabulary but adverse drug reactions are known only to a more aware and literate patient. Ciprofloxacin, when given for an ear-infection, may cause vertigo and amoxycillin, while fighting a throat infection, may hurt the stomach. Similarly, while chemotherapy given for cancer may lead to indigestion and hair fall, steroids administered continuously may lead to obesity and diabetes.

5. Drugs are meant to eliminate disease. In the quest for avoiding the misery of sickness, man has invented medicines that may themselves cause diseases. The illness caused by a drug may be short-term or long-term. Side effects are short-term and predictable. The unpredictable and bizarre reactions are termed as adverse reactions. A variety of drugs cure many ills but are also known to cause irregular heart beat and even sudden death.

6. A strong sense of responsibility on the physician's part and an attitude of extreme caution on the patient's part can substantially help in covering at least some of the risks of medicines, if not all. There are many factors that help a doctor in his choice and use of the drug. The medical history of a patient, age, sex, personality, environment and education contribute in deciding the course of treatment. The very old and the very young are likely to suffer as their bodies are less tolerant. Older children may sometimes be more tolerant than the adults. The elderly tend to respond better to standard drug dosage. But the lower body size, slow blood flow to vital organs, decreasing metabolic capacity and tendency to multiple physical problems contribute to adverse reactions.

(a) **According to the author, what must we familiarise ourselves with, among the following?**
   (i)   different types of viral diseases and their precautions.
   (ii) ailments caused due to a physician's negligence.
   (iii) working conditions of the paramedical staff.
   (iv) career choices for becoming a physician.

Ans. (ii) ailments caused due to a physician's negligence.

(b) **Select the option that suitably completes the dialogue with reference to paragraph 4.**

   Eric: I don't always believe in taking tablets when I am sick because I am afraid of all the horrible side-effects and reactions.

   Otis: Your fear is misplaced. You should rather ....
   (i)   educate yourself about the drugs and only take the doses prescribed by the physician.
   (ii) look for natural medicines and herbs whenever you feel sick.
   (iii) study and become a physician yourself so that you can understand drugs in detail.
   (iv) learn about the deadly side-effects of drugs and stay away from them.

Ans. (i) educate yourself about the drugs and only take the doses prescribed by the physician.

(c) **Choose the option that best conveys the message in - 'Cured yesterday of my disease, I died last night of my physician'.**
   (i)   Patients making a recovery overnight
   (ii) Physicians losing patients to irrational fear of drugs
   (iii) Patients dying of misguided treatment

   (iv) Physicians curing and then murdering patients

Ans. (iii) Patients dying of misguided treatment

(d) **What are the symptoms of an anaphylactic shock? Choose one option from the following:**
   (i)   Swelling of blood and lymph vessels.
   (ii) Sharp rise in the blood pressure.
   (iii) Hyperactivity and alertness.
   (iv) No signs of bronchoconstriction.

Ans. (i) Swelling of blood and lymph vessels.

(e) **Select the option with the underlined words that can suitably replace the word *dearth* (paragraph 1).**
   (i)   The water <u>supply</u> in our city is severely affected by the drought that happened this summer.
   (ii) Things have changed a lot since the <u>death</u> of our last diligent leader.
   (iii) We took as much eggs with us as we liked because there was no <u>scarcity</u> of it on the farm.
   (iv) His did not keep any <u>record</u> of the dead subjects in order to appease his superiors

Ans. (iii) We took as much eggs with us as we liked because there was no <u>scarcity</u> of it on the farm.

(f) **A Jargon is a literary term that is defined as the use of specific phrases and words in a particular situation, profession, or trade.**
   From the options given below, select a Jargon word that appears in the para 2.
   (i)   iatrogenic   (ii) havoc
   (iii) anaphylaxis   (iv) ciprofloxacin

Ans. (i) iatrogenic

(g) **Select the qualities from paragraph 6, that the author wants the physicians and patients to adopt.**
   Being:
   (1) haphazard   (2) responsible
   (3) cautious   (4) negligent
   (5) fastidious
   (i)   (1), (2) and (3)   (ii) (1), (3) and (4)
   (iii) (1), (2) and (5)   (iv) (2), (3) and (5)

Ans. (iv) (2), (3) and (5)

(h) **Which of the following is an outcome of continuous steroid use?**
   (i)   vertigo and stomach ache.
   (ii) indigestion and hair fall.
   (iii) obesity and diabetes.
   (iv) increased irritation and swelling.

Ans. (iii) obesity and diabetes.

(i) **What does the writer inform in paragraph 3?**

   (i) Anaphylaxis happens to pregnant women only.

   (ii) Many common drugs may cause anaphylaxis.

   (iii) Only rare drugs are known to cause anaphylaxis.

   (iv) Anaphylaxis occurs few days after the administration of drugs.

Ans. (ii) Many common drugs may cause anaphylaxis.

(j) **Choose the option that lists the quote best expressing the central idea of the passage.**

   (i) The power of community to create health is far greater than any physician, clinic or hospital. —Mark Hyman

   (ii) The good physician treats the disease; the great physician treats the patient who has the disease. —Sir William Osler

   (iii) Science has everything to say about what is possible. Science has nothing to say about what is permissible. —Charles Krauthammer

   (iv) Wherever the art of Medicine is loved, there is also a love of Humanity. —Hippocrates

Ans. (ii) The good physician treats the disease; the great physician treats the patient who has the disease. —Sir William Osler

4. **Read the passage and answer the questions that follow:**

1. Social media sites serve as a platform to connect with our friends and relatives. We share our happiness as well as sad moments on social media platforms to let those on our friend list know how we are feeling and what we are doing in life. People 'like' our status, updates and photographs and 'comment' on them to tell us how they feel about it all. This is a great way to socialise in this busy world. It makes us feel that everyone we love and want to be in touch with, is just a click away. However, social media becomes a problem when we get addicted to it.

2. Many people living in different parts of the world are suffering from social media addiction and are bearing their consequences too. Social media sites such as Instagram and Twitter may help us connect with our distant relatives and long-lost friends but social media addiction is distancing us from our immediate family and close friends. People addicted to social media are hooked to these platforms for hours. They do not care if their loved ones are sitting with them or trying to make a conversation. All they care about is who updated what on social media and how many people liked or commented on their posts.

3. Social media addicts frequently check updates and notifications on social media platforms. This can be as frequent as twenty-thirty times in an hour. Viewing a new notification, especially one involving their posts gives them a high. Lack of it, on the other hand, can make them feel sad and depressed.

4. All that the social media addicts care about is to maintain an attractive social media profile. They are mostly seen clicking pictures during social events, family gatherings and even during getaways with friends. They hardly enjoy the moment or talk to the people around them. They are only focused on collecting pictures that can be uploaded on their social media accounts or busy checking and commenting on the status updates of those on their friend list.

5. They post updates stating they are enjoying with their family or having fun with their friends while in reality, they do not even interact properly with anyone around. This is the grave reality of social media addicts. Social media addiction is becoming a big problem. It is ironic how a platform created to help people socialise is actually cutting them off from society.

(a) **What is the negative effect of social media?**

   (i) Connecting with friends

   (ii) Ignoring family

   (iii) Ignoring friends

   (iv) Making friends

Ans. (ii) Ignoring family

(b) **Choose the option that best captures the central idea of the passage from the given quotes.**

> **1.** "Don't use social media to impress people; use it to impact people."
> —Dave Willis

> **2.** "It takes discipline to not let social media steal your time." —Alexis Ohanian

> **3.** "Social media is addictive precisely because it gives us something which the real world lacks; it gives us immediacy, direction, and value as an individual."
> —David Amerland

> **4.** "It's not who you know in social media. It's how well you maintain and strengthen your relationships."
> —Stuart Davidson

(i) Option 1 (ii) Option 2
(iii) Option 3 (iv) Option 4

Ans. (iii) Option 3

(c) **According to the context of the passage, what does a social media addict care about?**
(i) Family
(ii) Children
(iii) Parents
(iv) Update about friends

Ans. (iv) Update about friends

(d) **Social media is distancing us from our immediate __________.**
(i) family (ii) house
(iii) car (iv) garden

Ans. (i) family

(e) **Social media addicts just want to maintain an attractive __________.**
(i) bank balance (ii) results
(iii) profile (iv) life

Ans. (iii) profile

(f) **Social media addicts do not like to __________ with people.**
(i) interact (ii) fight
(iii) argue (iv) exist

Ans. (i) interact

(g) **The biggest issue with social media is that it is becoming ______.**
(i) popular (ii) an addiction
(iii) intense (iv) expensive

Ans. (ii) an addiction

(h) **The synonym of 'bliss' as given in paragraph 1 is:**
(i) sadness (ii) happiness
(iii) misery (iv) ill-being

Ans. (ii) happiness

(i) **Choose the option that CORRECTLY states the two aspects of 'social media', as used in the passage.**
1. connects with friends
2. appreciates friends
3. share happiness and sad moments
4. share address
5. share property

(i) 1 and 3 (ii) 2 and 3
(iii) 3 and 4 (iv) 4 and 5

Ans. (i) 1 and 3

(j) **The antonym of 'repellent' as given in paragraph 4 is:**
(i) alluring (ii) charming
(iii) glamorous (iv) attractive

Ans. (iv) attractive

5. **Read the passage and answer the questions that follow:**

1. The difference between democracy and dictatorship is that in a democracy, people get to choose their leaders while in a dictatorship, a single individual or political entity rules the country. Democracy allows the free development of human personality whereas the other form of government hinders the development of human personality. Both are opposite political philosophies in terms of perception and approach and come with some merits and demerits.

2. The basic characteristics of democracy are equality, liberty and fraternity. It gives freedom of thought, speech and expression. It promises active participation and involvement of the governed in the governance. The chief principle of democracy is that power is implemented with respect to human rights. It makes people interested in the country and its democratic process. In democratic government, individuals' freedom and rights are given importance. Democracy gives right to eligible people to choose their leader but most people make irrational judgements. The majority of population in developing nations such as India is illiterate and the judgement made is not completely independent.

3. In dictatorship, the governed has no right to voice his/her opinion. While in dictatorship, the absolute power is concentrated in the hands of the dictator. A strong and well-run dictatorship can be very effective. It can prove to be better than democracy. But there is a fear that the dictator may become authoritarian and ruthless. As the power lies in the hands of a single individual, it is solely on the dictator as to how he uses the power. He can use it for the advancement of the nation or for purposes like exploiting people, terrorism and so on.

4. There is no guarantee that justice would be served in any form of government. The success of any form of government is based on the selection of rulers or political leaders selected by the people. Personally, I value the dignity of the individual, equality and justice. I believe democracy is any day better than the other alternatives.

(a) People get to choose their leaders in which government?

(i) Democracy

(ii) Dictatorship

(iii) Authoritarianism

(iv) Totalitarianism

Ans. (i) Democracy

(b) Choose the option that best captures the central idea of the passage from the given quotes.

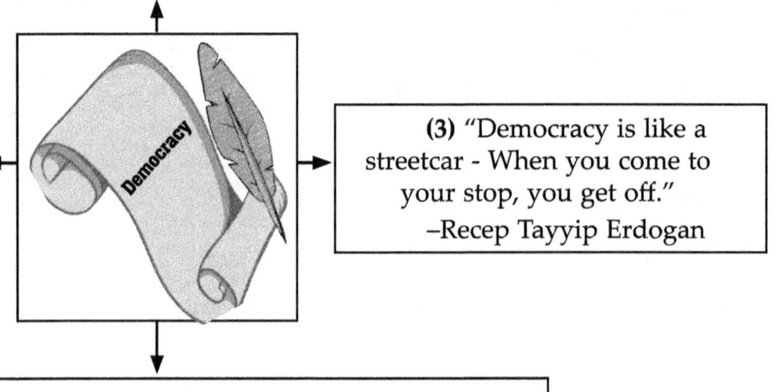

(i) Option 1

(ii) Option 2

(iii) Option 3

(iv) Option 4

Ans. (i) Option 1

(c) Which of these is not a basic characteristic of democracy?

(i) Religion

(ii) Equality

(iii) Liberty

(iv) Fraternity

Ans. (i) Religion

(d) The chief principle of democracy is that power is implemented with respect to human __________.

(i) rights

(ii) duties

(iii) violations

(iv) responsibilities

Ans. (i) rights

(e) In dictatorship, which type of power is concentrated in the hands of the dictator?

(i) Absolute

(ii) Nominal

(iii) Little

(iv) Maximum

Ans. (i) Absolute

(f) In democracy, __________ people chose their leaders.

(i) eligible

(ii) young

(iii) old

(iv) middle-aged

Ans. (i) eligible

(g) What kinds of people are there in developing nations?

(i) Literate

(ii) Illiterate

(iii) Poor

(iv) Rich

Ans. (ii) Illiterate

(j) Choose the option that correctly states the two different aspects of 'dictatorship', as used in the passage.

1. No right to the governed.

2. Dictatorship can be ineffective.

3. Dictatorship does not give freedom.

4. Dictatorship never succeeds.

5. Strong dictatorship can be effective.

(i) 1 and 4

(ii) 3 and 5

(iii) 1 and 5

(iv) 2 and 4

Ans. (iii) 1 and 5

(k) Which of the following words is an antonym for advancement?

(i) Progress

(ii) Growth

(iii) Going forth

(iv) Stagnation

Ans. (iv) Stagnation

(l) Which of the following is a fear related to dictators?

(i) Kind

(ii) Just

(iii) Ruthless

(iv) Uniform

Ans. (iii) Ruthless

6. Read the passage and answer the questions that follow:

1. On the last Sunday of November, among the ruins of the Phra Prang Sam Yot temple in Lopburi, Thailand, a bountiful banquet awaits the guests of honour, none of whom are humans. This feast is held in celebration of Lopburi's thousands of macaques, thought to bring good luck to the area and its people.

2. Located 93 miles away from Bangkok, archaeological evidence confirms that Lopburi has been continuously inhabited for at least 3,000 years—this makes it one of the oldest and most historic cities in Thailand. Due to a millennia-worth of human

habitation, the city boasts countless ancient sites dating from a variety of civilisations and dynasties.

3. From what began in 1989 by hotelier Yongyuth Kitwattananusont, the Monkey Buffet Festival was launched with the help of the Tourism Authority of Thailand. Over the years, the festival has expanded to include a large number of primates. In turn, it has seen an increase in the number of visitors who attend this unique event.

4. In the week leading up to the festival, locals pass out "invitations" to the monkeys with cashews attached to them as a small incentive. But, Lopburi's residents don't stop there when it comes to rolling out the red carpet for their furry neighbours.

5. The Monkey Buffet Festival kicks off with an opening ceremony that includes performances by dancers in monkey costumes. When the monkeys arrive, hosts remove sheets from the banquet tables, revealing decorative spreads of vibrantly hued fruits and vegetables. The macaques jump across tables and climb towering pyramids of watermelon, durian, lettuce, pineapple and more, indulging in the nearly two tons of offerings.

6. Respect for monkeys traces back at least 2,000 years to the epic tale of Rama, a divine prince, and his struggle to rescue his wife, Sita, from the clutches of a demon lord. According to the tale, the monkey king Hanuman and his army helped rescue Sita. Since that time, monkeys have been appreciated as a sign of good luck and prosperity. Lopburi's annual buffet is one way people mark their appreciation.

(Source: www. ripleys.com)

(a) The monkey buffet festival is celebrated to:
   (i) calm down the macaques
   (ii) pet the macaques
   (iii) mark good luck to the people through monkeys
   (iv) conserve the macaques

Ans. (iii) mark good luck to the people through monkeys

(b) Choose the option that best captures the central idea of the passage from the given quotes.

1.	"Appreciation is the highest form of prayer, for it acknowledges the presence of good wherever you shine the light of your thankful thoughts." —Alan Cohen
2.	"Be thankful for what you have and you'll end up having more." —Oprah Winfrey
3.	"You won't be happy with more until you're happy with what you've got." —Viki King
4.	"We should all be thankful for those people who rekindle the inner spirit." —Albert Schweitzer

   (i) Option 1   (ii) Option 2
   (iii) Option 3   (iv) Option 4

Ans. (i) Option 1

(c) The traditional monkey buffet festival holds relevance from:
   (i) a 2000-year-old epic tale of Lord Rama
   (ii) the episode when Rama rescued Sita with the help of King Hanuman
   (iii) the episode when King Hanuman had rescued Sita from the demon God
   (iv) the episode of offering food to the monkey in epic tales

Ans. (i) a 2000-year-old epic tale of Rama

(d) Lopburi, Thailand is famous:
   (i) for many ancient sites
   (ii) as a seat of many civilisations and dynasties
   (iii) for the Monkey Buffet Festival
   (iv) all of the above

Ans. (iii) for the Monkey Buffet Festival

(e) The locals attach cashew to the invitations to:
   (i) invite the monkeys
   (ii) attract monkeys
   (iii) feed the monkeys
   (iv) distract the monkeys

Ans. (i) invite the monkeys

(f) The residents of Lopburi make the buffet special by:
   (i) arranging the food in pyramids
   (ii) arranging the food in a decorative spread
   (iii) attaching cashew to the invitation
   (iv) both (i) and (ii)

Ans. (iv) both (i) and (ii)

(g) Lopburi's annual buffet is to appreciate _____ for their role in the epic called Ramayan.

(i) the people   (ii) the kings

(iii) the soldiers   (iv) the monkeys

Ans. (iv) the monkeys

(h) Choose the option that CORRECTLY states the two aspects related to appreciation in the passage.

1. Appreciation of humans by animals with a festival.
2. Appreciation of animals by inviting them to a feast.
3. Appreciation of primitive humans by the modern humans.
4. Appreciating the macaques through a feast to bring good luck and fortune.
5. Appreciation of the macaques by giving them bananas.

(i) 1 and 4   (ii) 2 and 3

(iii) 2 and 4   (iv) 3 and 5

Ans. (iii) 2 and 4

(i) Identify a word from the passage which means the opposite of 'inadequate'.

(i) arrange   (ii) towering

(iii) vibrant   (iv) bountiful

Ans. (iv) bountiful

(j) The Monkey Buffet Festival owes its commencement to:

(i) the locals

(ii) the earlier kings

(iii) hotelier Yongyuth Kitwattananusont

(iv) the monkey tamers

Ans. (iii) hotelier Yongyuth Kitwattananusont

7. Read the passage and answer the questions that follow:

1. Till 1988, the Pamban Bridge was the only surface transport that connected Tamil Nadu's island of Rameswaram to the mainland. Said to be an engineering marvel, the Pamban Bridge was once India's longest sea bridge, till the Bandra-Worli sea link came up in 2009. What makes Pamban Bridge more wonderful is that it was built more than 100 years ago.

2. The 2.057 km long bridge, also known as Bridge No. 346 in Indian Railway reference, consists of over 140 spans. The amazing feature of a double-leaf section that can be raised to allow movement of ships and boats was designed by German engineer Scherzer. The 114th span, midway along the bridge, is called the Scherzer span.

3. Interestingly, the Scherzer span is now being replaced by a modern one to improve the life of the bridge. Pamban Bridge is a cantilever bridge, that has structures that project horizontally into space, supported only on one end.

4. Until recently, the two leaves of the bridge were opened manually using levers by workers, says Indian Railways. Following cyclone-induced tragic train accident in 1964, Indian Railways installed devices to check the wind velocity across the Pamban via duct. Train movement on the bridge is halted when the wind speed exceeds 58 kmph.

5. The construction of the Pamban Bridge began in 1911 and it was opened in 1914. It was only in 2007 that the railway line on Pamban Bridge was converted from metre-gauge to broad-gauge.

6. According to Indian Railways, the famed Ramanathaswamy temple in Rameswaram and the Pamban Bridge draw scores of foreign tourists and inland pilgrims to the island.

7. Even as Indian Railways' Pamban Bridge continues to be an engineering marvel, yet another railway bridge that is likely to be a stunning site is coming up in Jammu and Kashmir. Said to be the world's highest railway bridge, the Chenab bridge, is set to be completed by 2019. The bridge will be taller than Paris' famous Eiffel Tower and is being built to withstand earthquakes.

8. Yet another bridge that will be a landmark is the Bogibeel Bridge - India's longest rail-cum-road bridge. The Bogibeel double-deck bridge is being built over the Brahmaputra in the Dibrugarh district of Assam and will connect the North and South banks of the river. The total length of the rail-cum-road bridge will be 4.9 km.

(Source: www.financialexpress.com)

(a) The Pamban bridge used to be:

(i) the only surface transport of India

(ii) the longest sea bridge

(iii) operated manually

(iv) all of the above

Ans. (iv) all of the above

(b) Choose the option that best captures the central idea of the passage from the given quotes.

1.	"Mistakes are the usual bridge between inexperience and wisdom." —Phyllis Theroux

2.	"The hardest thing in life is to know which bridge to cross, and which to burn." —David Russell

3. "What is great in man is that he is a bridge and not a goal." — Friedrich Nietzsches

4. "Travel is the bridge between you and everything." —Rumi

   (i) Option 1 (ii) Option 2
   (iii) Option 3 (iv) Option 4

Ans. (iv) Option 4

(c) **Which of the following is NOT TRUE about the Pamban Bridge?**

   (i) Pamban Bridge connects Tamil Nadu's island of Rameswaram to the mainland.
   (ii) Pamban bridge is longer than the Bandra-Worli sea link.
   (iii) Pamban bridge draws a lot of foreign tourists.
   (iv) Pamban bridge is also known as Bridge No. 346 in Indian Railway reference.

Ans. (ii) Pamban bridge is longer than the Bandra-Worli sea link.

(d) **The Chenab bridge:**

   (i) is over Brahmaputra river
   (ii) will be taller than the Eiffel tower in Paris
   (iii) is a rail-cum-road bridge
   (iv) is one of the oldest bridges

Ans. (ii) will be taller than the Eiffel tower in Paris

(e) **Which of the following statements is not true?**

   (i) The Bogibeel Bridge will be a single deck rail-cum-road bridge.
   (ii) The Pamban bridge was constructed in the twentieth century.
   (iii) Chenab Bridge is a railway bridge.
   (iv) The 114th span of the Pamban Bridge was named after its designer, the German engineer Scherzer.

Ans. (i) The Bogibeel Bridge will be a single deck rail-cum-road bridge.

(f) **The bridge that will connect the north and south bank of river Brahmaputra in Assam is:**
   (i) Pamban bridge
   (ii) Chenab bridge
   (iii) Bogibeel bridge
   (iv) Worli Sea link

Ans. (iii) Bogibeel bridge

(g) **The railway line on Pamban Bridge was converted from metre-gauge to broad-gauge in:**
   (i) 2008 (ii) 2009
   (iii) 2007 (iv) 2010

Ans. (iii) 2007

(h) **Choose the option that CORRECTLY states the two aspects of Pamban bridge.**

   1. Pamban Bridge was the only surface transport that connected Tamil Nadu's island of Rameswaram to the mainland.
   2. The amazing feature of a double-leaf section that can be raised to allow movement of ships and boats was designed by German engineer Scherzer.
   3. The Scherzer span is now being replaced by a modern one to improve the life of the bridge.
   4. Indian Railways installed devices to check the wind velocity across the Pamban via duct.
   5. Pamban Bridge is a cantilever bridge, that has structures that project horizontally into space, supported only on one end.

   (i) 1 and 5 (ii) 2 and 4
   (iii) 3 and 5 (iv) 3 and 4

Ans. (i) 1 and 5

(i) **Which of the following words means the opposite of 'started'?**
   (i) Installed (ii) Stunning
   (iii) Marvel (iv) Halted

Ans. (iv) Halted

(j) **Which of the following words means the same as 'eye-catching'?**
   (i) Stunning (ii) Marvel
   (iii) Landmark (iv) Velocity

Ans. (i) Stunning

Case Based Factual Passages

1. Read the passage and answer the questions that follow:

1. Neha is only 11 years old - and should be in school. In August 2009, when she was around one year old, the Indian parliament had passed the landmark Right to Education Act that made education free and compulsory for children between the ages 6 and 14. Neha's parents enrolled her in school when she was six, but she dropped out four years later, before completing elementary school. She had to help her mother with housework and look after her younger siblings.

2. School education in India has had its ups and down over the past few decades but one thing which has remained almost constant is the lopsided ratio between male and female students. Though the scene is not as dismal as it used to be, but we have a long way to go.

3. The All-India Survey of Higher Education published by the UGC last week shows the ratio of boys is higher than girls at almost every level of education. In broader terms, the student enrolment at the undergraduate level has 51% boys and 49% girls. The data reveals diploma too has a skewed gender distribution, with 66.8% boys and 33.2% girls. At the level of research streams also, male students outnumber females. In PhD courses across the country, 80.18% boys and 19.82% girls.

4. One of the most alarming fact is that the number of dropouts at school level is much higher in girls. In rural areas almost 50% of the girl students drop out after high school and almost 20% complete their higher secondary education. The number of girls completing their college education is merely 15% of the total female school going population, while female postgraduates in a rural area are a meagre 2% of that. However, the dropout rate among the girls is much lower in cities.

5. Literacy and level of education are basic indicators of the level of development achieved by a society. Higher levels of female literacy lead to a greater awareness and contributes to the improvement of economic and social conditions. It acts as a catalyst for social upliftment, population control and better health standards.

(a) The purpose of the Right to Education Act 2009 by Indian parliament was to provide _____. Choose the correct option.

(i) free and compulsory food for children between the ages 6 and 14.

(ii) free and compulsory books for children aged 6-14.

(iii) free and compulsory education for children aged 6-14.

(iv) free and compulsory shelter for children between the ages 6 and 14.

Ans. (iii) free and compulsory education for children aged 6-14.

(b) Select the option that is true for the two statements given below.

(1) The dropout rate among the girls is much lower in cities.

(2) At the level of research streams also, male students outnumber females.

(i) (2) is the reason for (1).

(ii) (1) contradicts (2).

(iii) (1) is independent of (2).

(iv) (2) is the result of (1)

Ans. (iii) (1) is independent of (2).

(c) Select the option that gives the correct meaning of the following statement.

"Higher levels of female literacy lead to a greater awareness."

(i) Women form half of the society and will have a lot more to contribute if they are educated.

(ii) Greater awareness should be spread around the nation to advocate for female literacy.

(iii) It has been proven that female literacy is more important than male literacy.

(iv) Female literacy is easier to achieve at higher levels and can be beneficial for society.

Ans. (i) Women form half of the society and will have a lot more to contribute if they are educated.

(d) According to the All-India Survey of Higher Education, there is a skewed gender distribution because____.

    (i) it is far more convenient to educate the male students.

    (ii) the data collected was not a proper indication of reality.

    (iii) girls are not interested in getting education as much as boys.

    (iv) girls are pressurised to drop out at an early age to be of domestic help at home.

Ans. (iv) girls are pressurised to drop out at an early age to be of domestic help at home.

(e) Select the option listing what the given sentence refers to 'the student enrolment at the undergraduate level has 51% boys and 49% girls.'

    (1) The percentage of female undergraduates is less than 49%.

    (2) The ratio of male to female undergraduates is balanced.

    (3) The percentage of male undergraduates is 51%.

    (4) The undergraduate enrolment is skewed towards male students.

    (5) The percentage of female undergraduates is less than 51%.

    (i) (2), (3) and (4)   (ii) (2), (4) and (5)

    (iii) (3), (4) and (5)   (iv) (1), (2) and (4)

Ans. (iii) (3), (4) and (5)

(f) For which of the following programs, the maximum percentage of female students from rural areas are enrolled?

    (i) postgraduate

    (ii) high school

    (iii) secondary education

    (iv) undergraduate

Ans. (ii) high school

(g) The passage lists an example proving that school education in India has _______.

    Select the correct option.

    (i) succeeded in terms of enrolling more female students

    (ii) little to no hope in improving the quality for women's education

    (iii) failed even after the introduction of Right to Education Act

    (iv) a lot of work to do in improving gender disparity

Ans. (iv) a lot of work to do in improving gender disparity

(h) Choose the correct option to answer the following:

According to paragraph 5, 'Literacy and level of education are basic indicators of the level of development achieved by a society'.

This is so because

    (i) literate people may not necessarily mean that they are educated.

    (ii) a developed society is driven by an educated majority.

    (iii) higher the level of education, lesser is their contribution towards the society.

    (iv) development of the society inversely relates to its literacy.

Ans. (ii) a developed society is driven by an educated majority.

2. **Read the passage and answer the questions that follow:**

1. The Indian pharma industry is flourishing overseas, touching almost every part of the world. With low cost, speed and high-quality advantage, India is gearing up to become the hub for contract research and manufacturing. Having a competitive edge is, one thing and maintaining it is another. Canada provides tax benefits up to 6% for research carried out within the country. Others like Korea and China without a large pool of scientists make up by facilitating foreign research in every conceivable way.

2. India does not do any of this and faces many hurdles - diseases that it has been inflicted with since independence like Malaria and TB while Indian companies have only focused on reverse engineering blockbuster drugs from MNCs, overseas scientists have displayed little interest in researching sub-continent specific diseases as there are more profits and public interest in lifestyle drugs such as obesity which in turn fund their research. In the interest of Indian research industry, a decision must be taken quickly on the implementation of data protection laws.

3. India is one of the few countries where data exclusivity provisions are not prevalent. Data protection is a contentious issue, wholly debated by the government and the industry. A pharma company wishing to market a drug is required to submit data to the drug controller to show that the drug is both effective and safe. The first (originator) company that makes the application for marketing approval has to submit its data relating to the clinical trials to the drug controller, who once satisfied that the drug is safe and effective will register it. Another drug company wishing to market the same drug only requires to show a bio-equivalence company. Thus, as per the prevailing laws, the regulator in India can rely on an innovator's data to approve the competitor's product.

4. While the system in general is responsible for maintaining the necessary secrecy, it is not accountable for the same—the competitor gets an unfair advantage over the innovator even when he is clandestinely abusing an innovator's intellectual property. Consequently research-based pharma companies are being forced to undertake vital clinical trials abroad. Huge expenditures are incurred overseas, draining precious foreign exchange when this could be done at home at a fraction of the cost.

(a) The Indian pharma companies prefer to research in ______. Choose the correct option.

   (a) reverse engineering discontinued drugs from MNCs.

   (b) sub-continent specific diseases and their cure.

   (c) cure for malaria and tuberculosis.

   (d) reverse engineering blockbuster drugs from MNCs.

Ans.   (d) reverse engineering blockbuster drugs from MNCs.

(b) Select the option that is true for the two statements given below.

   (1) The competitor gets an unfair advantage over the innovator.

   (2) The regulator in India can rely on an innovator's data to approve the competitor's product.

   (i) (2) is the reason for (1).

   (ii) (1) contradicts (2).

   (iii) (2) is independent of (1).

   (iv) (2) is the result of (1).

Ans.   (i) (2) is the reason for (1).

(c) Select the option that gives the correct meaning of the following statement.

"While the system in general is responsible for maintaining the necessary secrecy, it is not accountable for the same."

   (i) The system assures to safeguard intellectual properties of innovators at all cost.

   (ii) The system controls the intellectual properties but cannot guarantee if it gets copied.

   (iii) The system is not responsible for registering intellectual properties but protects them.

   (iv) The innovators can rely on the system because it assures the secrecy of their intellectual property.

Ans.   (ii) The system controls the intellectual properties but cannot guarantee if it gets copied.

(d) According to the data, overseas scientists don't research on diseases that affect third world countries because______.

   (i) they lack proper funds and knowledge for research in that field.

   (ii) there are more profits and public interest in lifestyle drugs.

   (iii) sub-continental diseases can be deadly hence riskier to work with.

   (iv) other scientists are already doing research on those diseases.

Ans.   (ii) there are more profits and public interest in lifestyle drugs.

(e) Select the option listing what the given sentence refers to.

'Another drug company wishing to market the same drug only requires to show a bio-equivalence company.'

   (1) The other drug company has to innovate from the start.

   (2) The other company can easily market someone else's drug.

   (3) The other drug company can easily copy the formula.

   (4) The innovator can do almost nothing to stop plagiarism.

   (5) The innovator can stop other companies from selling their drug.

   (i) (1), (3) and (4)   (ii) (2), (3) and (5)

   (iii) (2), (4) and (5)   (iv) (2), (3) and (4)

Ans.   (iv) (2), (3) and (4)

(f) How do Korea and China excel in the research field even without a large pool of scientists?

   (i) by facilitating foreign research.

   (ii) by avoiding foreign research.

   (iii) by copying foreign research material.

   (iv) by paying large sums of money to buy the ranks.

Ans.   (i) by facilitating foreign research.

(g) The passage discusses that the Indian pharma industry is flourishing overseas because________.

Select the correct option.

(i) Indian pharma companies are spending money to reverse engineer already successful drugs.

(ii) India provides low cost, speed and high-quality advantage in research and manufacturing.

(iii) Indian pharma industry promises secrecy when it comes to protecting new innovations.

(iv) Indian produced drugs cannot be used in foreign market because of unregulated protocol.

Ans. (ii) India provides low cost, speed and high-quality advantage in research and manufacturing.

(h) Choose the correct option to answer the following:

According to paragraph 4, 'Huge expenditures are incurred overseas, draining precious foreign exchange'. This is so because:

(i) research-based pharma companies are allowed to undertake vital clinical trials at home.

(ii) research-based pharma companies take bribes to undertake vital clinical trials.

(iii) research-based pharma companies are being forced to undertake vital clinical trials abroad.

(iv) research-based pharma companies don't have to undertake vital clinical trials for safety.

Ans. (iii) research-based pharma companies are being forced to undertake vital clinical trials abroad.

3. Read the passage and answer the questions that follow:

1. Scientists understand some of the reasons for sleep. But they do not understand everything about it. There are two kinds of sleep in mammals and birds. One is Rapid Eye Movement sleep, which we call REM sleep. The other is Non–Rapid Eye Movement sleep, which we call NREM or non–REM sleep. The American Academy of Sleep Medicine divides NREM sleep into three stages: N1, N2, and N3 sleep.

2. When people first go to sleep, they are in NREM sleep. The first stage of NREM sleep is N1 sleep. During N1 sleep, people get very drowsy. Some people have muscle twitches during this part of sleep. People are not very conscious of, or aware of, their surroundings during this stage of sleep. Brain monitors identify small, slow, and irregular brain waves during N1 sleep.

3. The second stage of sleep is N2 sleep. People are not at all conscious of their surroundings during N2 sleep. About 45%-55% of total adult sleep is N2 sleep. Brain monitors identify large brain waves with quick bursts of activity during N2 sleep.

4. The third stage of sleep is N3 sleep. It is very deep sleep. Brain monitors identify very slow brain waves during N3 sleep. Therefore, N3 sleep is called slow–wave sleep (SWS.) After N3 sleep, people cycle back to lighter N2 sleep before going into REM sleep. People cycle through the stages of NREM sleep 4 or 5 times each night and enter REM sleep several times during one night.

5. Scientists are not sure of all the reasons for sleep. They know that sleep helps the body heal and grow. Sleep helps the immune system – which helps people fight disease. Sleep helps the infant brain grow. It seems that REM sleep is especially important for babies' brain growth. It also seems that sleep is a time for processing memories. The National Sleep Foundation in the United States says that 7-9 hours of sleep daily is best for an adult. Seven to nine hours of sleep is good for memory, alertness, problem-solving, and health. Less than six hours of sleep affects the ability to think. Getting too much sleep may not be good for people either. Too much sleep is linked to sickness and depression.

(a) The purpose of the research by National Sleep Foundation in the United States was to study the_____. Choose the correct option.

(i) mechanism of how and why we dream while sleeping.

(ii) optimum amount of sleep an adult need.

(iii) immune action in body during sleep.

(iv) impact of sleep in an infant's brain growth.

Ans. (ii) optimum amount of sleep an adult need.

(b) Select the option that is true for the two statements given below.

(1) During N1 sleep, people get very drowsy.

(2) Brain monitors identify small, slow, and irregular brain waves during N1 sleep.

(i) (2) is the opposite of (1).

(ii) (2) contradicts (1).

(iii) (1) is independent of (2).

(iv) (1) is the reason for (2).

Ans. (iv) (1) is the reason for (2).

(c) Select the option that gives the correct meaning of the following statement.

"About 45%-55% of total adult sleep is N2 sleep."

(i) In a 9-hour sleep cycle, an adult goes through 5 hours of N3 sleep.

(ii) Almost all of the sleep cycle of an adult comprises of N2 sleep.

(iii) In an 8-hour sleep cycle, an adult approximately goes through 4 hours of N2 sleep.

(iv) The total adult sleep fluctuates a lot between N2 and N3 cycles.

Ans. (iii) In an 8-hour sleep cycle, an adult approximately goes through 4 hours of N2 sleep.

(d) According to the American Academy of Sleep Medicine research, the Non–Rapid Eye Movement sleep is ____.

(i) divided into three stages based on the difference in brain wave patterns.

(ii) sub-categorised into three types where people can see dreams.

(iii) where mammals and birds make rapid eye movements while sleeping.

(iv) followed by a cycle of REM sleep of N1, N2 and N3 type.

Ans. (i) divided into three stages based on the difference in brain wave patterns.

(e) Select the option listing what the given sentence refers to.

'People cycle through the stages of NREM sleep 4 or 5 times each night.'

(1) People go through N1 sleep several times a night.

(2) People experience N3 sleep only once in a night.

(3) The cycles of N1, N2 and N3 sleep happens 4-5 times.

(4) People do not stay in one stage of NREM sleep all night.

(5) The cycles of NREM happens randomly without any sequence.

(i) (1), (2) and (4)   (ii) (1), (3) and (5)

(iii) (1), (3) and (4)   (iv) (1), (2) and (3)

Ans. (iii) (1), (3) and (4)

(f) On what from the following did the scientists study the effects of sleep in helping people fight disease?

(i) brain growth   (ii) infants

(iii) dream patterns (iv) immune system

Ans. (iv) immune system

(g) The passage lists an example proving that sleep _______.

Select the correct option.

(i) follows only one pattern of brain wave cycles all night.

(ii) is necessary for the growth and health of every individual.

(iii) is beneficial only for over 10 long hours a day.

(iv) is the unconscious state of human body where nothing happens in the brain.

Ans. (ii) is necessary for the growth and health of every individual.

(h) Choose the correct option to answer the following:

According to paragraph 5, 'They know that sleep helps the body heal and grow.'

This is so because:

(i) they have been told so for generations.

(ii) scientists are not sure of all the reasons for sleep.

(iii) sleep is good for memory, alertness, problem-solving, and health.

(iv) too much sleep is linked to sickness and depression.

Ans. (iii) sleep is good for memory, alertness, problem-solving, and health.

4. Read the passage and answer the questions that follow:

1. Elephant babies like coconut oil. This discovery has saved the life of hundreds of orphaned, unweaned elephants, left behind when their mothers were killed, victims of the ivory wars that have catastrophically reduced elephant populations across Africa.

2. The discovery came after two decades of efforts by the renowned conservationist

Daphne Sheldrick, who has died aged 83. She devoted most of her life rescuing young elephants and releasing them back into the wild.

3. When she first made attempts to keep the orphaned babies alive, often at one or two years old, with other milk sources, they remained malnourished and faded into death. It was only after trying every combination she could find that she hit on one baby milk formula from Europe, which contained coconut oil that seemed to work. She and the elephants never looked back, and now more than 230 elephants in Kenya, and many others in Asia and other parts of Africa, are alive, and mostly in the wild, thanks to her hand-rearing.

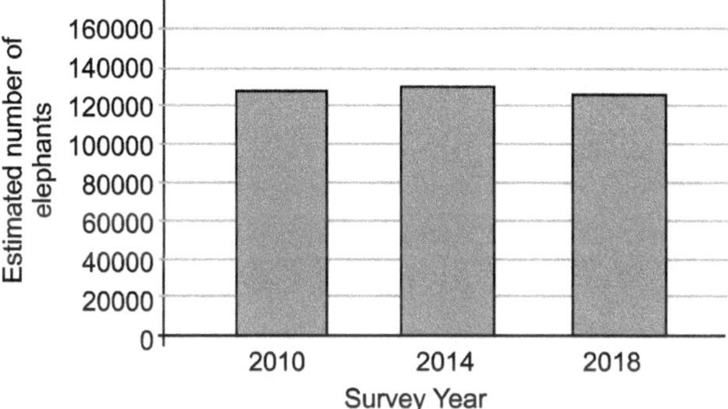

4. Her work grew from her care of orphaned elephants found by her husband, David Sheldrick, chief warden at the Tsavo National Park in Kenya in the 1960s. By the time her sanctuary was well-established, in the late 70s and 80s, each elephant had its own stall, as otherwise they would disturb one another, was bottle-fed every three hours, and was given blankets, raincoats and sunscreen as needed. A keeper slept with each animal under a year old, alternating lest the babies grow too dependent.

5. Often, the elephants arrived traumatised, having experienced the lethal violence and cruelty of poaching. It was crucial, in her view, to recognise their grief and help them to overcome it. "They are emotionally human animals," she told journalists. "You have to think in human terms. How does a child feel when it has lost its whole family and is suddenly in the hands of the enemy?"

6. Throughout her life, Sheldrick championed the ability of elephants to communicate and their capacity for feeling. Once, she recounted, a female wrenched the tusks from a newly killed bull elephant and threw them into the jungle, before the eyes of the poachers.   (Source: www.theguardian.com)

(a) Who was Daphne Sheldrick?

(i)   Doctor   (ii) Teacher

(iii) Conservationist (iv) Writer

Ans.   (iii) Conservationist

(b) How was Daphne Sheldrick able to save the lives of the orphaned elephants?

(i)   By giving them a shelter

(ii) By giving them food

(iii) By giving them formula milk

(iv) By giving them medicines

Ans.   (iii) By giving them formula milk

(c) Choose the option that lists the correct answers for the following:

1. Queenie was a popular attraction for 40 years, giving children up to 500 rides a day, feeding gently out of their hands, and performing acts and tricks for their amusement. She was an Indian (or Asian) elephant, and adults and children alike delighted in her antics, queuing for hours to meet and interact with her.

2. After 40 years of carrying people along the same route, performing the same tricks, and being fed from taunting human hands, Queenie finally reacted in the way her instincts dictated. Although a good-natured animal, her frustrations should have been anticipated, and her actions avoided. In 1944, she trampled her keeper, Wilfred Lawson, to death.

(i)   (1) She was the gentle giant (2) she trampled her keeper to death

(ii) (1) She was gentle and sweet (2) she succumbed to the frustration of humans taunting her

(iii) (1) She was an Asian elephant and (2) she reacted to instincts

(iv) (1) She had long years of service (2) she gave an anticipated end to the keeper

Ans.   (ii) (1) She was gentle and sweet (2) she succumbed to the frustration of humans taunting her

(d) Based on your understanding of the passage, choose the option that lists the inherent need to treat elephants with a greater understanding.

1. Hundreds of orphaned elephants.	2. Hand-rearing did not save many babies.

3. They can disturb one another.	4. Trauma experienced by elephants.	5. Angry animals.	6. Less caring needed.

(i) 1 and 3   (ii) 2 and 4
(iii) 1 and 4   (iv) 2 and 5

Ans. (iii)1 and 4

(e) What did Sheldrick say about elephants while referring to their emotional side?
(i) That they are babies
(ii) That they are weak
(iii) That they are like human beings
(iv) That they are like women

Ans. (iii) That they are like human beings

(f) Choose the correct option that lists the options that are TRUE from the ones given below:

1. The estimated number of elephants was more than 120000 in the year 2010.
2. The highest number of elephants were in the year 2018.
3. The difference between the survey conducted was of 4 years.
4. There is no difference found in the elephant population for any year.

(i) 1 and 3   (ii) 3 and 4
(iii) 2 and 4   (iv) 1 and 4

Ans. (i) 1 and 3

(g) The antonym of 'harmless' as given in paragraph 5 is:
(i) dangerous   (ii) lethal
(iii) fatal   (iv) innocent

Ans. (ii) lethal

(h) The synonym of 'pulled out forcefully' as given in paragraph 6 is:
(i) recounted   (ii) wrenched
(iii) championed   (iv) none of these

Ans. (ii) wrenched

5. Read the passage and answer the questions that follow:

1. For many during the lockdown, newspapers and TV anchors were the go-to source for coronavirus-related updates. News consumption indeed rose at that time, even more so in India, a global survey has found. This, even though Indians expressed less trust in the media than in public officials during the lockdown months.

2. As many as 76% respondents in India said they had watched or read more news of late than they did earlier, the survey by data research firm YouGov found. This was the highest, followed by Japan, with 61%.

3. You Gov ran its Covid-19 Consumer Monitor in 26 countries during the peak pandemic months. Around 220,000 respondents were asked about their news habits in the two weeks prior to the survey. In India, 8,218 participants from 200 cities and towns were interviewed in May and June.

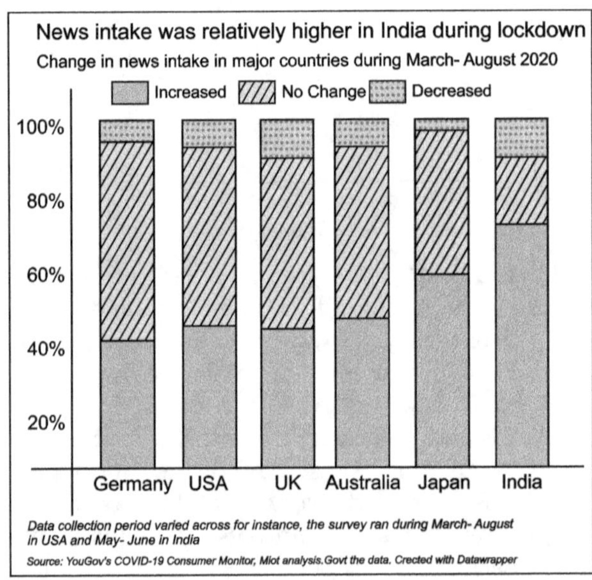

4. Crisis situations such as terrorist attacks or epidemics, in general, induce the public to watch more news, past research has shown. The uncertainty makes people anxious and they turn to the news to get rid of negativity. The YouGov data also reveals that those who held a negative view of the coronavirus situation, in India as well as the world, were more likely to increase their news intake than those who believed the situation was getting better.

5. Even on aspects of personal life, those who were more worried about the future were more likely to increase their news consumption, the survey found. For instance, in India, 59% of the respondents said they were concerned about their personal health

due to the pandemic, and 73% were worried about their friends and family. Among the set of people who were worried about sickness or death coming to themselves or their loved ones, four-fifths watched or read more news during the pandemic.

6. Among those who were not worried, this figure was 74%.

7. The pandemic brought economic woes along with a public health crisis. India recorded a historic contraction of 23.9% in its GDP in the June-ended quarter. This was bound to have an adverse impact on the economic outlook of people. Around 60% respondents from India felt the Indian economy would still be in a depression or recession by mid-year 2021.

8. The bleaker outlook of the economy seems to be coming from personal experience, and not just poor GDP numbers. Most Indian respondents said their household financial situation had worsened in the month prior to the day they were interviewed. Further, 82% were worried that going forward, their finances would be severely impacted, while 68% feared losing their job. Such people were more likely to have increased their news intake than those who were not worried about personal finances or job loss.

(Source: Livemint)

(a) From where did the people get their coronavirus updates?
(i) newspapers (ii) TV anchors
(iii) only (i) (iv) both (i) and (ii)

Ans. (iv) both (i) and (ii)

(b) India saw more news consumption despite:
(i) frequent power cuts
(ii) lack of trust in media
(iii) dependence on multimedia news
(iv) both (i) and (iii)

Ans. (ii) lack of trust in media

(c) Consider the following statements about the survey:
1. conducted by YouGov
2. across 26 countries
3. 220,000 respondents
4. collected data on news habits in the four weeks before the survey

Which of the following options is CORRECT?
(i) 1, 2, 4 (ii) only 4
(iii) 2, 3, 4 (iv) 1, 2, 3

Ans. (iv) 1, 2, 3

(d) In India, _________ were interviewed in May and June.

(i) 8,218 participants from 200 cities and towns
(ii) 8,218 participants from 209 cities and towns
(iii) 8,918 participants from 200 cities and towns
(iv) 8,218 participants from 210 cities and towns

Ans. (i) 8,218 participants from 200 cities and towns

(e) News consumption in India increased by almost 80% in comparison to USA's ____.
(i) 50%
(ii) 40%
(iii) 30%
(iv) oil companies and e-commerce giants

Ans. (ii) 40%

(f) What makes people watch more news?
(i) Terrorist attacks
(ii) Natural and man-made disasters
(iii) Only (i)
(iv) Both (i) and (ii)

Ans. (iv) both (i) and (ii)

(g) The people who felt more negatively toward the coronavirus situation saw _______ news than those who thought positively about it.
(i) less (ii) more
(iii) same (iv) negligible

Ans. (ii) more

(h) Which word in the passage means "hopeless"?
1. Woes 2. Bleaker
3. Adverse 4. Epidemics
5. Economic
(i) 1 and 2 (ii) only 2
(iii) 3 and 5 (iv) 4 and 5

Ans. (ii) only 2

6. **Read the passage and answer the questions that follow:**

1. The Arctic is warming more than twice as fast as the rest of the world, and some scientists believe that thawing permafrost — ground frozen since the last Ice Age — is about to release enormous amounts of climate-warming emissions. In the coldest regions of planet Earth, ice binds together soil, rock, sand and organic matter. This layer of permafrost can begin just centimetres below the Earth's surface. Anywhere cold enough to keep the ground frozen year-round for at least two years counts as permafrost. About a

quarter of the Northern Hemisphere contains permafrost.

2. Warmer temperatures in the Arctic are causing snow and ice to disappear. As ice covering the sea shrinks back, it exposes darker waters that absorb solar radiation rather than reflecting it back out of the atmosphere. This is called the albedo effect, and helps explain why the Arctic region is warming so much faster than the rest of the world. This chart shows how much average surface air temperatures have changed at different latitudes since 1960.

3. The Siberian Arctic town of Verkhoyansk in June registered a record high temperature of 38 degrees Celsius (100.4 Fahrenheit) during a prolonged heat wave. Record fires have also engulfed vast swathes of Siberian Russia, emitting more carbon dioxide than Switzerland or Norway do in a year.

4. The boreal forests of the Arctic have evolved to survive and thrive from occasional fires that would naturally occur every few decades or centuries in the region. But the more recent fires are different, scientists say. They are starting months earlier than they ever have before, and are smouldering through the winter as underground 'zombie fires.'

5. The more intense fires are also burning up peat bogs. A forest might grow back in a few decades and reabsorb the carbon it released when it burned; a peat bog is the accumulation of thousands of years of partial decomposition.

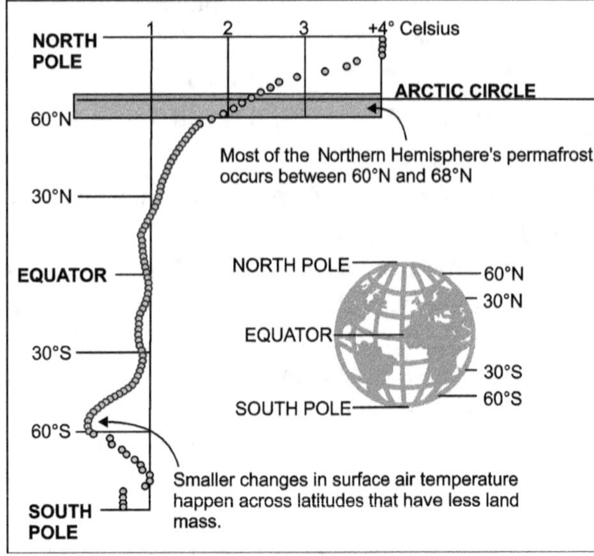

6. The best way to prevent permafrost from thawing is to limit climate change by reducing fossil fuel emissions and protecting forests, scientists say. But once permafrost thaws, there's nothing that can be done to stop the carbon from being released.

(Source: Reuters.com)

(a) **Consider the following statements about permafrost:**

1.	It is ground frozen since the Second Ice Age.
2.	It is ice, soil, rock, sand and organic matter bound together.
3.	It can begin just centimetres below the Earth's surface.
4.	It is year-round frozen ground for at least one year.

Which of the given statements is/are CORRECT?

(i) 1 and 2   (ii) 2 and 3
(iii) 1 and 3   (iv) 3 and 4

Ans. (ii) 2 and 3

(b) **Why is the exposure of darker waters spell disaster for the atmosphere?**
(i) It absorbs radiation instead of reflecting it back
(ii) It can lead to infectious diseases
(iii) It releases carbon dioxide
(iv) It releases oxygen

Ans. (i) It absorbs radiation instead of reflecting it back

(c) **Consider the following statements:**
(A): The Arctic region is warming faster than the rest of the world.
(R): The exposed layer of darker waters is absorbing radiation.
Which of the following options is correct with regards to Arctic warming?
(i) (A) is correct and (R) is the correct explanation of (A)
(ii) (A) is incorrect and (R) is not the correct explanation of (A)
(iii) (A) is correct and (R) is incorrect
(iv) (A) is incorrect and (R) is correct

Ans. (i) (A) is correct and (R) is the correct explanation of (A)

(d) **Which of the following are the consequences of heat waves?**
1. The Siberian Arctic town of Verkhoyansk in June registered a record high temperature of 39 degrees Celsius.

    2. Record fires engulf vast swathes of Siberian Russia.

(i) Both (1) and (2) (ii) Neither (1) nor (2)

(iii) Only (1)   (iv) Only (2)

Ans. (iv) Only 2

(e) How are the fires in boreal forests of the Arctic acting differently?

(i) Starting months before they normally do

(ii) Starting months later than they normally do

(iii) Fires stay for the entire year

(iv) Fires are stronger in intensity

Ans. (i) Starting months before they normally do

(f) What are 'zombie fires'?

(i) Fires in boreal forests which smoulder through the winter

(ii) Fires in boreal forests which smoulder through the summer

(iii) Underground fires

(iv) Fires that lasts long

Ans. (i) Fires in boreal forests which smoulder through the winter

(g) The best way to prevent permafrost from thawing is to:

(i) reduce fossil fuel emissions

(ii) protect forests

(iii) both (i) and (ii)

(iv) only (i)

Ans. (iii) both (i) and (ii)

(h) Which word in the passage means "becoming liquid or soft due to warming up"?

(i) Emissions   (ii) Thawing

(iii) Engulf   (iv) Thrive

Ans. (ii) Thawing

7. Read the passage and answer the questions that follow:

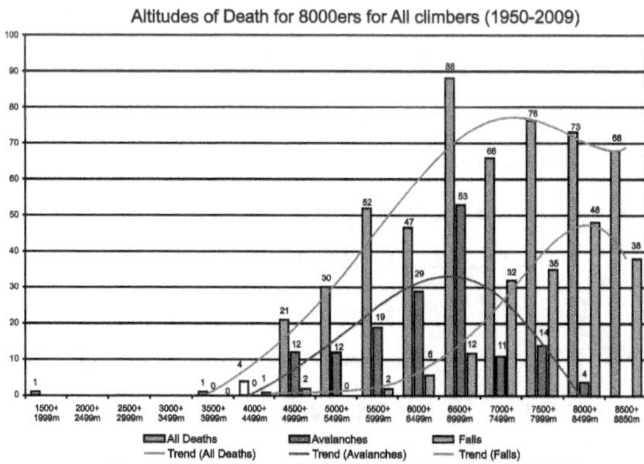

Chart D-15: Altitudes of death for all 8000ers from 1950-2009

1. High-altitude climbing is still a very dangerous task in spite of the availability of oxygen masks and other protective equipment, which modern climbers take with them. These, of course, are indispensable accessories of climbing, but more important than these is the stamina of the climber, which ultimately determines the success of his attempt. Throughout his journey, death is his constant companion, which he can keep at a distance only with his superb presence of mind.

2. He has to tread every inch of the ground with utmost care, for a false step may not only strike him a fatal blow, but also bring disaster to the whole expedition. That is why all expeditions invariably take with them local guides who are experienced climbers and who have a thorough knowledge of the nature of the terrain. Moreover, a huge amount of capital is needed for financing these expeditions, and this is generally provided by governments or rich private organisations.

3. The primary object of a mountaineering expedition is to get to the top of a high mountain, which, in the past has withstood all attempts to conquer it. But it should not be presumed that the expedition is a complete failure if it does not reach its destination. Sometimes operations are temporarily suspended because of bad weather, loss of some valuable equipment or the sudden death of a very important member of the party.

4. Every big expedition takes with it men who are interested in botany, biology, geology and various other branches of science, and these men carry with them equipment for recording their observations concerning the weather, the terrain, and different forms of life in higher altitudes. Other scientists, explorers and expeditionists utilise the fruits of their observations. Thus, every unsuccessful expedition contributes to the success of later expeditions.

5. The British Expedition led by Colonel Hunt would have found their way to Everest much more difficult had not earlier expeditions armed them with useful knowledge about the death-dealing weather which they had to encounter in the vicinity of the summit.

6. To ordinary people, mountaineering need not be a fearful journey in the land of snowstorms, where the brave adventurer is always face to face with death. They can scale less ambitious heights, rest their weary limbs under a quiet shelter and feast their eyes in the distant landscape. In the company of friends they can enjoy an outing near a waterfall or cross into the next valley with haversacks full of provisions dangling from their shoulders. All those who can afford to go to hill station should seek this innocent pleasure, for it can be had without any risk to life or limb. (Source: The Atlantic)

(a) Which of the following is one of the protective equipments used by modern climbers?

(i) Oxygen masks

(ii) Oxygen cylinders

(iii) Protective wear

(iv) Protective medicines

Ans. (i) Oxygen masks

(b) Which of the following ultimately is the secret to successful climbing of the mountains?

(i) Experience of the climber

(ii) Height of the mountain

(iii) Stamina of the climber

(iv) Health condition of the climber

Ans. (iii) Stamina of the climber

(c) Choose the option that lists the CORRECT answers for the following:

1. These people had found their way to the Everest but not much before learning in the earlier expeditions with the death-dealing weather. Who were they?

2. Some people utilize their observations for their future expeditions and they are a group of people. Who are they?

(i) (1) is a lot of travelers and (2) is a group of women achievers

(ii) (1) is a group of scientists and (2) is a group of students

(iii) (1) is the British expedition and (2) is a group of explorers

(iv) (1) is a group of workers and (2) is a few local guides

Ans. (iii) (1) is the British expedition and (2) is a group of explorers

(d) Based on your understanding of the passage, choose the option that lists the CORRECT aspects of mountaineering.

1. A mountaineer has to take each step carefully.

2. A mountaineer need not carry any equipments.

3. A mountaineer has the privilege to see the beautiful landscapes.

4. A mountaineer need not face any harsh weather.

5. A mountaineer is always alone with oxygen masks.

6. The expeditions are financed by the mountaineer himself.

(i) 1 and 3

(ii) 5 and 6

(iii) 2 and 4

(iv) 3 and 5

Ans. (i) 1 and 3

(e) Which of the following is one of the reasons for the temporary suspension of mountaineering expeditions?

(i) Bad weather

(ii) Bad company

(iii) Bad coach

(iv) Loss of money

Ans. (i) Bad weather

(f) Which of the following should be present in a person for going for a mountaineering expedition?

(i) Love for mountains

(ii) Love for nature

(iii) Love for the environment

(iv) All of the above

Ans. (iv) All of the above

(g) Which of the following is always there with regard to mountaineering?

(i) Risk to life

(ii) Risk of money

(iii) Risk of losing the group

(iv) Risk of going missing

Ans. (i) Risk to life

(h) Which of the following words means the opposite of 'energetic'?

(i) Feast

(ii) Quiet

(iii) Weary

(iv) Dangling

Ans. (iii) Weary

❏❏

WRITING

Letter of Order

(1) You are Advaya from, Karawan, Hyderabad. You are the head of the music department of your school. You have to write a letter to 'Sargam Music House' to place an order for Sitar and Tabla. You are a student of ABC International School, Hyderabad.

1. What should be the appropriate subject for this letter?

(a) To buy sitar and tabla

(b) Placement of order for musical instruments

(c) To place an order

(d) New purchases of musical instruments.

Ans. (b) Placement of order for musical instruments

2. What details of the instrument should Advaya include in the letter while placing an order?

(i) The number of instruments required

(ii) The brand makes

(iii) The packaging

(iv) The guarantee period

(a) (i), (ii), and (iv) (b) (i) and (iv)

(c) (i), (ii), (iii) and (iv) (d) (ii) and (iv)

Ans. (c) (i), (ii), (iii) and (iv)

3. What other demands could be made for the delivery of the instruments?

(i) Delivery timings

(ii) Discount

(iii) Delivery place

(iv).Gifts on purchase

(a) Only (iv) (b) (i), (ii) and (iii)

(c) (i) and (ii) (d) Only (i)

Ans. (b) (i), (ii) and (iii)

4. Should Advaya give instructions for transportation? If yes, what could that/those be?

(a) No, It is not in his rights to give any instructions.

(b) Transportation and tracking details should be given from time to time.

(c) Any damage caused during transportation shall rest with you.

(d) No extra charges for transportation will be paid.

Ans. (c) Any damage caused during transportation shall rest with you.

5. Advaya makes some statements regarding payments. Select the appropriate option.

The payment will be made __________

(a) online

(b) after delivery

(c) after using and checking the instruments

(d) through a crossed cheque to your agent just after the delivery

Ans. (d) through a crossed cheque to your agent just after the delivery.

6. Select the option that completes the concluding line accurately.

I hope in future ____________

(a) dealings will be done if this comes out to be perfect in quality.

(b) repairs and maintenance of the pieces of instruments will be provided by you satisfactorily.

(c) of our relationship with your company will be bright.

(d) deliveries will be done without any charges.

Ans. (b) repairs and maintenance of the pieces of instruments will be provided by you satisfactorily.

(2) You are Salil, a dealer in books for the new session and stationery. You need to order books for class X for the new session and stationery items for your shop. You reside in Amritsar. Write a letter to M/s Anubhav publishing house, Sector 16, Chandigarh.

1. While writing an order letter to a publishing house, Salil needs to start his letter with:

(a) Seller's Address

(b) Buyer's Address

(c) Items to be ordered

(d) The date when orders need to be delivered

Ans. (b) Buyer's Address

2. Which details are not required while ordering stationery and books in the letter?

(a) Number of copies/items needed

(b) Edition of books to be purchased

(c) Transportation details

(d) Both (a) and (b)

Ans. (d) Both (a) and (b)

3. What should be the appropriate subject of the letter?

(a) Order for books and stationery items

(b) Books and stationery items

(c) Need to buy a few books and stationery

(d) No subject is required

Ans. (a) Order for books and stationery items

4. Complete the sentence mentioning the requirements of the orders.

I want these books__________

(a) at discounted rate as we share an old customer-dealer relationship.

(b) in their latest edition and original print.

(c) at older prices.

(d) with one free copy as the sample.

Ans. (b) in their latest edition and original print.

5. Which option should Salil include appropriately for writing the main body of the letter?

(a) • Number of copies of books

 • Number of items of stationery

 • Rate of which it is to be bought

(b) • Edition, number, name of books and number of stationery items

 • Asking for discount

 • Asking to attach the bill

(c) • Name of brand of stationery items

 • Name of author of the books

 • Number of books

(d) • Address of buyer and seller.

 • Mentioning the names, price of books and stationery.

Ans. (b) • Edition, number, name of books and number of stationery items

 • Asking for discount

 • Asking to attach the bill

6. What is the most appropriate option related to the dispatch of the order?

(a) Send it by railways along with the bill, which will be cleared within two days of receiving the order.

(b) Payment has been made. Therefore, kindly dispatch the order at its earliest.

(c) Kindly have a check on broken or torn items, before dispatching the products and do the packaging accordingly. Payment will be made online after two days of receiving the order.

(d) None of the above.

Ans. (c) Kindly have a check on broken or torn items, before dispatching the products and do the packaging accordingly. Payment will be made online after two days of receiving the order.

(3) You are Ruhani, Head of the chemistry department of XYZ Senior Secondary School, Mohali. There is a need for various lab apparatuses and chemicals for the laboratory. Please place an order by writing a letter to M/s Shanti Scientific Works, Saharanpur, as your management has approved their quotation.

1. Select an appropriate opening sentence of the main body of the letter.

(a) This is regarding your quotation dated 21st January 20XX

(b) We want to buy some lab apparatuses.

(c) I request you to send the following _________

(d) Your subsequent offer of discount_________

Ans. (a) This is regarding your quotation dated 21st January 20XX

2. What are the do's of order letter that should be taken care of while writing it?

(a) Letter should be addressed to the person responsible for manufacturing the products.

(b) It can be handwritten or typed.

(c) Name of the person using the goods ordered.

(d) It should include all the terms and conditions agreed upon by both involved parties.

Ans. (d) It should include all the terms and conditions agreed upon by both involved parties.

3. The subject of the order letter should be:

(a) Brief, clear and relevant

(b) Stretched and with multiple meanings

(c) As long as possible

(d) None of the above

Ans. (a) Brief, clear and relevant

4. Which of the following options must be included in the given letter while placing an order?

1. Number of the particular apparatus to be purchased.

2. Quantity of chemicals to be purchased.

3. Explaining why particular apparatus is required.

4. The terms and conditions on which purchase will be made.

(a) 1 and 2 (b) 1, 2 and 4

(c) Only 1 (d) 1, 2, and 3

Ans. (b) 1, 2 and 4

5. Which among the following options should appropriately be included as the main part of the letter?

(a) • Reference letter No. and date

 • Mentioning discounts that are agreed upon

- List of goods required
- Demanding extra discount
- Dispatching requirements

(b)
- Reference letter No. and date
- Discounts per goods
- Demanding extra discounts
- Dispatching requirements

(c)
- List of apparatuses
- List of chemicals
- Separate rates of each product
- Dispatched requirements

(d)
- Reference letter No.
- Discounts
- Rates of each and every product
- Dispatched product details.

Ans. (a)
- Reference letter No. and date
- Mentioning discounts that are agreed upon
- List of goods required
- Demanding extra discount
- Dispatching requirements

6. Select the most appropriate concluding line for the given letter.

(a) Dispatch these products as early as possible.

(b) All items must reach in time.

(c) Kindly ensure that the above equipment is delivered within seven days.

(d) We expect more discount as we are your old customer.

Ans. (c) Kindly ensure that the above equipment is delivered within seven days.

(4) You are Aman / Anita, hostel warden, XYZ School, Vrindavan, Uttar Pradesh. Write a letter to the sales manager, Bharat Electronics, New Delhi, placing an order for fans, ovens, and geysers that you wish to purchase for the hostels. Also, ask for the discount permissible on the purchase.

1. Select the option with relevant aspects that Aman/Anita should select for this letter.

(i) Address of receiver

(ii) List of the goods

(iii) Personal information

(iv) Company details

(a) (i), (iii) and (iv)   (b) (i) and (ii)

(c) (iii) and (iv)   (d) (ii), (iii) and (iv)

Ans. (b) (i), (ii)

2. Select the appropriate subject for the letter.

(a) Complaint of order

(b) Quotation of order of electronic products

(c) Placement of order of electronic products

(d) Cancellation of order

Ans. (c) Placement of order

3. Which option should Aman/ Anita select to elaborate on the placement of order of electronic gadgets?

(a) List of products, price, quantity of products and delivery details

(b) Personal and financial information of Bharat Electronics

(c) Address of receivers and senders

(d) All of the above

Ans. (a) List of products, price, quantity of product and delivery details

4. Where should the name of the company placing an order be mentioned?

(a) Top left corner   (b) Top right corner

(c) Bottom left corner (d) Bottom right corner

Ans. (a) Top left corner

5. Select the option that completes the concluding portion of the letter appropriately.

We expect the same____________

(a) Delivery time as discussed

(b) Payment method

(c) Quality and quantity of the product

(d) Both (a) and (c)

Ans. (d) Both (a) and (c)

6. Which of these should not be mentioned in a letter while placing an order?

(a) Date   (b) Address of seller

(c) Age of owner   (d) Address of receivers

Ans. (c) Age of owner

(5) Write a letter to Haryana Sports, Haryana, to order sports articles like footballs, cricket balls, Tennis balls, and cricket bats to be supplied to your school. Sign as Ravindra/ Ravina, Sports Secretary.

1. Select the appropriate subject for the letter.

(a) Placement of order

(b) Placement of an order for different sports articles.

(c) Enquiry of order

(d) Quotation of order

Ans. (b) Placement of an order for different sports articles.

2. Select the option with relevant aspects that the undersigned must mention in the list of goods to be purchased.

(a) Product, quantity

(b) Product name, price, colour

(c) Product name, brand name, quantity to be purchased

(d) Quantity and quality

Ans. (c) Product name, brand name, quantity to be purchased

3. **Which of these is mentioned in a letter when an order is placed?**

(a) City of owner

(b) Nationality of senders and receivers

(c) Mode of payment

(d) Health of owner

Ans. (c) Mode of payment

4. **Select the option that correctly justifies the choice of starting the letter.**

(i) This has reference to the quotation dated

(ii) The payment will be made by

(iii) All the items should be in good condition

(a) Both (i) and (ii)   (b) Only (i)

(c) Only (ii)   (d) Both (ii) and (iii)

Ans. (b) Only (i)

5. **Select the appropriate option with relevant aspects to be mentioned in the body of the letter.**

(a) Condition of goods, delivery details, payment details

(b) List of products only

(c) Receivers and senders details

(d) Date and time of delivery

Ans. (a) Condition of goods, delivery details, payment details

6. **Select the option that correctly justifies the choice of the concluding portion of this letter.**

(a) We do expect the same delivery this time as well.

(b) Hope to receive the catalogue at the earliest

(c) Both (a) and (b)

(d) None of the above

Ans. (a) We do expect the same delivery this time as well.

(6) You are Laxmi of Bright Stars Senior Secondary School, Ghaziabad. Write a letter to the Sales Manager of The Books Point, Ghaziabad placing an order for some books for your school library.

Bright Star Senior Secondary School

Ghaziabad

15 July 20XX

The Sales Manager

The Books Point

Ghaziabad

Subject: Supply of books for the School Library

Dear Sir,

I am writing this letter in reference to the quotations that you sent for the books we asked for. I want to tell you that we intend to buy those books from you on the quoted amount by you.

Please send the following books by the end of this week. The quantity of each book is mentioned against the books in the list.

	Name	Author	Class	Quantity
1.	As you like it	Shakespeare	12	20
2.	Great Expectations		11	10
3.	Footprints Without Feet	Charles Dickens	10	25
4.	Timeline	Michael Crichton		5

You are requested to send the above books as per the terms and conditions. Kindly make sure the books to be in good condition, well–bound and packed properly. You are also requested to send the bill along with the books after applying the discount permissible to schools. Payment will be made soon after the receipt and checking of the books.

Damaged books will not be accepted nor any payment will be made for the same.

Thanking you

Yours faithfully

Laxmi

(7) Write a letter to the Manager, Kapoors Sports shop, Jalandhar, a well known firm in sports goods. In the letter ask them to supply trade catalogues at the earliest. You are Suresh, The Sports Secretary of Horizon School.

Horizon School

Jalandhar

11 May, 20XX

The Manager

Kapoors Sports Shop

Jalandhar.

Subject: Trade Catalogue for Sports Goods.

Dear Sir,

We need sports material in bulk for our sports department. We are renewing our sports department for which we need sports accessories and sports equipments.

We intend to buy hockey sticks and balls, goalkeeper's full kit, cricket bats and balls, footballs and volleyballs, table tennis racquets, skates, skates kit, mats, gloves, rope, gymnastic equipments, etc.

I request you to send us the latest catalogue. Kindly mention the price for the above mentioned items and also include in the catalogue the items you have other than above mentioned related to games and sports with their respective prices. Please do tell us the term of payment. Hope to receive the catalogue at the earliest for us to place the order for the sports goods well in advance.

Yours faithfully

Suresh (Sports Secretary)

(8) You are Kritika, Proprietor of M/S Shiv shakti surgicals, Partik Vihar, Amritsar. Write a letter to the Manager, M/S Guru Nanak Surgicals & CO., Hall Gate, Amritsar to place an order for surgical instruments.

M/S Shiv Shakti surgicals

Partik Vihar

Amritsar

22 May, 20XX

The Manager

M/S Guru Nanak Surgical & Co

Subject: Placing an an order for surgical instruments.

Dear Sir,

We intend to buy surgical instruments from you for our company. We have been with you in the business for years. So we want to continue the same with you too because as you know quality is our priority as is yours. We can't afford to have cheap quality products as these are used by health department.

Thus we have always appreciated the quality of surgical instruments bought from your shop all these years and the current year is no exception. So we are pleased to place the order for the following surgical instruments. Kindly send these items to our firm at the above address through your transport carefully.

Name of the items	No. of items
Scalpels	75
Metzenbaum scissors, mayo scissors	50
Forceps	50
Clamps	20

We need haemostatic instruments too which we have ordered already but those were out of stock at that time. If you need the list again of those instruments please imitate. All the items should be in good condition and well packed. Any damage during transportation will be your responsibility. Kindly give us a suitable discount too being a regular customer.

Yours faithfully

Kritika

(9) You are Karan, Hostel warden, Apex Public School, Moga. Write a letter to the Sales manager, Raahat furnitures, Firozpur placing an order for new beds, chairs, tables and other stuff that you wish to purchase for the hostel. Also ask for the discount permissible on the purchase.

Apex Public School

Moga

18th March, 20XX

Sales Manager

Raahat Furnitures

Firozpur

Subject: Required furniture goods for hostel

Dear Sir

We need some piece of furniture for our hostel. Our new session is going to start soon. So for that we need the following items in furniture at its earliest as we have constructed new rooms and we need this furniture for our new rooms for our students. Please arrange to supply the following items at an early date:

Items	Quantity
Full Size Almirah with lockers and mirrors- wardrobe type	15
Folding beds	20
Plastic chairs	30
Mattress	20
Pillows	20

You are also requested to send the bill after allowing the discount permissible for schools. Payment will be made after the consignment is received and checked by the Hostel Committee of the school.

Further, please ensure the quality of the consignment. No defective product will be received and no payment will be made for the same. If you want more clarity on any issue you can contact.

Thanking you

Yours faithfully

Karan

(Hostel Warden)

(10) You are Lokesh. You want to order eatables from the Red Velvet Bakers for your father's surprise birthday party. You reside at D-52 , Mahapalika Vihar, Malad. Place an order for

your desired bakery items for the party. Also ask for the discount.

D-52 , Mahapalika Vihar,
Malad
November 16,2021

The manager
Red velvet Bakers
Malad
Subject: Order for bakery items
Dear sir,
I want to order some bakery items from you. I am organizing my father's surprise birthday party next Sunday. I want the food items to be delectable and hygienically made. I have heard a lot about the ways of your food preparation and quality of food and its taste. So I want the eatables for the party to come from you. You are requested to deliver the following items on Sunday by 5:00 pm.

Items	Quantity
Birthday cake	10 pounds
Pizzas large	20
Cream roll	40
Cheese Patties	40
Dry fruit cookies	10 packets

Please make sure all the items are freshly baked and made. Kindly do the delivery on time. I will give the Paytm Rs 500 on your given number as advance. Final payment will be made after delivery. Please send the bill along with delivery. As this will be my first order from you and the first order itself is big, I expect a generous discount too.

Thanking you

Yours sincerely
Lokesh

□□

Letter of Enquiry

(1) Smriti, a student of class 12th and residence of 11, British colony, New Delhi, wants to be a choreographer. She writes to the National Institute of Choreography, Mumbai, seeking information about their course, admission procedure, eligibility criteria and other necessary details.

1. **Select the appropriate subject for the letter.**
   (a) Details of courses
   (b) Letter of details
   (c) Enquiry regarding courses in choreography
   (d) Request letter

Ans. (c) Enquiry regarding courses in choreography

2. **Which of these details is not required in the above mentioned letter of enquiry?**
   (a) Details of institute administrative
   (b) Demanding for prospectus
   (c) Details of courses
   (d) Details of eligibility criteria

Ans. (a) Details of institute administrative

3. **Select the appropriate option that completes the beginning line of the letter appropriately. Refer red to your advertisement regarding _______**

   (a) I am very much interested in your institute
   (b) electric fixtures in our newly built school hostels
   (c) courses offered by your institute
   (d) the post of a choreographer

Ans. (c) courses offered by your institute

4. **Select the option with relevant aspects that Smriti should select for this letter.**
   (i) Administration details
   (ii) Details about courses
   (iii) Fees details
   (iv) Details about teachers
   (a) (i), (ii), (iii)   (b) (ii), (iii)
   (c) (i), (iii), (iv)   (d) (ii), (iii), (iv)

Ans. (b) ii, iii

5. **Select the option that correctly justifies the choice of the concluding portion of this letter.**
   (a) Kindly send us the latest prospectus of the institute
   (b) We request credit in terms of payment
   (c) Details of institute infrastructure
   (d) Kindly reply to my request of hiring a choreographer

Ans. (a) Kindly send us the latest prospectus of the institute

6. **Which of the following statement is true in respect of the given letter?**
   I. General enquiry letters do not result in any business returns.
   II. Above letter of enquiry is related to seeking information about the courses and other necessary details.
   (a) Only II   (b) Only I
   (c) Both I and II   (d) None of these

Ans. (a) Only II

(2) You are Rajini, a resident of 59, Sector 3, JK colony, Banglore. You are interested in joining the course in communication skills advertised by the Elite School of Language, North Extension-I. Write a letter of enquiry for the same.

1. **Where should the firm's name and address be mentioned in a letter of enquiry?**
   (a) Top left corner   (b) Top right corner
   (c) Bottom left corner (d) Bottom right corner

Ans. (a) Top left corner

2. **Select the appropriate subject for the letter.**
   (a) Enquiry of course
   (b) Elite School of Language
   (c) Quotation for course
   (d) All of the above

Ans. (a) Enquiry of course

3. **Select the appropriate option that completes the beginning line appropriately. This refers to_______**
   (a) your new course
   (b) the advertisement in the newspaper
   (c) development in my communication skills
   (d) your communication school

Ans. (b) the advertisement in the newspaper

4. **Select the option with relevant aspects to be mentioned in the body of the letter.**

(i)   Details about the course
(ii) Your qualification
(iii) Your personal details
(iv) Financial details of school
(a) Both (i) and (iii)   (b) Both (iii) and (iv)
(c) Both (i) and (ii)   (d) Both (ii) and (iv)

Ans. (c) Both (i) and (ii)

5. **Select the option that correctly justifies the choice of the concluding portion of this letter.**
   (a) Kindly provide the details of the course at the address mentioned.
   (b) Would you please let me know the duration of the course?
   (c) I can decide about enrolling.
   (d) None of the above

Ans. (a) Kindly provide the details of the course at address mentioned.

6. **In letter writing format, a title "Respected Sir/ Ma'am" is an example of______**
   (a) Signed named   (b) Letter body
   (c) Salutation   (d) Introduction

Ans. (c) Salutation

(3) **You are interested in learning fashion technology through a correspondence course. Write a letter to the Principal of National Fashion Institute D.R. Das Road, Rampur, enquiring about the details of the fees and duration of the correspondence course in Fashion Technology offered by them. Imagine yourself to be Vishal, who is living at sector 19, Sangeet Bhavan, Rampur.**

1. **Select the appropriate subject for the letter.**
   (a) Information regarding the correspondence course in fashion technology
   (b) Enquiry for details of the courses
   (c) Enquiry for the details of correspondence course in fashion technology
   (d) Details about National Fashion Institute

Ans. (c) Enquiry for the details of correspondence course in fashion technology

2. **Select the appropriate option that completes the beginning line appropriately.**
   I am interested in ____________.
   (a) joining the fashion technology course offered by your institute
   (b) your institute courses
   (c) courses advertised
   (d) none of the above

Ans. (a) joining the fashion technology course offered by your institute

3. **Select the option with relevant aspects to be included in the body of the letter.**

(i)   About institute
(ii) Details of the courses
(iii) Your qualification
(iv) Duration and fee structure of the course
(a) (i) and (ii)   (b) (i) and (iv)
(c) (ii), (iii), (iv)   (d) (i), (ii), (iii)

Ans. (c) (ii), (iii), (iv)

4. **Where should the courteous leaving–taking be mentioned in a letter of enquiry?**
   (a) Top left corner   (b) Top Right corner
   (c) At the end   (d) Bottom right corner

Ans. (c) At the end

5. **Select the option that correctly justifies the choice of the concluding portion of this letter.**
   (a) Looking forward to an early response
   (b) Kindly send me the details
   (c) I have just cleared my class XII examination
   (d) I am interested in the course of Fashion Technology

Ans. (a) Looking forward to an early response

6. **Which option should Vishal select to elaborate on the enquiry regarding the course?**
   (i)   Duration of the course
   (ii) Course content and fees structure
   (iii) Student list who are joining
   (iv) Lodging facility, if available
   (a) (i) and (ii)   (b) (iii) and (iv)
   (c) (i), (ii) and (iv)   (d) (ii), (iii) and (iv)

Ans. (c) (i), (ii) and (iv)

(4) **You are Simran, a student of class X and resident of 25 C, Lawrence Road, Kolkata, and wants to be a painter. Write a letter to the director, Elite Institute of painting, New Delhi, seeking information about their course, admission procedure, eligibility criteria and other necessary details.**

25 C, Lawrence road

Kolkata

11 Nov., 2021

The Director

Elite Institute of Painting

New Delhi

Subject: Inquiry regarding course in painting

Respected Sir

I am writing this letter to know about the courses in painting offered by your reputed institute as I have an immense interest in painting.

I want to state that I am currently in X class. I want to take painting as a career. I have also searched about the good institutes and found yours to be the best. I would feel glad to be part of it. Kindly send me the prospectus and the application form. I would be very grateful if you could provide me with the following information:

- The courses available
- Duration of each course
- Admission fee
- Scholarships available if any
- Faculty
- Hostel facility

Please find the draft of ₹300/- for the brochure enclosed herewith.

I am looking forward for your answer at its earliest so that I can start the class as soon as possible.

Yours faithfully

Simran

(5) You are Tarleen residing at, 27, Orient Tower, near Indian Oil petrol pump, Guwahati, Assam and studing at a coaching centre in New Delhi. You need accommodation for yourself. Write a letter to the Manager of Paying Guest Services, D-113, Block D, East of Kailash, Delhi, inquiring about the details you need for your comfortable stay there.

27, Orient tower

Assam

Guwahati

15 Nov, 2021

The Manager

D-113 Block-D

East of Kailash

Delhi 1100XX

Subject: Enquiry about the accommodation

Respected Sir,

I am student here at Zenith coaching centre. I am preparing for the entrance test of UPSC. I basically hail from Assam. I have come to Delhi for my studies. I am looking here for rented accommodation. I saw the advertisement of your paying guest services in the Tribune of 13th Nov, 2021. I would like to know in detail about the services offered by you.

I want to be accommodated near to my coaching centre as it would save my travel time and I would be less tired and thus will be able to give more time to my studies. My coaching centre is in Model Town and I would like to be accommodated near it to save travel time. Kindly send me the details about the type of

accommodation offered, monthly charges, food provisions, facilities available like attached bathrooms, Wi–Fi facility and other basic facilities. Any other condition that you think should be informed in advance, please do share. I assure you that the rental payments shall be made on time.

Thanking you.

Yours faithfully

Tarleen

(6) You are Riya of C- 70, Rajouri Garden, Delhi. You are a health conscious person. You came across an advertisement in the newspaper on fitness classes in your surroundings. Write a letter to the organisers enquiring about the course and other relevant details.

C-70, Rajouri Garden

Delhi 1100XX

12 December, 20XX

The Organizer

Fitness World

RK Puram,

New Delhi 1100XX

Subject: Enquiry about fitness classes

Dear Sir,

I saw your advertisement in the Indian Express dated 11th October. I am writing this letter to know the details about the Fitness classes offered by you.

I am a student and it makes me uncomfortable to see the growing unhealthy lifestyle, unhealthy eating habits and thus increasing diseases and many health issues. Being from a doctor family, I understand the importance of exercise. Thus I wish to know the details, including the courses offered, their duration and the fee structure so that I can make my friends and other people to join this course along with me .

Thanking you in anticipation.

Yours faithfully

Riya

(7) You are Hritika, the Secretary of the Science Society of Mahananda Senior Secondary School, Uttrakhand. You want to take a group of thirty-five students of your school on a trip from Uttrakhand to Delhi by a deluxe bus. Write a letter to Fast and Safe Travels, Delhi, enquiring about their terms and conditions for package tours.

Science Society

Mahananda Senior Secondary School

Uttrakhand 4000XX

13 October 20XX

The Manager

Fast and Safe Travels

New Link Road

Delhi

Subject: Enquiry regarding package tour to Delhi

Dear Sir,

I am planning to take a group of thirty five students to Delhi by a deluxe bus. The trip will be of about 10 days in November. We intend to sightseeing the route. This is the reason we have chose this mode of travelling. We also wish to do camping at night at the place suitable for the same .

We expect the complete tour package arrangement from your side. Also, please suggest if we will be able to visit the famous places in these days or more days would be required. I want you to arrange for the deluxe bus, our boarding and lodging, and sightseeing. And let us know if you can make hotel arrangements. Please tell your charges too. We shall expect the discount given to large groups and to students. Also, indicate what mode of payment will be acceptable to you.

I look forward for an early response so that we may finalise our programme.

Yours sincerely

Hritika

(8) **You are Nishant, managing director of Apex Studies institute, Jalandhar. You are in urgent need of 10 laptops for teaching practical aspects of soft skills to students. Write a letter to Mr Sahil, manager of Optimax technologies Ltd., Jalandhar to give you information about the laptops of particular specifications you need.**

Nishant

Managing Director

Apex Studies institute

Jalandhar

Date: November 5th, 2021

Manager

Optimax Technologies Ltd.

Jalandhar

Subject: Enquiry Letter for Laptops

Dear Mr Sahil,

I am writing this letter to know about the laptops. Our institute is in urgent need of 10 laptops. We need laptops to teach our students the soft skills with its practical application. I heard of your reputed company from my friend, who is an old customer of yours. So in the expectation of receiving as good quality and services from your side I am writing the specifications I need information about

- The brand name
- The RAM size
- The processor
- The memory size
- About the anti-virus
- Period of warranty
- Anti-virus warranty period
- The price along with brands
- Hard drive size

We would like to know the details of different models available under the specifications we are looking for.

Thanking in anticipation

Yours Sincerely

Nishant

Analytical Paragraph

Analytical Paragraphs Based On Charts, Graphs, Cues, Hints Etc.

1. **Write an analytical paragraph based on the following table:**

Different types of schools in India	Year-wise percentage of attendance	Year-wise percentage of attendance	Year-wise percentage of attendance
Year	2000	2005	2010
City govt. schools	59%	65%	67%
Village govt. schools	31%	35%	39%
General English medium schools	58%	55%	60%
Public schools	75%	77%	79%

The 'Table' shows year wise percentage of attendance in four different types of schools of India. The percentage of attendance is recorded with a gap of 5 years.

As it is clear from the given data, from 2000 to 2010 there is a steady and positive increase in the percentage of attendance in all the four types of schools. The attendance in public schools is much higher compared to the other three types of schools. Initially, the village schools show a noticeably poor percentage in attendance. At the same time, the 'General English Medium' schools witnessed less attendance than the public schools. All in all, the continuous higher percentage indicates that the relevant authorities are concerned about improving the country's education. Therefore, the 'Government' must have taken an effective measure to improve the literacy in the villages. Noteworthy, public school attendance indicates solid infrastructure and focuses on the healthy growth of the corresponding authorities.

2. The two pie charts below show the online shopping trends in Delhi.

Write an analytical paragraph based on the given information by selecting and reporting the main features and making relevant comparisons.

2. **Write an analytical paragraph based on the following bar chart:**

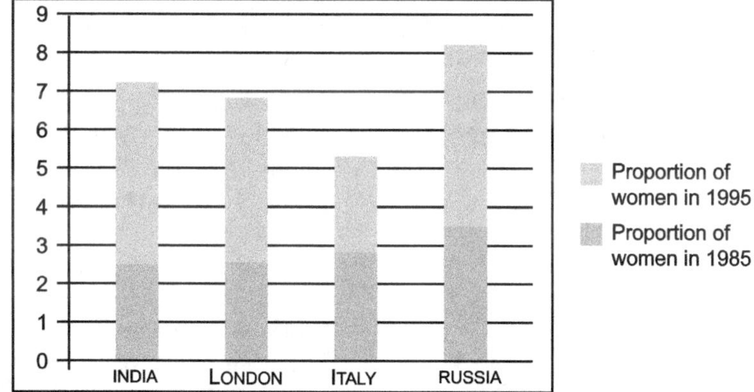

The bar chart shows the percentage of females entering higher education in the years 1985 and 1995. The chart shows the percentages in four countries, India, London, Italy, Russia. The data is shown in millions. Overall, the proportion of women in higher education is increased in the four countries.

In general, there were more female students in 1995 than in 1985, with more than half of women in higher education in all of the four countries. In addition, in four of the countries, the percentage of women going into higher education rose.

The most dramatic change was in India, where the percentage is more than doubled. The least of all change was seen in London change. The only country where there was no increase was Italy. Although the percentage of Australian women going into higher education remained the same.

Russia's highest percentage of women went for higher education, which sustained its position even after a decade.

3. Analyse the picture in your own words.

Rising pollution- a serious cause of concern

Our world is suffering a great deal because of the rising problem of pollution. It is really painful to see the city and its environment suffering for years. There used to be trees on the city roads. Also, a few vehicles were plying on them. Life was peaceful and free. Now it has become a thing of the distant future. The smoke emitted by vehicles has become a health hazard causing many respiratory diseases like asthma, bronchitis etc. Also, noise pollution has greatly increased. The smoke being emitted from chimneys of factories contains poisonous gases like carbon dioxide and carbon monoxide. These cause various breathing-related problems and later serious diseases. The trees look diseased and withered. The drains used to be cleaned. But now, they are seldom cleaned. Mounds of sewage are seen piled up on thoroughfares. Thus the city has become unfit for healthy living. It is all due to increasing environmental pollution. This all calls for immediate steps by all of us to check the increasing environmental pollution. If immediate steps are not taken in this direction, the world may soon become unsuitable for living.

4. Write an analytical paragraph on whether the Internet is useful or not based on cues given below.

Hints:
- Internet widely used
- Interconnection
- Easy and quick
- Made our life easier
- Various uses
- E-commerce
- No access in a few places

The Internet is a modern international computer network system. It is an interconnection method that makes access easy from anywhere. Internet is one of the greatest creative and popular inventions in the history of science. Its functions are easy and quick. A number dialled from the computer and a link to the Internet will soon connect to the outside. It has made our lives easier. The Internet has various uses like communication, learning, exchanging information, entertainment, etc. It is a milestone in the modern world of communication. It also plays an effective role in the field of trade and commerce. Today e-commerce has become very popular with customers. Because online shopping applications have brought a revolution in the world, which saves time and gives millions of options of one product at their convenience. Nowadays, millions of people have access to the internet facility. But many people in some areas of the world still don't have access to the Internet.

5. The line graph shows Delhi Metro station passengers. Write an analytical paragraph on the information provided by the graph and make comparison where relevant.

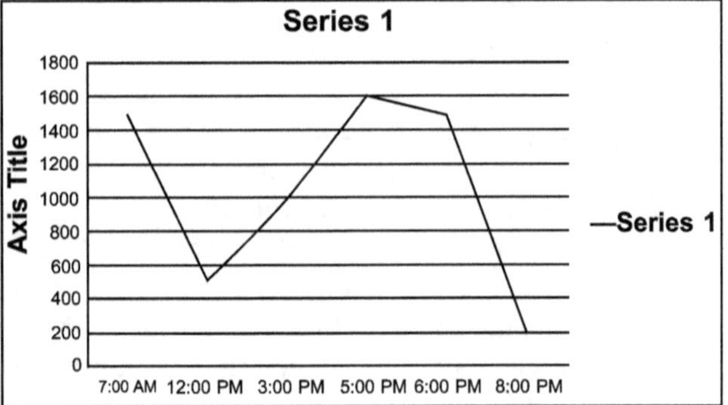

The line-graph depicts the number of people using a metro station in New Delhi over a given day of a year.

The number of passengers rises sharply in the morning reaching a peak of 1500 at 7 am. After the morning peak there is a steady drop to 800 at around 9 am and less than 500 at 12 in the noon. After 12 there is a steady increase in the number of passengers. 1000 passengers boarded the train at 3:00 pm .The evening brings a huge increase from 1200 at 4 pm to almost 1600 at 5 pm. The number of passengers tapers off slightly after 5 pm, but falls quickly to 200 by 8 pm.

All in all, the time series show that the greatest number of passengers gather in the station early in the morning and also early in the evening when it is their time to go to work and in the evening when they come back from work and take the train to home. In between the travelling is less mostly by those who are going to or coming from some personal business.

GRAMMAR

Tenses

Chapter 7

Tenses & Uses

The Verb Tenses may be categorised according to the time frame.

1. Present Tense   2. Past Tense
3. Future Tense

The Verb Tenses may also be categorised according to aspect.

Aspect refers to the nature of the action described by the verb. There are four aspects:

- ➤ indefinite or simple
- ➤ continuous or progressive
- ➤ perfect
- ➤ perfect continuous

Basic Rules

Abbreviation used :

S = Subject ;   O = object ;
V1 = First form of the verb ;
V2 = Second form of the verb ;
V3 = Third form of the verb;

Simple Present : The simple present tense in English is used to describe an action that is regular, true or normal.

1. If subject is singular $S + V1 + s/es + O$
   e.g. Alex sells cakes.
2. If subject is plural $S + V1 + O$
   e.g. Children perform on the stage.

Uses :

1. To express a habitual action.
   e.g. I take butter milk after lunch every day.
2. To express universal truth.
   e.g. Water is the life line of living beings.
3. To express an action taking place in the immediate present.
   e.g. The pickup van arrives within five minutes.
4. To indicate the present period.
   e.g. Simran teaches in DAV public school.
5. To express a future fixed action.
   e.g. The national news telecasts at 7 in the evening.

Present Continuous : The Present Continuous is mainly used to express the idea that something is happening at the moment of speaking. The Present Continuous also describes activities generally in progress.

1. If subject is singular
   $S + is/am + V1 + ing + O$
   e.g. He is drinking milk.
2. If subject is plural
   $S + are + V1 + ing + O$
   e.g. They are drinking milk.

('am' is used with 'I' ; ' is' is used with ' he/ she'; 'are' is used with 'we/ they/ you')

Uses :

1. For an action , going at the time of speaking.
   e.g. My father is watching a movie.
2. To talk about activities happening in the near future, especially for planned future events.
   e.g. Susan is coming for dinner tomorrow.
3. With "always, forever, constantly", to describe and emphasise a continuing series of repeated actions to express annoyance .
   e.g. You are always interrupting me when I'm talking.

Present Perfect : It is used when an action that happened in the past continues to have a strong connection in the present.

1. If the subject is singular
   $S + has + V3 + O$
   e.g. He has finished his work.
2. If the subject is plural
   $S + have + V3 + O$
   e.g. They have finished their work.

Uses :

1. To indicate completed action in the immediate past.
   e.g. He has just taken his dinner. (Now he is full, he cannot take anything).
2. To express past action whose time is not defined.
   e.g. Anita has gone to Japan for a project.
3. To express a past action, the effect of which still continues.
   e.g. I have lost my wallet. (I don't have my wallet now; can you help me find it?)

Present Perfect Continuous : This tense is used to talk about an action or actions that started in the past and continued until recently or that continue into the future:

1. If subject is singular

   S + has + been + V1 + ing + since/ for + O

   e.g. She has been teaching for four hours.

2. If subject is plural

   S + have + been + V1 + ing + since/ for + O

   e.g. They have been teaching for four hours.

Uses :

1. For an action which began at some point of time in the past and still continues.

   e.g. Sunayan has been studying since 4 am .

2. For an unfinished action

   e.g. I've been waiting for him for 30 minutes and he still hasn't arrived.

Simple Past : The simple past is used to talk about a completed action. The time of the action can be in the recent past or the distant past. Whether the subject is singular or plural, rule remains the same.

S + V2 + O   e.g. John bought two chairs.

Uses :

1. To indicate an action completed.

   e.g. I went to meet my friend.

2. For past habits or repeated actions.

   e.g. He always fought for pretty matters.

Past Continuous : It is used to express a continued or ongoing action in past, an ongoing action which occurred in past and completed at some point in past.

1. If subject is singular

   S + was + V1 + ing + O

   e.g. He was eating fruits.

2. If subject is plural

   S + were + V1 + ing + O

   e.g. They were flying kites.

Uses :

1. To denote an action going on at some time in the past.

   e.g. Ridhi was weeping bitterly when the result was declared.

2. We use past continuous tense to describe a past action over a period of time.

   e.g They were practicing for the event all day.

3. We use past continuous to say that an action in the past was temporary.

   e.g. They were living in a small house for a year.

Past Perfect : The past perfect refers to a time earlier than before now. It is used to make it clear that one event happened before another in the past. It does not matter which event is mentioned first - the tense makes it clear which one happened first.

Whether the subject is singular or plural, rule remains the same.   S + had +V3 + O

eg. He had killed the snake.

Uses :

1. A completed action before something else in the past.

   e.g. When we arrived, the film had started. (= first the film started, then later we arrived)

2. To explain or give a reason for something in the past.

   e.g. I'd eaten dinner so I wasn't hungry.

   It had snowed in the night, so the bus didn't arrive.

3. As part of the third conditional.

   e.g. If I had known you were ill, I would have visited you.

Past Perfect Continuous : The past perfect continuous shows that an action that started in the past continued up to the another time in the past.

Whether the subject is singular or plural, rule remains the same.

S + had + been V1 + ing + since / for + O

eg. They had been talking for over an hour.

Uses :

1. Duration of a Past Action

   e.g. The maids had been quarrelling for half an hour when we arrived home.

2. Showing Cause

   e.g. The road was wet because it had been raining.

3. Used in third conditional sentences

   e.g. If it hadn't been raining, we would have gone to the park.

Simple Future : The simple future refers to a time later than now and expresses facts or certainty.

Whether the subject is singular or plural, rule remains the same.

S + will / shall + V1 + O

e.g. She will go there in the evening.

Uses :

1. To predict a future event

   e.g. It will be a holiday tomorrow.

2. To express a spontaneous decision

   e.g. I'll pay for the tickets by credit card.

3. To express willingness and in the negative form, to express unwillingness

   e.g. I'll cook dinner for everyone.

   The baby won't sleep in the cradle.

4. To make a suggestion

   e.g. Shall we go for shopping ?

Future Continuous : The future continuous refers to an unfinished action or event that will be in progress at a time later than now.

Whether the subject is singular or plural, rule remains the same.

S + will / shall + be + V1 + ing + O

eg. The boys will be running tomorrow.

Uses :

1. For an action that lasts a period of time in the future.

   e.g. His father will be working the whole day tomorrow.

2. For an action that has been planned.

   e.g. They will be going to London for vacation this summer.

3. To express an action that will be in progress at a certain or specified time in the future.

   e.g. We will/shall be sleeping by the time you return.

4. To ask for information

   e.g. Will you be joining the drinking session tonight?

Future Perfect : The future perfect tense refers to a completed action in the future. When we use this tense we are projecting ourselves forward into the future and looking back at an action that will be completed sometime later than now. It is most often used with a time expression.

Whether the subject is singular or plural, rule remains the same.

S + will/ shall + have + V3 + O

eg. Jane will have finished the work.

Uses :

1. Talks about future actions that will be finished before some specified point in the future.

   e.g. Before they come, we will have cooked the dinner.

2. Talks about actions which will last after a given point in the future.

   e.g. Simran will have lived in USA for 10 years by 2016.

3. To express conviction that something happened in the near past.

   e.g. Our relatives will have arrived at the hotel by now. (I'm sure our relatives have arrived at the hotel)

Future Perfect Continuous : It refers to the events or actions in a time between now and some future time which are unfinished. It is most often used with a time expression.

Whether the subject is singular or plural, rule remains the same.

S + will / shall + have + been + V1 + ing + O

Jane will have been dancing on the stage tomorrow.

Below is a recap of the tense table :

Example : Verb 'go' in Active Voice.

Tense	Simple (Indefinite)	Continuous	Perfect	Perfect Continuous
Present Tense	go goes	am going is going are going	has gone have gone	has been going have been going
Past Tense	went	was going were going	had gone	had been going
Future Tense	will go shall go	will be going shall be going	will have gone shall have gone	will have been going shall have been going

Exercise-1

Choose the correct option:

1. Every boy and girl __________ in the class today.

   (a) are present   (b) is present

   (c) have present   (d) had present

Ans. (b) is present

2. By the next month, we shall ________ the project.

   (a) has completed   (b) completing

   (c) completed   (d) have completed

Ans. (d) have completed

3. He was only joking, as he _____ many times before.

   (a) is doing   (b) are done

   (c) has doing   (d) had done

Ans. (d) had done

4. Sudha or her brothers __________ to be blamed.

  (a) is   (b) has

  (c) are   (d) was

Ans. (c) are

5. The wise leader and politician____ assassinated.

  (a) are   (b) has been

  (c) have been   (d) have had been

Ans. (b) has been

6. The news __________ not updated timely.

  (a) were   (b) have

  (c) is   (d) are

Ans. (c) is

7. Mr Yew ______ Jessie good advice but Jessie did not take his advice.

  (a) has given   (b) had given

  (c) are given   (d) have given

Ans. (b) had given

8. Choose the correct sentence.

  (a) When I woke up, he has already eaten breakfast.

  (b) When I woke up, he had already eaten breakfast.

  (c) When I had woken up, he had already ate breakfast.

  (d) When I had woken up, he has already ate breakfast.

Ans. (b) When I woke up, he had already eaten breakfast.

9. Each of the four army soldiers __________ for the mission.

  (a) were ready   (b) are ready

  (c) was ready   (d) have been ready

Ans. (c) was ready

10. The thief and the eye-witness __________.

  (a) has escaped   (b) has been escaping

  (c) was escaping   (d) have escaped

Ans. (d) have escaped

11. The quality of products __________ over time.

  (a) are degrading

  (b) has been degrading

  (c) have degrading

  (d) were degraded

Ans. (b) has been degrading

12. Choose the sentence with the future perfect tense.

  (a) They shall have arrived by then.

  (b) They shall be arriving by then.

  (c) They shall arrive by then.

  (d) They shall have been arriving by then.

Ans. (a) They shall have arrived by then.

13. I __________ working all afternoon and have just finished the assignment.

  (a) have been   (b) had been

  (c) shall be   (d) am

Ans. (b) had been

14. Rohan __________ the movie before he read the review.

  (a) watches   (b) have watched

  (c) had watched   (d) was watching

Ans. (c) had watched

15. He __________ daily for a year now.

  (a) exercises

  (b) was exercising

  (c) has been exercising

  (d) have been exercising

Ans. (c) has been exercising

16. He __________ in the States but he still does not have a command over the English language.

  (a) have been living   (b) has been living

  (c) have lived   (d) living

Ans. (b) has been living

17. According to the prevailing rate, two dozen __________ rupees one hundred.

  (a) costs   (b) cost

  (c) costing   (d) costed

Ans. (b) cost

18. I __________ this book since morning.

  (a) had been reading   (b) has been reading

  (c) have had read   (d) shall be reading

Ans. (a) had been reading

19. The Council __________ made its decision.

  (a) have   (b) have had

  (c) has   (d) having

Ans. (c) has

20. "I ______ to Mrs. Suze about your matter. She wants you to see her as soon as possible," Mr. Goh said.

  (a) have spoken   (b) has spoken

  (c) had spoken   (d) are spoken

Ans. (a) have spoken

21. I ______ along the road for a kilometre when I realized that I was on the wrong road.

  (a) have driven   (b) am driven

  (c) has driven   (d) had driven

Ans. (d) had driven

22. **Neither of the paintings __________ sold.**
    (a) have been   (b) were
    (c) are   (d) was

Ans. (b) were

23. **The Chief guest, with his wife, __________.**
    (a) has left   (b) are leaving
    (c) have left   (d) left

Ans. (a) has left

24. **They __________ into their cars and drove away.**
    (a) has got   (b) have got
    (c) gets   (d) got

Ans. (d) got

25. **By the end of the 15th century, the Portuguese ______ to Malacca.**
    (a) had come   (b) has come
    (c) are come   (d) have come

Ans. (a) had come

26. **Identify the tense used in the underlined phrase. "The weatherman forecasted that it is going to rain."**
    (a) Present indefinite tense
    (b) Future indefinite tense
    (c) Future perfect continuous tense
    (d) Future continuous tense

Ans. (b) Future indefinite tense

27. **Choose the past perfect continuous tense form of the sentence. "The children played in the park throughout the evening."**
    (a) The children played in the park throughout the evening.
    (b) The children have been playing in the park throughout the evening.
    (c) The children had played in the park throughout the evening.
    (d) The children had been playing in the park throughout the evening.

Ans. (d) The children had been playing in the park throughout the evening.

28. **The boy was sorry that he ______ asleep.**
    (a) are fallen   (b) have fallen
    (c) has fallen   (d) had fallen

Ans. (d) had fallen

29. **Back in my native place, I __________ a smartphone.**
    (a) did not have   (b) do not have
    (c) did not had   (d) do not had

Ans. (a) did not have

30. **I __________ the medicine as prescribed by the doctor for a week now.**
    (a) takes   (b) have been taking
    (c) would have taken   (d) have had been taking

Ans. (b) have been taking

31. **You and I __________ the obligations.**
    (a) am fulfilled   (b) has been fulfilling
    (c) have fulfilled   (d) has fulfilled

Ans. (c) have fulfilled

32. **Two-thirds of the food supply __________ for the month.**
    (a) has been used   (b) were used
    (c) have been using   (d) has been using

Ans. (a) has been used

33. **Identify the tense used in the sentence. "Her brother will walk her down the aisle."**
    (a) Future indefinite tense
    (b) Future tense
    (c) Present indefinite tense
    (d) Present perfect tense

Ans. (b) Future tense

34. **We ______ to visit you last month.**
    (a) have planned   (b) had planned
    (c) were planned   (d) are planned

Ans. (b) had planned

35. **Rohan __________ to attend the programme.**
    (a) did not wanted   (b) did not want
    (c) do not wanted   (d) does not wanted

Ans. (b) did not want

36. **Fill in the blank with the present perfect tense form of the verb given in the bracket. "Jack __________ to visit her grandmother." (go)**
    (a) have been going   (b) had gone
    (c) has gone   (d) has been going

Ans. (c) has gone

37. **Shall we ______ you cut the vegetables ?" we asked Mother.**
    (a) help   (b) helps
    (c) helped   (d) to help

Ans. (a) help

38. **Fill in the blank with the present perfect continuous tense form of the verb given in the bracket. "Anirudh __________ a health regime everyday." (follow)**
    (a) follows
    (b) have been following
    (c) has been following
    (d) has followed

Ans. (c) has been following

39. Ali accidentally _______ his mother's vase while playing in the hall just now.

(a) break   (b) breaks

(c) broke   (d) broken

Ans. (c) broke

40. The technique of paraphrasing _________.

(a) are practised

(b) has to be practised

(c) have to be practised

(d) is practising

Ans. (b) has to be practised

41. "Shyam and his brothers" _________ a famous sweet shop in our neighbourhood.

(a) are   (b) have been

(c) is   (d) have

Ans. (c) is

42. The boys _______ going to visit their classmate who is sick and in the hospital.

(a) have   (b) are

(c) has   (d) had

Ans. (b) are

43. Identify the tense used in the sentence. "While he was in the military, he still regularly wrote to me."

(a) Past indefinite tense

(b) Past perfect tense

(c) Present indefinite

(d) Past perfect continuous tense

Ans. (a) Past indefinite tense

44. Identify the tense used in the underlined phrase. "He is <u>reading the newspaper</u>."

(a) Present indefinite tense

(b) Present perfect continuous tense

(c) Present continuous tense

(d) Present perfect tense

Ans. (c) Present continuous tense

45. Fill in the blank with the future perfect continuous tense form of the verb given in the bracket. "We _________ for an hour now." (wait)

(a) shall have been waiting

(b) have been waiting

(c) shall be waiting

(d) had been waiting

Ans. (a) shall have been waiting

46. By the time she was fifteen, she ________ a beautiful singer.

(a) shall become   (b) become

(c) had become   (d) has becoming

Ans. (c) had become

47. Neither she nor I _________ at home.

(a) were   (b) was

(c) has been   (d) be

Ans. (b) was

48. None of the children _______ the answer to the question.

(a) knows   (b) know

(c) has known   (d) knowing

Ans. (a) knows

49. My friends and I _________ stuck there.

(a) had been   (b) was

(c) has been   (d) have had been

Ans. (a) had been

50. It had started to rain just before the guests _______.

(a) arrive   (b) arrives

(c) arrived   (d) arriving

Ans. (c) arrived

Exercise-2

(1) Fill in the blanks with the correct form of the verb given in the bracket.

Forgot your passport on way to the airport? Relax as De La Rue, a Britain-based commercial banknote printer and passport manufacturer, (a)______(be) working on a technology that can store "paperless passports" in smartphones. The technology would allow travellers to do without the booklets and switch to "paperless passports" that would act similar to mobile boarding cards enabling a tourist to travel through an airport without documents of any kind, the Telegraph reported. "Paperless passports (b)________(be) one of many initiatives that we are currently (c) (look) at, but at the moment it is a concept that is at the very early stages of development," a spokesman of the company said. However, the potential for forgery, global barriers and the distinct possibility of (d)______(lost) one's smartphone mean the security challenges present big hurdles, the report added. "Digital passports on your phone will require new hardware on the device in order to securely store the electronic passport so it cannot be (e) (copy) from the phone," David Jevans from security company. Proof point was quoted as saying. The "paperless passport" service is already under the (f)______ (test) mode.

Answers:

(a) is   (b) are

(c) looking   (d) losing

(e) copied   (f) testing

(2) The following passage has not been edited. A word has been omitted/an error in each line. Write the missing word along with the word that comes before and the word after it in your answer sheet against the correct blank number. Ensure that the word that forms your answer is underlined.

Yesterday I saw Rebecca after a long time. She been away   (a)___________

for more than a decade. I surprised at meeting her.   (b)___________

Rebecca show me her new car which her brother bought   (c)___________

in Delhi. It quite spacious but   (d)___________

it was small size.   (e)___________

Answers:

(a) she <u>had</u> been away

(b) I <u>was</u> surprised

(c) Rebecca <u>showed</u> me

(d) It <u>was</u> quite spaciouse

(e) small <u>in</u> size.

(3) Insert the correct form of the verb in the following sentences.

1. His health has improved since he ___________ from the military camp.

(a) will return   (b) returned

(c) would return

Ans. (b) returned

2. He said that he ___________ not believe it even if he saw it with his own eyes.

(a) will   (b) would

(c) might

Ans. (c) might

3. It ___________ a lot where you live.

(a) rains   (b) raining

(c) would rain

Ans. (a) rains

4. The rescue plane, ___________ to arrive from Chennai.

(a) scheduled   (b) would scheduled

(c) had scheduled

Ans. (c) had scheduled

5. Musical instruments of the Air Force band ___________ among the wreckage.

(a) was found   (b) were found

(c) will find

Ans. (b) were found

6. Bats navigate by emitting shrill squeaks that ___________ back to their ears from insect prey or obstacles in their path.

(a) are reflected   (b) was reflected

(c) is reflected

Ans. (a) are reflected

7. The old man ___________ with a great effort and took the bowl between his shaking hands.

(a) rise   (b) rose

(c) will rise

Ans. (b) rose

8. The poor mother ___________ her child when it cried for more food.

(a) embrace   (b) embraced

(c) embracing

Ans. (b) embraced

9. Mala ___________ nonsense in her dream which her mother could hardly understand.

(a) was talking   (b) is talking

(c) will be talking

Ans. (a) was talking

10. The children ___________ at the insane man on the road.

(a) is mocking   (b) were mocking

(c) mocking

Ans. (b) were mocking

11. The teacher asked the boys if they ___________ the assignment.

(a) completed   (b) had completed

(c) have completed

Ans. (b) had completed

12. Although they ___________ in the election, they did not lose heart.

(a) defeated   (b) were defeated

(c) had defeated

Ans. (b) were defeated

13. I ___________ in the garden all morning and it's already 11.30 a.m.

(a) have been working

(b) had been working

(c) would have been working

Ans. (b) had been working

14. The workers ___________ a pay rise last month.

(a) were given   (b) was given

(c) has given

Ans. (a) were given

15. The school building _____________ right now.

    (a) is being painted   (b) was painted

    (c) had painted

Ans. (a) is being painted

16. I knew that Ramesh _____________ Jaipur before, so I asked him to recommend a good hotel.

    (a) had visited   (b) has been visiting

    (c) visited

Ans. (a) had visited

17. I saw that she _____________ to hold back her tears when she got the message of her father's demise.

    (a) tries   (b) is trying

    (c) was trying

Ans. (c) was trying

18. I wanted to see her but I didn't know if she _____________ in her apartment.

    (a) is   (b) was

    (c) had been

Ans. (b) was

19. Rishi told me that he visited Rini and Riddhi when he _____________ from Spain.

    (a) has returned   (b) returned

    (c) will return

Ans. (b) returned

20. My daughter learned in class yesterday that the Earth _____________ around the Sun.

    (a) revolves   (b) is revolving

    (c) revolved

Ans. (a) revolves

Exercise-3

Fill in the blanks choosing the most appropriate words from the given options :

Last Sunday our school (a) .... a fete. There (b) .... stalls selling edible items. People (c) .... at all these stalls. There (d) ....to be an unending rush. Suddenly. I (e)............... a child crying. I (f) .... around and saw a pretty little girl who was crying.

    (a) (i) organises   (ii) organised

        (iii) will organise   (iv) was organising

    (b) (i) was   (ii) were

        (iii) has been   (iv) have been

    (c) (i) throng   (ii) throngs

        (iii) thronged   (iv) will throng

    (d) (i) seem   (ii) will seem

        (iii) seemed   (iv) had seemed

    (e) (i) hear   (ii) heard

        (iii) will hear   (iv) will have heard

    (f) (i) look   (ii) looking

        (iii) have looked   (iv) looked

Answers :

(a) (ii) organised   (b) (ii) were

(c) (iii) thronged   (d) (iii) seemed

(e) (ii) heard   (f) (iv) looked

Exercise-4

Last Saturday our school (a)_______for the summer vacation. My brother, Ashish, who (b) _______in a hostel in Gwalior (c)_______by the Shatabdi Express. Mother (d) _______me to go to the railway station and (e)_______him up. I (f)_______ my scooter and left.

    (a) (i) closes   (ii) closed

        (iii) will close   (iv) is closing

    (b) (i) stays   (ii) stayed

        (iii) will stay   (iv) will be staying

    (c) (i) comes   (ii) came

        (iii) was coming   (iv) has come

    (d) (i) tells   (ii) told

        (iii) is telling   (iv) had told

    (e) (i) pick   (ii) picked

        (iii) is picking   (iv) will pick

    (f) (i) look   (ii) will take

        (iii) am taking   (iv) took

Answers :

(a) (ii) closed   (b) (i) stays

(c) (iii) was coming   (d) (ii) told

(e) (i) pick   (f) (iv) took

Exercise-5

Drug addiction (a) _______a serious problem and the reasons for it (b) _______not difficult to find. The home environment (c) _______a major contributory factor. Modern life (d) _______very hectic. When both the parents (e) _______working hands, they (f) _______spare time for their children. Lonely youngsters try to experiment with drugs. The parents realise the fact only when they become drug addicts.

(a) (i) becomes   (ii) became
  (iii) has become   (iv) will become

(b) (i) is   (ii) am
  (iii) are   (iv) will be

(c) (i) is   (ii) am
  (iii) are   (iv) are being

(d) (i) became   (ii) becomes
  (iii) is being become   (iv) has become

(e) (i) are   (ii) were
  (iii) have been   (iv) had been

(f) (i) do not find   (ii) are not finding
  (iii) have not found   (iv) had not found

Answers :

(a) (iii) has become   (b) (iii) are

(c) (i) is   (d) (iv) has become

(e) (i) are   (f) (i) do not find

Exercise-6

The status of women in India (a)_______a gradual change. Earlier women (b) _______to the house. They (c) _______after the household affairs only. But now they (d) _______out of the threshold of the house and (e) _______shoulder to shoulder with men. While this (f) _______a good sign and an indication of their emancipation, yet it has led to a number of problems.

(a) (i) undergo   (ii) undergoes
  (iii) is undergoing   (iv) has undergone

(b) (i) confined   (ii) confines
  (iii) was confined   (iv) were confined

(c) (i) looks   (ii) looked
  (iii) were looking   (iv) had looked

(d) (i) step   (ii) are stepping
  (iii) have stepped   (iv) have been stepping

(e) (i) work   (ii) are working
  (iii) have worked   (iv) have been working

(f) (i) is   (ii) are
  (iii) has been   (iv) will be

Answers :

(a) (iv) has undergone

(b) (iv) were confined

(c) (ii) looked

(d) (iii) have stepped

(e) (ii) are working

(f) (i) is

Modals

Modals are used with great frequency and has wide range of meanings. They express ideas, such as willingness and ability; permission and refusal; obligation and prohibition; suggestion, necessity, promise and intention.

Characteristics :

➤ There is no –s in the third person.

E.g. you cannot say he cans or she wills.

➤ There is no do/does in the question.

E.g. Do you can swim? Incorrect

Can you swim ? Correct

➤ There is no don't/ doesn't in the negative.

E.g. You don't should tell him. Incorrect

You shouldn't tell him. Correct

➤ They are followed by an infinitive without 'to' (the exception is ought).

E.g. You ought to study more if you want to pass the exam.

You must to go. Incorrect

You must go. Correct

➤ They don't have past form or infinitives or – ing forms. Other verbs are used instead.

➤ All modals except 'may and 'shall' can contract with 'not'.

E.g. She shouldn't tell her.

She mayn't come .

➤ All modals (will/would/shall/should/can/could/may/might/must) and the semi-modals (ought to/ have to) have only one form.

Degree of Possibility

Can/could (indicate ability in present and past).

E.g. He can / could go to school.

Might : He might go to school.

May : He may go to school.

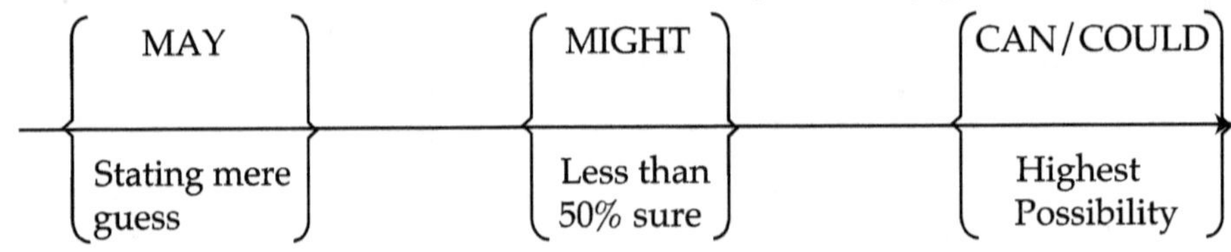

(Lowest possibility)

Ought to : (Obligation / Duty); I ought to finish my work today.

Must : (Necessity) ; I must finish my work today.

Obligation or Promise

Shall : (Promise); I shall finish my work today.

Should : (Obligation/ Duty); I should finish my work today.

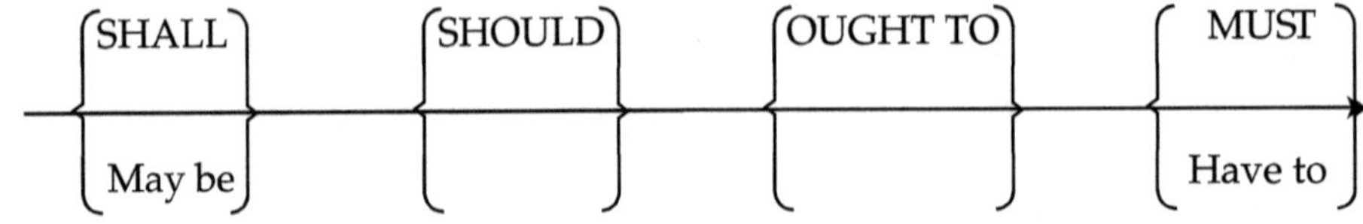

Prediction

May/ Might : The world may/ might end in 2018.

Shall : The world shall end in 2018.

Will : The world will end in 2018.

Degree of predictability :

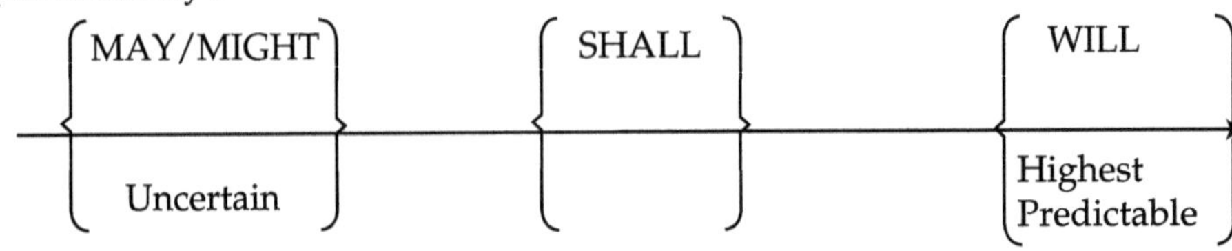

Exercise-1

Choose the correct option.

1. You _________ borrow my books for your research.
   - (a) need to
   - (b) can
   - (c) have to
   - (d) ought to

   Ans. (b) can

2. You _________ ask your mom before submitting the application.
   - (a) would
   - (b) could
   - (c) can
   - (d) should

   Ans. (d) should

3. You _________ have read the terms and conditions before you signed the document.
   - (a) could
   - (b) should
   - (c) would
   - (d) might

   Ans. (b) should

4. We _________ either host lunch or dinner.
   - (a) may
   - (b) could
   - (c) ought to
   - (d) shall

   Ans. (a) may

5. If you are nervous, _________ I speak to her?
   - (a) shall
   - (b) would
   - (c) can
   - (d) could

   Ans. (a) shall

6. _________ you please bring me a chair?
   - (a) Might
   - (b) Would have
   - (c) Would
   - (d) Can

   Ans. (c) Would

7. People _________ be interested to learn about his struggle.
   - (a) could
   - (b) might
   - (c) would
   - (d) should

   Ans. (b) might

8. I _________ believe my eyes!
   - (a) might not
   - (b) must not
   - (c) couldn't
   - (d) shouldn't

   Ans. (c) couldn't

9. The class is dismissed. You _________ leave now.
   - (a) should
   - (b) can
   - (c) need to
   - (d) ought to

   Ans. (b) can

10. He is our colleague. We _________ invite him.
    - (a) can
    - (b) must
    - (c) dare to
    - (d) will

    Ans. (b) must

11. You _________ follow the court orders.
    - (a) could
    - (b) might
    - (c) can
    - (d) must

    Ans. (d) must

12. It was a grand party. They _________ have spent a lot.
    - (a) might
    - (b) need to
    - (c) could
    - (d) must

    Ans. (d) must

13. I missed my last appointment. I _________ visit the doctor this weekend.
    - (a) must
    - (b) used to
    - (c) can
    - (d) could

    Ans. (a) must

14. Had he wanted, he _________ have completed the project by now.
    - (a) should
    - (b) might
    - (c) could
    - (d) must

    Ans. (c) could

15. I _________ wake up early to catch the flight tomorrow.
    - (a) must
    - (b) can
    - (c) could
    - (d) would have

    Ans. (a) must

16. _________ we hire a tour guide?
    - (a) Could
    - (b) Should
    - (c) Would
    - (d) Might

    Ans. (b) Should

17. We _________ finish our meals before we leave.
    - (a) dare to
    - (b) ought to
    - (c) could
    - (d) would

    Ans. (b) ought to

18. I _________ appreciate your presence there.
    - (a) can
    - (b) should
    - (c) will have
    - (d) would

    Ans. (d) would

19. During the college days, I _________ beat them all in the race!
    - (a) could
    - (b) should
    - (c) can
    - (d) might

    Ans. (a) could

20. Do you _________ fight with those goons?
    - (a) ought to
    - (b) might
    - (c) dare to
    - (d) must

    Ans. (c) dare to

21. The train is running late. We _________ reach on time.
    - (a) should not
    - (b) might not
    - (c) could not
    - (d) need not

    Ans. (b) might not

22. I_________have been there if I had the address.

(a) would   (b) could

(c) should   (d) might

Ans. (a) would

23. It is big news! We_________definitely celebrate.

(a) should   (b) could

(c) would   (d) might

Ans. (a) should

24. The soup is hot. You _________ be careful.

(a) should   (b) could

(c) would   (d) might

Ans. (a) should

25. You _________ baby-sit your sister as her elder brother.

(a) will   (b) can

(c) could   (d) ought to

Ans. (d) ought to

26. She _________ make any mistake. She's an expert in her field.

(a) couldn't   (b) wouldn't

(c) shouldn't   (d) might not

Ans. (b) wouldn't

27. I have decided that I _________ go to Bali this year definitely.

(a) should   (b) will

(c) can   (d) could

Ans. (b) will

28. I am busy right now. I _________ call you later.

(a) could   (b) ought to

(c) dare to   (d) shall

Ans. (d) shall

29. How _________ we assist you?

(a) would   (b) can

(c) should   (d) will

Ans. (b) can

30. It's high time. I _________ take this anymore.

(a) should not   (b) will not

(c) can not   (d) may not

Ans. (c) can not

31. Rohan _________ be here anytime soon.

(a) can   (b) would

(c) will   (d) may

Ans. (c) will

32. You _________ go to the picnic but on some condition.

(a) should   (b) could have

(c) would have   (d) can

Ans. (d) can

33. We are the organisers. We _________ welcome the guests.

(a) could   (b) might

(c) ought to   (d) would

Ans. (c) ought to

34. You _________ bring more food. We have enough supplies already.

(a) shall not   (b) need not

(c) could not   (d) would not

Ans. (b) need not

35. It was a long day. You _________ be hungry.

(a) must   (b) might

(c) need to   (d) should

Ans. (a) must

36. _________ you be able to convince him?

(a) Could   (b) Will

(c) Should   (d) May

Ans. (b) Will

37. We _________ disturb the committee for such a trivial matter.

(a) dare not   (b) can not

(c) should not   (d) will not

Ans. (b) can not

38. It's not a hectic job. You _________ stress.

(a) can not   (b) need not

(c) dare not   (d) will not

Ans. (b) need not

39. We _________ apologised if we had been at fault.

(a) could have   (b) should have

(c) ought to have   (d) would have

Ans. (d) would have

40. We _________ afford a new car this year.

(a) should   (b) might

(c) may   (d) can

Ans. (d) can

41. She _________ deposit the cheque on time to get it cleared.

(a) dare to   (b) must

(c) might   (d) could

Ans. (b) must

42. We_________tease each other during childhood.

(a) used to   (b) need to

(c) should   (d) Will

Ans. (a) used to

43. They _________ decided by now.

(a) should have   (b) could have

(c) will have   (d) ought to have

Ans. (a) should have

44. I __________ talk to your guardian if you don't behave properly.

    (a) could have   (b) ought to have

    (c) shall   (d) should

Ans. (c) shall

45. __________ I invite her for a meal?

    (a) Would   (b) Must

    (c) Can   (d) Need

Ans. (c) Can

46. There's not much time left. I________ start packing for the tour.

    (a) need to   (b) might

    (c) can   (d) could

Ans. (a) need to

47. We __________ touch the antique pieces.

    (a) should not   (b) dare not

    (c) need not   (d) can not

Ans. (b) dare not

48. We __________ take a detour before we reach the destination.

    (a) would   (b) should

    (c) might   (d) will

Ans. (c) might

49. __________ I call the witness?

    (a) Could   (b) Can

    (c) Should   (d) May

Ans. (d) May

50. You __________ pay attention in the class.

    (a) can   (b) should

    (c) may   (d) might

Ans. (b) should

Exercise-2

1. Complete the sentences with a suitable modal. Negative forms are also possible. There may be more than one correct answer.

1. I like Saturdays because I________get up early.

2. You________play football on the road. It's dangerous.

3. I'm not quite sure about his age. He________ be 40 or 50.

4. I________do some exercise. I'm getting very unfit.

5. Passengers________smoke anywhere on the train.

6. In England, you________be eighteen to vote.

7. ________you pass me that book, please?

8. I ________take my dog to the vet yesterday. He was very ill.

9. Liz ________use a computer so she's going to computer classes.

10. You ________smoke in the library.

Answers :

1. don't have to   2. must not

3. might   4. should

5. must not   6. must

7. can   8. had to

9. can not   10. must not

2. Complete the sentences using modal verbs as directed in parenthesis.

1. I ________go to bed now or I won't be able to get up for work. **(obligation)**

    (a) must   (b) have to

    (c) can   (d) may

Ans. (a) Must is used when the feeling of obligation comes directly from the speaker, who feels she or he wants to emphasize its importance.

2. I'm afraid I can't come to your birthday party. The boss has told me I________go away on business. (*obligation*)

    (a) must   (b) have to

    (c) can   (d) may

Ans. (b) Have to expresses obligation but usually describes what other people, not the speaker, require (*i.e.,* the external obligation).

3. You really________stop driving so fast or you'll have an accident. **(obligation)**

    (a) can   (b) will

    (c) have to   (d) must

Ans. (c) Have to expresses obligation but usually describes what other people, not the speaker, require (*i.e.,* the external obligation).

4. This is going to be an expensive month because I ________pay the telephone bill. **(obligation)**

    (a) may   (b) can

    (c) might   (d) must

Ans. (d) Must is used when the feeling of obligation comes directly from the speaker, who feels she or he wants to emphasize its importance

5. Now, people________use computers to view their accounts and pay their bills. **(ability)**

    (a) can   (b) could

    (c) may   (d) might

Ans. (a) Make a request or ability —can, could

6. The literature________be organized by date, author or argument. **(ability)**

    (a) may   (b) might

    (c) will   (d) can

Ans. (d) Make a request or ability—can, could

7. You________use mobile phones inside the aircraft. **(prohibition)**

  (a) had to   (b) can

  (c) could   (d) mustn't

Ans.(d) Express prohibition

8. There is someone at the door. It________be the courier. **(assumption)**

  (a) had to   (b) must

  (c) ought   (d) shall

Ans.(b) Express assumption

9. We sent the parcel by express courier. It________ to have reached Pamela by now. **(deduction or conclusion)**

  (a) may   (b) shall

  (c) ought   (d) could

Ans.(c) Ought to is used to express two principal meanings: (i) duty, necessity, obligation; (ii) deduction or conclusion to a given situation.

10. When I was in college, I________study eight to nine hours in a day. **(past habits no longer in use)**

  (a) used to   (b) could

  (c) might   (d) will

Ans.(a) Express a habit that is no longer in use.

3. Complete the sentences using modal verbs as directed in parenthesis.

1. You don't look well. You________see a doctor. **(Advice)**

  (a) are not   (b) could

  (c) need to   (d) should

Ans. (d) should

2. ________lending me your CD player for a couple of days? **(Request)**

  (a) Can you   (b) Could you

  (c) Would you   (d) Would you mind

Ans.(d) Would you mind

3. Whose bag is this? – I am not sure. It ________ be Ann's. **(Possibility)**

  (a) might   (b) must

  (c) should   (d) would

Ans.(a) might

4. She________home yesterday because her little son was sick. **(Necessity)**

  (a) could have stayed

  (b) had to stay

  (c) must have stayed

  (d) should have stayed

Ans. (b) had to stay

5. You________leave work at 3:30 today. **(Permission)**

  (a) can   (b) could

  (c) might   (d) will

Ans.(a) can

6. Though he was ill and weak, he ________get out of the burning building. **(Ability)**

  (a) could   (b) might

  (c) should   (d) was able to

Ans. (d) was able to

7. The windows look clean. You________wash them. **(Absence of necessity)**

  (a) can't   (b) don't have to

  (c) must not   (d) are not to

Ans. (b) don't have to

8. You________disturb him during his work! **(Prohibition)**

  (a) could not   (b) don't have to

  (c) must not   (d) should not

Ans.(c) must not

9. Whose car is this? ________it be Anton's. I think I saw him driving a red car like this one. **(Strong probability)**

  (a) Might   (b) Could

  (c) Must   (d) Would

Ans.(c) Must

10. I don't believe it. It________be true. **(Impossibility)**

  (a) can't   (b) mustn't

  (c) shouldn't   (d) wouldn't

Ans.(a) can't

4. There is a modal missing in each line against the blank given. Write the missing modal along with the word that comes before and the word that comes after it. Ensure that the modal you have supplied is underlined.

I like you to know the story of Helen Keller,

(a) ________who neither see nor hear from the time she was a baby.

(b) ________She was unable to play with other children and not hear

(c) ________what was said to her. Doctors do nothing to make her hear

(d) ________and see again for the first time, Helen learnt that things have

(e) ________names under Ann Sullivan's guidance.

Answers :

  (a) I <u>would</u> like

  (b) who <u>could</u> neither

  (c) and <u>could</u> not

(d) Doctors <u>could</u> do

(e) things <u>must</u> have

5. What is the Communicative Intention behind these dialogues?

____

___________________   ___________

Answers :

1. Possibility ; Probability

2. Ability

3. Logical Necessity ; Obligation / Compulsion

6. Complete the following dialogue by filling in appropriate modals.

Customer : (a) __________ you show me some warm clothes, please?

Shopkeeper : Which type of warm clothes (b) __________ you like to see? Light winter clothes or a heavy one?

Customer : I (c) __________ rather see some light winter clothes as in Hyderabad winter is not severe.

Shopkeeper : All right , madam, then you (d) __________ see this latest brand which will perfectly suit to your requirement.

Customer : Light jacket! It's good. (e) __________ you get me the brown colour?

Shopkeeper : Sure!

Answers :

(a) Can/Could   (b) would

(c) would   (d) must

(e) could

❑❑

Subject-Verb Concord

Concord :

Concord refers to the agreement or relationship between two grammatical units. It is defined as "the relationship between two grammatical units such as one of them displays a particular features (e.g., plurality) that accords with a displayed (or semantically implicit) feature in the other".

Basic Rules :

1. A singular subject takes a singular verb; whereas a plural subject takes a plural verb.

   E.g. A grammar book <u>helps</u> you to learn English well.

   Grammar books <u>help</u> you learn English well.

2. When a subject consists of two or more nouns it takes a plural verb.

   E.g. Jack and Jill <u>are</u> going up the hill.

3. When two or more singular nouns take/represent a compound name of one thing/expresses one idea; the compound is thought of as singular and it takes a singular verb.

   E.g. Bread and butter <u>is given</u> in the breakfast.

   All work and no play <u>makes</u> jack a dull boy.

4. When a plural number applies to weight, distance and rupees and represents a single figure, it is treated as singular and takes a singular verb.

   E.g. Forty thousand rupees <u>is</u> the school fees.

   Ten thousand dollars <u>is</u> a lot of money.

   Two kg of sugar <u>costs</u> eighty rupees.

5. When two nouns qualified by each other, require a singular verb.

   E.g. Every boy and every girl <u>is</u> responsible for their misdeeds.

6. If the nouns are taken as different units, a plural verb is used.

   E.g. Bread and butter <u>have been charged</u> separately.

7. Subject containing 'one of', 'each of', 'everyone of', 'neither/either of', 'none of' are followed by a singular verb.

   E.g. One of my friends <u>has gone</u> to Canada.

   None of my sisters <u>likes</u> watching television.

8. Two or more singular nouns connected by 'and' are normally followed by a plural verb.

   E.g. Tobacco and alcohol <u>are</u> injurious to heath.

   Oil and water <u>do not mix</u>.

9. If two nouns refer to two different things or persons, the determiner should be repeated and the verb should be used in plural.

   The industrialist and the politician <u>have been invited</u> to the function.

10. Subjects connected by neither-nor, either-or, are followed by singular verb.

    When subjects connected by OR or NOR are of different persons, the verb should agree in person with the subject nearest/closer to it.

    E.g. Neither he nor I <u>have</u> any objection to your plan.

    Either you or Lakshmi <u>has</u> to own the responsibility for the mishap.

11. A collective noun, which means a noun referring to more than one person or ideas, can be used collectively as well as severally. In the former case verb should be singular and in the latter it should be plural.

    E.g. The police <u>is</u> organising a raid on this business house.

    The committee <u>is</u> examining the details of this deal.

    The jury <u>are</u> divided in opinion.

12. When two subjects are joined by as well as, with, in addition to, or, and not, together, the verb agrees with the first subject.

    E.g. Pramod with his servants <u>was</u> arrested.

    Rohini as well as her sons <u>is coming</u> from Jaipur.

Exercise-1

Choose the correct option:

1. Each and every member __________ to vote.

   (a) has   (b) have

   (c) having   (d) are

Ans. (a) has

2. Much ___________ been speculated about the arrival of the King.

   (a) were   (b) have

   (c) has   (d) was

Ans. (c) has

3. Either you or I should __________ the lead.

   (a) takes   (b) take

   (c) taking   (d) took

Ans. (b) take

4. A school of fish__________ spotted in the lake.

   (a) are   (b) have

   (c) has   (d) was

Ans. (d) was

5. Physics ___________ difficult to understand.

   (a) were   (b) are

   (c) is   (d) have been

Ans. (c) is

6. A pair of scissors__________been bought from the stationery.

   (a) have   (b) has

   (c) were   (d) is

Ans. (b) has

7. Half of the class __________ empty.

   (a) were   (b) was

   (c) has   (d) have

Ans. (b) was

8. My applications__________not been approved.

   (a) were   (b) have

   (c) are   (d) has

Ans. (b) have

9. The quality of food here__________gone down.

   (a) have   (b) has

   (c) is   (d) are

Ans. (b) has

10. The teacher and the students__________ arrived.

   (a) has   (b) have

   (c) will   (d) are

Ans. (b) have

11. Neither she nor I _________ involved.

   (a) am   (b) are

   (c) is   (d) were

Ans. (a) am

12. Two-thirds of the pantry __________ full.

   (a) are   (b) were

   (c) have   (d) is

Ans. (d) is

13. Joshua, with his members,_________really well.

   (a) sing   (b) singing

   (c) have sung   (d) sings

Ans. (d) sings

14. Much__________been said in the news reports.

   (a) were   (b) have

   (c) has   (d) was

Ans. (c) has

15. All means of communication_____shut down.

   (a) was   (b) has

   (c) have   (d) is

Ans. (c) have

16. The pieces of information being circulated _______ true.

   (a) were   (b) was

   (c) are   (d) have been

Ans. (c) are

17. My glasses ___________ nowhere to be found.

   (a) is   (b) are

   (c) have   (d) has

Ans. (b) are

18. Either of the two horses shall ___________ win the race.

   (a) winning   (b) win

   (c) wins   (d) won

Ans. (b) win

19. The United States of America __________ going to conduct elections soon.

   (a) are   (b) is

   (c) have   (d) has

Ans. (b) is

20. That woman ___________vegetables.

   (a) sell   (b) selling

   (c) sells   (d) have sold

Ans. (c) sells

21. Gold and silver ________ precious metals.

   (a) is   (b) am

   (c) are   (d) was

Ans. (c) are

22. The orphanage_______good care of its employees.

   (a) take   (b) took

   (c) takes   (d) taking

Ans. (c) takes

23. The quality of the content _______ not good.

   (a) was   (b) were

   (c) has   (d) have

Ans. (a) was

24. All possible means _________ been tried.

   (a) are   (b) were

   (c) have   (d) has

Ans. (c) have

25. Every boy and girl _______ asked to wear black clothes.

   (a) are   (b) was

   (c) were   (d) have

Ans. (b) was

26. The wages of his sin ______ death.

   (a) are   (b) were

   (c) have   (d) is

Ans. (d) is

27. Time and tide ______ for none.

   (a) is waiting   (b) waits

   (c) waited   (d) wait

Ans. (b) waits

28. They shall _________ soon.

   (a) come   (b) comes

   (c) coming   (d) came

Ans. (a) come

29. The board of directors __________ anxious.

   (a) are   (b) have been

   (c) has been   (d) were

Ans. (b) have been

30. Some of the food __________ still left.

   (a) is   (b) are

   (c) has   (d) have

Ans. (a) is

31. Few participants _________ backed out at the last moment.

   (a) have   (b) has

   (c) were   (d) are

Ans. (a) have

32. The Committee_______divided on their views.

   (a) is   (b) are

   (c) were   (d) has

Ans. (b) are

33. The United States _________ a big army.

   (a) are   (b) were

   (c) have   (d) has

Ans. (d) has

34. The Principal, teachers, staff members _______ discussing the event.

   (a) is   (b) are

   (c) were   (d) have

Ans. (b) are

35. Our happiness or our sorrow ______ largely due to our own actions.

   (a) is   (b) are

   (c) were   (d) have

Ans. (a) is

36. Neither Ramesh nor Suresh ______ the culprit.

   (a) is   (b) are

   (c) were   (d) have

Ans. (a) is

37. Ten kilometres ______ a long distance.

   (a) are   (b) were

   (c) have   (d) is

Ans. (d) is

38. Public speaking __________ a skill.

   (a) are   (b) have

   (c) has   (d) is

Ans. (d) is

39. Tuberculosis__________a common disease among the workers here.

   (a) are   (b) is

   (c) were   (d) has

Ans. (b) is

40. Each of the innocent ones ______ released.

   (a) are   (b) were

   (c) have   (d) is

Ans. (d) is

41. The thief and the lawyers ______ missing.

   (a) are   (b) were

   (c) have   (d) is

Ans. (a) are

42. The Three Musketeers______written by Dumas.

   (a) are   (b) were

   (c) have   (d) is

Ans. (d) is

43. That evening everyone at the party ______ stunned.

   (a) are   (b) was

   (c) were   (d) have

Ans. (b) was

44. Hundred rupees______ too much for this fabric.

   (a) are   (b) were

   (c) have   (d) is

Ans. (d) is

45. There ______ many views against the motion.

   (a) are   (b) were

   (c) have   (d) is

Ans. (a) are

Exercise-2

1. Look at the subjects below and supply the correct verb. The first one is done for you.

E.g. The bag of apples _______ (is/are) ripe.

Answer : is

1. The bags of apples ______ (is/are) ready for collection.

2. Several of us ______ going to watch the movie.

3. Neither the dog nor the cat ______ (enjoy/enjoys) being thrown into the swimming pool.

4. Neither the dogs nor the cat ______ (likes/like) the food.

5. Everybody ______ (know/knows) the answer to that question.

6. More than 5000 bags of flour ______ (be) damaged due to flood.

7. Fish and chips______ (be) usually liked by children.

8. The teacher as well as her students______ (have) been here all day.

9. His song (has/have) a theme which______ (be) difficult to understand.

10. A list of names______ (have/has) been sent to you.

11. Many buses______ (is/are) owned by Bhim Joshi.

12. He says that the pair of trousers______ (be) not yet dry.

13. Neither Peter nor his wife______ (be) at home.

14. Most of us ______ (be) happy with the result.

15. Here ______ (comes/come) Patricia and her brother.

16. One of my sisters usually______ (help/helps) me.

17. The athletes of this club ______(is/are) mostly the winners.

18. Playing on harmonium and singing ______(is/are) quite easy.

19. The sceneries of Mahabaleshwar ______(is/are) more beautiful than that of Darjeeling.

20. These days bread and butter______(is/are) difficult to earn.

Answers :

1. are 2. are 3. enjoys
4. like 5. knows 6. are
7. is 8. has 9. has/is
10. has 11. are 12. is
13. is 14. are 15. comes
16. helps 17. are 18. is
19. are 20. is

2. Fill in the blanks with verbs that suffice subject verb agreement. The first one is done for you.

1. The sacks of onions ________ (is/are) lying by the roadside.

   The sacks of onions are lying by the roadside.

2. Each of the pupils _________ (have/has) a special creative skills.

3. The notable patriot and orator ________ (is/are) no more.

4. No scholarship or reward ________ (was/were) given to the student who stood first in the examination.

5. Politics __________ (is/are) a dirty game.

6. These spectacles, perhaps you know,________ (are/is) of fine quality.

7. His power and influence __________ (is/are) immense.

8. The cattle ________ (are/is) grazing in the field.

9. Some ill people ________ (refuse/refuses) to take medicine.

10. Caroline is the only one of those students who ______ (has/have) lived up to the potential described in the yearbook.

11. Rupees 2 lakhs _______(is/are) enough to restock the library.

12. Not only the students but also their instructor______ (has/have) been called to the Principal's office.

13. Most of the milk ______ (has/have) gone bad. Six gallons of milk ______ (are/is) still in the refrigerator.

14. Each and every student and instructor in this building _______(hope/hopes) for a new facility by next year.

15. The students and instructors each _______ (hope/hopes) for a new facility by next year.

16. Rice and rajma, _______ (is/are) my favourite dish.

17. Four years ______(is/are) a long time to spend away from your friends and family.

18. There ________ (was/were) fifteen candies in that bag. Now there _____ (are/is) only one left !

19. Tobacco and alcohol ______ (are/is) injurious to health.

20. Bread and butter _________ (have/has) been charged separately.

Answers :

2. has (each is singular, so it will take a singular verb).

3. is (when two singular nouns connected by 'and' express one idea they take a singular verb).

4. was (when two singular nouns connected by 'and' express one idea they take a singular verb.)

5. is (Politics is a plural noun considered as singular so they generally take a singular verb).

6. are (spectacles is a plural noun which take plural verb).

7. is (When two singular nouns are practically synonymous one being added to the other for emphasis, the verb is singular).

8. are (When the singular noun is a mass/collective noun, the verb is always in the plural).

9. refuse (Some (plural) so it will take plural verb).

10. has (The 'who' refers, in this case, to 'the only one,' which is singular).

11. is (a plural number applies to distances, weights or amounts of money, represents a single figure or quantity. It takes singular verb).

12. has (With paired conjunctions such as either ... or and not only ... but also, the subject closer to the verb -- in this case, the singular 'instructor' -- determines whether the verb will be singular or plural).

13. has ('Most' is not a countable noun here (you can't count 'the milk' in the first sentence), so the verb must be singular. You can count the gallons of milk, though, so the subject in the second sentence is plural).

14. hopes (The subject of the verb is 'each and every,' which is singular : the correct verb choice, then, is 'hopes').

15. hope (When 'each' or 'every' comes after the compound subject, a plural verb -- 'hope' -- is appropriate).

16. is (Rice and rajma' is one dish, so we need a singular verb to agree with it).

17. is (The quantity of 'four years' here is meant to be taken as a whole, as one quantity, so the verb should be singular).

18. were, is (Candies' is plural so 'were' is correct and 'one' is singular so 'is' is correct).

19. are (Two or more singular nouns connected by 'and' are normally followed by a plural verb).

20. have (If nouns are taken as different units, a plural verb is used).

3. **Complete the passage given below by choosing the appropriate options.**

Christmas (a) _________ (are/is/was) fondly remembered as the time Santa Claus (b) _________ (makes/make) an appearance while children (c) _________ (sleeps/sleep). Gifts are traditionally left under the Christmas tree. Letter writing to Santa (d) ___ (was/is) another tradition followed by children even now, where they state their wish-list assuring him that they (e) _________ (has/have) been good throughout the year. To keep the Christmas spirit going, some postal services (f)_________ (offer/offers) the option of writing letters to Santa with the promise of delivering responses from Santa himself ! With technology at its peak, Santa even (g) _________ (respond/responds) via e-mail or IMs with Santa Tracking websites hoping to encourage children to explore the world, enhancing their knowledge of geography.

Answers :

  (a) is   (b) makes   (c) sleep

  (d) is   (e) have   (f) offer

  (g) responds

4. **In the following extract there are errors in the agreement between subject and verb. Identify the errors and write the correct version.**

The Melbourne players was not downhearted by their recent cup defeat. John Smith, the captain, have spoken for all the team when he said that they would be trying for the trophy again next year. He congratulated the supporters who was magnificent. Neither the manager nor he himself was feeling downcast and they was all looking forward to the next season. Each of the team members were keen to challenge the title next season. Everybody were confident.

Answers :

The Melbourne players **were** not downhearted by their recent cup defeat. John Smith, the captain, **has** spoken for all the team when he said that they would be trying for the trophy again next year. He congratulated the supporters who **were** magnificent. Neither the manager nor he himself was feeling downcast and they **were** all looking forward to the next season. Each of the team members **was** keen to challenge the title next season. Everybody **was** confident.

5. Circle the correct verb so that it agrees with the subject.

1. The girls from villages (sell, sells) vegetables at the weekly market.
2. My brother (is, are) a friendly and loving person.
3. My neighbours (is, are) very cooperative .
4. Mr. Smith (drive, drives) his motor boat every Sunday.
5. Jessica and Thomas (take, takes) the bus to school every day.
6. Squirrels (like, likes) to munch on nuts when they are hungry.
7. Both Steve and Bella (want, wants) to study Russian in Russia.
8. The fans in the hallway (has, have) stopped working.
9. Mrs. Selena (travel, travels) to Montgomery very often.
10. Brian, Sandra and Suzzie (wear, wears) sunglasses outside.
11. My friend Ethan (go, goes) to the same university as me.
12. The bee (buzz, buzzes) around the flowers in the garden.
13. This band (play, plays) music I like.
14. The mother and son (resemble, resembles) one another.
15. Dogs (is, are) loyal pets.
16. Dogs (show, shows) more attention than cats.
17. Most households (has, have) at least one car.
18. Jason and I (is, are) always in argument over scientific matters.
19. The number of students registering for the excursion (has, have) increased.
20. Michael and his partner (deserve, deserves) the best.
21. My class (like, likes) the new Physics teacher.
22. One of us (is, are) completely wrong !
23. A range of music systems (is, are) available.
24. The whole family (is, are) meeting up at seven in the evening for dinner.
25. My friend (start, starts) working tomorrow.

Answers :

1. sell	2. is	3. are
4. drives	5. take	6. like
7. want	8. have	9. travels
10. wear	11. goes	12. buzzes
13. plays	14. resemble	15. are
16. show	17. have	18. are
19. has	20. deserves	21. likes
22. is	23. is	24. is
25. starts		

Determiner

Chapter 10

Determiners are used before a noun to determine, limit or fix its meaning.

Kinds of determiners :

1. Articles – a, an, the
2. Demonstratives – this, that, these, those
3. Possessives – my, your, his, her, our, their
4. Infinite Adjectives or Quantifiers - some, any, much, many, little, few, less, more etc...

1. **Articles :** The definite and indefinite articles are all determiners.

   ➤ Definite article—**the**

   ➤ Indefinite article—**a,** or **an** (a is used before a consonant sound; an is used before a vowel sound).

Examples :

Close **the** door, please.

I've got **a** friend in Canada.

2. **Demonstratives :** There are four **demonstrative determiners** in English and they are : this, that, these and those.

   Note that demonstrative determiners can also be used as demonstrative pronouns. When they are used as determiners they are followed by the nouns they modify. Compare :

   This is my camera. (Demonstrative used as a pronoun, subject of the verb 'is')

   This camera is mine. (Demonstrative used as a determiner modifying the noun 'camera'.)

3. **Possessives : Possessive adjectives**—my, your, his, her, its, our, your, their—modify the noun following it in order to show possession.

   Possessive determiners are different from possessive pronouns—mine, his, hers, yours, ours, their.

   ➤ Possessive pronouns can stand alone and are not followed by nouns.

   ➤ Possessive determiners, on the other hand, are followed by nouns.

   Compare : This is my house. ('my' is a possessive determiner. It is followed by the noun house which it modifies.)

   Is that car yours ? ('yours' is a possessive pronoun. It is not followed by a noun.)

4. **Infinite Adjectives or Quantifiers :** Infinite adjectives or Quantifiers are followed by nouns which they modify. Examples of quantifiers include : some, any, few, little, more, much, many, each, every, both, all, enough, half, little, whole, less etc.

   Quantifiers are commonly used before either countable or uncountable nouns.

   He knows more people than his wife.

   Little knowledge is a dangerous thing.

Exercise-1

Choose the correct option:

1. _______ of my colleagues are going on the trip.
   - (a) No
   - (b) None
   - (c) Neither
   - (d) Either

   Ans. (b) None

2. Is there _______ at the door?
   - (a) nobody
   - (b) somebody
   - (c) someone
   - (d) everybody

   Ans. (c) someone

3. _______ Shatabdi express will arrive at eight o'clock.
   - (a) A
   - (b) Any
   - (c) Some
   - (d) The

   Ans. (d) The

4. Can I borrow _______ sugar?
   - (a) much
   - (b) some
   - (c) a little
   - (d) a few

   Ans. (b) some

5. _______ of you should attend the conference.
   - (a) Both
   - (b) Each
   - (c) Every
   - (d) Many

   Ans. (a) Both

6. _______ of the two sisters is married.
   - (a) Both
   - (b) Every
   - (c) Each
   - (d) Any

   Ans. (c) Each

7. _______ of the candidates pass this exam.
   - (a) Enough
   - (b) Fewer
   - (c) Either
   - (d) Most

   Ans. (d) Most

8. They have spent _________for their son's wedding.
   - (a) many
   - (b) enough
   - (c) all
   - (d) the little

   Ans.(b) enough

9. Not ________ is known about these legends.
   - (a) little
   - (b) all
   - (c) many
   - (d) much

   Ans.(d) much

10. __________ experience of yours is of no use!
    - (a) Some
    - (b) The few
    - (c) The little
    - (d) A little

    Ans.(c) The little

11. __________ of their customers complain.
    - (a) Many
    - (b) Much
    - (c) Enough
    - (d) Most

    Ans.(b) Much

12. __________ English is widely spoken around the world.
    - (a) The
    - (b) An
    - (c) A
    - (d) None of the above

    Ans.(d) None of the above

13. She has eaten ________ the chocolates in the box.
    - (a) each
    - (b) every
    - (c) all
    - (d) none

    Ans.(c) all

14. We should inform ________ of them.
    - (a) many
    - (b) every
    - (c) few
    - (d) all

    Ans.(d) all

15. He should work ________ and take a break.
    - (a) less
    - (b) little
    - (c) a little
    - (d) more

    Ans.(a) less

16. __________ wealthy should be generous.
    - (a) A
    - (b) An
    - (c) The
    - (d) Some

    Ans.(c) The

17. ________ those students were punished.
    - (a) All
    - (b) Much
    - (c) Enough
    - (d) Some

    Ans.(a) All

18. ________participants left the meeting in between.
    - (a) Several
    - (b) Much
    - (c) The few
    - (d) Little

    Ans.(a) Several

19. You can pick ________ of two.
    - (a) many
    - (b) more
    - (c) either
    - (d) some

    Ans.(c) either

20. There isn't ________ cash left with us.
    - (a) some
    - (b) many
    - (c) more
    - (d) much

    Ans.(d) much

21. It looks like I have seen you __________.
    - (a) somewhere
    - (b) anywhere
    - (c) nowhere
    - (d) everywhere

    Ans.(a) somewhere

22. I don't like __________ of them.
    - (a) neither
    - (b) both
    - (c) either
    - (d) much

    Ans.(c) either

23. Can I have __________ bowl of soup?
    - (a) more
    - (b) another
    - (c) enough
    - (d) little

    Ans.(b) another

24. Has __________ left?
    - (a) few
    - (b) many
    - (c) several
    - (d) anyone

    Ans.(d) anyone

25. The exam is compulsory for ________ students.
    - (a) several
    - (b) many
    - (c) much
    - (d) all

    Ans.(d) all

26. There are not__________ students in the class.
    - (a) much
    - (b) some
    - (c) many
    - (d) most

    Ans.(c) many

27. Only______toys have been sold since morning.
    - (a) few
    - (b) a few
    - (c) little
    - (d) the few

    Ans.(b) a few

28. __________ has been looking for you.
    - (a) Everyone
    - (b) Anyone
    - (c) Several
    - (d) A few

    Ans.(a) Everyone

29. I don't have __________ to say.
    - (a) much
    - (b) most
    - (c) some
    - (d) all

    Ans.(a) much

30. We can take __________ of the routes.
    - (a) several
    - (b) no
    - (c) any
    - (d) either

    Ans.(d) either

31. He is __________ head of the family.
    - (a) the
    - (b) a
    - (c) either
    - (d) all

    Ans.(a) the

32. __________ of the two halves is equal.
    - (a) Every
    - (b) All
    - (c) Each
    - (d) None of the above

    Ans.(c) Each

33. __________ of the money we had, has been used.
    - (a) Many
    - (b) All
    - (c) Enough
    - (d) Every

Ans. (b) All

34. **Due to his tours, he got to meet __________ of people.**
    - (a) a lot
    - (b) much
    - (c) little
    - (d) several

Ans. (a) a lot

35. **The poor beggar had __________ to go.**
    - (a) anywhere
    - (b) somewhere
    - (c) nowhere
    - (d) everywhere

Ans. (c) nowhere

36. __________ exam copies are still unchecked.
    - (a) A few
    - (b) Few
    - (c) Little
    - (d) Much

Ans. (a) A few

37. **One of __________ books that I borrowed is missing.**
    - (a) a
    - (b) the
    - (c) several
    - (d) many

Ans. (b) the

38. __________ Taj Hotel is famous world-wide.
    - (a) A
    - (b) Many
    - (c) The
    - (d) All

Ans. (c) The

39. **Fortunately, __________ of the children were hurt.**
    - (a) few
    - (b) some
    - (c) none
    - (d) no

Ans. (c) none

40. **He has __________ evidence to prove his innocence.**
    - (a) many
    - (b) all
    - (c) either
    - (d) enough

Ans. (d) enough

41. __________ orchestra band that you called has arrived.
    - (a) An
    - (b) A
    - (c) The
    - (d) Some

Ans. (c) The

42. __________ is waiting in the lobby.
    - (a) Anyone
    - (b) All
    - (c) Several
    - (d) Everyone

Ans. (d) Everyone

43. __________ but one was against the proposal.
    - (a) Everyone
    - (b) All
    - (c) None
    - (d) No

Ans. (b) All

44. **She has done __________ mistake.**
    - (a) none
    - (b) any
    - (c) much
    - (d) no

Ans. (d) no

45. __________ Indus has five main tributaries.
    - (a) The
    - (b) A
    - (c) An
    - (d) All

Ans. (a) The

46. **He is __________ early bird.**
    - (a) the
    - (b) a
    - (c) an
    - (d) some

Ans. (c) an

47. __________ business men want to be rich.
    - (a) Many
    - (b) Many a
    - (c) More
    - (d) Enough

Ans. (a) Many

48. __________ event is scheduled according to the plan.
    - (a) Each
    - (b) Several
    - (c) All
    - (d) Every

Ans. (d) Every

49. **They have always helped __________.**
    - (a) another
    - (b) several
    - (c) all
    - (d) each other

Ans. (d) each other

50. __________ is known about her achievements.
    - (a) Few
    - (b) Little
    - (c) A little
    - (d) None

Ans. (b) Little

Exercise-2

1. **Fill in the blanks with the correct use of 'some/any'.**

1. Do you need __________ help ?
2. You're feeling cold. Have __________ hot coffee ?
3. I wasn't given __________ instructions.
4. Hamid doesn't have __________ job at present.
5. __________ girls are still in the playground.
6. Don't you have __________ friends.
7. I didn't have __________ money, so I had to borrow __________ from my friend.
8. Can I have __________ milk in the coffee, please ?

Answers :

1. some	2. some	3. any
4. any	5. Some	6. any
7. any, some	8. some.	

2. **Fill in the blanks with 'much/many/more/most.**

1. You didn't eat __________, did you ?
2. We didn't spend __________ money.
3. __________ people drive very fast.
4. He won __________ prizes.
5. I have already done enough for her. What __________ can I do ?
6. How __________ kilograms have you lost ?

7. He is the __________ handsome boy in our class.

8. She is __________ capable than Salma.

Answers :

1. much   2. much   3. Many

4. many   5. more   6. many

7. most   8. more

3. Fill in the blanks with 'much/many/few/little'.

1. How __________ people were there in the meeting ?

2. My hands are so full of work that I have _______ time for outdoor activities.

3. How ______time do you need to solve this sum ?

4. She's lucky. She has ________ problems.

5. Very _______ people are as honest as Ram is.

Answers :

1. many   2. little   3. much

4. few   5. few

4. Fill in the blanks with correct use of 'each/every'.

1. Read __________ of these questions carefully.

2. The Asian Games are held ________ four years.

3. __________ ball has a different colour.

4. I play tennis __________ sunday morning.

5. There is a bus to Delhi __________ five minutes.

6. Those coconuts cost 30 rupees ________.

Answers :

1. each   2. every   3. Each

4. every   5. every   6. each

4. Fill in the blanks with 'either/neither'.

1. __________ of the two boys has broken the glass. Both of them were present there when the glass broke.

2. __________ the monitor nor the teacher saw it being broken.

3. The headmaster told them that __________ they should replace the glass or be ready for suspension.

4. Still __________ of them owned up to the crime.

5. It seems that __________ of them had the courage to speak the truth.

Answers :

1. Either   2. Neither   3. either

4. neither   5. neither

5. Fill in the blanks with correct determiners.

1. ________ (both/all) these restaurants are equally good. You can dine at ________ (either/neither) of them.

2. I called _______ (several/all) times. But ________ (each/every) time her mother picked up the phone.

3. Today morning I saw an accident. ________ (one/several) car drove into the back of ________ (other/another). Fortunately ________ (neither/either) were the drivers injured, nor the occupants, but _______ (both/all) the cars were badly damaged.

4. She answered _______ (all/every) the questions correctly.

5. He lost ________ (both/either) his parents.

6. "Do you want a pen or a pencil ?" _______ (Either/Neither), I really don't mind."

7. "What day is today....Monday or Tuesday?" __________ (Either/Neither), it is ________ Wednesday."

8. "Where did you go for the holidays—Mussorie or Dehradun ?" "We went to ______ (both/all). A week in Dehradun and a week in Mussorie".

Answers :

1. Both, either   2. several, every

3. one, another, neither, both

4. all   5. both   6. Either

7. Neither   8. both

7. Choose the best word from the options given to complete the following conversation.

BOOKSELLER : (1)_______ (Every/First/Both/Either) of these books are equally good. You can buy (2)________ (neither/either/all/several) of them.

STUDENT: They're good, no doubt but (3)__________ (neither/either/any/most) of them serves my needs. Can you please show me (4)________ (more/another/other/ an) book, which covers the full syllabus.

BOOKSELLER : Yes, There's the (5)_______ (another/other/both/one) that covers (6)________ (many/both/most/enough) of the syllabus. This is the latest edition with (7)________ (several/most/another/any) new chapters added to it.

STUDENT : Hmm ! Let me see ! It looks OK. Fine! Give me this book.

BOOKSELLER : Here it is ! ₹ 500 please.

STUDENT : Five Hundred ? I am afraid I don't have (8)______ (many/most/ enough/any) money with me.

BOOKSELLER : Oh, don't worry; you can pay the balance later. Is there any (9)______ (other/ either/another/one) book you need ?

Answers :

1. Both   2. either   3. neither

4. another   5. one   6. most

7. several   8. enough   9. other.

❑❑

Reported Speech

We often report a conversation between two people to a third person. In such case, we have seen that we do not repeat the exact words spoken by the two people, instead we report what they said in our own words. What is actually spoken by a person is Direct Speech. When it is reported later by someone else, it becomes Indirect Speech.

Here, conversation between Bob and Lisa, is reported by Lisa to her friends.

Bob said 'I practice English every day !'

Bob (he) said that he practiced English every day.

In the first sentence, the exact words of Bob are given. This is called Direct speech.

In the second sentence, a report is given without quoting Bob's exact words.

This is called Reported (or indirect) speech.

In changing from direct to indirect speech we notice certain changes :

1. Inverted commas are removed.

2. Change in the tense of the reported speech.

3. Change in the pronoun of the reported speech.

4. Use of connector (that) between the reporting verb and the speech.

5. Change in certain words denoting distance and time. (In the above comic strip it is not applicable.)

1. Inverted commas are always removed while changing a sentence from direct to indirect speech.

2. Change of tense : The most significant aspect of reported speech is the back shifting of the tenses in the past form.

play	played
is playing	was playing
has played	had played
has been playing	had been playing

Simple past changes to past perfect

played	had played

Changes in modals auxiliaries

can	—	could
may	—	might
will	—	would
shall	—	should

3. Change in pronouns

• Second person (you) and first person (I, We) changes into the third person (he/she/they).

Mrs. Jose said , "I saw you at the bus stop yesterday."

Mrs. Jose said that she had seen him at the bus stop the day before.

- If the person spoken to report the speech, second person (you) changes to first person (I).

My mother said to me, "You shall not watch movies during exams."

My mother said that I should not watch movies during the exams.

4. Changes in other words

now	—	then
yesterday	—	the day before
this	—	that
last night	—	the night before
ago	—	before
these	—	those
today	—	that day
tomorrow	—	the next day

5. If reporting verb is in Present or Future Tense, the tense of the verb in the reported speech is not changed.

She says, 'I eat a mango'.

She says that she eats a mango.

Rohit will say, 'I was absent'.

Rohit will say that he was absent.

6. If the reported speech expresses universal truth or habitual fact the tense of the verb in the reported speech is not changed into the corresponding past.

E.g. Ram said, ' The Earth moves round the sun'.

Ram said that the Earth moves round the sun.

7. Neutral verbs : SAY and TELL

'SAY' is never followed by an indirect object (*e.g.,* him, us, them, my sister) whereas we have to use an indirect object after 'TELL'.

We choose SAY when the person who was spoken to is unimportant or already known. We choose TELL when we wish to draw attention specifically to the person who is being addressed.

E.g.   He said that he was busy.

He told me (that) he was busy.

8. First person pronoun in reported speech *i.e.,* I, we, me, us, mine, or our, is not changed if the pronoun (Subject) of reporting verb is also first person pronoun *i.e.,* I or we.

9. If something is said and reported at the same time, the time expressions can remain the same.

Example : "I will go on holiday tomorrow," he told me today.

He told me today he would go on holiday tomorrow.

We have seen that we make changes to the actual words spoken in reported speech. It is because often the words spoken in one place are reported in another place at different time and sometimes by different person. So there are grammatical differences between the actual spoken words (direct speech) and the reported speech.

Type of sentence within the quotation mark	Changed form of Reporting Verb 'said'	Conjunction to replace Inverted Commas
(i) Statements	said, told, agreed, explained, declared, remarked, admitted, mentioned	that
(ii) Questions	asked, inquired	(a) if/whether for YES/NO answer type questions. (b) Wh-word for information seeking question.
(iii) Commands and request	asked, suggested, advised, ordered, commanded, requested	'to' [followed by V₁]
(iv) Exclamations	cried, shouted (with joy), exclaimed, complained	that
(v) Wish/Prayer	wished, prayed	that

Exercise-1

Instructions for question 1 to question 25:

Select the most appropriate option to change the sentences from Direct Speech to Reported Speech.

1. Nancy said, "I may leave tomorrow."
   (a) Nancy said that she might leave the next day.
   (b) Nancy said that she might leave tomorrow.
   (c) Nancy asked if she should leave the next day.
   (d) Nancy informed me to leave tomorrow.

Ans. (a) Nancy said that she might leave the next day.

2. Keshav said, "Rita is busy right now."
   (a) Keshav said Rita was busy.
   (b) Keshav informed that Rita was busy then.
   (c) Keshav said Rita had been busy.
   (d) Keshav informed that Rita is busy.

Ans. (b) Keshav informed that Rita was busy then.

3. The teacher said, "You are suspended!."
   (a) The teacher exclaimed that I am suspended.
   (b) The teacher exclaimed to me to suspend.
   (c) The teacher informed me that I was suspended.
   (d) The teacher exclaimed that I was suspended.

Ans. (d) The teacher exclaimed that I was suspended.

4. He said, "I have been a great mentor."
   (a) He said that he had been a great mentor.
   (b) He said that he was a great mentor.
   (c) He exclaimed that he was a great mentor.
   (d) He said that he has been a great mentor.

Ans. (a) He said that he had been a great mentor.

5. Vidushi said, "We went for a summer trip."
   (a) Vidushi said that they went for a summer trip.
   (b) Vidushi said that they were on a summer trip.
   (c) Vidushi said that they had gone for a summer trip.
   (d) Vidushi said they went for a summer trip.

Ans. (c) Vidushi said that they had gone for a summer trip.

6. Rahul said, "I will manage hereafter."
   (a) Rahul said that he would manage hereafter.
   (b) Rahul said that he will manage thereafter.
   (c) Rahul said that he would manage thereafter.
   (d) Rahul said that he will manage hereafter.

Ans. (c) Rahul said that he would manage thereafter.

7. "I am going out tonight." Manisha said.
   (a) Manisha said that she was going out tonight.
   (b) Manisha said that she was going out that night.
   (c) Manisha said she was going out that night.
   (d) Manisha said that she will be going out that night.

Ans. (b) Manisha said that she was going out that night.

8. The guard asked, "Who are you?"
   (a) The guard asked who he was.
   (b) The guard asked me who he was.
   (c) The guard asks me who he was.
   (d) The guard asked who I was.

Ans. (d) The guard asked who I was.

9. Ravi said, "The concert ended yesterday."
   (a) Ravi said that the concert had ended yesterday.
   (b) Ravi said that the concert ended the day before.
   (c) Ravi said that the concert had ended the previous day.
   (d) Ravi said that the concert ended already.

Ans. (c) Ravi said that the concert had ended the previous day.

10. She said, "Bring a glass of water, please."
   (a) She commands me to bring a glass of water.
   (b) She requested me to bring a glass of water.
   (c) She asked me to brought a glass of water.
   (d) She ordered me to bring her a glass of water.

Ans. (b) She requested me to bring a glass of water.

11. The landlord said, "You should leave if you cannot pay the rent."
   (a) The landlord asks me to leave if I didn't pay the rent.
   (b) The landlord warned me to leave if I couldn't pay the rent.
   (c) The landlord asked me to leave if I would not be paying the rent.
   (d) The landlord asked me to leave or pay the rent.

Ans. (b) The landlord warned me to leave if I couldn't pay the rent.

12. The salesman said, "Are you interested in the scheme?"
   (a) The salesman said that if I was interested in the scheme.
   (b) The salesman said that if I were interested in the scheme.
   (c) The salesman asks if I am interested in the scheme.

(d) The salesman asked me if I was interested in the scheme.

Ans. (d) The salesman asked me if I was interested in the scheme.

13. She said, "Shut the door!"
(a) She asked me whether I would shut the door.
(b) She ordered me to shut the door.
(c) She said that I should shut the door.
(d) She shouted and said to shut the door.

Ans. (b) She ordered me to shut the door.

14. She said, "They will be leaving soon."
(a) She said that they would leave soon.
(b) She said that they are leaving.
(c) She said that they would be leaving soon.
(d) She said that they will leave soon.

Ans. (c) She said that they would be leaving soon.

15. "Alas! It can't be this bad." He said.
(a) He exclaimed with sorrow that that couldn't be that bad.
(b) He grieved that it couldn't be that bad.
(c) He said that it was really that bad.
(d) He said with sorrow that that was bad.

Ans. (a) He exclaimed with sorrow that that couldn't be that bad.

16. The teacher said, "The wind is a renewable energy source."
(a) The teacher said that the wind was a renewable energy source.
(b) The teacher said that the wind is a renewable energy source.
(c) The teacher told that the wind is a renewable energy source.
(d) The teacher tells that the wind was a renewable energy source.

Ans. (b) The teacher said that the wind is a renewable energy source.

17. The secretary said, "Is Mr. Fisher in his office?"
(a) The secretary said that if Mr. Fisher was in his office.
(b) The secretary enquired if Mr. Fisher was in his office.
(c) The secretary enquired that if Mr. Fisher was in his office.
(d) The secretary asked if Mr. Fisher had been in his office.

Ans. (b) The secretary enquired if Mr. Fisher was in his office.

18. The policeman said, "Don't cross the speed limit."
(a) The policeman said not to cross the speed limit.
(b) The policeman asked if I would cross the speed limit.
(c) The policeman warned me not to cross the speed limit.
(d) The policeman asks if I had crossed the speed limit.

Ans. (c) The policeman warned me not to cross the speed limit.

19. Richard said, "I must attend the meeting."
(a) Richard said that he had to attend the meeting.
(b) Richard said that it was must that he attend the meeting.
(c) Richard said if he must attend the meeting.
(d) Richard said that he would attend the meeting.

Ans. (a) Richard said that he had to attend the meeting.

20. She said, "What a beautiful view!"
(a) She said that the view was beautiful.
(b) She exclaimed that the view is beautiful.
(c) She exclaimed with joy and said that the view was beautiful.
(d) She exclaimed that the view was beautiful.

Ans. (d) She exclaimed that the view was beautiful.

21. David said, "Can we go tomorrow?"
(a) David said if we can go tomorrow.
(b) David asked if we could go the following day.
(c) David asked if we could go tomorrow.
(d) David said whether we could go tomorrow.

Ans. (b) David asked if we could go the following day.

22. The student said, "Ma'am, please extend the deadline."
(a) The student asked the teacher to extend the deadline.
(b) The student said if the teacher would extend the deadline.
(c) The student requested ma'am to extend the deadline.
(d) The student said that ma'am should extend the deadline.

Ans. (c) The student requested ma'am to extend the deadline.

23. He said, "Ah! You are here."
(a) He exclaimed with delight that I was there.
(b) He said that he was delighted that I was there.
(c) He exclaimed with joy to see me there.
(d) He said it was a joy to see me there.

Ans. (a) He exclaimed with delight that I was there.

24. The maid said, "I gave them the address."
(a) The maid asked whether she should have given the address to them.
(b) The maid informed me that she had given the address to them.
(c) The maid said that she would give them the address.
(d) The maid said to give the address to them.

Ans. (b) The maid informed me that she had given the address to them.

25. The driver said, "Do you want to halt for a while?"

   (a) The driver said if we wanted a halt for a while.

   (b) The driver asked if we want to halt for a while.

   (c) The driver asks if we wanted to halt for a while.

   (d) The driver asked if we wanted to halt for a while.

Ans. (d) The driver asked if we wanted to halt for a while.

26. He said, "I was writing letters".

   (a) He told her that I was writing letters.

   (b) He said that he had been writing letters.

   (c) He asked her that he had been writing letters.

   (d) He said that he was writing letters.

Ans. (b) He said that he had been writing letters.

27. Reeta said, "Her cousin snores throughout the nights."

   (a) Reeta said that her cousin snores throughout the night.

   (b) Reeta said that her cousin has snored throughout the night.

   (c) Reeta asked that her cousin snored throughout the night.

   (d) Reeta said that her cousin had been snoring throughout the night.

Ans. (a) Reeta said that her cousin snores throughout the night.

Read the following conversation and choose the right answer to the questions that follow:

Sana: Your watch is pretty.

Anubha: Thanks. My father gave it on my anniversary.

Sana: When does your anniversary fall on?

Anubha: 17th September.

Sana told Anubha (3) ______ . Anubha said (4) ________ . Sana enquired of (5) ________ Anubha informed that it falls on 17th September every year.

28. (a) that your watch is pretty.

   (b) that her watch was pretty.

   (c) that her watch is pretty.

   (d) that your watch was pretty.

Ans. (b) that her watch was pretty.

29. (a) that her father has given it on her anniversary.

   (b) that my father has given it on her anniversary.

   (c) that her father had given it on her anniversary.

   (d) that my father had given it on her anniversary.

Ans. (c) that her father had given it on her anniversary.

30. (a) when your anniversary falls on

   (b) when her anniversary falls on

   (c) when her anniversary fell on

   (d) when your anniversary fell on

Ans. (c) when her anniversary fell on

31. Vidushi said, "I will manage hereafter."

   (a) Vidushi said that she will manage hereafter.

   (b) Vidushi said that she would manage hereafter.

   (c) Vidushi said that she would manage after that.

   (d) Vidushi said that she will manage after that.

Ans. (c) Vidushi said that she would manage after that.

32. He said, "May God grant peace to the departed soul."

   (a) He prayed that may God grant peace to the departed soul.

   (b) He prayed that God would grant peace to the departed soul.

   (c) He wished by God to grant peace to the departed soul.

   (d) He wished that God should grant peace to the departed soul.

Ans. (b) He prayed that God would grant peace to the departed soul.

33. My brother said, "The sun is a renewable energy source."

   (a) My brother said that the sun was a renewable energy source.

   (b) My brother said that the sun is a renewable energy source.

   (c) My brother said that sun is a renewable energy source.

   (d) My brother said that sun was a renewable energy source.

Ans. (b) My brother said that the sun is a renewable energy source.

Exercise-2

Choose the correct option:

1. Girlsh : I have invited my friends to dinner.

  Nidhi : I'll invite my Friends also.

  Girish : What should we have for dinner?

Girish told Nidhi (1) ______ Nidhi said. (2) ______ Girish asked her (3) ______

Question 1.

   (a) that I have invited my friends to dinner.

   (b) that he has invited his friends to dinner.

(c) that I had invited my friends to dinner.

(d) that he had invited his friends to dinner.

Question 2.

(a) that I would invite my friends also.

(b) that she would invite her friends also.

(c) that she will invite my friends also.

(d) that I will invite any friends also.

Question 3.

(a) what they shall have for dinner.

(b) what we should have for dinner.

(c) what they should have for dinner.

(d) what we shall have for dinner.

Answers :

1. (d) that he had invited his friends to dinner.

2. (b) that she would invite her Friends also.

3. (c) what they should have for dinner.

2. Doctor: Do you go for a morning walk?

Sagar : I don't have enough time in the morning.

Doctor: But morning walk is very essential for you.

Sagar : I walk many miles a day during the course of my work.

The doctor asked Sagar (1) _______Sagar told him (2) _______enough time in the morning. the doctor insisted that (3) _______Sagar told him that he walked many miles a day during the course of his work.

Question 1.

(a) if you went for a morning walk

(b) if he went for a morning walk

(c) it you go for a morning walk

(d) if he goes for a morning walk

Question 2.

(a) that I do not have

(b) that I did not have

(c) that he did not have

(d) that he does not have

Question 3.

(a) Morning walk had been very essential for him.

(b) Morning walk has been very essential for him.

(c) Morning walk was very essential for him.

(d) Morning walk is very essential for him.

Answers :

1. (b) if he went for a morning walk

2. (c) that he did not have

3. (d) Morning walk is very essential for him.

3. Doctor :   How are you feeling now?

Raghu :   Much better, sir.

Doctor :   Are you taking the medicines regularly?

Raghu :   Yes, sir.

The doctor asked Raghu (1)_______then. Raghu replied that (2)_______ much better. The doctor further asked Raghu (3) _______the medicines regularly. Raghu replied in affirmative.

Question 1.

(a) that how he was feeling

(b) how he was feeling

(c) how you are feeling

(d) how was he feeling

Question 2.

(a) I am feeling   (b) I was feeling

(c) he is feeling   (d) he was feeling

Question 3.

(a) if you are taking   (b) if he is taking

(c) that he was taking (d) if he was taking

Answers :

1.   (b) how he was feeling

2.   (d) he was feeling

3.   (d) if he was taking

4. Father :   Sonu, don't pull the cat's tail. It'll hurt the cat.

Sonu :   Daddy, I am not doing anything. I'm simply holding the cat's tail.

Father asked his son, Sonu (1) _______ because (2) _______Sonu wittingly told his father (3) _______He was simply holding the cat's tail. He supported his statement saying (4) _______

Question 1.

(a) not pull the cat's tail

(b) don't pull the cat's tail

(c) not to pull the cat's tail

(d) not to pulled the cat's tail

Question 2.

(a) it should hurt the cat

(b) it shall hurt the cat

(c) it will hurt the cat

(d) it would hurt the cat

Question 3.

(a) that he is not doing anything

(b) that I am not doing anything

    (c) that he was not doing anything

    (d) that I was not doing anything

Question 4.

    (a) that the cat is putting its tail.

    (b) that the cat has pulled its tail.

    (c) If the cat will pull its tail.

    (d) that the cat was pulling its tail.

Answers :

1. (c) not to pull the cat's tail

2. (d) it would hurt the cat

3. (c) that he was not doing anything

4. (d) that the cat was putting its tail.

5. Doctor : How many times did you take the medicine?

    Patient :   As per your prescription?

    Doctor :   What was my prescription?

    Patient: Three times a day.

The doctor asked the patient (1) _______ Patient replied (2)_______The doctor cross questioned (3) _______The patient informed that it was about three times a day.

Question 1.

    (a) how many times you have taken the medicine.

    (b) how many times he had taken the medicine.

    (c) how many times you had taken the medicine.

    (d) how many times he has taken the medicine.

Question 2.

    (a) that I have taken it as per his prescription

    (b) that I had taken it as per his prescription

    (c) that he has taken it as per his prescription

    (d) that he had taken it as per his prescription

Question 3.

    (a) what my prescription has been

    (b) what his prescription had been

    (c) what his prescription has been

    (d) what my prescription had been

Answers :

1. (c) how many times he had taken the medicine

2. (d) that he had taken it as per his prescription

3. (b) what his prescription had been

Exercise-3

1. Jim said, "I had read this book before."

2. Jane said, " I will read this book."

3. Surabhi said, " The sun rises in the east."

4. Jack said, "I need a new research project."

5. Rohit said, "I have done the painting."

6. The teacher said, "The students will collect money for the picnic."

7. Simran said, "My grandmother is going to cook dinner for us."

8. Jovi said to me, "You are late, I have been waiting for you since morning."

9. 'The book is interesting," Rohit said.

10. The student said, "Oil floats on water".

11. He said, "Sunil is going to learn programming."

12. The traveller said, "Can you tell me the way to the police station."

13. Jane said, "Mohan is preparing for the exam."

14. Jessica said "I'm going to clean the kitchen."

15. Henry said, "Abby and Jonath will travel to Alaska."

16. Ivan and Jane : "We need new story books."

17. Latifa said, "I have been teaching Physics for five years."

18. Rahim said, " I have played polo for two years."

19. Father said to Arun, "Avoid bad company."

20. Hetal said, "I cannot swim."

21. The old aunt asked the girl if she could use her mobile for a minute.

22. He prayed that God might bless her with good health.

23. He confessed with regret that he was destroyed by the people he had made.

24. He bade goodbye to his friends.

25. The boss said to the employee that he should do extra duty for two days.

26. He says, "He is burning the midnight oil to get the first position in the exams."

27. The teacher said, "two and Two makes four."

28. I said, "I will finish my work as quickly as I can."

29. He said to us, "I advise you all to do your work wholeheartedly."

30. He said to me, "The rain has been falling since daybreak."

31. "What a terrible storm it is!" she said.

    She _____ that it _____ a terrible storm.

32. The officer said, "Let them see the doctor."

    The officer_____ that _____ should see the doctor.

33. The preacher said, "The lust for fame is a bane."

    The preacher said that ___________.

34. Meenakshi said to Dheeraj, "Let us go home."

    Meekanshi said to Dheeraj that ________.

35. "Shoot the murderer, "said the king.

    The king ordered ________

36. She asked him where Gauri lived.

37. She asked if I could type.

38. Ramya asked if I had been to Dubai before.

39. He asked me if I also worked from home during the lockdown.
40. She enquired us whether we had finished the project yet.
41. She asked me where I usually went for dining.
42. Nira wanted to know how much pocket money her brother got.
43. The shopkeeper said to Meera, "How much rice do you want?"
44. Kiara said, "What will you do now?'
45. Madhu said to me, "Have you received the parcel?"
46. She said to me, "Can you spare some time for me?"
47. Her mother said to her, "Has the teacher not given you any homework?"
48. "Do you think it will rain?" he said
49. "Are you free tonight?" I said

Answers :

1. Jim said that he had read that book before .
2. Jane said that she would read that book.
3. Surabhi said that the sun rises in the east.
4. Jack said that he needed a new research project.
5. Rohit said that he had done the painting.
6. The teacher said that the students would collect money for the picnic.
7. Simran said that her grandmother was going to cook dinner for them.
8. Jovi said that I am late. She had been waiting for me since morning.
9. Rohit said that the book was interesting.
10. The student said that the oil floats on water.
11. He said that Sunil was going to learn programming.
12. The traveller asked if I could tell him the way to the police station.
13. Jane said that Mohan was preparing for the exam.
14. Jessica said that she was going to clean the kitchen.
15. Henry said that Abby and Jonath would travel to Alaska.
16. Ivan and Jane remarked that they needed new story books.
17. Latifa said that she had been teaching Physics for five years.
18. Rahim said that he had played polo for two years.
19. Father advised Arun to avoid bad company.
20. Hetal said that she could not swim.
21. The old aunt said to the girl, "Can I use your mobile for a minute?"
22. He said to her, " May God bless you with good health!"
23. He said, "Alas! I am destroyed by the people I made."
24. He said to his friends, "Goodbye!"
25. The boss said to the employee, "You should do extra duty for two days."
26. He says that he was burning the midnight oil to get the first position in the exams.
27. The teacher said that two and two makes four.
28. I said that I would finish my work as quickly as I could.
29. He advised us to do our work wholeheartedly.
30. He told me that the rain had been falling since daybreak.
31. (i) said (ii) was
32. (i) said (ii) they
33. (i) The lust for fame was a bane.
34. (i) they should go home.
35. (i) to shoot the murderer.
36. She said to him, "Where does Gauri live?"
37. She said to me, "Can you type?"
38. Rama said to me, "Have you been to Dubai before?"
39. He said to me, "Do you also work from home during the lockdown?"
40. She said to us, "Have you finished the project yet?"
41. She said to me, "Where do you usually go for dining?"
42. Nira said to me, "How much pocket money does her brother get?"
43. The shopkeeper asked Meera how much rice she wanted.
44. Kiara enquired what would I do then.
45. Madhu enquired whether I had received the parcel.
46. She asked whether I could spare some time for her.
47. Her mother enquired if her teacher had not given her any homework.
48. He asked me if I thought it would rain.
49. I asked him if he was free that night.

❏❏

Reported Speech— Commands and Requests

Chapter 12

Find out which of the following sentence are commands.

Choose the correct option:

1. (a) Get in the class, students.
   (b) Students are getting in the class.
   (c) Students will get in the class.
   (d) Students need to get in the class.

Ans. (a) Get in the class, students.

2. (a) You will have to go to the bank.
   (b) I am going to the bank.
   (c) Go to the bank
   (d) I may go to the bank.

Ans. (c) Go to the bank.

3. (a) He told me not to walk on the grass.
   (b) He ordered me not to walk on the grass.
   (c) He asked me not to walk on the grass.
   (d) He told me that I could walk on the grass.

Ans. (b) He ordered me not to walk on the grass.

4. (a) Policeman ordered them not to move.
   (b) Policeman said to them not to move.
   (c) Policeman requested them not to move.
   (d) Policeman told them that they cannot move.

Ans. (a) Policeman ordered them not to move.

5. (a) He told them that don't make a noise.
   (b) He asked them not to make a noise.
   (c) He told them not to make the noise.
   (d) He told them not to make a noise.

Ans. (d) He told them not to make a noise.

6. (a) The teacher said, "Be quiet, Boys."
   (b) The teacher pleaded, "Be quiet, Boys!"
   (c) The teacher requested, "Boys! Please be quiet."
   (d) The teacher said, "Boys! Please be quiet."

Ans. (a) The teacher said, "Be quiet, Boys."

Change the following statement into Indirect Speech.

7. **"Do your homework!", My mom told me.**
   (a) My mom asked me to do my homework.
   (b) My mom told me to do my homework.
   (c) My mom requested me to do my homework.
   (d) My mom told me to complete my homework.

Ans. (b) My mom told me to do my homework.

8. **She said, "Leave me alone."**
   (a) She urged me to leave him alone.
   (b) She said to leave me alone.
   (c) She told me to leave her alone.
   (d) She told me leave her alone.

Ans. (c) She told me to leave her alone.

9. **Her mother said, "Tidy your room!"**
   (a) Her mother told her to tidy the room.
   (b) Her mother told her to tidy the room.
   (c) Her mother asked her to tidy her room.
   (d) Her mother requested her to tidy our room.

Ans. (a) Her mother told her to tidy her room.

10. **"Get off the bike!" said the policeman.**
    (a) The policeman ordered him to get off the bike.
    (b) The policeman told him to get off the bike.
    (c) The policeman ordered him to get off his bike.
    (d) The policeman said him that he had to get off his bike.

Ans. (a) The policeman ordered him to get off the bike.

11. **The thief said to us, "Don't move!"**
    (a) The thief said to us, don't move.
    (b) The thief said to us that we should not move.
    (c) The thief said that we might not move.
    (d) The thief warned us not to move.

Ans. (d) The thief warned us not to move.

12. **My mother said to the maid, "Clean the kitchen now."**
    (a) My mother said to the maid to clean the kitchen now.
    (b) My mother commanded the maid to clean the kitchen then.
    (c) My mother told the maid that she should clean the kitchen now.
    (d) My mother said to maid clean the kitchen now.

Ans. (b) My mother commanded the maid to clean the kitchen then.

13. **Nakul said to Arjun, "Go away."**
    (a) Nakul ordered Arjun to go away.
    (b) Nakul said Arjun go away.
    (c) Nakul said Arjun to go away.
    (d) Nakul ordered Arjun to leave.

Ans. (a) Nakul ordered Arjun to go away.

14. 'Call the eye witness', said the judge.
   (a) The judge said that call the eye witness.
   (b) Call the eye witness said this judge.
   (c) The judge commanded them to call the eyewitness.
   (d) The judge said to call the eye witness.
Ans.(c) The judge commanded them to call the eyewitness.

15. He said, "Bring a glass of juice now."
   (a) He said that bring a glass of juice.
   (b) He requested me to bring a glass of juice.
   (c) He pleaded me to bring a glass of juice.
   (d) He commanded me to bring a glass of juice then.
Ans.(d) He commanded me to bring a glass of juice, then.

16. The examiner said, "Stop writing."
   (a) The examiner said stop writing.
   (b) The examiner told not to write.
   (c) The examiner ordered me to stop writing.
   (d) The examiner said that they should stop writing.
Ans.(c) The examiner ordered me to stop writing.

17. The boss said, "Complete your project right now."
   (a) The boss ordered me to complete my project right then.
   (b) The boss ordered me to complete my project quickly.
   (c) The boss got angry and asked me to complete my project quickly.
   (d) The boss told me to complete my project now.
Ans.(a) The boss ordered me to complete my project right then.

18. Maisha said, "Please lend me your car."
   (a) Maisha ordered me to lend a car to her.
   (b) Maisha begged me to lend her my car.
   (c) Maisha asked if I could lend her a car.
   (d) Maisha requested me to lend her my car.
Ans.(d) Maisha requested me to lend her my car.

19. Tany said, "Help me to complete my project."
   (a) Tany requested me to help him to complete his project.
   (b) Tany asked to help me to complete my project.
   (c) Tany told me to help him to complete my project.
   (d) Tany ordered me to help him to complete my project.
Ans.(a) Tany requested me to help him to complete his project.

20. The maid said, "Kindly grant me leave for one day."
   (a) The maid said that she wanted to leave for one day.
   (b) The maid said that she needed to leave for one day.
   (c) The maid requested me to grant her leave for one day.
   (d) The maid asked her to grant me a leave for one day.
Ans.(c) The maid requested me to grant her leave for one day.

21. Tahira said, "Ma'am, please extend the deadline."
   (a) Tahira said that ma'am, please extend the deadline.
   (b) Tahira requested her ma'am to extend the deadline.
   (c) Tahira asked the teacher to extend the deadline.
   (d) Tahira said that ma'am should extend the deadline.
Ans.(b) Tahira requested her ma'am to extend the deadline.

22. Amit said to me, "Please open the window."
   (a) Amit said that open the window.
   (b) Amit said to open the window.
   (c) Amit asked me to open the window.
   (d) Amit requested me to open the window.
Ans.(d) Amit requested me to open the window.

23. "Please carry my bag," my friend said.
   (a) My friend requested me to carry her bag.
   (b) My friend told me to please carry my bag.
   (c) My friend told me to please carry my bag.
   (d) My friend told me to carry my bag.
Ans.(a) My friend requested me to carry her bag.

Find out which of the following options represent the statement of request.

24. (a) Please stay.
   (b) She stayed here.
   (c) Stay here.
   (d) She should stay here.
Ans. (a) Please stay.

25. (a) Remove the chair.
   (b) Would you please remove the chair?
   (c) Remove the chair from here.
   (d) She asked me to remove the chair.
Ans.(b) Would you please remove the chair?

26. (a) He asked me to pass the salt.

    (b) He said to me to pass the salt.

    (c) Would you please pass me the salt?

    (d) Pass me the salt.

Ans. (c) Would you please pass me the salt?

27. (a) Kindly help me in finding my keys.

    (b) Will you help me find my keys?

    (c) Help me to find the lost key

    (d) He told me to find his keys.

Ans. (a) Kindly help me in finding my keys.

28. (a) No one should disturb me. I want to work.

    (b) Let me work. Do not disturb.

    (c) He asked me to let him work.

    (d) Would you please let me work? Do not disturb.

Ans. (d) Would you please let me work? Do not disturb.

29. **Which one is the correct Reported Speech?**

She said, "Get me the charger from another room, please.!"

    (a) She requested me to get her the charger from another room.

    (b) She requested to get the charger from another room.

    (c) She asked me to get the charger from another room, please.

    (d) She said that she wanted a charger from another room.

Ans. (a) She requested me to get her the charger from another room.

Fill in the blanks with the correct option:

30. **Kanak said to him, "Please help me in doing my homework."**

Kanak (i)________him to help (ii)______ in doing (iii) _____homework.

    (a) (i) said (ii) her (iii) my

    (b) (i) requested (ii) her (iii) her

    (c) (i) requested (ii) my (iii) my

    (d) (i) said (ii) my (iii) her

Ans. (b) (i) requested (ii) her (iii) her

31. **Sanjay said to me, "Get me the medicine as I am feeling unwell".**

Sanjay (i) _______ me to get (ii) _________ the medicine as (iii) _____ feeling unwell.

    (a) (i) requested (ii) him (iii) he was

    (b) (i) requested (ii) me (iii) I was

    (c) (i) said (ii) him (iii) he was

    (d) (iv) said (ii) me (iii) I was

Ans. (a) (i) requested (ii) him (iii) he was

32. **Jahnvi said to me, "Please turn off the TV as I need to study for my exams."**

Jahnvi (i) ______ me to turn off the TV as (ii) ______ needed to study for (iii) ____ exams.

    (a) (i) ordered (ii) I (iii) her

    (b) (i) ordered (ii) she (iii) her

    (c) (i) said (ii) I (iii) my

    (d) (i) requested (ii) she (iii) her

Ans. (d) (i) requested (ii) she (iii) her

33. **The student said, "Ma'am, please extend the deadline."**

    (a) The student asked the teacher to extend the deadline.

    (b) The student said if the teacher would extend the deadline.

    (c) The student requested ma'am to extend the deadline.

    (d) The student said that ma'am should extend the deadline.

Ans. (c) The student requested ma'am to extend the deadline.

34. **She said, "Bring a glass of water, please."**

    (a) She commands me to bring a glass of water.

    (b) She requested me to bring a glass of water.

    (c) She asked me to brought a glass of water.

    (d) She ordered me to bring her a glass of water.

Ans. (b) She requested me to bring a glass of water.

35. **She said, "Shut the door!"**

    (a) She asked me whether I would shut the door.

    (b) She ordered me to shut the door.

    (c) She said that I should shut the door.

    (d) She shouted and said to shut the door.

Ans. (b) She ordered me to shut the door.

36. **The policeman said, "Don't cross the speed limit."**

    (a) The policeman said not to cross the speed limit.

    (b) The policeman asked if I would cross the speed limit.

    (c) The policeman forbade me to cross the speed limit.

    (d) The policeman asks if I had crossed the speed limit.

Ans. (c) The policeman forbade me to cross the speed limit.

37. **"Don't make noise in the library." the librarian said.**
    (a) The librarian said not to make noise in the library.
    (b) The librarian ordered me not to make noise in the library.
    (c) The librarian said to be quiet while in the library.
    (d) The librarian asks me to not make any noise.
Ans. (b) The librarian ordered me not to make noise in the library.

38. **Maria said, "Please lend me a pen."**
    (a) Maria ordered me to lend a pen.
    (b) Maria begged me to lend her a pen.
    (c) Maria asked if I could lend her pen.
    (d) Maria requested me to lend her a pen.
Ans. (d) Maria requested me to lend her a pen.

39. **Ranjan said, "You can not park here!"**
    (a) Ranjan said that I may not park here.
    (b) Ranjan said to me that I was unable to park there.
    (c) Ranjan exclaimed that I couldn't park there.
    (d) Ranjan forbade me to park there.
Ans. (c) Ranjan exclaimed that I couldn't park there.

40. **The boss said, "Call him right now."**
    (a) The boss shouted and said to call him right then.
    (b) The boss ordered me to call him quickly.
    (c) The boss told me to call him now.
    (d) The boss ordered me to call him right then.
Ans. (d) The boss ordered me to call him right then.

41. **He said, "Guard the door."**
    (a) He pleaded with me to guard the door.
    (b) He asked if I could guard the door.
    (c) He enquired whether I may guard the door.
    (d) He commanded me to guard the door.
Ans. (d) He commanded me to guard the door.

40. **The Captain said to his men, "Stand at ease."**
    (a) The Captain urged his men to stand at ease.
    (b) The Captain wanted his men to stand at ease.
    (c) The Captain told his men that they should stand at ease.
    (d) The Captain commanded his men to stand at ease
Ans. (a) The Captain urged his men to stand at ease.

43. **"Get out of the car!" said the policeman.**
    (a) The policeman ordered him to get out of the car.
    (b) The policeman advised him to get out of the car.
    (c) The policeman requested him to get out of the car.
    (d) The policeman told him to get out of the car.
Ans. (a) The policeman ordered him to get out of the car.

44. **"Could you please be quiet," she said.**
    (a) She requested me to be quiet.
    (b) She told me to be quiet.
    (c) She ordered me to be quiet.
    (d) She advised me to be quiet.
Ans. (a) She requested me to be quiet.

45. **He said, "Open the door!"**
    (a) He told me to open the door.
    (b) He requested me to open the door.
    (c) He advised me to open the door.
    (d) He ordered me to open the door.
Ans. (d) He ordered me to open the door.

46. **The officer said, "Move fast."**
    (a) The officer commanded them to move fast.
    (b) The officer requested them to move fast.
    (c) The officer advised them to move fast.
    (d) The officer said them to move fast.
Ans. (a) The officer commanded them to move fast.

47. **Mahima said to Anubhav, "Please give me a new book."**
    (a) Mahima advised Anubhav to give her a new book.
    (b) Mahima requested Anubhav to give her a new book.
    (c) Mahima ordered Anubhav to give her a new book.
    (d) Mahima asked Anubhav to give her a new book.
Ans. (b) Mahima requested Anubhav to give her a new book.

❑❑

Reported Speech— Statements

Choose the correct option:

1. **The leader said to the team that he had thought of an alternate solution.**

   (a) The leader said, "He has been thinking of an alternate solution".

   (b) The leader said, "He has an alternate solution".

   (c) The leader said to the team, "I have thought of an alternate solution".

   (d) The leader said to the team, "I had thought of an alternate solution."

   Ans. (c) The leader said to the team, "I have thought of an alternate solution".

2. **He exclaimed with joy that it was his first victory.**

   (a) He said, "I have been waiting for my first victory."

   (b) He said, "It is my first victory."

   (c) He said, "Hurray! It is my first victory."

   (d) He exclaimed, Oh! It is my first victory."

   Ans. (c) He said, "Hurray! It is my first victory."

3. **Heena said that she would be visiting Josh the following day.**

   (a) Heena said, "I shall be visiting Josh the next day."

   (b) Heena said, "I would visit Josh tomorrow."

   (c) Heena said, "I may visit Josh tomorrow."

   (d) Heena said, "I will be visiting Josh tomorrow."

   Ans. (d) Heena said, "I will be visiting Josh tomorrow."

4. **Jessica said that she had a few things to buy.**

   (a) Jessica said, "She has a few things to buy."

   (b) Jessica said, "She had few things to buy."

   (c) Jessica said, "She had had few things to buy."

   (d) Jessica said, "She has had few things to buy."

   Ans. (a) Jessica said, "She has a few things to buy."

5. **Kashvi said that she had been watching cricket.**

   (a) Kashvi said, "I have been watching cricket."

   (b) Kashvi said, "I should watch cricket."

   (c) Kashvi said, "I would be watching cricket."

   (d) Kashvi said, "I have watched cricket."

   Ans. (a) Kashvi said, "I have been watching cricket."

6. **She said to her husband that they should buy a new oven.**

   (a) She said, "Hubby! Let us buy a new oven."

   (b) She said to her husband, "We shall buy a new oven."

   (c) She tells her husband, "We can buy a new oven."

   (d) She said to her husband, "We may buy a new oven."

   Ans. (b) She said to her husband, "We shall buy a new oven."

7. **Reena told me that she had often warned me not to play with a knife.**

   (a) Reena said, "I have often been warning you not be play with a knife."

   (b) Reena said to me, "I had often warned you not to play with a knife."

   (c) Reena said to me, "I have often warned you not to play with a knife."

   (d) Reena said to me, "I often warned you not to play with a knife".

   Ans. (c) Reena said to me, "I have often warned you not to play with a knife."

8. **He said that all is well that ends well.**

   (a) He said, "All is well that ends well."

   (b) He said, "All is well that ended well."

   (c) He said, "All was well that ended well."

   (d) He said, "All was well that ends well."

   Ans. (a) He said, "All is well that ends well."

9. **Fill the blank with the right choice of options:**

   Rani said, "I was cooking dinner yesterday."

   Rani said that she (i)______cooking lunch (ii)______

   (a) (i) was, (ii) yesterday

   (b) (i) had been (ii) yesterday

   (c) (i) was (ii) the day before

   (d) (i) had been (ii) the day before

   Ans. (d) (i) had been (ii) the day before

10. **Choose the correct options:**

    Mohan said, "I can speak different languages."

    Mohan said that he______speak different languages

(a) can   (b) could

(c) should   (d) may

Ans. (b) could

11. **Riyaz:** Can I borrow your pen?

    Jai: Sure you can.

    Riyaz asked Jai (i) if he _______ borrow his pen.

    Jai replied that (ii) ________.

    (a) (i) can (ii) he could

    (b) (i) could (ii) he can

    (c) (i) can (ii) he can

    (d) (i) could (ii) he could

Ans. (d) (i) could (ii) he could

12. **Sanjna said, "My stomach is aching."**

    Sanjna said that (i) _______ stomach (ii) _______ aching.

    (a) (i) her (ii) was   (b) (i) my (ii) is

    (c) (i) my (ii) was   (d) (i) her (ii) is

Ans. (a) (i) her (ii) was

13. **Ankit said that he couldn't come to school in the morning.**

    Ankit (i)______, "He (ii) _____ come to school in the morning".

    (a) (i) told (ii) can't   (b) (i) said (ii) couldn't

    (c) (i) said (ii) can't   (d) (i) told (ii) couldn't

Ans. (c) (i) said (ii) can't

14. **He said, "I work in a laboratory."**

    (a) He said that he had worked in a laboratory.

    (b) He asked that he work in a laboratory.

    (c) He said that he works in a laboratory.

    (d) He said that he has worked in a laboratory.

Ans. (c) He said that he works in a laboratory.

15. **Meena said, "My father is highly educated."**

    (a) Meena asked if her father was highly educated.

    (b) Meena said that my father was highly educated.

    (c) Meena said that her father was highly educated.

    (d) Meena said that my father is highly educated.

Ans. (c) Meena said that her father was highly educated.

16. **He said, "I must go at once."**

    (a) He said he must go at once.

    (b) He said he had to go at once.

    (c) He says he will have to go at once.

    (d) He said that he had to go at once.

Ans. (d) He said that he had to go at once.

17. **My grandfather said, "May you succeed."**

    (a) My grandfather prayed that I might succeed.

    (b) My grandfather said that I might succeed.

    (c) My grandfather prayed that you might succeed.

    (d) My grandfather said that I might succeed.

Ans. (a) My grandfather prayed that I might succeed.

18. **She said, "I will meet you tomorrow."**

    (a) She said that I would meet you the next day.

    (b) She said that she would meet you the next day.

    (c) She said that she would meet me the next day.

    (d) She said that she could meet me the next day.

Ans. (c) She said that she would meet me the next day.

19. **Maria said, "Honesty is the best policy."**

    (a) Maria said that honesty is the best policy.

    (b) Maria said that honesty was the best policy.

    (c) Maria said honesty was the best policy.

    (d) Maria said honesty is always the best policy.

Ans. (a) Maria said that honesty is the best policy.

20. **He said, "I saw him in the hotel."**

    (a) He said that I had seen him in the hotel.

    (b) He said that he had seen him in the hotel.

    (c) He said that he has saw him in the hotel.

    (d) He said that he had been seeing him in the hotel.

Ans. (b) He said that he had seen him in the hotel.

21. **Surbhi said, "I take bath daily."**

    (a) Surbhi said that she would take bath daily.

    (b) Surbhi said that she had taken bath daily.

    (c) Surbhi said that she takes bath daily.

    (d) Surbhi said she take bath daily.

Ans. (c) Surbhi said that she takes bath daily.

22. **Raji said, "I have bought a new dress yesterday."**

    (a) Raji said that I had bought a new dress the previous day.

    (b) Raji said that she had bought a new dress yesterday.

    (c) Raji said that she has bought a new dress the previous day.

    (d) Raji said that she bought a new dress the previous day.

Ans. (d) Raji said that she bought a new dress the previous day.

23. The boss said to the employee, "I cannot pay you more salary".

(a) The boss told the employee that he could not be paid more salary.

(b) The boss told the employee that he could not pay him more salary.

(c) The boss forbade the employee to pay more salary.

(d) The boss warned the employee that he could not pay him more salary.

Ans. (b) The boss told the employee that he could not pay him more salary.

By changing into direct speech, choose the correct option:

24. Nishant told me that he would do it then or never.

(a) Nishant said to me, "I will do it now or never."

(b) Nishant said, "He will do it them or never".

(c) Nishant said, "He would do it now or never".

(d) Nishant said to me, "I would do it then or never".

Ans. (a) Nishant said to me, "I will do it now or never."

25. The tourist told the vendor that he was looking for a hotel.

(a) The tourist said to the vendor, "He was looking for a hotel."

(b) The tourist said to the vendor, "I am looking for a hotel."

(c) The tourist said to the vendor, "I was looking for a hotel."

(d) The tourist said to the vendor, "I have been looking for a hotel."

Ans. (b) The tourist said to the vendor, "I am looking for a hotel."

26. He warned him calmly that he would shoot him if he didn't give him the money.

(a) "If he doesn't give him the money, he will shoot him, " he said to him in a calm voice.

(b) "If he didn't give him the money, he would shoot him, " he said to him in a calm voice.

(c) "If you don't give me money, I will shoot you, " he said to him in a calm voice.

(d) If you didn't give him money, I would shoot you, " he said to him in a calm voice.

Ans. (c) "If you don't give me money, I will shoot you, " he said to him in a calm voice.

27. He said that he ate pizzas and a burgers.

(a) He said, "I eat pizzas and burgers."

(b) He said, "He eats pizzas and burgers."

(c) He said, "He ate pizzas and burgers."

(d) He said, "He has eaten pizzas and burgers."

Ans. (a) He said, "I eat pizzas and burgers."

28. Yashika said that she drank juice after lunch.

(a) Yashika said, "She drinks juice after lunch."

(b) Yashika said, "I drink juice after lunch."

(c) Yashika said, "She drank juice after lunch."

(d) Yashika said, "I had drink juice after lunch."

Ans. (b) Yashika said, "I drink juice after lunch."

29. She told her friend that she knew where everyone was.

(a) She said to her friend, "I know where everyone is".

(b) She said to her friend, "I knew where is everyone is"

(c) She said, "I know where is everyone."

(d) She said to her friend, "I knew where everyone is."

Ans. (a) She said to her friend, "I know where everyone is".

30. Yash says that the earth is round.

(a) Yash says, "The earth was round."

(b) Yash says, "Earth will be round."

(c) Yash said, "The earth is round."

(d) Yash says, "The earth is round."

Ans. (d) Yash says, "The earth is round."

31. Sunita said that she had been studying a lot.

(a) Sunita said, "She had been studying a lot."

(b) Sunita said, "She has been studying a lot."

(c) Sunita said, "I have been studying a lot."

(d) Sunita said, "She was studying a lot."

Ans. (c) Sunita said, "I have been studying a lot."

32. Jarman said he would be there at 5 pm.

(a) Jarman said, "I will be there at 5 pm."

(b) Jarman said, "I would be there at 5 pm."

(c) Jarman said, "He will be there at 5 pm."

(d) Jarman said, "He would be there at 5 pm."

Ans. (a) Jarman said, "I will be there at 5 pm."

Fill in the blanks with the right option.

33. "She always wears bangles," He said.

He said that (i) _______ always (ii) ______ bangles

(a) (i) I (ii) wear

(b) (i) she (ii) wore

(c) (i) she (iii) worn

(d) (i) I (ii) wore

Ans. (b) (i) she (ii) wore

34. He says, "I will finish my work in three days".

He says that (i) ______ (ii) _____ finish (iii) _____ work in three days.

(a) (i) he (ii) will (iii) his

(b) (i) I (ii) will (iii) my

(c) (i) he (ii) would (iii) my

(d) (i) he (ii) would (iii) his

Ans. (d) (i) he (ii) would (iii) his

35. Kritika said "I saw her last night."

Kritika said that (i) ______ (ii) _______ (iii) _____ her (iv) ______ .

(a) (i) she (ii) had (iii) seen (iv) the night before

(b) (i) I (ii) had (iii) seen (iv) the night before

(c) (i) she (ii) has (iii) seen (iv) last night

(d) (i) I (ii) have (iii) seen (iv) last night

Ans. (a) (i) she (ii) had (iii) seen (iv) the night before

36. She says, "I have got a singing lesson today."

She said that (i) ______ (ii) _______ got a singing lesson (iii) _____

(a) (i) she (ii) has (iii) today

(b) (i) I (ii) have (iii) that today

(c) (i) she (ii) had (iii) that day

(d) (i) I (ii) had (iii) that today

Ans. (c) (i) she (ii) had (iii) that day

37. Meena said that she had been walking along the street.

Meena said, "(i) _____ (ii) _____ walking along the street."

(a) (i) I (ii) was   (b) (i) She (ii) was

(c) (i) I (ii) had   (d) (i) She (ii) had

Ans. (a) (i) I (ii) was

38. She said that Ravi might get a ticket the next day.

She says, "Ravi (i) _____ get a ticket (ii) _____."

(a) (i) may (ii) the next day

(b) (i) might (ii) the next day

(c) (i) can (ii) tomorrow

(d) (i) may (ii) tomorrow

Ans. (d) (i) may (ii) tomorrow

39. She said that she had to go to the bank to deposit some documents.

She says, "I _____ go to the bank to deposit some money."

(a) had to   (b) must

(c) can   (d) may

Ans. (b) must

40. He says that he was going to the gym.

He says, "(i) _____ (ii)______ going to the gym.

(a) (i) I (ii) was   (b) (i) He (ii) was

(c) (i) I (ii) am   (d) (i) He (ii) is

Ans. (c) (i) I (ii) am

41. He told us that they had visited their grandfather the last week.

He told us, "They______ visited their grandfather the last week."

(a) have   (b) had

(c) None   (d) has

Ans. (a) have

42. She said, "They may invite us for dinner."

She said that (i) _____ (ii) ______ invite us for dinner.

(a) (i) He (ii) may   (b) (i) they (ii) might

(c) (i) He (ii) may   (d) (i) He (ii) might

Ans. (b) (i) they (ii) might

43. Ravi said, "The concert ended yesterday."

(a) Ravi said that the concert had ended yesterday.

(b) Ravi said that the concert ended the day before.

(c) Ravi said that the concert had ended the previous day.

(d) Ravi said that the concert ended already.

Ans. (c) Ravi said that the concert had ended the previous day.

44. The lawyer said, "The law always believes in the evidence."

(a) The lawyer said that the law always believed in the evidence.

(b) The lawyer said that the law should always believe in the evidence.

(c) The lawyer said that the law always believes in the evidence.

(d) The lawyer said that the law has always believed in the evidence.

Ans. (c) The lawyer said that the law always believes in the evidence.

45. Jen said, "I like drawing sketches."

(a) Jen said that she liked drawing sketches.

(b) Jen said that she has liked drawing sketches.

(c) Jen said that she liked to draw sketches.

(d) Jen said that she likes drawing sketches.

Ans. (d) Jen said that she likes drawing sketches.

46. Julia said, "I can not attend your wedding."

(a) Julia said that she might not attend our wedding.

(b) Julia said that she could not attend our wedding.

(c) Julia said that she can not attend our wedding.

    (d) Julia said that she wished she could attend our wedding.

Ans. (b) Julia said that she could not attend our wedding.

47. Tina said, "I may postpone the trip to the next year."

    (a) Tina said that she may have to postpone the trip to the next year.

    (b) Tina said that she might have to postpone the trip to the next year.

    (c) Tina said that she might postpone the trip to the following year.

    (d) Tina said that she may postpone the trip to the following year.

Ans. (c) Tina said that she might postpone the trip to the following year.

6. Omar said, "I had always wanted to be a teacher."

    (a) Omar said that he had always wanted to be a teacher.

    (b) Omar said that he had had always wanted to be a teacher.

    (c) Omar said that he have always wanted to be teacher.

    (d) Omar said that he wanted to be a teacher ever since.

Ans. (a) Omar said that he had always wanted to be a teacher.

48. She said, "You have been late. Everybody's here already."

    (a) She said that I had been late and everybody was there already.

    (b) She said that I was late and that everyone was there already.

    (c) She said I got late so that everybody was there already.

    (d) She said that I am late and everybody got there already.

Ans. (a) She said that I had been late and everybody was there already.

49. Meera said, "It's time. I must go now."

    (a) Meera said that it is time and she should leave.

    (b) Meera said that it was time and she had to go then.

    (c) Meera said that it was time to go then.

    (d) Meera said it is time and she may go.

Ans. (b) Meera said that it was time and she had to go then.

50. Tim said, "I may teach you if you will show sincerity."

    (a) Tim said that he might teach me if I would show sincerity.

    (b) Tim said that he may teach me at a condition.

    (c) Tim said that he could teach me had I shown sincerity.

    (d) Tim said that he will teach me if I was to show sincerity.

Ans. (a) Tim said that he might teach me if I would show sincerity.

51. Philip said, "I was playing football."

    (a) Philip said that he was playing football.

    (b) Philip said that he would be playing football.

    (c) Philip said that he had been playing football.

    (d) Philip said that he plays football.

Ans. (a) Philip said that he was playing football.

❑❑

Reported Speech— Questions

Chapter 14

1. **The supervisor asked, "Who is he?"**
   (a) The supervisor asked who he was.
   (b) The supervisor asked me who he was.
   (c) The supervisor asked who are you.
   (d) The supervisor told who is he.
   Ans. (a) The supervisor asked who he was.

2. **The shopkeeper said to me, "Are you interested in buying this shirt?"**
   (a) The shopkeeper said that if I was interested in buying this shirt.
   (b) The shopkeeper said that if I were interested in buying this shirt.
   (c) The shopkeeper asks if I am interested in buying that shirt.
   (d) The shopkeeper asked me if I was interested in buying that shirt.
   Ans. (d) The shopkeeper asked me if I was interested in buying that shirt.

3. **Rajan said, "Is Mr. Vikrant in his cabin?"**
   (a) Rajan requested that if Mr. Vikrant was in his cabin.
   (b) Rajan enquired if Mr. Vikrant was in his cabin.
   (c) Rajan enquired that if Mr. Vikrant was in his cabin.
   (d) Rajan asked if Mr. Vikrant had been in his cabin.
   Ans. (b) Rajan enquired if Mr. Vikrant was in his cabin.

4. **Aunt said, "What's the time by your watch?"**
   (a) Aunt asks me what time it was by my watch.
   (b) Aunt asked me what the time was by my watch.
   (c) Aunt asked me what the time by my watch was.
   (d) Aunt asked me what time it was by my watch.
   Ans. (c) Aunt asked me what the time by my watch was.

5. **Anthony said, "Where have Rachel been?"**
   (a) Anthony asked where Rachel had been.
   (b) Anthony told me where Rachel should have been.
   (c) Anthony told me where Rachel was.
   (d) Anthony said that Rachel had not been there.
   Ans. (a) Anthony asked where Rachel had been.

6. **Jyotika said, "How much more is to be done?"**
   (a) Jyotika asked how much more was to be done.
   (b) Jyotika asked how much had been left to be done.
   (c) Jyotika asked how much was still to be done.
   (d) Jyotika asked how much more was left to be done.
   Ans. (a) Jyotika asked how much more was to be done.

7. **She said, "Why are you not dancing?"**
   (a) She said, that why am I not dancing.
   (b) She asked me why I was not dancing.
   (c) She asked me why I am not dancing.
   (d) She asked whether I was dancing.
   Ans. (b) She asked me why I was not dancing.

Change the following into Direct Speech.

8. **Victoria asked Joan if he was free that evening.**
   (a) Victoria said to Joan, "Are you free this evening?"
   (b) Victoria asked Joan, "Will you be free this evening?"
   (c) Victoria said to Joan, "If you are free this evening?"
   (d) Victoria said to Joan, "Be free this evening."
   Ans. (a) Victoria said to Joan, "Are you free this evening?"

9. **The husband asked his wife whether she was ready for the party or not.**
   (a) The husband said to his wife, "Is she ready for the party or not?"
   (b) The husband said to his wife, "Are you ready for the party or not?"
   (c) The husband said to his wife, "Were you ready for the party or not?"
   (d) The husband said to his wife, "Are you ready, or shall I wait?"
   Ans. (b) The husband said to his wife, "Are you ready for the party or not?"

10. Mother enquired who had been responsible for the mess.

   (a) Mother said, "Who was responsible for the mess?"

   (b) Mother said, "Who has been responsible for the mess?"

   (c) Mother said, "Who is responsible for this mess?"

   (d) Mother said, "Who shall be responsible for this?"

Ans. (b) Mother said, "Who has been responsible for the mess?"

11. Our teacher asked us who was not wearing a proper uniform.

   (a) Our teacher said, "Who was not wearing a proper uniform?"

   (b) Our teacher said, "Who has not worn a proper uniform?"

   (c) Our teacher said, "Who is not wearing a proper uniform?"

   (d) Our teacher asked, "Who had not worn a proper uniform?"

Ans. (c) Our teacher said, "Who is not wearing a proper uniform?"

12. He asked if she had finished her work.

   (a) He said, "Has she finished her work?"

   (b) He asked, "Have she finished her work?"

   (c) He asked, "Had she finished her work?"

   (d) He said, "Has she finished the work?"

Ans. (a) He said, "Has she finished her work?"

13. He inquired him whether his profession was not a doctor.

   (a) He asked, "Whether his profession was not a doctor?"

   (b) He said, "Whether his profession is not a doctor?"

   (c) He said to him, "Is your profession not a doctor?"

   (d) He said, "Was your profession, not doctor?"

Ans. (c) He said to him, "Is your profession not a doctor?"

14. She asked me where I lived.

   (a) She said to me, "Where do you live"

   (b) She said to me, "Where you live'?

   (c) She asked me "Where do I live"?

   (d) She asked "Where did I lived"?

Ans. (a) She said to me, "Where do you live"

15. Esther asked him whether he had any children.

   (a) Esther said to him, "Do you have any children?

   (b) Esther said to him, "Have you had any children?"

   (c) Esther asked, "Had he had any children?"

   (d) Esther said, "Has he had any children?"

Ans. (a) Esther said to him, "Do you have any children?

Fill in the blanks with the right option.

16. Susan said, "Which car do you plan to buy?"

Susan asked (i) _____ which car (ii) _____ (iii)_________ to buy.

   (a) (i) that (ii) do (iii) you

   (b) (i) me (ii) I (iii) planned

   (c) (i) me (ii) do (iii) you

   (d) (i) to me (ii) do (iii) planned

Ans. (b) (i) me (ii) I (iii) planned

17. The Guard said, "Do you really come from Afghanistan?"

The Guard asked ________ he really (ii) ______ from Afghanistan.

   (a) (i) if (ii) come

   (b) (i) if (ii) will come

   (c) (i) whether (ii) came

   (d) (i) whether (ii) did come

Ans. (c) (i) whether (ii) came

18. The lady inquired if he was quite well.

The lady said, "____ you quite well?"

   (a) Are   (b) Do

   (c) Will   (d) Have

Ans. (a) Are

19. Reeta asked Seeta if she had read the book.

Reeta said to Seeta, "(i) _____ (ii) ______ read the book?"

   (a) (i) Has (ii) she   (b) (i) Have (ii) you

   (c) (i) Do (ii) you   (d) (i) Had (ii) she

Ans. (b) (i) Have (ii) you

20. He said, "Where is the letter?"

He (i) ______ me where the letter (ii) _____.

   (a) (i) asked (ii) was   (b) (i) said (ii) is

   (c) (i) asked (ii) is   (d) (i) said (ii) was

Ans. (a) (i) asked (ii) was

21. My father said to me, "Has your brother returned from Delhi?"

My father asked me (i) ______ (ii) ______ brother (iii) ______ returned from Delhi.

(a) (i) if (ii) my (iii) has

(b) (i) that (ii) your (iii) has

(c) (i) if (ii) your (iii) had

(d) (i) if (ii) my (iii) had

Ans. (d) (i) if (ii) my (iii) had

22. The lady at the reception asked what she could do for him.

The lady at the reception (i) _______, "What (ii) _____ (iii)_____ do for you?"

(a) (i) said (ii) she (iii) can

(b) (i) said (ii) can (iii) I

(c) (i) asked (ii) she (iii) can

(d) (i) asked (ii) she (iii) could

Ans. (b) (i) said (ii) can (iii) I

25. Change into Reported Speech by choosing the right option.

My brother said to his colleague, "Why are you so lazy today?"

(a) My brother said to his colleague, that why are you so lazy today.

(b) My brother asked his colleague why he had been so lazy that day.

(c) My brother asked his colleague why he was so lazy that day.

(d) My brother asked his colleague he were he so lazy this day.

Ans. (c) My brother asked his colleague why he was so lazy that day.

Exercise-1

Choose the correct option:

1. The guard asked, "Who are you?"

(a) The guard asked who he was.

(b) The guard asked me who he was.

(c) The guard asks me who he was.

(d) The guard asked who I was.

Ans. (d) The guard asked who I was.

2. Grandpa said, "What's the time by your watch?"

(a) Grandpa asked me what time it was by my watch.

(b) Grandpa asked me what was the time by my watch.

(c) Grandpa asked me what the time was by my watch.

(d) Grandpa asks me what time it was by my watch.

Ans. (b) Grandpa asked me what was the time by my watch.

3. Harish said, "Will you accompany me there?"

(a) Harish asked me if I would accompany him there.

(b) Harish asked if I could accompany him there.

(c) Harish enquired whether I will accompany him there.

(d) Harish said to me that I accompany him there.

Ans. (a) Harish asked me if I would accompany him there.

4. Daniel said, "Where have you been?"

(a) Daniel asked me where I had been.

(b) Daniel told me where I should have been.

(c) Daniel told me where I was.

(d) Daniel said that I had not been there.

Ans. (a) Daniel asked me where I had been.

5. He said, "How much is left to do?"

(a) He asked how much had been left to do.

(b) He asked how much had been left to be done.

(c) He asked how much was left to be done.

(d) He asked how much was still left.

Ans. (c) He asked how much was left to be done.

6. Jacob said, "Have you read this book?"

(a) Jacob asked me if I have read this book.

(b) Jacob asked me if I had read that book.

(c) Jacob asked me if I would read this book.

(d) Jacob asked me if I had been reading this book.

Ans. (b) Jacob asked me if I had read that book.

7. The driver said, "Do you want to halt for a while?"

(a) The driver said if we wanted a halt for a while.

(b) The driver asked if we want to halt for a while.

(c) The driver asks if we wanted to halt for a while.

(d) The driver asked if we wanted to halt for a while.

Ans. (d) The driver asked if we wanted to halt for a while.

8. David said, "Can we go tomorrow?"

(a) David said if we can go tomorrow.

(b) David asked if we could go the following day.

(c) David asked if we could go tomorrow.

(d) David said whether we could go tomorrow.

Ans. (b) David asked if we could go the following day.

9. The secretary said, "Is Mr. Fisher in his office?"

(a) The secretary said that if Mr. Fisher was in his office.

(b) The secretary enquired if Mr. Fisher was in his office.

(c) The secretary enquired that if Mr. Fisher was in his office.

(d) The secretary asked if Mr. Fisher had been in his office.

Ans. (b) The secretary enquired if Mr. Fisher was in his office.

10. The salesman said, "Are you interested in the scheme?"

(a) The salesman said that if I was interested in the scheme.

(b) The salesman said that if I were interested in the scheme.

(c) The salesman asks if I am interested in the scheme.

(d) The salesman asked me if I was interested in the scheme.

Ans. (d) The salesman asked me if I was interested in the scheme.

Exercise-2

1. Nishant : "Do you speak French ?"
2. Rony : "Have you got a computer ?"
3. Father asked, "Did you come by train ?"
4. Devi : "Have you been to London ?"
5. Susan : "Does Manish work in an office ?
6. Elizabeth : "Will Jovi have lunch with Anne ?"
7. Frank : "How much pocket money does Lisa get?"
8. Sophia : " Did you watch the latest movie ?"
9. Anne : "Must I do shopping ?"
10. Ronald : "Where does Pinki park her car ?"
11. Joseph : "May I ask you a question ?"
12. "Have you set your alarm clock", he asked me.
13. "How long have you been working in here", Sonam asked me.
14. "Shall I tell you the story of ghosts" , Ruma asked the child.

15. "What do you want", Rohit asked his brother.
16. Mum asked, "How often do you phone your friend ?"
17. Alex : "What do you think of the new movie ?"
18. Dev : "Did you have enough time to finish your assignment ?"
19. Jane : "Why are Rishi and Rini still sleeping ?"
20. "Don't you like to read comics", Sunita asked Ramu.

Answers :

1. Nishant asked if I spoke French.
2. Rony wanted to know whether I had a computer.
3. Father wanted to know whether I had come by train.
4. Devi asked if I had been to London.
5. Susan asked if Manish worked in an office.
6. Elizabeth asked if Jovi would have lunch with Anne.
7. Frank wanted to know how much pocket money Lisa got.
8. Sophia asked if I had watched the latest movie.
9. Anne asked if she had to do shopping.
10. Ronald asked me where Pinki parked her car.
11. Joseph requested if he might ask me a question.
12. He asked me if/whether I had set my alarm clock.
13. Sonam asked me how long I had been working there.
14. Ruma asked the child whether she should tell the story of ghosts.
15. Rohit asked his brother what he wanted.
16 Mum wondered how often I phone my friends.
17. Alex wanted to know what I thought of the new movie.
18. Dev asked if I had enough time to finish my assignment.
19. Jane wanted to know why Rishi and Rini were still sleeping.
20. Sunita asked Ramu if he didn't like to read comics.

LITERATURE
FIRST FLIGHT
[PROSE]

Glimpses of India

Chapter 7

I. A Baker from Goa—*by Lucio Rodrigues*

Summary :

This is a pen portrait of a baker of Goa. Lucio Rodrigues tells of the Portuguese influence to bread-making and how the tradition is still continuing. The baker is an important person in town as bread and its varieties are a must for different occasions. The baker would come to the narrator's house twice a day and all the children would vie for a sight of the breads in his basket. The typical dress that a baker wears and that he is called a pader are some of the interesting things the narrator tells us through this pen picture.

Extract Based Questions

I. Read the given extract to attempt the questions that follow:

During our childhood in Goa, the baker used to be our friend, companion and guide. He used to come at least twice a day. Once, when he set out in the morning on his selling round, and then again, when he returned after emptying his huge basket. The jingling thud of his bamboo woke us up from sleep and we ran to meet and greet him. Why was it so? Was it for the love of the loaf? Not at all. The loaves were bought by some Paskine or Bastine, the maid-servant of the house! What we longed for were those bread-bangles which we chose carefully. Sometimes it was sweet bread of special make.(Glimpses of India)

1. What according to the narrator was the reaction of the children on hearing the baker's bamboo thud?

1. They avoid the loud noise and would turn around and sleep.
2. They would wake up from their sleep.
3. They would jump out of bed quickly.
4. They would run to meet and greet him.
5. They would go to buy loaves.

Choose the correct option from the following:

(a) (1) and (5)   (b) (2), (3) and (4)

(c) (2) and (3)   (d) (3) (4)and (5)

Ans. (b) (2), (3) and (4)

2. Select the option which displays an example of "jingling"

(a) The hawker pushed through the crowd in the market.

(b) The little boy ran across the road to fetch the ball.

(c) The ice-cream vendor began ringing a small bell attached to his cart on the beach.

(d) The two old women were strolling in the park

Ans. (c) The ice-cream vendor began ringing a small bell attached to his cart on the beach.

3. From the options given below, identify the attitude of the children in the extract:

(a) Frightened   (b) Restless

(c) Excited   (d) Hesitant

Ans. (c) Excited

4. '*Not at all*' in the above extract means...

Choose one from the following to answer:

(a) Of course   (b) In every respect

(c) By no means   (d) Absolutely

Ans. (c) By no means

5. Select the most appropriate option for (1) and (2).

(1) Paskine or Bastine were male servants of the house.

(2) The narrator ate only the sweet bread bangles.

(a) (1) is true and (2) is false.

(b) (2) is the opposite of (1).

(c) (1) furthers the meaning of (2).

(d) Both (1) and (2) cannot be inferred from the extract.

Ans. (d) Both (1) and (2) cannot be inferred from the extract.

II. *We kids would be pushed aside with a mild rebuke and the loaves would be delivered to the servant. But we would not give up. We would climb a bench or the parapet and peep into the basket, somehow. I can still recall the typical fragrance of those loaves. Loaves for the elders and the bangles for the children. (Glimpses of India)*

1. **Why were the children reproached when the baker arrived?**
   1. So that the children could not smell the fragrance.
   2. So that the loaves would be delivered to the servant.
   3. So that the loaves would be delivered to the elders.
   4. So that the bangles could be given to the servant.
   5. So that the elders get the loaves and the children the bangles.

   Choose the correct option from the following:
   (a) (1) and (5)   (b) (1), (3) and (4)
   (c) Only 2   (d) (2) and (5)

Ans. (c) Only 2

2. **Select the option which displays an example of *'would not give up'*.**
   (a) Jack trekked along despite injuries and reached the mountain top
   (b) I had a lot of losses and can't bear to lose anymore
   (c) People saw the smoke coming from the shop and ran helter-skelter.
   (d) Raj jumped in to the pool and swam back safely.

Ans. (a) Jack trekked along despite injuries and reached the mountain top

3. **Select the most appropriate option for (1) and (2).**
   (1) We would climb a bench or the parapet and peep into the basket.
   (2) The children would yield to the rebuking.
   (a) (1) is true and (2) is false.
   (b) (2) is the opposite of (1).
   (c) (1) furthers the meaning of (2).
   (d) Both (1) and (2) cannot be inferred from the extract.

Ans. (a) (1) is true and (2) is false.

4. **From the options given below, identify the attitude of the children in the extract:**
   (a) Scared   (b) Restless
   (c) Determined   (d) Hesitant

Ans. (c) Determined

5. **What do you understand from the statement when the narrator says the following?**

   I can still recall the typical fragrance of those loaves.

Choose one from the following to answer:
(a) The narrator is hungry when he sees the loaves.
(b) The narrator remembers the fragrance of the loaves.
(c) The narrator is unsure of the fragrance of the loaves.
(d) The narrator has the memory of the baker.

Ans. (b) The narrator remembers the fragrance of the loaves.

Multiple Choice Questions

1. **Our elders think ___________ about those good old Portuguese days.**
   (a) favourably   (b) fondly
   (c) scornfully   (d) casually

Ans. (b) fondly

2. **In the lesson 'A Baker from Goa', what does *'reminiscing nostalgically'* indicate?**
   (a) Thinking about the present.
   (b) Thinking about the carnival.
   (c) Thinking fondly about the past.
   (d) Thinking about the improvement.

Ans. (c) Thinking fondly about the past.

3. **What was the famous topic of the elders of Goa according to the narrator?**
   (a) Portuguese and their rule.
   (b) Portuguese and their loaf of bread.
   (c) Portuguese and their forts.
   (d) Portuguese and their loaves of bread.

Ans. (d) Portuguese and their loaves of bread.

4. **According to the author the elders think fondly of the Portuguese because of:**
   (a) their famous movie stars
   (b) their famous sports
   (c) their famous loaves of bread
   (d) their famous buildings

Ans. (c) their famous loaves of bread

5. **Which option correctly replaces the underlined word in the line 'Might have vanished' from the lesson *A Baker from Goa*?**
   (a) Unlikely to have   (b) Sure
   (c) Confident   (d) Perhaps

Ans. (d) Perhaps

6. **With reference to the lesson 'A Baker from Goa', relate the given words**
   loaves: baker: furnace___________
   (a) bread   (b) mixer
   (c) fire   (d) pader

Ans. (c) fire

7. **Identify the apt option that does not describe the making of loaves.**
   (a) moulders   (b) mixers
   (c) furnace   (d) eaters

Ans. (d) eaters

8. **What does the narrator of the chapter 'A Baker from Goa' aptly imply by 'age-old' in the line 'Those age-old, time-tested furnaces still exist'.**
   (a) Worn out   (b) Ancient
   (c) Year old   (d) Exhausted

Ans. (b) Ancient

9. **Which among the following poetic device is used in the line--- 'The thud and jingle of the baker's bamboo'?**
   (a) Simile   (b) Repetition
   (c) Onomatopoeia   (d) Personification

Ans. (c) Onomatopoeia

10. **What did the author actually mean by the line –' the fire in the furnace still exists?'**
    (a) People still buy loaves of bread from the friendly village baker.
    (b) The elders gather together to reminiscence nostalgically about Goa.
    (c) The author's fond memory of the fragrance of bread loaves.
    (d) The Old Portuguese traditions of Goa are not wholly extinct.

Ans. (d) The Old Portuguese traditions of Goa are not wholly extinct.

11. **What was the real purpose of the specially made bamboo staff carried by the baker?**
    (a) Bang the ground to announce his arrival.
    (b) Place the basket of loaves on the bamboo staff.
    (c) The staff denoted a mark of identity.
    (d) It was used to scare away dogs.

Ans. (a) Bang the ground to announce his arrival.

12. **The narrator says that 'the fire in the furnaces has not yet been extinguished' because...**
    (a) The eaters of loaves have vanished.
    (b) The bakers still exist.
    (c) The baking tradition doesn't exist.
    (d) the loaves are no more needed.

Ans. (b) The bakers still exist.

13. **The purpose of the thud and jingle of the traditional baker's bamboo, might be to _____.**
    (a) wake the people up.
    (b) announce his arrival.
    (c) frighten the children.
    (d) play with the children.

Ans. (b) announce his arrival.

14. **What are the bakers known as in Goa?**
    (a) Pader   (b) Pekar
    (c) Portugese   (d) Baker

Ans. (a) Pader

15. **The word 'heralding' aptly means:**
    (a) Declaring   (b) Pronouncing
    (c) Announcing   (d) Yelling

Ans. (c) Announcing

16. **'During our childhood in Goa, the baker used to be our friend, companion and guide'. This meant that he was a good__________________.**
    (a) mentor   (b) foe
    (c) attendant   (d) captor

Ans. (a) mentor

17. **How many times did the baker come every day?**
    (a) Once   (b) Thrice
    (c) Twice   (d) Varies daily

Ans. (b) Thrice

18. **Which amongst the following figure of speech does, 'musical entry' denote?**
    (a) Metaphor
    (b) Simile.
    (c) Hyperbole
    (d) Transferred Epithet

Ans. (d) Transferred Epithet

19. **The baker would say 'Good morning' to the lady of the house. What would that mean?**
    (a) A mockery   (b) A greeting
    (c) A joke   (d) A remark

Ans. (b) A greeting

20. **The baker would place his basket on the ______ bamboo.**
    (a) Horizontal   (b) Parallel
    (c) Vertical   (d) Perpendicular

Ans. (c) Vertical

21. **We kids would be pushed aside with _________**
    (a) A gentle push   (b) A hard stare
    (c) A mild rebuke   (d) A warning

Ans. (c) A mild rebuke

22. **We kids would be pushed aside because:**
    (a) They were in the way
    (b) They were teasing
    (c) They were stealing
    (d) They were naughty
Ans. (a) We were in the way

23. *'But we would not give up'.* 'We' refers to_____.
    (a) The elders   (b) The children
    (c) The bakers   (d) The maid-servants
Ans. (b) The children

24. **What does *'would not give up'* imply?**
    (a) The children were meek.
    (b) The children were strong.
    (c) The children were determined.
    (d) The children were docile.
Ans. (c) The children were determined

25. **Why the children in 'A Baker from Goa', did not care to brush their teeth or wash their mouths properly?**
    (a) The children wanted to take the bangles
    (b) The children were afraid they would not get the bangles
    (c) The children were enchanted by the fragrance of the bangles.
    (d) The children were eager to meet the baker and get the bangles.
Ans. (d) The children were eager to meet the baker and get the bangles.

26. **In the lesson 'A Baker from Goa', relate the words.**
    children: tiger: mango-leaf: __________
    (a) bangle bread   (b) toothbrush
    (c) bol   (d) Loaves
Ans. (b) toothbrush

27. **Why does the author not feel the need to brush his teeth?**
    (a) He was like a tiger
    (b) It was troublesome
    (c) He was carefree
    (d) He was only going to take the bangles
Ans. (b) It was troublesome

28. **Which among the following can be said to be most disliked by the author as a child?**
    (a) Children were rebuked by the baker for approaching his basket.
    (b) The twigs and the leaves were used for the purpose of brushing the teeth.
    (c) A general requirement of brushing teeth.
    (d) The virtual disappearance of the concept of the village baker.
Ans. (c) A general requirement of brushing teeth.

29. **What type of trait did the children attribute to in the chapter 'A Baker from Goa'?**
    (a) Child like   (b) Carefree
    (c) Wild   (d) Caged
Ans. (b) Carefree

30. **The early morning entry of the Baker would usher in________**
    Fill in the appropriate phrase from the options given below.
    (a) cackle of activities
    (b) bubble of activities
    (c) noisy chuckling of kids
    (d) babble of activities
Ans. (b) bubble of activities

31. **According to the author, marriage gifts are meaningless without_______.**
    (a) baker   (b) bolinhas
    (c) bread   (d) bol
Ans. (d) bol

32. **What can the symbolism of baker's furnace be associated to in a Goan village?**
    (a) All social occasions demanded the presence of baker's products.
    (b) The village women loved the loaves made by the baker.
    (c) The children woke up early.
    (d) There was a government regulation, which demanded that all villages should have a bakery.
Ans. (a) All social occasions demanded the presence of baker's products.

33. **The lady of the house must prepare sandwiches on the occasion of her daughter's engagement as a.**
    (a) Compulsion   (b) Tradition
    (c) Business   (d) Profession
Ans. (b) Tradition

34. **Other than cake what is a must for Christmas?**
    (a) Bol   (b) Kabai
    (c) Bangles   (d) Bolinhas
Ans. (d) Bolinhas

35. Which option correctly replaces the underlined word in the give line from *A Baker from Goa*? 'Absolutely essential'.

(a) Necessary   (b) Extremely important

(c) Wanted   (d) Must have

Ans. (b) Extremely important

36. The bakers of the good old Portuguese days had a peculiar dress known as__________

(a) Bolinhas   (b) Pader

(c) Kabai   (d) Bol

Ans. (c) Kabai

37. *The baker's dress was a single-piece long frock.* What does the author imply by the underlined word?

(a) A suit   (b) A one piece

(c) A gown   (d) Unscathed

Ans. (b) A one piece

38. When did the baker usually collect his bills?

(a) End of the week

(b) Every fortnight

(c) End of the month

(d) Beginning of the month

Ans. (c) End of the month

39. Where were the monthly accounts of the baker recorded?

(a) In a copy, with a pencil

(b) On a wall, with a pencil

(c) On a board, with a pencil

(d) On a tree trunk, with a pencil

Ans. (b) On a wall, with a pencil

40. In the lesson 'A Baker from Goa', relate the words fruitless: productive: loss: _______.

(a) useless   (b) soaring

(c) profit   (d) vain

Ans. (c) profit

41. How was the baking profession in the monetary sense in the good old days?

(a) Roaring   (b) Profitable

(c) Loss   (d) Fruitless

Ans. (b) Profitable

42. The profession of the baker was so profitable that his family and his servants were:

(a) Greedy and prosperous

(b) Starving and prosperous

(c) Happy and prosperous

(d) Sad and prosperous

Ans. (c) Happy and prosperous

43. What was the main reason for the baker and his family to be prosperous?

(a) The family never starved.

(b) There was round the year demand for bread loaves.

(c) The baker and his servants usually sported a healthy plum body reflecting prosperity.

(d) All of the above.

Ans. (b) There was round the year demand for bread loaves.

44. What was the testimony of the baker in the good old days?

(a) Lean physique

(b) Plump physique

(c) Muscular physique

(d) Thin physique

Ans. (b) Plump physique

45. Even today any person with a __________ physical appearance is easily compared to a baker.

(a) Muskmelon like   (b) Watermelon like

(c) Jackfruit like   (d) Banana like

Ans. (c) Jackfruit like

46. What does the word bangles imply in the phrase *'bangles for the children'* from the chapter 'A Baker from Goa'?

(a) An ornament   (b) A wrist band

(c) A sweet bread   (d) A toast

Ans. (c) A sweet bread

47. Under which category can the lesson *'A Baker From Goa'* be listed?

(a) Historical   (b) Factual

(c) Descriptive   (d) Nostalgic

Ans. (d) Nostalgic

Text Book Questions

Oral Comprehension Check :

48. What are the elders in Goa nostalgic about?

Ans. The elders in Goa are nostalgic about the good old Portuguese days, the Portuguese and their famous loaves of bread.

49. Is bread-making still popular in Goa? How do you know?

Ans. Yes, bread-making is still popular in Goa. When the narrator says that the sons have carried on the tradition, it means that Goa still has bread makers. Also, we hear of the famous bread making industry in Goa.

50. What is the baker called?

Ans. The baker is called 'pader'.

51. When would the baker come everyday? Why did the children run to meet him?

Ans. During the narrator's childhood, the baker would come everyday. The children ran to meet him to look into his basket for the bread bangles.

52. Match the following. What is a must:

(i) as marriage gifts?	(a) cakes and bolinhas
(ii) for a party or a feast?	(b) sweet bread called bol
(iii) for a daughter's engagement?	(c) bread
(iv) for Christmas?	(d) sandwiches

Ans. (i)-b, (ii)-c, (iii)-d, (iv)-a

53. What did the bakers wear: (i) in the Portuguese days? (ii) when the author was young?

Ans. (i) During the Portuguese days the bakers wore a peculiar dress known as the kabai. It was a single-piece long frock reaching down to the knees.

(ii) When the author was young, he had seen the bakers wearing shirt and trousers which were shorter than full-length ones and longer than half pants.

54. Who invites the comment — "he is dressed like a pader"? Why?

Ans. Anyone who wears a half pant which reaches just below the knee invites the comment that he is dressed like a pader!

55. Where were the monthly accounts of the baker recorded?

Ans. The monthly accounts of the baker were recorded on some wall in pencil.

56. What does a 'jack fruit - like appearance' mean?

Ans. Jack fruit-like appearance means a plump physique, someone who is not thin but round like a jack fruit.

Thinking about the Text

57. Which of these statements are correct?

(i) The pader was an important person in the village in old times. True

(ii) Paders still exist in Goan villages. True

(iii) The paders went away with the Portuguese. False

(iv) The paders continue to wear a single-piece long frock. False

(v) Bread and cakes were an integral part of Goan life in the old days. True

(vi) Traditional bread-baking is still a very profitable business. True

(vii) Paders and their families starve in the present times. False

58. Is bread an important part of Goan life? How do you know this?

Ans. Bread is an important and integral part of Goan life because some or the other form of bread is a must during various ceremonies and occasions in Goa.

59. Tick the right answer. What is the tone of the author when he says the following?

(i) The thud and the jingle of the traditional baker's bamboo can still be heard in some places. (nostalgic, hopeful, sad)

Ans. nostalgic

(ii) Maybe the father is not alive but the son still carries on the family profession. (nostalgic, hopeful, sad)

Ans. hopeful

(iii) I still recall the typical fragrance of those loaves. (nostalgic, hopeful, naughty)

Ans. nostalgic

(iv) The tiger never brushed his teeth. Hot tea could wash and clean up everything so nicely, after all. (naughty, angry, funny)

Ans. funny

(v) Cakes and bolinhas are a must for Christmas as well as other festivals. (sad, hopeful, matter-of-fact)

Ans. matter of fact

(vi) The baker and his family never starved. They always looked happy and prosperous. (matter-of-fact, hopeful, sad)

Ans. matter of fact

Reference to Context Questions

Read the extract given below and answer the questions that follow :

60. *Our elders are often heard reminiscing nostalgically about those good old Portuguese days, the Portuguese and their famous loaves of bread. Those eaters of loaves might have vanished but the makers are still there. We still have amongst us the mixers, the moulders and those who bake the loaves.*

(a) How can you say that bread-making is still popular in Goa ?

(b) Is bread an important part of Goan life ? How do you know this ?

Ans. (a) Bread-making is still popular in Goa because the bread makers are still there and so are their mixers, moulders and furnaces.

(b) Yes, bread is an important part of Goan life even today. This we can definitely say because bread is a part of important occasions like Christmas, festivals, weddings and engagements. These occasions are incomplete without a special preparation for each event, made from bread.

61. *Pranjol's father slowed down to allow a tractor, pulling a trailer-load of tea leaves, to pass. 'This is the second flush or sprouting period, isn't it, Mr. Barua ?'*

Rajvir asked, 'It lasts from May to July and yields the best tea.'

'You seem to have done your homework before coming,' Pranjol's father said in surprise. 'Yes, Mr. Barua,' Rajvir admitted. 'But I hope to learn much more when I'm here.'

(a) Why did Mr. Barua feel surprised ?

(b) What information was given by Pranjol's father to Rajvir about Assam Tea State ?

Ans. (a) Mr. Barua was surprised that Rajvir knew so much about tea plantations, despite the fact that it was his first visit to Assam. He appreciated the fact that Rajvir had collected a considerable amount of information before coming.

(b) Pranjol's father agreed to Rajvir's information about it being the second-flush or sprouting period.

II. Coorg—*by Lokesh Abrol*

Summary :

Lokesh Abrol gives a beautiful description of Coorg, the smallest district in Karnataka. It is the home of the Kodavas, a martial clan possibly descended from the Arabs or the Greek. Their traditional dress hints at a connection to the Arabs and the Kurds. The Kodavas are a brave clan with many joining the army. The natural beauty is worth a visit with animals from elephants to langurs and exotic birds. The best season to visit is from September to March—when it doesn't rain. Another attraction is the Buddhist settlement right in the heart of the area.

Extract Based Questions

I. **Read the given extract to attempt the questions that follow:**

Coorg, or Kodagu, the smallest district of Karnataka, is home to evergreen rainforests, spices and coffee plantations. Evergreen rainforests cover thirty per cent of this district. During the monsoons, it pours enough to keep many visitors away. The season of joy commences from September and continues till March. The weather is perfect, with some showers thrown in for good measure. The air breathes of invigorating coffee. Coffee estates and colonial bungalows stand tucked under tree canopies in prime corners.

(Glimpses of India- Coorg)

1. How is the narrator trying to describe the environment of Coorg?

1. Mangrove forest
2. By its deciduous forests
3. By its evergreen rainforests
4. The smell of coffee
5. Perfect weather

Choose the correct option from the following

(a) (1) and (5)   (b) (3), (4) and (5)
(c) (2) and (3)   (d) (1) (2)and (3)

Ans. (b) (3), (4) and (5)

2. From the options given below, identify the word in the extract that means the same as prevent?

(a) Commences   (b) Invigorating
(c) Good measure   (d) Keep away

Ans. (d) Keep away

3. Select the most appropriate option for (1) and (2).

(1) During the monsoons it is a pleasant place for visitors.

(2) September to March is the season of joy.

(a) (1) is false and (2) is true.

(b) (2) is the opposite of (1).

(c) (2) furthers the meaning of (1).

(d) Both (1) and (2) cannot be inferred from the extract.

Ans. (a) (1) is false and (2) is true.

4. Select the option which displays an example of 'some showers' in the extract.

(a) The little boy was dirty and mother asked him to take a bath.

(b) The boy ran and took shade under a tree to avoid getting wet from the unexpected rain.

(c) The woman washed her soiled clothes with the water from the pool.

(d) The woman washed her feet in the flowing stream.

Ans. (b) The boy ran and took shade under a tree to avoid getting wet from the unexpected rain.

5. 'Colonial bungalows' in the above extract signifies bungalows built during the ...

Choose one from the following to answer:

(a) Pre-British era   (b) Modern era

(c) Post British era   (d) British era

Ans. (d) British era

II. *The fiercely independent people of Coorg are possibly of Greek or Arabic descent. As one story goes a part of Alexander's army moved South along the coast and settled here when return became impractical. These people married amongst the locals and their culture is apparent in the martial traditions, marriage and religious rites, which are distinct from the Hindu mainstream. Coorgi homes have a tradition of hospitality, and they are more than willing to recount numerous tales of valour related to their sons and fathers. The Coorg Regiment is one of the most decorated in the Indian Army, and the first Chief of the Indian Army, General Cariappa, was a Coorgi. Even now, Kodavus are the only people in India permitted to carry firearms without a license.*

(Glimpses of India-Coorg)

1. **How is the narrator trying to describe the special quality of the people of Coorg?**

   1. Ferocious

   2. Fiercely independent

   3. Greek or Arabic descent

   4. dependent

   5. not independent

   Choose the correct option from the following

   (a) (1) and (5)   (b) (3), (4) and (5)

   (c) Only 2   (d) (2) and (3)

Ans. (d) (2) and (3)

2. **Select the most appropriate option for (1) and (2).**

   (1) Alexander's army married amongst the locals .

   (2) Their culture is apparent in the martial traditions, marriage and religious rites, and are indistinct from the Hindu mainstream.

   (a) (1) is true and (2) is false.

   (b) (2) is the opposite of (1).

   (c) (2) furthers the meaning of (1).

   (d) Both (1) and (2) cannot be inferred from the extract.

Ans. (a) (1) is true and (2) is false.

3. **From the options given below, find a word from the extract that means the same as relating to war.**

(a) Hospitable   (b) Fiercely

(c) Martial   (d) Humility

Ans. (c) Martial

4. **Select the option which displays an example of 'valour'.**

   (a) Jane picked up a bag found on the street and handed it over to the police.

   (b) Raj patiently helped the old woman cross the road.

   (c) Sam jumped into the water and saved the little boy from drowning.

   (d) The ragged woman shared her food with the street children.

Ans. (c) Sam jumped into the water and saved the little boy from drowning.

5. **Which group of people in India are allowed to carry firearms without licence?**

   Choose one from the following to answer:

   (a) Gorkha   (b) Nagas

   (c) Kodavus   (d) Toda

Ans. (c) Kodavus

Multiple Choice Questions

1. **What is the apt term for 'Midway'?**

   (a) Nearby   (b) Equidistant

   (c) At a distance   (d) Not very far from

Ans. (b) Equidistant

2. **What is the exact location of Coorg?**

   (a) Between Mangalore and the coastal town of Bangalore

   (b) Between Mysore and the coastal town of Bangalore

   (c) Between Mysore and the coastal town of Kerala

   (d) Between Mysore and the coastal town of Mangalore

Ans. (d) Between Mysore and the coastal town of Mangalore

3. **The author refers to which place as piece of heaven?**

   (a) Mangalore   (b) Mysore

   (c) Coorg   (d) Croog

Ans. (c) Coorg

4. **'*piece of heaven*' can be attributed to which amongst the following figure of speech?**

   (a) Metapho   (b) Simile

   (c) Hyperbole   (d) Transferred Epithet

Ans. (a) Metaphor

5. Which option correctly replaces the underlined word in the given line from Coorg? Must have drifted.

(a) Unlikely to have   (b) Sure to have

(c) Confident   (d) likely to have

Ans. (d) likely to have

6. The cause of the drifting of the piece of heaven from the kingdom of God is……..

(a) Certainly Gods were angry

(b) Uncertain

(c) Unsure about God's rage

(d) Certain

Ans. (b) Uncertain

7. Coorg is the land of rolling hills? This means.

(a) It is surrounded by hills

(b) It is a land of hills

(c) It has no vegetation

(d) It is barren

Ans. (a) It is surrounded by hills

8. The author refers to the men of Coorg as martial men. What do you understand by it?

(a) Humble men   (b) Martial art men

(c) Men of war   (d) Fierce men

Ans. (c) Men of war

9. The other name for Coorg is __________.

(a) Kodgau   (b) Kadgou

(c) Kodagu   (d) Kudago

Ans. (c) Kodagu

10. In the lesson 'Coorg', relate the words Mangalore: coastal town: Coorg: __________

(a) Country   (b) State

(c) District   (d) Town

Ans. (c) District

11. As quoted by the author, Coorg is a home to ________ .

(a) Wild animals

(b) Fierce men

(c) Evergreen rainforests

(d) Evergreen canopies

Ans. (c) Evergreen rainforests

12. The evergreen rainforests cover______per cent of Coorg.

(a) 50 per cent   (b) 75 per cent

(c) 30 per cent   (d) 25 per cent

Ans. (c) 30 per cent

13. *During the monsoon, it pours enough to keep many visitors away.* What do you conclude?

(a) Visitors enjoy the rains

(b) Visitors shun the rains

(c) Visitors avoid coming during the rains

(d) Visitors enjoy this pleasant weather

Ans. (c) Visitors avoid coming during the rains

14. Identify the phrase from the text that have the same meaning.

During monsoons it rains so heavily that tourists do not visit Coorg.

(a) During monsoons the downpour keeps away the visitors.

(b) During monsoons it pours enough to keep many visitors away.

(c) The weather is not perfect and keeps many visitors away.

(d) Some showers thrown in good measure keeps many visitors away.

Ans. (b) During monsoons it pours enough to keep many visitors away.

15. Identify the word used by the author that means 'start' or 'begin'.

(a) From   (b) Some

(c) Commence   (d) Inhabit

Ans. (c) Commence

16. The season of joy refers to the period ________

(a) From September to February

(b) Between September and March

(c) From December to March

(d) Between December and February

Ans. (b) Between September and March

17. What is the appropriate synonym for the word invigorating?

(a) Rejuvenating   (b) Tiring

(c) Sapping   (d) Wearying

Ans. (a) Rejuvenating

18. *Tucked under tree canopies in prime corners.* Here Prime implies______

(a) Good   (b) Best

(c) Beginning   (d) First

Ans. (b) Best

19. Coorg is a ________according to its referral by the author.

(a) Tourist place   (b) Historical place

(c) Hill station   (d) Vacation place

Ans. (c) Hill station

20. What does the author have to say about the inhabitants of Coorg?

(a) Fiercely Independent and Portuguese descent.

(b) Independent and Greek and Arabic descent.

(c) Fiercely independent and Greek or Arabic descent.

(d) Fiercely dependent and Greek or Arabic descent

Ans. (c) Fiercely independent and Greek or Arabic descent.

21. Identify the word that is the synonym to 'not sure'.

(a) Hopefully   (b) Perhaps

(c) Maybe   (d) Possibly

Ans. (d) Possibly

22. Identify the phrase from the text that has the same meaning.

Some people say that Alexander's army moved south along the coast and settled there.

(a) As the story goes, Alexander's army moved south along the coast and settled here.

(b) As one story goes, Alexander's army moved north along the coast and settled here.

(c) As one story goes, a part of Alexander's army moved south along the coast and settled here.

(d) As the story goes, a part of Alexander's army moved south along the coast and settled here.

Ans. (c) As one story goes, a part of Alexander's army moved south along the coast and settled here.

23. The apt word for embroidered is________

(a) Tailored with thread

(b) Stitched with thread

(c) Ornamented with thread

(d) Sewn with thread

Ans. (c) Ornamented with thread

24. Who are the Kodavus in Coorg?

(a) The personel security in Coorg.

(b) The personel of the Coorg Regiment in the Indian Army.

(c) The locals of Coorg.

(d) The farmers of Coorg.

Ans. (c) The locals of Coorg.

25. Identify the other word for Tradition used in the lesson Coorg.

(a) Culture   (b) Mainstream

(c) Rites   (d) Martial

Ans. (a) Culture

26. Identify the phrase from the text that has the same meaning.

The theory of the Arab origin is supported by the long coat with embroidered waist- belt they wear.

(a) The theory is that the Arab origin is supported from the long coat with embroidered waist- belt they wear.

(b) The theory of Arab origin draws support from the long coat with embroidered waist- belt they wear.

(c) The theory behind the long coat with embroidered waist- belt they wear is drawn from the theory of the Arab origin.

(d) The theory is that long coat with embroidered waist- belt they wear is drawn from the theory of the Arab origin.

Ans. (b) The theory of Arab origin draws support from the long coat with embroidered waist-belt they wear.

27. The author says the kuppia worn by the Kodavus resembles the__________worn by the Arabs.

(a) Kufia   (b) Kaffia

(c) Kuffia   (d) Kauffi

Ans. (c) Kuffia

28. What makes the Coorg society different from rest of Indians?

(a) Their Greek -Arab descent.

(b) Their martial heritage.

(c) Their tradition of hospitality.

(d) Though being Hindus, the religious rites followed by them differ from the mainstream.

Ans. (d) Though being Hindus, the religious rites followed by the people of Coorg differ from the mainstream.

29. What exactly is the author trying to highlight through this passage?

(a) The evergreen rain forests of Coorg.

(b) The beautiful hills of Coorg.

(c) The subtle aroma of coffee associated with Coorg.

(d) The martial society and the lifestyle of the people of Coorg.

Ans. (d) The martial society and the lifestyle of the people of Coorg.

30. **Identify the phrase from the text that has the same meaning.**

    The Coorg people are always ready to tell stories of their son's and father's valour.

    (a) The people of Coorg have a tradition of recounting numerous tales of valour related to their sons and fathers.

    (b) The people of Coorg traditionally recount numerous tales of valour related to their sons and fathers.

    (c) The Coorg people are more than willing to recount numerous stories of valour related to their sons and fathers.

    (d) The people of Coorg never recount the tales of valour related to their sons and fathers.

    Ans.(c) The Coorg people are more than willing to recount numerous stories of valour related to their sons and fathers.

31. **By tales of valour the author tells us about____**

    (a) History of the brave people of the past

    (b) Freedom fighters

    (c) Stories of courage and bravery usually in war

    (d) Heroic deeds of freedom fighters.

    Ans.(c) Stories of courage and bravery usually in war

32. **By most decorated the author relates to_____**

    (a) Having received the maximum number of medals for sports

    (b) Having received maximum number of awards for bravery

    (c) Having received rewards for extracurricular activities.

    (d) Having received rewards for archery

    Ans.(b) Having received maximum number of awards for bravery

33. **Which of these indicates a profound recognition of martial nature of the Kodavus by India?**

    (a) The first Chief of the Indian Army was from Coorg.

    (b) The Coorgi regiment is one of the most decorated in the Indian Army.

    (c) No license is required by the people of Coorg to carry fire arms.

    (d) Coorg people are believed to be of Greek and Arab descendance.

    Ans.(c) No license is required by the people of Coorg to carry fire arms.

34. **The hills and forests of Coorg is from where the river________ obtains its water.**

    (a) Godavari   (b) Krishna

    (c) Kaveri   (d) Yamuna

    Ans.(c) Kaveri

35. **The river Kaveri abounds in Mahaseer which is a large________**

    (a) Monkeys   (b) Freshwater fish

    (c) Langurs   (d) Elephant

    Ans.(b) Freshwater fish

36. **Kingfisher is a type of _______ that dives as revealed by the author.**

    (a) Airlines   (b) Sea farer

    (c) Fish   (d) Bird

    Ans.(d) Bird

37. **What do langurs and squirrels enjoy doing mischievously?**

    (a) Throwing away partially eaten fruits in the muddy water.

    (b) Throwing away partially eaten fruits in the clear water.

    (c) Throwing away partially spoilt fruits in the dustbins.

    (d) Throwing away partially stolen fruits in the clear water.

    Ans. (b) Throwing away partially eaten fruits in the clear water.

38. *The most laidback individuals become converts.* **What is the quality of the individual according to the author?**

    (a) Aggressive   (b) Demanding

    (c) Relaxed   (d) Stubborn

    Ans.(c) Relaxed

39. *Individuals become converts.* **What does convert mean here?**

    (a) Change of attitude

    (b) Change of religion

    (c) Remain the same

    (d) Change of apparel

    Ans.(a) Change of attitude

40. **Pick the odd man out which does not refer to High-energy adventure.**

    (a) Canoeing   (b) Mountain biking

    (c) Rappelling   (d) Horse riding

    Ans.(d) Horse riding

41. Rappelling is __________ .

(a) Trekking

(b) Sliding down a rope from a cliff

(c) Travelling on a raft

(d) Travelling on a narrow boat

Ans. (b) Sliding down a rope from a cliff

42. What in author's mind is the best way to enjoy Coorg?

(a) Visit a local family

(b) Take a dive into Kodavu cuisine

(c) Enjoy the wild life

(d) Take part in outdoor activities

Ans. (d) Take part in outdoor activities.

43. Which of these can best describe the idea behind the phrase, *'The most laidback individuals......'*?

(a) Coorg is not for relaxing

(b) People who prefer to do active sports cannot enjoy Coorg

(c) Coorg is only for activity

(d) Even the people who prefer to chill will try adventure sports

Ans. (d) Even the people who prefer to chill will try adventure sports

44. What do you think about this with reference to a trail?

(a) Every path is a trail

(b) Every trail is a path

(c) Every trail is not a path

(d) Not every trail is a path.

Ans. (d) Not every trail is a path.

45. From which place in Coorg could you get the panoramic view of the misty landscapes?

(a) Mountain   (b) Bylakuppe

(c) Brahmagiri   (d) Nisargadhama

Ans. (c) Brahmagiri

46. A walk across the rope bridge leads to the sixty-four-acre island of __________ .

(a) Bylakuppe   (b) Nisargadhama

(c) Mysore   (d) Coorg

Ans. (b) Nisargadhama

47. What is the bonus that the author is talking about:

(a) Running into some macaques.

(b) Running into some langurs.

(c) Running into Buddhists monks.

(d) Running into some mountain trekkers.

Ans. (c) Running into Buddhists monks.

48. The ochre colour is nearest to which of the following options?

(a) Dark chocolate   (b) Teak colour

(c) Clay earth   (d) Coconut

Ans. (c) Clay earth

Text Book Questions

Thinking about the Text :

49. Where is Coorg?

Ans. Coorg is the smallest district of Karnataka and is situated midway between Mysore and the coastal town of Mangalore.

50. What is the story about the Kodavu people's descent?

Ans. Coorgis are possibly of Greek or Arabic descent. As one story goes, a part of Alexander's army moved to south along the coast and settled there when their return became impractical. These people married amongst the locals and their culture is apparent in the martial traditions, marriage and religious rites, which are distinct from the Hindu mainstream.

51. What are some of the things you now know about :

(i) the people of Coorg?

Ans. They are the only ones permitted to carry firearms.

(ii) the main crop of Coorg?

Ans. coffee

(iii) the sports it offers to tourists?

Ans. river rafting, canoeing, rappelling, rock climbing, mountain biking and trekking

(iv) the animals you are likely to see in Coorg?

Ans. Elephants, Macaques, Malabar squirrels, langurs, slender loris, birds, bees and butterflies

(v) its distance from Bangalore and how to get there?

Ans. 260 kms, by road via Mysore or Neelamangal

52. Here are six sentences with some words in italics. Find phrases from the text that have the same meaning. (Look in the paragraphs indicated)

(i) During monsoons it rains so heavily *that tourists do not visit Coorg.*   **(para 2)**

Ans. to keep many visitors away.

(ii) *Some people say that* Alexander's army moved south along the coast and settled there. **(para 3)**

Ans. As one story goes.

(iii) The Coorg people *are always ready to tell stories of their sons' and fathers' valour.* **(para 4)**

Ans. they are more than willing to recount

(iv) *Even people who normally lead an easy and slow life get smitten by the high-energy adventure sports of Coorg.* **(para 6)**

Ans. The most laid-back individuals become converts

(v) The theory of the Arab origin *is supported by the long coat with embroidered waist-belt they wear.* **(para 3)**

Ans. draws support from

(vi) Macaques, Malabar squirrels *observe you carefully* from the tree canopy. **(para 7)**

Ans. keep a watchful eye

Thinking about Language

53. Which of the following nouns can collocate with which of the adjectives given below?

unique   terrible   unforgettable   serious   ancient   wide   sudden

(i) culture : unique culture, ancient culture

(ii) monks: ancient monks, serious monks, unforgettable monks

(iii) surprise: unforgettable surprise, terrible surprise

(iv) experience : unforgettable experience, terrible experience

(v) weather : terrible weather

(vi) tradition : ancient tradition, unique tradition

Short Answer Type Questions

20-30 Words

54. What did excite Rajvir? Why did Pranjol not share his excitement?

Ans. The beautiful scenery and wide range of green tea gardens excited Rajvir. Pranjol did not share his excitement since he was born and brought up in Assam, a place familiar to him.

55. Why were the children fascinated by the baker? How did they show their eagerness to see him?★

★ **are board exam questions from previous years**

Ans. The baker or the pader used to be an essential part of the Goan's life. He sold bread in different shapes and tastes which was a popular part of the Goan cuisine. The children were not fascinated by the baker's jingle or by the loaves of bread he sold but attracted by the bread bangles or the special sweet bread that he sold. The children would know about his arrival from the 'jhang, jhang' sound of his bamboo stick. They would run to meet and greet him. They tried to surround the basket but were pushed aside until the bread was delivered to the maid. Then they were allowed to choose their bread-bangles.

The bread-bangles fascinated the children and made them eager for the arrival of the baker.

56. How did the baker make his presence known in the morning?

Ans. The baker came in the morning with the 'jhang jhang' sound of his bamboo staff. He carried his basket on his head supported with one hand and in the other hand he had the bamboo staff which he banged on the ground. This sound marked his presence in the mornings.

57. Baking was considered essential in a traditional Goan village. What reasons does the writer give to support his point ?

Ans. Baking was considered important and essential in a Goan village, since the time of the Portuguese. Bread is an essential item for everyday and for every occasion. Marriage gifts were considered meaningless without sweet bread and festivals and celebrations were incomplete without cakes.

58. What do we learn about the financial condition of the bakers of Goa ?

Ans. The bakers of Goa led a prosperous life. As bakers never starved, baking was a profitable profession in the old days. The families and servants of these bakers always looked happy and prosperous. Their plum physique is an open testimony to their prosperity.

Long Answer Type Questions

100-120 words

59. Give the two legends about the discovery of tea.

Ans. The Indian legend for the discovery of tea: There was a Buddhist ascetic named Bodhidharma. He often fell asleep during meditation. To stop this he cut off his eyelids. It is said that ten tea plants grew out of the eyelids. The leaves of this plant are put in hot water and drunk to banish sleep. The legend connects the energising quality of tea with the ascetic's problem of sleep.

The Chinese legend: There was a Chinese emperor who always had boiled water. Once a few leaves from a twig fell into his boiling water. They gave a delicious flavour to his water and from then, tea became popular in China.

60. Write a paragraph on Coorg.

Ans. Coorg is the smallest district in Karnataka, situated about 260 kms from Bangalore. It is situated between Mysore and Mangalore. There are hills all around the town which appears like a piece of heaven broken down from the Kingdom of God. It is the land of the brave martial clan of the Kodavus. There are coffee plantations in the area. The Coorgis are very hospitable people. They are a brave community with the first Army chief of our country being a Coorgi. The flora and fauna of the area is unique and one can easily encounter elephants, Malabar squirrels, langurs, loris etc. The best time to visit Coorg is from September to March when the rains have stopped. Coorg is also a haven for adventure sport enthusiasts.

Reference to Context Questions

Read the extract given below and answer the questions that follow :

61. The theory of Arab origin draws support from the long, black coat with an embroidered waist-belt worn by the Kodavus.

(a) Choose the answer that lists the correct option about the dress of the Arabs.

1. The Arabs wore a short coat.

2. The Arabs wore a long coat.

3. The Arabs wore a waist-coat.

4. The Arabs wore a long coat with an embroidered waist-coat.

(i) Option 1   (ii) Option 2

(iii) Option 3   (iv) Option 4

(b) The people of Coorg are known for their

  (i) hospitality

  (ii) martial art

  (iii) descendancy from Alexander

  (iv) descendancy from the Arabs

(c) One can get a panoramic view of Coorg from the _______ hills.

  (i) Bylakuppe

  (ii) Brahmagiri Hills

  (iii) Mariani junction

  (iv) None of these

(d) A walk across the rope bridge leads to the island of _______.

  (i) Tibet

  (ii) Bylakuppe

  (iii) Nisargadhama

  (iv) All of these

(e) Which of the following words expresses the exact meaning of the phrase – 'draws support'?

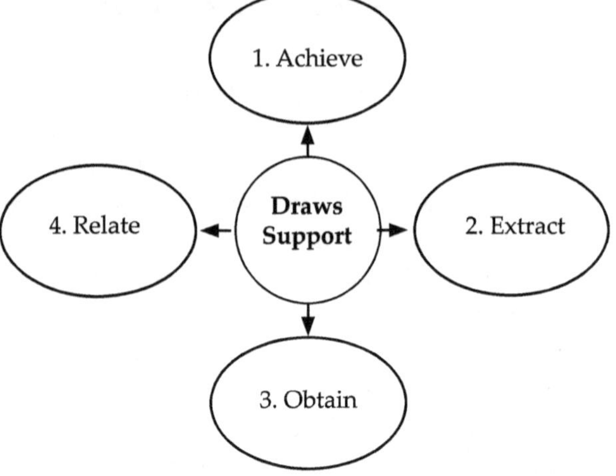

(i) Option 1   (ii) Option 2

(iii) Option 3   (iv) Option 4

Ans. (a) (iv) option 4

    (b) (i) hospitality

    (c) (ii) Brahmagiri Hills

    (d) (iii) Nisargadhama

    (e) (iii) option 3

III. Tea from Assam—*by Arup Kumar Datta*

Summary :

Pranjol, a youngster from Assam, is Rajvir's classmate at school in Delhi. Pranjol's father is the manager of a tea-garden in Upper Assam and Pranjol has invited Rajvir to visit his home during the summer vacation. This dialogue is between Rajvir and Pranjol on their train journey to the tea estate. The boys talk about the history of tea, how it came to India and the legends behind its discovery. Rajvir is very excited the sight of tea gardens on the hills of Assam and is looking forward to learning more about how tea is grown and the rigours of growing it.

Extract Based Questions

I. Read the given extract to attempt the questions that follow:

CHAI-GARAM... garam-chai," a vendor called out in a high-pitched voice. He came up to their window and asked,"Chai, sa'ab?" "Give us two cups," Pranjol said. They sipped the steaming hot liquid. Almost everyone in their compartment was drinking tea too. "Do you know that over eighty crore cups of tea are drunk every day throughout the world?" Rajvir said. "Whew!" exclaimed Pranjol. "Tea really is very popular."

1. In the chapter 'Tea from Assam' what does the narrator want to highlight?

  1. The country as a whole.

  2. The natives of India.

  3. The brewing of the drink.

  4. The origin of the popular drink .

  5. The population of India

Choose the correct option from the following:

  (a) (1) and (5)   (b) (3) and (4)

  (c) (2) and (4)   (d) (1), (2) and (3)

Ans. (b) (3) and (4)

2. Select the most appropriate option for (1) and (2).

  (1) "Chai –Garam….garam-chai" a vendor called out.

  (2) Chai, sa'ab?" "Give us two cups,"

  (a) (1) is true and (2) is false.

  (b) (2) is the opposite of (1).

  (c) (2) is the result of (1).

  (d) Both (1) and (2) cannot be inferred from the extract.

Ans. (c) (2) is the result of (1).

3. Select the option which displays an example of 'compartment' in the extract.

  (a) The little boy put his hands on his head in despair.

  (b) I put the soap in the softener slot of the washing machine by mistake.

  (c) The woman used her towel to shield herself from the sun.

  (d) The boy tried to board the running bus and was injured.

Ans. (b) I put the soap in the softener slot of the washing machine by mistake.

4. From the options given below, the narrator's expression "Whew!" in the extract is of _______

  (a) anxiety   (b) surprise

  (c) greetings   (d) sympathy

Ans. (b) surprise

5. Synonym of the word 'famous' in the above extract is ...

Choose one from the following to answer.

  (a) general   (b) unusual

  (c) rare   (d) popular

Ans. (d) popular

II. *"Tell me another!" scoffed Pranjol. "We have an Indian legend too. Bodhidharma, an ancient Buddhist ascetic, cut off his eyelids because he felt sleepy during meditations. Ten tea plants grew out of the eyelids. The leaves of these plants when put in hot water and drunk banished sleep. "Tea was first drunk in China," Rajvir added, "as far back as 2700 B.C.! In fact words such as tea, 'chai' and 'chini' are from Chinese. Tea came to Europe only in the sixteenth century and was drunk more as medicine than as beverage."*

1. "Tell me another!" scoffed Pranjol. By this it is meant that Pranjol spoke _____________

Choose the right option:

  (a) Excitingly   (b) Surprised

  (c) Mockingly   (d) Angrily

Ans. (c) Mockingly

2. In the lesson 'Tea from Assam' Why does Pranjol scoffed at Rajvir?

  1. Pranjol was ignorant about the legends.

  2. Rajvir had read about Assam.

  3. Rajvir knew all about the history of Tea.

  4. Pranjol was sleepy.

  5. Pranjol was excited

Choose the correct option from the following.

(a) (1) and (5)   (b) (3) and (4)

(c) (2) and (4)   (d) (1), (2) and (3)

Ans. (d) (1), (2) and (3)

3. **Select the most appropriate option for (1) and (2).**

(1) A Buddhist ascetic Bodhidharma felt sleepy during meditations.

(2) A Buddhist ascetic Bodhidharma cut off his eyelids.

(a) (1) is true and (2) is false.

(b) (2) is the opposite of (1).

(c) (2) is the result of (1).

(d) Both (1) and (2) cannot be inferred from the extract.

Ans. (c) (2) is the result of (1).

4. **Select the option which displays an example of 'meditation' in the extract.**

(a) The teacher asked Ram to run an extra round as a punishment.

(b) The group of women were practicing Yoga in the park.

(c) The woman was tired and lay down to sleep.

(d) The boy ran after the ball to save a run.

Ans. (b) The group of women were practicing Yoga in the park.

5. **Synonym of the word *'banished'* in the above extract is ...**

Choose one from the following to answer:

(a) take away   (b) replace

(c) abandon   (d) vanished

Ans. (d) Vanished

Multiple Choice Questions

1. **Identify the incorrect statement with reference to the lesson, "Tea from Assam".**

(a) Pranjol is a youngster.

(b) Rajvir is Pranjol's classmate.

(c) Rajvir's father is a manager of a tea garden in Upper Assam.

(d) Pranjol's father is a manager of a tea garden in Upper Assam.

Ans. (c) Rajvir's father is a manager of a tea garden in Upper Assam.

2. **The vendor was calling out in a high-pitched voice because_________**

(a) he was angry and wanted attention.

(b) he was addressing people and wanted attention.

(c) he was begging and wanted attention.

(d) he was selling tea and wanted attention.

Ans. (d) he was selling tea and wanted attention.

3. **What was the tone of tea vendor when he asked,"*Chai, sa'ab?***

(a) Aggressive   (b) Humble

(c) Proud   (d) Stern

Ans. (b) Humble

4. **Who said these words and to whom? *"Give us two cups said"* __________**

(a) Pranjol to the tea vendor.

(b) Rajvir to the tea vendor.

(c) Pranjol's father to the tea vendor.

(d) Rajvir's father to the tea vendor.

Ans. (a) Pranjol to the tea vendor

5. **What was ordered by Pranjol?**

(a) Two cups of Tea   (b) Two cups of Coffee

(c) Two Chapatis   (d) None of these

Ans. (a) Two cups of Tea

6. **What was the purpose behind sipping the steaming hot tea?**

(a) It was very hot

(b) to make it cold

(c) It had no taste

(d) They had burned their tongue.

Ans. (a) It was very hot

7. **Think and choose the right answer.**

(a) Tea is very popular all over the world as 80 crore cups of the brew are drank every day.

(b) Tea is not so popular as only 80 crore people of the world drink it every day.

(c) Tea is highly popular in certain parts of the world and nearly 80 crore people drink it daily.

(d) None

Ans. (c) Tea is highly popular in certain parts of the world and nearly 80 crore people drink it daily.

8. **Pranjol's expression *"whew"* suggests an_____.**

(a) Expression of seriousness

(b) Expression of joking

(c) Expression of anger

(d) Expression of surprise

Ans. (d) Expression of surprise

9. **In the lesson 'Tea from Assam', relate the words leaves: hot: steaming: famous: __________**

(a) Cold   (b) Shrug

(c) Dejected   (d) Popular

Ans. (d) Popular

10. **Which option correctly replaces the underlined word in the given line from Tea from Assam? Pranjol buried his nose in his detective book again.**
    - (a) Engrossed
    - (b) Ashamed
    - (c) Bored
    - (d) Stuck up

Ans. (a) Engrossed

11. **What is the other word for passionate used in this lesson.**
    - (a) Engrossed
    - (b) Ardent
    - (c) Sturdy
    - (d) Keener

Ans. (b) Ardent

12. **Identify the apt option that describes interest.**
    - (a) Keener
    - (b) Buried
    - (c) Magnificent
    - (d) Sturdy

Ans. (a) Keener

13. **Was Rajvir a fan of detective stories?**
    - (a) Yes
    - (b) No
    - (c) Maybe
    - (d) Don't know

Ans. (a) Yes

14. **The narrator states that he was keener on looking at the beautiful scenery since________.**
    - (a) He was keen of sceneries
    - (b) It was green everywhere
    - (c) There were plantations all around
    - (d) he had never before seen such greenery

Ans. (d) he had never before seen such greenery

15. **In the lesson Tea from Assam, what does 'sea of tea bushes' indicate?**
    - (a) Floating tea plants
    - (b) Flourishing tea plants
    - (c) Florescent tea plants
    - (d) Tea plants surrounded by water.

Ans. (b) Flourishing tea plants

16. **How does the author describe the tea plantations?**
    - (a) A sea of Tea bushes.
    - (b) A house of Tea bushes.
    - (c) A continent of Tea bushes.
    - (d) A greenery of Tea bushes.

Ans. (a) A sea of Tea bushes.

17. **_Sea of Tea bushes_ can be identified as which figure of speech?**
    - (a) Metaphor
    - (b) Simile
    - (c) Hyperbole
    - (d) Transferred Epithet

Ans. (a) Metaphor

18. **Dwarfing the tiny tea plants were tall sturdy shade-trees. Means__________**
    - (a) The tall trees were overshadowing the tea plants
    - (b) The tall trees were dominating the tea plants
    - (c) The tall trees were not allowing the tea plants to grow
    - (d) The tall trees were protecting the tea plants.

Ans. (a) The tall trees were overshadowing the tea plants

19. **What do you think the ugly building with chimney was?**
    - (a) Factory
    - (b) Old shanty building having a go down
    - (c) A tea leaf processing plant
    - (d) A building hoisting the canteen for the tea plantation workers

Ans. (c) A tea leaf processing plant

20. **The author says Rajvir cried excitedly when he saw the tea garden, He meant that Rajvir__________.**
    - (a) Was sad
    - (b) Was horrified
    - (c) Was surprised
    - (d) Was dejected

Ans. (c) Was surprised

21. **Why does the author say Pranjol didn't share Rajvir's excitement? Since __________.**
    - (a) Rajvir was born and brought up on a plantation.
    - (b) Rajvir knew a lot about the plantation
    - (c) Pranjol was born and brought up on a plantation
    - (d) Pranjol was bored seeing the plantation.

Ans. (c) Pranjol was born and brought up on a plantation

22. **Which option correctly replaces the underlined word in the given line from Tea from Assam? Concentration of plantations.**
    - (a) Attentiveness
    - (b) Estates
    - (c) liquidity
    - (d) Absorption

Ans. (b) Estates

23. **Legends in Tea from Assam refers to __________**
    - (a) Fairy tales
    - (b) Folk tales
    - (c) Science
    - (d) Technology

Ans. (b) Folk tales

24. **The legends surprised and excited __________.**
    - (a) Rajvir and his dad

(b) Pranjol

(c) Pranjol and his dad

(d) Rajvir

Ans. (b) Pranjol

25. Bodhidharma was _____________.

(a) A Chinese emperor

(b) A Chinese ascetic

(c) A Buddhist king

(d) A Buddhist ascetic

Ans. (d) A Buddhist ascetic

26. The reason for the ascetic to cut off his eyelids was____________.

(a) To keep him awake during meditations

(b) To plant tea plants

(c) To avoid distraction

(d) To see clearly far and wide

Ans. (a) To keep him awake during meditations

27. How many legends did Rajvir recall on the way to the plantation?

(a) 1   (b) 2

(c) 3   (d) Many

Ans. (b) 2

28. The origin of drinking tea goes back to _______.

(a) India   (b) Japan

(c) China   (d) Korea

Ans. (c) China

29. The narrator refers to the words like 'chai' and 'chini' are from...

(a) India   (b) Japan

(c) China   (d) Korea

Ans. (c) China

30. What conclusion can you draw from the statement –'tea arrived late in Europe and the beverage was drunk more as a medicine'?

(a) Tea is not very popular in Europe.

(b) Though tea was being drunk in China from 2500 BC, nobody thought of selling it to the Europeans.

(c) It was the British who introduced Tea to Europe from India after the 16th century.

(d) None

Ans. (c) It was the British who introduced Tea to Europe from India after the 16th century.

31. Identify the apt option that describes refreshment.

(a) Tea   (b) Coffee

(c) Medicine   (d) Beverage

Ans. (d) Beverage

32. The junction the train clattered into was ______.

(a) Mariami   (b) Mariani

(c) Miriani   (d) Maniari

Ans. (b) Mariani

33. What do you conclude when the author says the boys pushed their way?

(a) They were excited

(b) They were frightened

(c) They were searching

(d) They were lost

Ans. (a) They were excited

34. The children were welcomed from the station by _________.

(a) Rajvir's parents   (b) Rajvir's father

(c) Pranjol's parents   (d) Mr Barua

Ans. (c) Pranjol's parents

35. Identify the location of the tea-garden managed by Pranjol's father.

(a) Nisargadhama   (b) Brahmagiri

(c) Dhekiabari   (d) Mariani

Ans. (c) Dhekiabari

36. Which option correctly replaces the underlined word in the given phrase 'the car veered sharply'.

(a) Abruptly   (b) Strongly

(c) Cutting   (d) Deeply

Ans. (a) Abruptly

37. Identify the apt word used for change of direction.

(a) Clatter   (b) Cross

(c) Veer   (d) Drive

Ans. (c) Veer

38. Identify the apt option that does not refer to a cattle- bridge.

(a) A bridge made for cattle passing

(b) A bridge built over a ditch

(c) A bridge built of metal

(d) A bridge made for smooth flow of traffic

Ans. (a) A bridge made for cattle passing

39. The tea bushes were on both sides of the____________.

(a) The cattle bridge   (b) The veering roads

(c) The gravel roads   (d) Railway junction

Ans. (c) The gravel roads

40. As per as your understanding of the passage match the following:

(a) Second Flush   a. Awake

(b) Assam   b. Sprouts

(c) Tea   c. Plantations

(d) Chinese Emperor   d. Tea

Ans. (a)-b; (b)-c; (c)-a; (d)-d

41. In the lesson 'Tea from Assam', relate the words Scoffed: Compliment: passionless: _________ .

(a) Bored   (b) Ardent

(c) Keener   (d) Horrified

Ans. (b) Ardent

42. *"You seem to have done your homework before coming,"* said Pranjol's father. What do you infer?

(a) Holiday homework

(b) Project work

(c) Knowledge about Assam

(d) Geography

Ans. (c) Knowledge about Assam

Text book Questions

Thinking about Language

43. Look at these words: upkeep, downpour, undergo, dropout, walk-in. They are built up from a verb (keep, pour, go, drop, walk) and an adverb or a particle (up, down, under, out, in).

Use these words appropriately in the sentences below. You may consult a dictionary.

(i) A heavy <u>downpour</u> has been forecast due to low pressure in the Bay of Bengal.

(ii) Rakesh will <u>undergo</u> major surgery tomorrow morning.

(iii) My brother is responsible for the <u>upkeep</u> of our family property.

(iv) The <u>dropout</u> rate for this accountancy course is very high.

(v) She went to the Enterprise Company to attend a <u>walk-in</u> interview.

44. Now fill in the blanks in the sentences given below by combining the verb given in brackets with one of the words from the box as appropriate.

over   by   through   out   up   down

(i) The Army attempted unsuccessfully to <u>overthrow</u> the Government. (throw)

(ii) Scientists are on the brink of a major <u>breakthrough</u> in cancer research. (break)

(iii) The State Government plans to build a <u>by-pass</u> for Bhubaneswar to speed up traffic on the main highway. (pass)

(iv) Gautama's <u>outlook</u> on life changed when he realised that the world is full of sorrow. (look)

(v) Rakesh seemed unusually <u>downcast</u> after the game. (cast)

45. Think of suitable -ing or -ed adjectives to answer the following questions.

How would you describe

(i) a good detective serial on television ?

Ans. thrilling

(ii) a debate on your favourite topic 'Homework Should Be Banned' ?

Ans. exciting

(iii) how you feel when you stay indoors due to incessant rain ?

Ans. bored

(iv) how you feel when you open a present?

Ans. surprised

(v) how you feel when you watch your favourite programme on television ?

Ans. excited

(vi) the look on your mother's face as you waited in a queue ?

Ans. tired

(vii) how you feel when tracking a tiger in a tiger reserve forest ?

Ans. scared

(viii) the story you have recently read, or a film you have seen ?

Ans. thrilling

Short Answer Type Questions

46. Why is Coorg called the land of rolling hills?

Ans. Coorg is called the land of rolling hills because it has a lot of hills and is itself a hill station. The hills seem to roll down in a panoramic view.

47. What legends are associated with the origin of tea?

Ans. There are a few legends associated with tea. The Chinese legend describes how a few leaves of the twigs burning under the pot, fell into the boiling water and lend it some flavor. While the Indian legend describes how Bodhidharma cut off his eyelids during meditation because he felt sleepy. He threw these eyelids on the earth. Out of those eyelids grew ten tea plants, which when boiled with water and drunk, banished sleep.

48. What is the Arab theory about the descent of the Kodavu people?

Ans. The Coorgis wear a coat called kuppia. It has an embroidered belt. This kuppia resembles the kuffia worn by the Arabs. Thus, it is believed that the Kodavu people are descendants of the Arabs.

49. How are the tea pluckers different from the other farm labourers?★

Ans. Tea pluckers are mostly women and hired labourers, while farm labourers are mostly males and they can be hired or can be the farm owners themselves. Tea pluckers mainly pluck the tea leaves whereas farm labourers go through the entire process of farming, right from ploughing to sowing and then to reaping.

50. What is the Indian legend about the discovery of tea?

Ans. There was a Buddhist ascetic named Bodhidharma. He often fell asleep during meditation. To stop this, he cut off his eyelids. It is said that ten tea plants grew out of the eyelids. The leaves of this plant are put in hot water and drunk to banish sleep.

❑❑

★ are board exam questions from previous years

Madam Rides the Bus

Chapter

9

Summary :

'Madam Rides the Bus' is a sensitive story about an eight year old village girl Valliammai whose way to have fun and pass time is to stand at her door and watch the passersby. Valli, as everybody calls her, loves to watch the city bus stop in front of her house every hour. As days go by, she starts to crave to take the bus ride to the city. She discreetly gets all the information about the fare and the time of journey and after saving enough money, sets out one day in the bus. She pays the full fare and much to the amusement of the conductor, expects to be treated as a grown up. She loves every bit of her onward journey and enjoys looking out of the window at the sights. She is amused by a cow running right in front of the bus. She does not get off at the city but pays the fare again to go back to her village. She is wide eyed at the shops and sights of the city. Her travel back is equally exciting except for the sad sighting of a dead cow on the roadside. She enters her home, with her mother none the wiser about her little afternoon excursion.

Extract Based Questions

I. **Read the given extract to attempt the questions that follow:**

But for Valli, standing at the front door was every bit as enjoyable as any of the elaborate games other children played. Watching the street gave her many new unusual experiences. The most fascinating thing of all was the bus that travelled between her village and the nearest town. It passed through her street each hour, once going to the town and once coming back. The sight of the bus, filled each time with a new set of passengers, was a source of unending joy for Valli. (Madam Rides the Bus)

1. **Standing at the front door and watching the street, makes Valli __________**

   (a) curious   (b) courteous

   (c) shy   (d) unique

Ans. (a) curious

2. **From the options given below, find a word from the extract that means the same as *not very common.***

   (a) Elaborate   (b) Fascinating

   (c) Unusual   (d) Habitual

Ans. (c) Unusual

3. **What did Valli get from watching the street?**

   Choose one from the following to answer:

   (a) Boredom

   (b) Fascination

   (c) Unusual Experience

   (d) apathetic

Ans. (c) Unusual Experience

4. **What fascinated Valli the most?**

   1. The bus conductor.
   2. The colour of the bus.
   3. The bus driver.
   4. The sight of the bus.
   5. The bus travelling between her village and the town.

   Choose the correct option?

   (a) (1), (2), and (3)   (b) (2), (3), and (4)

   (c) (4) and (5)   (d) (3), (4), and (5)

Ans. (c) (4) and (5)

5. **Select the option which displays an example of 'fascinating'.**

   (a) The terminal exams result was announced and the students were tensed.

   (b) The children tiredly looked at their online classroom program on their computers.

   (c) Anna visited the mall with her friends.

   (d) The flying display of the air force planes on Independence Day.

Ans. (d) The flying display of the air force planes on Independence Day.

II. *The bus slowed down to a crawl, and the conductor, sticking his head out the door, said, "Hurry then! Tell whoever it is to come quickly." "It's me," shouted Valli. "I'm the one who has to get on." By now the bus had come to a stop, and the conductor said, "Oh, really! You don't say so!" "Yes, I simply have to go to town," said Valli, still standing outside the bus, "and here's my money." She showed him some coins. "Okay, okay, but first you must get on the bus," said the conductor, and he stretched out a hand to help her up. "Never mind," she said, "I can get on by myself.*

You don't have to help me." The conductor was a jolly sort, fond of joking. "Oh, please don't be angry with me, my fine madam," he said. "Here, have a seat right up there in front. Everybody move aside please — make way for madam".

(Madam Rides the Bus)

1. Why did the bus slowed down to a crawl?

The bus slowed down because:

(1) People had to get into the bus.

(2) Valli shouted and stopped the bus.

(3) Valli wanted to board the bus.

(4) Valli had to get off the bus.

(5) Conductor had asked Valli to get off the bus.

Choose the correct option from the following:

(a) (1) and (5) (b) (1), (3) and (4)

(c) (2) and (3) (d) (2), (4) and (5)

Ans. (c) (2) and (3)

2. Select the most appropriate option for (1) and (2).

(1) The bus slowed down to a crawl.

(2) The bus came to an abrupt halt.

(a) (1) is true and (2) is false.

(b) (2) is the opposite of (1).

(c) (1) furthers the meaning of (2).

(d) Both (1) and (2) cannot be inferred from the extract.

Ans. (c) (1) furthers the meaning of (2).

3. From the options given below, identify Valli's tone in the extract.

(a) Cool (b) Eager

(c) Shy (d) timid

Ans. (b) Eager

4. Select the option which displays an example of 'stretched out a hand' similar in meaning to the text used in the extract.

(a) He was dancing to the music stretching out his hands and shaking his feet.

(b) The teacher asked the students to stretch out their hands during the Physical training session.

(c) The old lady slipped while walking in the rain, Jane seeing her helped her up to her feet.

(d) The little beggar boy stretched out his hands asking for alms.

Ans. (c) The old lady slipped while walking in the rain, Jane seeing her helped her up to her feet.

5. What do we get to know about Valli, when she says the following?

"I can get on by myself. You don't have to help me."

Choose one from the following to answer:

(a) She is frightened of the conductor.

(b) She is trying to show that she is self-dependent.

(c) She is unsure of her own thoughts.

(d) She is afraid of the crowd.

Ans. (b) She is trying to show that she is self-dependent.

III. *Valli devoured everything with her eyes. But when she started to look outside, she found her view cut off by a canvas blind that covered the lower part of her window. So she stood up on the seat and peered over the blind. The bus was now going along the bank of a canal. The road was very narrow. On one side there was the canal and, beyond it, palm trees, grassland, distant mountains, and the blue, blue sky. On the other side was a deep ditch and then acres and acres of green fields — green, green, green, as far as the eye could see. Oh, it was all so wonderful!*

(Madam Rides the Bus)

1. What did not block Valli's view from seeing outside the window of the bus?

1. The seats

2. The canvas blind

3. The conductor

4. The driver

5. Mountains

Choose the correct option from the following

(a) (1) and (5) (b) (1), (3), (4) and (5)

(c) (1) and (4) (d) (2) and (5)

Ans. (b) (1), (3), (4) and (5)

2. Select the most appropriate option for (1) and (2).

(1) Valli was very excited about the ride.

(2) Valli devoured everything with her eyes.

(a) (1) is true and (2) is false.

(b) (2) is the opposite of (1).

(c) (1) furthers the meaning of (2).

(d) Both (1) and (2) cannot be inferred from the extract.

Ans. (c) (1) furthers the meaning of (2).

3. From the options given below, identify the word that is the synonym of 'grasped the maximum' in the extract.

(a) Wonderful (b) Peered

(c) Blind (d) Narrow

Ans. (b) Peered

4. Select the option which displays an example of 'peered' in the extract.

(a) The child curiously noticed the monkey eating bananas from behind a tree.

(b) The child stood and watched the cartoons on television.

(c) The teacher asked her to join her peers to complete the project.

(d) My sister went with her peers for a movie.

Ans. (a) The child curiously noticed the monkey eating bananas from behind a tree.

5. What do you understand from the statement when Valli exclaimed *Oh, it was all so wonderful!*

Choose one from the following to answer:

(a) Valli was excited.

(b) Valli felt dejected.

(c) Valli was annoyed.

(d) Valli was disturbed.

Ans. (a) Valli was excited.

IV. *"Hey, lady," said the conductor, "aren't you ready to get off? This is as far as your thirty paise takes you." "No," Valli said, "I'm going back on this same bus." She took another thirty paise from her pocket and handed the coins to the conductor. "Why, is something the matter?" "No, nothing's the matter. I just felt like having a bus ride, that's all." "Don't you want to have a look at the sights, now that you're here?" "All by myself? Oh, I'd be much too afraid." Greatly amused by the girl's way of speaking, the conductor said, "But you weren't afraid to come in the bus." "Nothing to be afraid of about that," she answered.... "No, I don't have enough money. Just give me my ticket, that's all."*

(Madam Rides the Bus)

1. Why did the conductor ask Valli "aren't you ready to get off?

1. He thought she had forgotten the destination

2. He wanted to guide her.

3. He jokingly asked her.

4. He casually asked her as the other passengers had left.

5. He thought she was too young and had lost her way.

Choose the correct option from the following:

(a) (1), (2) and (5)   (b) (2), (3) and (4)

(c) Only 2   (d) (2) and (5)

Ans. (a) (1), (2) and (5)

2. Select the most appropriate option for (1) and (2).

(1) "I'm going back on this same bus."

(2) She took another thirty paise from her pocket and handed the coins to the conductor.

(a) (1) is true and (2) is false.

(b) (2) is the opposite of (1).

(c) (2) further relates to (1).

(d) Both (1) and (2) cannot be inferred from the extract.

Ans. (c) (2) further relates to (1).

3. From the options given below, identify why Valli didn't get off the bus when she reached her destination?

(a) She was frightened.

(b) She had come for a bus ride.

(c) She had not enough money.

(d) She had not informed her mother.

Ans. (b) She had come for a bus ride.

4. What can be inferred from the following line?

"Why, is something the matter?"

(a) Concern of the passengers for Valli.

(b) Concern of the driver for Valli.

(c) Valli's concern for the conductor.

(d) The conductor's concern for Valli.

Ans. (d) The conductor's concern for Valli.

5. Select the option which displays an example of 'amused' in relation with the extract.

(a) The boy tried impressing his friends with his jokes.

(b) The little boy jumped over the hedge and was injured.

(c) The little girl went on a trek with her friends.

(d) The teacher was impressed with the young boy's quick-witted answers.

Ans. (d) The teacher was impressed with the young boy's quick-witted answers.

Multiple Choice Questions

1. What exactly is the writer trying to portray from this story?

(a) Limitations of a poor family

(b) Life in an Indian village

(c) Mature perspective of an eight year old Indian village child.

(d) Bus travel is rare in villages.

Ans. (c) Mature perspective of an eight year old Indian village child.

2. **What is the symbolism of the bus in the story?**
   (a) The vehicle took passengers from stagnated village to a modern town.
   (b) Only sign of modernity in the village.
   (c) Only means of fast transport.
   (d) It was the link that helped to bridge the chasm between curiosity and realisation.

   Ans.(d) It was the link that helped to bridge the chasm between curiosity and realisation.

3. **What best describes Valliammai *'watching what was happening in the street outside'*.**
   (a) Arrogant in nature (b) Defensive
   (c) Curious   (d) Unconcerned

   Ans.(c) Curious

4. **Identify the apt option that best describes a hobby.**
   (a) Curious   (b) Pastime
   (c) Watching   (d) Experiences

   Ans.(b) Pastime

5. **Identify the option that does not describe Valliammai's feelings of experiences while watching the street.**
   (a) Extraordinary   (b) Unusual
   (c) Weary   (d) Curious

   Ans. (c) Weary

6. **What is the most important thing the author wants to convey about Valli?**
   (a) Valli's self respect is worth noting.
   (b) Valli's mental perspective undergoes enlightenment.
   (c) She was intelligent and remarkably courageous.
   (d) Valli was brave with an inquisitive mind.

   Ans.(b) Valli's mental perspective undergoes enlightenment.

7. **Which option correctly replaces the underlined word in the given line from Madam Rides the Bus 'between her village and the nearest town'?**
   (a) Up and down
   (b) Back and forth
   (c) In and out
   (d) Backward and forward

   Ans. (b) Back and forth

8. **What was the most catching to Valli's eyes?**
   (a) The timely movement of the bus.
   (b) The hourly movement of the bus.
   (c) The conductor in the bus.
   (d) The driver of the bus.

   Ans.(b) The hourly movement of the bus.

9. **What most excited Valli was __________.**
   (a) The change of drivers
   (b) The change of conductors
   (c) The change of passengers
   (d) The change of color of the bus.

   Ans.(c) The change of passengers

10. **What does the author mean by *day after day*?**
    (a) Alternately   (b) Often
    (c) Repeatedly   (d) Mostly

    Ans.(c) Repeatedly

11. **Fill in with the appropriate word. *Gradually a tiny _____ crept into her head and grew there.***
    (a) Idea   (b) Wish
    (c) Hair   (d) Hope

    Ans.(b) Wish

12. **Identify the word that has the same meaning as 'slowly'.**
    (a) Immediately   (b) Suddenly
    (c) Gradually   (d) Frequently

    Ans.(c) Gradually

13. **The urge that crept into Valli's mind was.**
    (a) To jump in and out of the bus
    (b) To ride on that bus.
    (c) To watch that bus
    (d) To ask her mother to take her on that bus

    Ans.(b) To ride on that bus.

14. **In the lesson 'Madam Rides the Bus', relate the words stronger: overwhelming: wish: _______.**
    (a) Ride   (b) Dreams
    (c) Desire   (d) longings

    Ans.(c) Desire

15. **Identify the word that means the same as 'Longingly'.**
    (a) Desirably   (b) Wistfully
    (c) Wishfully   (d) Hopefully

    Ans.(b) Wistfully

16. **The word__________means the same as 'set a blaze'.**
    (a) Longing   (b) Wistful
    (c) Kindle   (d) Jealous

    Ans.(c) Kindle

17. **What would set a kindle in Valli?**
    (a) The faces of the children
    (b) The faces of the passengers
    (c) The face of the conductor
    (d) The face of the driver

    Ans.(b) The faces of the passengers

18. **What would make Valli jealous?**
    (a) Strangers ravelling by bus
    (b) Hearing stories of her friend's bus journey
    (c) Her mother travelling the bus
    (d) All of the above

Ans.(b) Hearing stories of her friend's bus journey

19. **Valli feels___________if any of her friends spoke about their bus ride.**
    (a) Proud   (b) Casual
    (c) Jealous   (d) Angry

Ans.(c) Jealous

20. **Which option correctly replaces the underlined word in the given line from Madam Rides the Bus? <u>Really understood</u>.**
    (a) Proud   (b) Comprehend
    (c) Confusion   (d) Comprise

Ans.(b) Comprehend

21. **The children used the word "Proud! proud!" as a ___________.**
    (a) As a taunting expression
    (b) As a jealous expression
    (c) As a slang expression
    (d) As an angry expression

Ans.(c) As a slang expression

22. **Another important aspect about Valli clearly understood from the excerpt was:**
    (a) She was very confident about her thoughts and actions.
    (b) She was very proud.
    (c) She could be shy when people's attention was drawn towards her.
    (d) She was scared of her mother.

Ans.(a) She was very confident about her thoughts and actions.

23. **Valli listened carefully to conversations of the frequent travelers. This meant that she was very.**
    (a) Inquisitive   (b) Snoopy
    (c) Attentive   (d) Intruder

Ans.(c) Attentive

24. **In the lesson Madam Rides the Bus identify and relate the words fare: paisa: journey:________.**
    (a) Time   (b) Distance
    (c) Cost   (d) Details

Ans.(b) Distance

25. **Valli was attentive to the conversation of regular travelers and asked discreet questions? What do you not agree with about her behaviour?**
    (a) She was not interested
    (b) She was eager to know about the journey
    (c) She needed to plan her journey
    (d) She needed to know the expenses

Ans.(a) She was not interested

26. **In this lesson Madam Rides the Bus what does 'discreet questions' indicate?**
    (a) Irrelevant questions
    (b) Unnecessary questions
    (c) Careful questions
    (d) Interrogative questions

Ans.(c) Careful questions

27. **What does the author mean by saying "which is almost nothing at all".**
    (a) It is easy   (b) It is costly
    (c) Worthless   (d) Not much

Ans.(d) Not much

28. **From whom did Valli hear "which is almost nothing at all"?**
    (a) A well-dressed woman
    (b) A well-dressed man
    (c) A Conductor
    (d) A Driver

Ans.(b) A well-dressed man

29. **In the lesson Madam Rides the Bus, pick the apt word which means overwhelming desire.**
    (a) immense   (b) Huge
    (c) Large   (d) Feeble

Ans.(a) immense

30. **The ideal word for luck in the passage is________.**
    (a) Chance   (b) Destiny
    (c) Fortune   (d) Rich

Ans.(c) Fortune

31. **How did she collect information about the bus?**
    (a) By checking the bags of passengers every time.
    (b) By asking some discreet questions.
    (c) By checking the luggage of passengers every time.
    (d) None of these

Ans.(b) By asking some discreet questions.

32. **What was the one way fare from the village to the town?**
    (a) 1 rupee   (b) 50 paise
    (c) 40 paise   (d) 30 paise

Ans.(d) 30 paise

33. **What was the timing of the afternoon nap taken by Valli's mother?**
    (a) 1 to 3   (b) 1 to 4
    (c) 2 to 4   (d) 2 to 3

Ans.(b) 1 to 4

34. How long would it take Valli to complete her journey on the bus as calculated by her?

(a) An hour and a quarter minutes

(b) One and a half hour

(c) One hour and forty-five minutes

(d) Two hours

Ans.(c) One hour and forty-five minutes

35. What was the next challenge once she'd saved enough money?

(a) Tell her mom about it

(b) Know about the timings

(c) Buy a ticket

(d) To sneak out of the house

Ans.(d) To sneak out of the house

36. What was the season when Valli did travel?

(a) Summer　　　　(b) Winter

(c) Spring　　　　(d) Monsoon

Ans.(c) Spring

37. The bus crawled to a halt____.

(a) To avoid a crash

(b) A woman halted the bus

(c) A tiny hand was raised

(d) To take in passengers

Ans.(c) A tiny hand was raised

38. The first thing Valli did on stopping the bus.

(a) Shout at the driver

(b) Hand over the fare

(c) Jump into the bus

(d) Ask the conductor the route

Ans.(b) Hand over the fare

39. In the lesson Madam Rides the Bus, pick the apt word which means stretched out a hand in the context?

(a) Exercise　　　　(b) Extend

(c) Expand　　　　(d) Relax

Ans.(b) Extend

40. "Never mind," she said, "I can get on by myself. You don't have to help me." How would you describe Valli's character traits?

(a) Frightened　　　　(b) Self-conscious

(c) Self-dependent　　(d) Feeble

Ans.(c) Self-dependent

41. What did the conductor call Valli?

(a) Cute Girl　　　　(b) Madam

(c) First Passenger　(d) None of these

Ans.(b) Madam

42. "Oh, please don't be angry with me, my fine madam," said the conductor _______

(a) Respectfully　　(b) Annoyingly

(c) Jokingly　　　　(d) Wittingly

Ans.(c) Jokingly

43. In the lesson 'Madam Rides the Bus', relate the words jolly: angry: slack: __________.

(a) Less　　　　　(b) Busy

(c) Careless　　　(d) Loose

Ans.(b) Busy

44. Valli tried to avoid everyone's eyes since____

(a) She was overcome with anger

(b) She was overcome with fear

(c) She was avoiding stares

(d) She was overcome with shyness

Ans.(d) She was overcome with shyness

45. Instead of an old rickety bus in the excerpt, the writer chose to describe a new freshly painted bus. What can the reason be for this?

(a) The writer wanted Valli to be happy riding a new bus.

(b) A new bus always will be fast, so that Valli could return home in time.

(c) The writer wanted to emphasize that modernity was well ensconced all around the village, except the village itself.

(d) The writer wants us to focus on the contrast between the old village and the new bus.

Ans.(c) The writer wanted to emphasize that modernity was well ensconced all around the village, except the village itself.

46. What does the sentence 'Valli devoured everything with her eyes' in the Madam Rides the Bus specify according to the author?

(a) She was constantly eating and watching

(b) She was just looking out

(c) She was enjoying the ride

(d) She was bored through the ride.

Ans.(c) She was enjoying the ride

47. ______________was hindering Valli's views from the window.

(a) The tall trees

(b) The windshield

(c) The Canvas blind

(d) The Shining overhead bars

Ans.(c) The Canvas blind

48. Why did Valli stand up?

(a) She wanted to enjoy the ride

(b) She wasn't able to look outside properly

(c) She liked standing

(d) She was tired of sitting

Ans.(b) She wasn't able to look outside properly

49. 'So she stood up on the seat and peered over the blind' showed that______.

(a) Valli was adamant

(b) Valli was angry

(c) Valli was disturbed

(d) Valli was destructive

Ans.(a) Valli was adamant

50. *The bus was now going along the bank of a canal.* **Here bank refers to______**

(a) Edge (b) Financial Institution

(c) Bridge (d) Flyover

Ans.(a) Edge

51. But she was annoyed by his attention. Whose attention is it referred to __________.

(a) The conductor of the bus

(b) The driver of the bus

(c) The elderly man in the bus

(d) The elderly woman in the bus

Ans.(c) The elderly man in the bus

52. Identify the word in the passage that describes pride.

(a) Chimed (b) Comfortable

(c) Haughty (d) Glance

Ans.(c) Haughty

53. The conductor __________in when Valli retaliated to the elderly man asked her to sit.

(a) Intervened (b) Chimed

(c) Joked (d) Intercede

Ans.(b) Chimed

54. The conductor often joked and mimicked Valli. This meant that he wanted to __________her.

(a) Irritate her

(b) Make her feel comfortable

(c) To protect her

(d) To make her feel lost

Ans.(b) Make her feel comfortable

55. *"But if you stand on the seat, you may fall and hurt yourself when the bus makes a sharp turn or hits a bump. That's why we want you to sit down, child." Said the conductor.* **It was a matter of _____**

(a) Manners (b) Rules

(c) Concern (d) Command

Ans.(c) Concern

56. The one thing Valli failed to understand was __________.

(a) The scenery was beautiful to her eyes

(b) The passengers were concerned for her

(c) The seat was for sitting

(d) That it was a public transport.

Ans.(b) The passengers were concerned for her

57. *"Valli found the woman absolutely repulsive".* **What do you mean by "repulsive"?**

(a) Causing strong dislike

(b) Showing displeasure

(c) Extremely attractive

(d) Admirable

Ans.(a) Causing strong dislike

58. What could a symbolic meaning of Valli paying for the short bus ride?

(a) Bus rides are not free.

(b) Free public transport doesn't exist.

(c) Progress to modernity comes at a cost.

(d) For Valli, it was a matter of pride to pay for the ride.

Ans.(c) Progress to modernity comes at a cost.

59. Amongst all passengers why do you think the author had stressed on the character of the old woman?

(a) The old woman's concern for young displays the heart of Indian Culture.

(b) The old woman was an obstacle for Valli

(c) The old woman represented a different generation.

(d) The character of the old woman is symbolic of Valli's village roots contrasted with Valli's efforts to reach out to modernity.

Ans.(d) The character of the old woman is symbolic of Valli's village roots contrasted with Valli's efforts to reach out to modernity.

60. Why did the old lady ask Vali so many questions?

(a) She was bothered about Valli

(b) She liked Valli

(c) She was poking her nose

(d) She was bored

Ans.(a) She was bothered about Valli

61. *"But lo! somehow it passed on smoothly, leaving all obstacles safely behind".* **What could be the embedded symbolism of this line?**

(a) The bus was supposed to move on.

(b) Progress from stagnation to modernity was irrevocable.

(c) Valli was growing up fast.

(d) Time was short and Valli had to make it fast to home.

Ans.(b) Progress from stagnation to modernity was irrevocable.

62. The train rushed fast the crossing gate with a:

(a) thud (b) crashing speed

(c) tremendous roar (d) lightning roar

Ans.(c) tremendous roar

63. How much money did Valli pay for her to and fro journey?
   (a) Fifty paise   (b) Sixty paise
   (c) Seventy paise   (d) Hundred paise
Ans. (b) Sixty paise

64. Why did Valli not get off the bus for sight-seeing?
   (a) She was afraid
   (b) She didn't want to
   (c) She didn't have the time
   (d) She didn't like the city
Ans. (a) She was afraid

65. What did the conductor offer Valli at the bus stop in the town?
   (a) Water   (b) Soft Drink
   (c) Pizza   (d) Burger
Ans. (b) Soft Drink

66. What does it tell you about Valli when she refused to accept the conductor's treat?
   (a) She was responsible
   (b) She was stubborn
   (c) She was rude
   (d) She was disrespectful
Ans. (a) She was responsible

67. The dead cow was a rude jolt for Valli. Why?
   (a) For Valli, this was a horror she had not taken cognizance of during her planning.
   (b) Valli was very sad to see the dead cow, as she was very young.
   (c) Valli got a taste of horrors associated with life.
   (d) Valli had never expected to see death so closely .
Ans. (a) For Valli, this was a horror she had not taken cognizance of during her planning.

68. Who was a "real chatterbox"?
   (a) Valli   (b) Conductor
   (c) Her aunt   (d) All of these
Ans. (c) Her aunt

69. The whole story points to the transformation and progress of the old to the new through Valli's eyes. What do you think the author wants Valli's mother and aunt to represent?
   (a) Represent the family of Valli, deeply grounded in the village.
   (b) Represent a village which by and large desired modernity but lacked the will to reach it.
   (c) Represent a world which Valli wanted to get away from.
   (d) The author just wanted to fill details in by posting the characters of Valli's mother and aunt.
Ans. (b) Represent a village which by and large desired modernity but lacked the will to reach it.

Text Book Questions

Oral Comprehension Check

I

70. What was Valli's favourite pastime?
Ans. Valli's favourite pastime was standing in the front doorway of her house and watching what was happening in the street outside.

71. What was a source of unending joy for Valli? What was her strongest desire?
Ans. The sight of the bus, that travelled between her village and the nearest Town and filled each time with a new set of passengers, was a source of unending joy for Valli. Her strongest desire was to ride the bus.

72. What did Valli find out about the bus journey? How did she find out these details?
Ans. Valli listened carefully to the conversations between her neighbours and the people who regularly used the bus and she also asked a few discreet questions here and there. This way she picked up various small details about the bus journey. The town was six miles away from her village. The fare was thirty paise for one way. The trip to the town took forty-five minutes. On reaching the town, if she stayed in her seat and paid another thirty paise, she could return home on the same bus.

73. What do you think Valli was planning to do?
Ans. Valli was planning to take a bus ride to the city and come back in the same bus.

II

74. Why does the conductor call Valli 'madam'?
Ans. The conductor is amused to see an eight year old who wants to behave like a grown up and in jest he calls her madam.

75. Why does Valli stand up on the seat? What does she see now?
Ans. Valli found her view cut off by a canvas blind that covered the lower part of her window. So she stood up on the seat and peered over the blind. On one side, she sees the canal and beyond it, palm trees, grasslands, distant mountains and the blue sky. On the other side, she sees a deep ditch and then acres of green fields.

76. What does Valli tell the elderly man when he calls her a child?
Ans. When the elderly man calls her a child she gets annoyed and says that she is not a child as she has paid the full fare.

77. Why didn't Valli want to make friends with the elderly woman?

Ans. The elderly woman was repulsive to Valli with big holes in her ear lobes and ugly earrings in them. She could smell the betel nut the woman was chewing and see the betel juice that was threatening to spill over her lips at any time. So she did not want to become friends with the elderly woman.

III

78. How did Valli save up money for her first journey? Was it easy for her?

Ans. Valli had saved up the money for her first journey by resisting every temptation to buy peppermints, toys, balloons etc. At the village, fair she had resolutely stifled a strong desire to ride the merry go-round, even though she had the money. Saving the money had not been easy for her.

79. What did Valli see on her way that made her laugh?

Ans. On her journey to the city, Valli saw a young cow, tail high in the air, running very fast, right in the middle of the road, in front of the bus. The driver sounded his horn loudly but the more he honked, the more frightened the animal became and the faster it galloped — always right in front of the bus. This sight of the cow running made her laugh.

80. Why didn't she get off the bus at the bus station?

Ans. Valli didn't get off the bus because she was too scared to get down. Also, she just wanted to take a ride in the bus and was going back to her village by the same bus.

81. Why didn't Valli want to go to the stall and have a drink? What does this tell you about her?

Ans. Valli didn't want to get down at the city stop and go to the stall for a drink because she was scared and also, had not planned for it. This tells us that she was careful not to venture into something she had no idea about.

Thinking about the Text

82. What was Valli's deepest desire? Find the words and phrases in the story that tell you this.

Ans. Valli's deepest desire was to ride on the city bus, for just once.

"Day after day she watched the bus pass by and gradually a tiny wish crept into her head and grew there. This wish became stronger and stronger, until it was an overwhelming desire. Valli would stare wistfully at the people who got on or off the bus".

83. How did Valli plan her bus ride? What did she find out about the bus and how did she save up the fare?

Ans. Valli listened carefully to conversations between her neighbours and people who regularly used the bus and she also asked a few discreet questions here and there. This way, she picked up various small details about the bus journey. The town was six miles from her village. The fare was thirty paise one way. The trip to the town took forty-five minutes. On reaching town, if she stayed in her seat and paid another thirty paise, she could return home on the same bus. With all this information, she planned her ride on the bus during the hour in the afternoon when her mother took a nap.

Valli had saved up the money for her first journey by resisting every temptation to buy peppermints, toys, balloons etc. At the village fair she had resolutely stifled a strong desire to ride the merry go-round, even though she had the money.

84. What kind of a person is Valli? To answer this question, pick out the following sentences from the text and fill in the blanks. The words you fill in are the clues to your answer.

(i) "Stop the bus! Stop the bus!" And a tiny hand was raised <u>commandingly</u>.

(ii) "Yes, I <u>simply have to</u> go to town," said Valli, still standing outside the bus.

(iii) "There's nobody here <u>who's a child,</u>" she said haughtily. "I've paid my thirty paise like everyone else."

(iv) "Never mind," she said, <u>"I can get on by myself.</u> You don't have to help me." I'm not a child, I tell you," she said, irritably.

(v) "You needn't bother about me. <u>I can take care of myself,</u>" Valli said, turning her face toward the window and staring out.

(vi) Then she turned to the conductor and said, "Well, sir, I hope <u>to see you again.</u>"

Ans. Though Valli is small, she is a very confident girl. She researches about the journey and then undertakes it. She doesn't like being called a child as she believes that she is a grown up and can travel on her own. She is careful not to be friendly with strangers, though she does come to trust the conductor by the end of the journey. She gets irritated very soon.

85. Why does the conductor refer to Valli as 'madam'?

Ans. The conductor is amused to see an eight year old wanting to behave like a grown up and in jest he calls her 'madam'.

86. Find the lines in the text which tell you that Valli was enjoying her ride on the bus.

Ans. Struck dumb with wonder, Valli gaped at everything.

Valli clapped her hands with glee.

Oh, it was all so wonderful!

87. Why does Valli refuse to look out of the window on her way back?

Ans. Valli sees a young cow lying dead by the roadside. The memory of the dead cow haunts her, dampening her enthusiasm and so she refuses to look out of the window on the way back.

88. What does Valli mean when she says, "I was just agreeing with what you said about things happening without our knowledge."

Ans. Valli has just come back from a bus ride into the city without her mother knowing anything about it. In this context, she agrees with her mother when she says that there are things that happen without one's knowledge.

89. The author describes the things that Valli sees from an eight-year-old's point of view. Can you find evidence from the text for this statement?

Ans. Sometimes the bus seemed on the point of gobbling up another vehicle that was coming towards them or a pedestrian crossing the road

    __ Valli devoured everything with her eyes.

    __ palm trees, grassland, distant mountains, and the blue, blue sky.

    __ then acres and acres of green fields — green, green, green, as far as the eye could see. Oh, it was all so wonderful!

Short Answer Type Questions

20-30 Words

90. How did Valli fulfil her desire to ride a bus to the town and back?★

____

★ **are board exam questions from previous years**

Ans. Valli was an eight-year-old girl who had a strong desire to take a bus ride. She heard the people around talking about bus rides and silently gathered all the information required before she took her first ride. She saved every single penny possible so that she could take a return journey in the bus. Eventually, one afternoon when Valli's mother was taking an afternoon nap post lunch, Valli sneaked out of the house for her first bus ride.

She boarded the bus on her own and shunned the conductor when he offered help and called her 'madam'. She stood up on the seat to enjoy the views around the bus when she could not see them clearly while sitting.

On her return journey, she enjoyed the same natural sights around but her face fell when she saw a dead cow hit by a fast moving vehicle. The memory of the dead cow haunted Valli. She no longer wanted to see out of the window and kept sitting on her seat until her village came. She got down and wished the conductor to see him again. The conductor smiled. He told Valli that whenever she felt like riding the bus she could come and join them.

91. Why did Valli shout in English 'proud, proud'?

Ans. If one of her friends happened to ride the bus and tried to describe the sights of the town to her, Valli would be too jealous to listen and would shout, in English: "Proud! proud!" Neither she nor her friends really understood the meaning of the word but they used it often as a slang expression of disapproval.

92. How did Valli slip out of the house without her mother's knowledge?

Ans. Every day after lunch her mother would nap from about one to four or so. Valli always used these hours for her 'excursions' and this is when she slipped out of the house without her mother's knowledge.

93. Why does Valli stand upon the seat ? What does she see now ?★

Ans. Valli's view was obstructed by a canvas blind which covered the lower part of the window and so she was forced to stand up on the seat. She noticed the canal on one side, palm trees, grassland, distant mountains and the blue sky and a deep ditch and acres of green fields on the other side.

94. Why didn't Valli want to go to the stall and have a drink? What does it tell you about her?★

Ans. Valli had accumulated only sixty paise, which was the cost of her bus ride between her village and the nearest town, and did not have enough money to spend at the stall. This shows that Valli was a firm and decisive little girl.

95. What made Valli sad?

Ans. On the ride to the city Valli was amused by a cow who was running right in the middle of the road in front of the bus. On the way back she saw the same cow dead by the roadside hit by a speeding vehicle. This saddened her.

96. How did Valli react when she saw the dead cow by the roadside ?

Ans. Valli was extremely excited about her bus journey. She had carefully planned and saved money for this journey. On her return journey, when she saw the dead cow on the roadside, she turned somber. She lost her enthusiasm on seeing the dead cow. She became pensive and built negative views towards life.

Long Answer Type Questions

100-120 words

97. An eight year old girl travelling alone in a bus. Is it right on the girl's part to take this journey? What would have happened if she had informed her mother before leaving?

Ans. An eight year old girl travelling alone in a bus does not happen too often these days. It was not right on Valli's part to have undertaken this journey alone. Anything could have gone wrong. The bus may not have returned by the same route or the same day. She had not informed her mother about it so, if the bus had been delayed due to unknown reasons her family wouldn't have known where to look for her. She was lucky to get good people as passengers, the conductor and the driver.

If Valli had informed her mother before leaving, either her mother would have refused to let her do so or she would have herself taken her on the ride.

98. Describe Valli's planning for the bus ride.

Ans. Valli craved to take the bus ride. She planned her ride meticulously. She started by finding out about the fare and the timings of the bus. She made arrangements for the fare and also decided what time will be suitable for her. Once she had done all the necessary preparation and she was ready for her secret excursion. She also found out how much time it took to go to the city and back. She had learnt that one could remain

sitting in the bus and come back to the village in the same bus. She saved money for the fare by resisting all temptations like peppermints, toys and even a ride on the merry-go-round at the village fair. She planned her excursion when her mother took her afternoon nap.

99. Once we decide to achieve something, so many difficulties come in our way. With focused attention we can make that achievement. How did Valli succeed in fulfilling her desire of riding a bus ?★

Ans. Eight-year-old Valli's desire was to ride the bus that travelled between her village and the nearest town. Her desire was so strong that it overcomes her fears prompting her to plan her trip meticulously. She collects all the details of the journey and saves every coin that comes her way. She maintains her will power so much that she does not even get tempted to go shopping. After taking all the precautions to ensure that she has a safe journey, she fulfills her dream of riding a bus. Despite her young age, she returns back home safely. Valli teaches us that once we decide to achieve something, many difficulties may come our way but with courage and confidence, we can accomplish the task.

100. Whenever we want to achieve something difficulties always come in our way. What did Valli have to do to go and ride in a bus?★

Ans. Ambition is the key to fulfillment of one's needs. One must always be ambitious in life. Valli was a simple girl who also had ambitions. Her greatest ambition or her growing desire was to ride a bus. This desire stemmed from watching the bus pass through her village everyday. All this intrigued her. To undertake her first bus journey, she did her bit of research. She watched the bus, took a note of its schedule and listened to people's conversations about their journey by bus. She even found out the fare of the bus, which was 30 paise for a trip. Gradually, she used all of this information to collect money for the bus fare as well as to undertake her first bus journey.

Reference to Context Questions

Read the extract given below and answer the questions that follow :

101. *Day after day she watched the bus, and gradually a tiny wish crept into her head and grew there: she* *wanted to ride on that bus, even if just once. This wish became stronger and stronger, until it was an overwhelming desire. Valli would stare wistfully at the people who got on or off the bus when it stopped at the street corner. Their faces would kindle in her longings, dreams, and hopes.*

(a) What was a source of unending joy for Valli? What was her strongest desire?

(b) What do you think Valli was planning to do?

Ans. (a) Valli enjoyed watching the bus and its new set of passengers every time it crossed the village. It gave her a never ending joy. Her strongest desire was to travel in the bus and take a ride to the nearby town and back.

(b) Valli was planning secretively to fulfill her desire of travelling by bus without her mother noticing.

102. *It was the slack time of day, and there were only six or seven passengers on the bus. They were all looking at Valli and laughing with the conductor. Valli was overcome with shyness. Avoiding everyone's eyes, she walked quickly to an empty seat and sat down. May we start now, madam?" the conductor asked, smiling. Then he blew his whistle twice, and the bus moved forward with a roar. It was a new bus, its outside painted a gleaming white with some green stripes along the sides. Inside, the overhead bars shone like silver. Directly in front of Valli, above the windshield, there was a beautiful clock. The seats were soft and luxurious.*

(a) One word that Valli and her friends often used as a slang expression of disapproval.

   (i) Jealous

   (ii) Proud

   (iii) Never mind

   (iv) Okay

(b) What is the word in the extract that is not similar to busy time of the day?

   (i) Rush hour

   (ii) Interval

   (iii) Slack

   (iv) Busy

(c) Valli was avoiding everyone's eyes since_____.

   (i) option 1

   (ii) Option 2

   (iii) option 3

   (iv) Option 4

(d) The conductor referred Valli with respect calling her:

   (i) Baby

   (ii) Girly

   (iii) Madam

   (iv) Sir

(e) Choose the correct option that describes the bus.

(i) Option 1   (ii) Option 2
(iii) Option 3   (iv) Option 4

Ans. (a) (ii) Proud
(b) (iii) Slack
(c) (ii) Option 2
(d) (iii) Madam
(e) (iii) Option 3

103. *"May we start now, madam?" the conductor asked, smiling. Then he blew his whistle twice, and the bus moved forward with a roar. It was a new bus, its outside painted a gleaming white with some green stripes along the sides. Inside, the overhead bars shone like silver. Directly in front of Valli, above the windshield, there was a beautiful clock. The seats were soft and luxurious. Valli devoured everything with her eyes. But when she started to look outside, she found her view cut off by a canvas blind that covered the lower part of her window. So she stood up on the seat and peered over the blind.*

(a) Why does the conductor call Valli 'madam'?

(b) Why does Valli stand up on the seat?

Ans. (a) Well prepared and proud Valli got annoyed if someone called her a child or treated her like one. On the other hand, the bus conductor was of the joking sort and began addressing her 'madam' as she was grown enough, bought her ticket and could take care of herself.

(b) Valli was short in height and thus, when she tried looking out of the window, the window blinds would come in her way obstructing her outside view. Thus, she decided to stand on her seat.

❑❑

The Sermon at Benares

—By Betty Renshaw

Summary :

This is the story of Gautam Buddha and a woman named Kisa Gotami. Gautam Buddha is born into royalty and lives the first twenty five years as such. However, when he is exposed to human suffering, he leaves all his wordly duties and looks for enlightenment. He attains it under a peepal tree. He gives his first sermon to share his understandings at Benares. In his sermon, he tells about a woman whose son dies. She goes from house to house asking for a medicine to save him but is sent away by all as her son is already dead. One person guides her to Buddha saying that he will resolve her problem. Buddha sends her in search of mustard seeds from a house where there never has been a death. She goes from house to house and realises that everyone has lost a loved one sometime or the other. Thus, she understands the secret of life and death. All mortals have to meet their death whether they are rich or poor, wise or foolish, young or old. The earlier one accepts it, the earlier one finds peace.

Extract Based Questions

I. Read the given extract to attempt the questions that follow:

GAUTAMA Buddha (563 B.C. – 483 B.C.) began life as a prince named Siddhartha Gautama, in northern India. At twelve, he was sent away for schooling in the Hindu sacred scriptures and four years later he returned home to marry a princess. They had a son and lived for ten years as befitted royalty. At about the age of twenty-five, the Prince, heretofore shielded from the sufferings of the world, while out hunting chanced upon a sick man, then an aged man, then a funeral procession, and finally a monk begging for alms. These sights so moved him that he at once went out into the world to seek enlightenment concerning the sorrows he had witnessed.

(The Sermon at Benares)

1. What does the extract state about Gautama Buddha?

1. Gautama Buddha was a Prince.
2. Gautama Buddha lived a princely life.
3. Gautama Buddha was home schooled.
4. Gautama Buddha learned the Hindu sacred scriptures.
5. Gautama Buddha continued living in royalty.

Choose the correct option from the following:

(a) (1), (2) and (4)   (b) (2), (3) and (4)
(c) Only 2   (d) (2) and (5)

Ans. (a) (1), (2) and (4)

2. What could be inferred from the word *"heretofore"* in the extract?

(a) From Now On   (b) Hence Forth
(c) Upto This Time   (d) Afterwards

Ans. (c) Upto This Time

3. Select the option which displays an example of *'chanced upon'* in relation with the extract.

(a) Jack played football with his friends in the neighbouring grounds.
(b) Jack found some old valuable coins in a box while cleaning the attic.
(c) The little girl took a try and jumped over the fence.
(d) The little girl's painting was picked up as the winning one by a panel of judges.

Ans. (b) Jack found some old valuable coins in a box while cleaning the attic.

4. Select the most appropriate option for (1) and (2).

(1) Gautama Buddha ruled his people with justice.
(2) He left the palace with his wife and son.

(a) (1) is true and (2) true.
(b) (2) is the opposite of (1).
(c) (2) further relates to (1).
(d) Both (1) and (2) cannot be inferred from the extract.

Ans. (d) Both (1) and (2) cannot be inferred from the extract.

5. From the options given below, identify the reason for Gautama Buddha to leave his royal lifestyle.

(a) He was shielded from the suffering of the world.

(b) He had wanted to see the outside world.

(c) He wanted to witness the sorrow.

(d) He wanted to understand the sorrows he had witnessed.

Ans. (d) He wanted to understand the sorrows he had witnessed.

II. *Kisa Gotami met a man who replied to her request, "I cannot give thee medicine for thy child, but I know a physician who can." And the girl said, "Pray tell me, sir; who is it?" And the man replied, "Go to Sakyamuni, the Buddha. Kisa Gotami repaired to the Buddha and cried, "Lord and Master, give me the medicine that will cure my boy." The Buddha answered, "I want a handful of mustard seed." And when the girl in her joy promised to procure it, the Buddha added, "The mustard-seed must be taken from a house where no one has lost a child, husband, parent or friend."* **(The Sermon at Benares)**

1. What made Kisa Gotami approach the Buddha?

1. She was told that Gautama Buddha was a prophet.

2. She was told that Gautama Buddha was a physician.

3. She was told that Gautama Buddha was caring.

4. She was told that Gautama Buddha could cure.

5. She was told that Gautama Buddha was enlightened.

Choose the correct option from the following

(a) (1), (2) and (4)   (b) (2), (3) and (4)

(c) (1), (3), and (5)   (d) (2) and (4)

Ans. (d) (2) and (4)

2. Select the most appropriate option for (1) and (2).

(1) Kisa Gotami was an old woman.

(2) She had a deceased son.

(a) (1) is false and (2) true.

(b) (2) is the opposite of (1).

(c) (2) further relates to (1).

(d) Both (1) and (2) cannot be inferred from the extract.

Ans. (a) (1) is false and (2) true.

3. Which literary device is used in the line-'*Kisa Gotami repaired to the Buddha*' in the extract?

(a) Irony   (b) Symbolism

(c) Stylistic   (d) Paradox

Ans. (c) Stylistic

4. Select the option which is the synonym of '*went to*' in the extract.

(a) Preserve   (b) Repaired

(c) Procure   (d) Surrender

Ans. (b) Repaired

5. From the options given below, identify what exactly Buddha wanted to tell the woman in "*The mustard-seed must be taken from a house where no one has lost a child, husband, parent or friend.*"

(a) It is possible to cure her son.

(b) Bring a handful of mustard seed.

(c) No human being is immortal.

(d) Man has to undergo illness.

Ans. (c) No human being is immortal.

III. *The Buddha said, "the life of mortals in this world is troubled and brief and combined with pain. For there is not any means by which those that have been born can avoid dying; after reaching old age there is death; of such a nature are living beings. As ripe fruits are early in danger of falling, so mortals when born are always in danger of death. As all earthen vessels made by the potter end in being broken, so is the life of mortals. Both young and adult, both those who are fools and those who are wise, all fall into the power of death; all are subject to death.*

(The Sermon at Benares)

1. What does the Buddha emphasise in the extract?

1. Life can be taken care of.

2. All living things have an end.

3. Living beings cannot reign over death.

4. Mortals have to face death.

5. Earthen vessels are not subjected to destruction.

Choose the correct option from the following

(a) (1), (2) and (4)   (b) (2), (3) and (4)

(c) (1), (3), and (5)   (d) (2) and (5)

Ans. (b) (2), (3) and (4)

2. Which word in the extract means "*hurt feelings*" in the extract?

(a) mortality   (b) death

(c) pain   (d) danger

Ans. (c) pain

3. From the options given below, identify the conclusion of the Buddha's saying:

(a) One can live if they take care of themselves.

(b) Fools fall into the power of death.

(c) Death is inevitable.

(d) Wise can prevail over death.

Ans. (c) Death is inevitable.

4. **Select the option which displays 'death'.**
   (a) The branch of a tree fell on the little girl who was standing under it and was injured.
   (b) James was swimming on the beach and was caught in a whirlpool. He did not survive.
   (c) Rita saved her friend by rushing her to the hospital in the nick of time.
   (d) The boy was playing with a sharp object and had a bleeding finger. His mother bandaged it and the wound healed.

Ans.(b) James was swimming on the beach and was caught in a whirlpool. He did not survive.

5. **Select the most appropriate option for (1) and (2).**
   (1) All living beings are subject to death.
   (2) The wise can never fall into the power of death.
   (a) (1) is true and (2) false.
   (b) (2) is the opposite of (1).
   (c) (2) further relates to (1).
   (d) Both (1) and (2) cannot be inferred from the extract.

Ans.(a) (1) is true and (2) false

IV. *"Not from weeping nor from grieving will anyone obtain peace of mind; on the contrary, his pain will be the greater and his body will suffer. He will make himself sick and pale, yet the dead are not saved by his lamentation. He who seeks peace should draw out the arrow of lamentation, and complaint, and grief. He who has drawn out the arrow and has become composed will obtain peace of mind; he who has overcome all sorrow will become free from sorrow, and be blessed."* **(The Sermon at Benares)**

1. **What does the Buddha emphasise in the following words?**
   "Not from weeping nor from grieving will anyone obtain peace of mind; his pain will be the greater and his body will suffer."
   1. Everyone must grieve for a lost one.
   2. Weeping will cause pain.
   3. Grieving will keep away one's serenity.
   4. The body will suffer.
   5. Grieving and sorrow will bring tranquility.
   Choose the correct option from the following.
   (a) (1), (2) and (4)   (b) (2), (3) and (4)
   (c) (1), (3), and (5)   (d) (2) and (5)

Ans.(b) (2), (3) and (4)

2. **Select the most appropriate option for (1) and (2).**
   (1) He who seeks peace should continue lamenting.
   (2) He who seeks peace should draw out the arrow of lamentation.
   (a) (1) is true and (2) false .
   (b) (2) is the opposite of (1).
   (c) (2) further relates to (1).
   (d) Both (1) and (2) cannot be inferred from the extract.

Ans.(b) (2) is the opposite of (1)

3. **Which word in the extract means *'express sadness over something'* ?**
   (a) Sick   (b) Pale
   (c) Lamentation   (d) Blessed

Ans.(c) lamentation

4. **Select the option which displays an example of *'physical weakness'*.**
   (a) Ram had dengue and was looking sick and pale.
   (b) James slipped into the pool. He did not know how to swim.
   (c) Little Rita could not keep the kettle down since it was at a height and filled with hot water.
   (d) Jane wanted to take her dog for a walk but couldn't since it was raining heavily.

Ans.(a) Ram had dengue and was looking sick and pale.

5. **From the options given below, identify to what is the conclusion of the Buddha's saying.**
   (a) By grieving for your loved ones you can stay happy and blessed.
   (b) You are responsible for death.
   (c) Death can be avoided.
   (d) One must not grieve at something bound to happen.

Ans.(d) One must not grieve at something bound to happen.

Multiple Choice Questions

1. **When was Budhha sent for Schooling?**
   (a) At the age of eight
   (b) At the age of ten
   (c) At the age of twelve
   (d) At the age of fourteen

Ans.(c) At the age of twelve

2. **The phrase, *'befitted royalty'* may be best replaced by:**
   (a) Expected of royalty
   (b) Suiting royalty
   (c) Royalty itself
   (d) As per royal requirements

Ans.(a) Expected of royalty

3. **How old was Siddhartha when he renounced the princely life?**
   (a) 22 (b) 32
   (c) 35 (d) 25

Ans. (d) 25

4. *Gautama was__________shielded from the sufferings of the world. Indicate the closest meaning to before now.*
   (a) henceforth (b) from before
   (c) heretofore (d) earlier

Ans. (c) heretofore

5. **Why do you think the Prince was shielded from the sufferings of the world?**
   (a) As a prince he was not expected to cure the sufferings of people.
   (b) He was considered very weak by his parents.
   (c) The negativities of life could to prove to be detrimental for the prince.
   (d) He was mentally hinged ,so Royal court was apprehensive

Ans. (c) The negativities of life could to prove to be detrimental for the prince.

6. **What motivated the Prince to wander away?**
   (a) The sights of sorrow and pain.
   (b) The desire to find remedies to sorrow and pain of his people.
   (c) He was tired of palace life.
   (d) He didn't care about his family.

Ans. (b) The desire to find remedies to sorrow and pain of his people.

7. **'Vowed to stay until enlightenment came'. What does this exactly mean?**
   (a) The wandering hermit was expecting a Guru to guide him.
   (b) He was tired after wandering and so he rested.
   (c) Promised himself to seek enlightenment through meditation.
   (d) He was lost and decided not to return to the palace.

Ans. (c) Promised himself to seek enlightenment through meditation.

8. **In the passage, enlightenment of the Prince can be most equated to:**
   (a) fruits of meditation
   (b) unraveling
   (c) seeking light
   (d) realisation

Ans. (d) realisation

9. **Where did he vow to stay until his enlightenment came?**
   (a) His palace (b) Under peepal tree
   (c) Under banyan tree (d) Under a tree

Ans. (b) Under peepal tree

10. *Siddhartha decided to________ enlightenment.* **Fill in the blank identifying the correct word that means the same as Quest in the passage.**
    (a) Search (b) Look
    (c) Seek (d) Find

Ans. (c) Seek

11. **Which option correctly replaces the underlined word in the title The Sermon at Benares?**
    (a) Lecture by a professor
    (b) Lecture by a teacher
    (c) Lecture by a preacher
    (d) Lecture by a student

Ans. (c) Lecture by a preacher

12. **Benares is the holy place for dipping in the River ________.**
    (a) Indus (b) Yamuna
    (c) Godavari (d) Ganges

Ans. (d) Ganges

13. *In the lesson 'The Sermon at Benaras', relate the words suffering: agony: mysterious: __________*
    (a) incomprehensible (b) misery
    (c) inscrutable (d) unimaginable

Ans. (c) inscrutable

14. **The sermon at Benares has been preserved and is given here. What is the sermon about?**
    (a) Mystery of death.
    (b) Mystery of suffering.
    (c) A woman named Kisa Gotami.
    (d) How Buddha revived the dead.

Ans. (c) A woman named Kisa Gotami

15. **Why was Kisa Gotami carrying her dead child to all her neighbours?**
    (a) She was overcome with grief
    (b) She was not ready to accept the fact of her child's death.
    (c) She needed medicines
    (d) She was building up the hysteria

Ans. (b) She was not ready to accept the fact of her child's death.

16. **Identify the apt word in the sentence** *'Kisa Gotami carried her dead son asking for medicine. People said she has lost her senses'* **it meant that she ____.**
    (a) was possessed (b) was mystified
    (c) was insane (d) was perplexed

Ans. (c) was insane

17. The man who tried to help Kisa Gotami addressed the Buddha as__________ (choose the apt word)

(a) doctor   (b) sage

(c) physician   (d) healer

Ans. (c) physician

18. The man asked the girl to go to Sakyamuni which is the name of ______________.

(a) A jungle   (b) A monastery

(c) A physician   (d) Buddha

Ans. (d) Buddha

19. What quantity of Mustard seeds did Buddha ask for?

(a) A sackful   (b) A handful

(c) A pinch   (d) A cup

Ans. (b) A handful

20. Buddha asked Kisa Gotami to collect a handful of mustard seeds from the house where death was never experienced. Buddha wanted her to understand the truth__________.

(a) that grief was natural

(b) that Death is not avoidable

(c) grief cannot revive death

(d) her selfishness

Ans. (b) that Death is not avoidable

21. Kisa Gotami repaired to the Buddha as per the context of the lesson it meant that she____________.

(a) hurried   (b) went to

(c) addressed   (d) adored

Ans. (b) went to

22. Kisa Gotami was happy when Buddha told her to get a handful of mustard seed with a condition *"The mustard-seed must be taken from a house where no one has lost a child, husband, parent or friend."* She ________.

(a) She never realised what it meant in her grief

(b) She thought she would procure it in her grief

(c) She was confident she would get it in her grief

(d) She was happy, it was a simple task in her grief

Ans. (a) She never realised what it meant in her grief

23. Kisa Gotami was ___________ at first when she was asked to bring a handful of mustard seed.

(a) Hopeful   (b) Happy

(c) Confused   (d) Dismissive

Ans. (b) Happy

24. *"The mustard-seed must be taken from a house where no one has lost a child, husband, parent or friend."* What was the Buddha trying to tell that kisa Gotami did not understand in her grief? Pick the odd one out

(a) Death is common.

(b) Death is rare.

(c) There is no one who has no grief.

(d) There is no place where there is no grief.

Ans. (b) Death is rare

25. Kisa Gotami went from house to house. The people __________.

(a) welcomed her

(b) were annoyed with her

(c) they pitied her

(d) they comforted her

Ans. (c) they pitied her

26. Hearing the comments *"Alas! the living are few, but the dead are many. Do not remind us of our deepest grief."*

Kisa Gotami was_______ (describe in one word)

(a) desperate   (b) exhausted

(c) frustrated   (d) tired

Ans. (c) frustrated

27. What view actually opened Kisa Gotami's mind about life?

(a) Buddha's words

(b) The flickering lights

(c) The deaths

(d) The night

Ans. (b) The flickering lights

28. Kisa Gotami saw *'lights .. extinguished again'.* What does the writer exactly mean by this?

(a) Kisa Gotami found the ray of hope slowly dying away.

(b) It was getting late in the night.

(c) Kisa Gotami, will have to wait till dawn.

(d) It was getting late and she must hurry to get the mustard seeds.

Ans. (a) Kisa Gotami found the ray of hope slowly dying away.

29. What did Kisa Gotami finally realise?

(a) She was unnecessarily grieving her child's death.

(b) No point in grieving as her child was already dead.

(c) It was foolish to grief.

(d) She realized that the experience of death in this world was not unique for her alone.

Ans. (d) She realised that the experience of death in this world was not unique for her alone.

30. **Kisa Gotami realises her __________ when she hears that there is no house that has not experienced death.**
    (a) dismay (b) confusion
    (c) frustration (d) selfishness
Ans. (d) Selfishness

31. **Considering her selfish grief Kisa Gotami realised that there is ....**
    (a) inevitable misery
    (b) inevitable grief
    (c) inevitable death
    (d) inevitable mortality
Ans. (c) inevitable death

32. **In the lesson 'the Sermon at Benares', relate the words Lights: extinguish: life: __________.**
    (a) ages (b) death
    (c) revives (d) flickers
Ans. (b) death

33. **What did Kisa Gotami overlook in her own grief according to the Sermon at Benares?**
    (a) The torture she was inflicting on others.
    (b) The torture she was inflicting on herself.
    (c) Death is inevitable.
    (d) Death was avoidable.
Ans. (b) The torture she was inflicting on herself.

34. **How selfish am I in my grief! Were Kisa Gotami's thoughts. Since......**
    (a) in her grief she was thinking about her own loss
    (b) in her grief she asked for help
    (c) in her grief she was awakening the grief of death in others
    (d) in her grief she was reminding the others of their grief of a lost one.
Ans. (d) In her grief she was reminding the others of their grief of a lost one.

35. **In the lesson The Sermon at Benares, which symbols have been used to create a positive effect on Kisa Gotami?**
    (a) Mustard seed; death
    (b) Mustard seed: life
    (c) Light: flickering
    (d) Light: extinguished
Ans. (d) Light: extinguished

36. **Which option correctly replaces the underlined word in the given line from Sermon at Benares? Valley of desolation.**
    (a) Area filled with joy.
    (b) Area filled with sorrow.
    (c) Area filled with beauty.
    (d) Not clear.
Ans. (b) Area filled with sorrow.

37. **What was the lesson Kisa Gotami learned from the collection of mustard seeds?**
    (a) Death is inevitable.
    (b) Life can be prolonged.
    (c) Dead can be revived.
    (d) Overcome death.
Ans. (a) Death is inevitable.

38. **Kisa Gotami's consideration was that of:**
    (a) Life and death
    (b) Fate of men
    (c) The darkness of night
    (d) The flickering lights
Ans. (b) Fate of men

39. **Kisa Gotami finally realised that______.**
    (a) death can be averted
    (b) grief is the ultimate solution
    (c) death is common and the ultimate truth
    (d) death is reversible.
Ans. (c) death is common and the ultimate truth

40. **Indicate which of these is an incorrect statement is relating to the sermon of Buddha.**
    (a) Humans are troubled and weep over death.
    (b) Humans are combined their grief and instil pain.
    (c) Humans are immortal.
    (d) Humans are in danger of death.
Ans. (c) Humans are immortal.

41. **Buddha tried to tell Kisa Gotami______indicate the incorrect statement.**
    (a) all humans need to grieve
    (b) grief increases the pain
    (c) there is no point in grieving over the dead.
    (d) by grieving one cannot save the dead.
Ans. (a) all Humans need to grieve

42. *As ripe fruits are early in danger of falling so also mortals when born are always in danger of death.* **Means____.**
    (a) there is an end to everything
    (b) there is an end to mortals
    (c) there is no end to mortals
    (d) there is no end to any thing
Ans. (a) there is an end to everything

43. **How did Buddha suggest a way to overcome sorrow due to death?**
    (a) By crying out loud in grief.
    (b) By accepting death as a natural process of life.

(c) By talking to friends about grief and sharing of facts could ease pain.

(d) By shutting away from the world and meditating for a brief while.

Ans. (b) By accepting death as a natural process of life.

44. The Buddha in his sermon compares life of mortal men to a living and non-living thing identify the right answer.

(a) Earthen Pot and raw fruits.

(b) Earthen Pot and old man.

(c) Earthen pot and ripe fruits.

(d) Ripe fruits and mortal man.

Ans. (c) Earthen pot and ripe fruits.

45. *"Of those who, overcome by death, __"*

(a) depart from life.   (b) become immortal.

(c) become free.   (d) become dead.

Ans. (a) depart from life.

46. *While relatives are looking on and lamenting deeply, one by one mortals are carried off, like an ox that is led to the slaughter.* **What is the ideal meaning?**

(a) The dead are carried and relatives lament while the ox is alive and taken to be killed no lamentation.

(b) There is grieving for the dead and grieving for the life that is going to be dead.

(c) There is no point of grieving over any life.

(d) Humans lament for the dead while no one laments for life.

Ans. (c) There is no point of grieving over any life.

47. Buddha in the lesson 'Sermon at Benares' specifies that there is no______for death. Select the appropriate word.

(a) similarity   (b) discrimination

(c) distinction   (d) mediocrity

Ans. (c) distinction

48. Identify the apt word for *afflicted* **from the following:**

(a) relieved   (b) distressed

(c) comforted   (d) solace

Ans. (b) distressed

49. Buddha advises people that a wise man who______natures functioning should never be upset at the happenings.

(a) thinks of   (b) understands

(c) ignores   (d) adheres to

Ans. (b) understands

50. The wise do not grieve since they know the ______ of the world.

(a) conditions   (b) terms

(c) nature   (d) atmosphere

Ans. (a) conditions

51. In the lesson 'Sermon at Benares' relate the words livings: living: nonliving: wise; ________.

(a) unwise   (b) fools

(c) Sane   (d) insane

Ans. (b) fools

52. The Buddha indirectly tries to tell the grieving Kisa Gotami in comparison to her grieving …….. Identify the incorrect statement.

(a) wise men understand the law of nature

(b) wise men do not grieve

(c) grieving and lament can revive a mortal

(d) grieving spoils one's health and increases pain.

Ans. (c) grieving and lament can revive a mortal

53. What should the primary focus of humans be according to the Sermon at Benares?

(a) Focus on sorrow and overlook things that keep us happy.

(b) Focus on things that make us happy and grieve for lost ones.

(c) Focus on both sorrow and things that make us happy.

(d) Neglect sorrows and focus on things that make us happy.

Ans. (d) Neglect sorrows and focus on things that make us happy.

54. In the lesson Sermon at Benares, what does *'composed'* **indicate?**

(a) In a state of tranquility.

(b) In a state of being ruined.

(c) In a state of mourning.

(d) In a state of discomfort.

Ans. (a) In a state of tranquility.

55. He who seeks peace should draw out the arrow of lamentation, complaint and grief is to_____.

(a) stay composed

(b) stay poised

(c) stay self-centered

(d) stay overwrought

Ans. (a) stay composed

56. According to the Sermon at Benares sorrow __________man's suffering leading to physical and mental torture.

(a) decreases   (b) adds to

(c) accelerates   (d) slows down

Ans. (c) Accelerates

57. To obtain peace of mind one has to avoid:
   (a) luxuries
   (b) the things of this world
   (c) lamentation and grief
   (d) addiction
Ans. (c) lamentation and grief

58. In the lesson 'Sermon at Benares' relate the words Pain: suffering: grief:________
   (a) trouble   (b) death
   (c) affliction   (d) lamentation
Ans. (d) lamentation

59. What is the meaning of lamentation?
   (a) expression of sorrow.
   (b) expression of gratefulness.
   (c) expression of joy.
   (d) expression of laughter.
Ans. (a) expression of sorrow.

60. Buddha taught the simple meaning that ____________ in his Sermon at Benares.
   (a) Man has to succumb to death to get peace of mind
   (b) Man can get peace of mind by lamenting
   (c) Man cannot get peace of mind by grieving
   (d) Man can grieve and be happy
Ans. (c) Man cannot get peace of mind by grieving

Text Book Questions

Thinking about the Text

61. When her son dies, Kisa Gotami goes from house to house. What does she ask for? Does she get it? Why not?

Ans. When her son dies, Kisa Gotami goes from house to house asking for medicine to cure her son. She does not get any because there is no medicine to bring back the dead.

62. Kisa Gotami again goes from house to house after she speaks with the Buddha. What does she ask for, the second time around? Does she get it? Why not?

Ans. Kisa Gotami again goes from house to house in search of mustard seeds from a house where no death has ever taken place. She does not find such a house because there can be no family where they haven't lost a loved one.

63. What does Kisa Gotami understand the second time that she failed to understand the first time? Was this what the Buddha wanted her to understand?

Ans. The second time around Gotami understands the truth about life. She realises that death is common to all. No mortal is above death. Buddha wanted her to understand this truth of life.

64. Why do you think Kisa Gotami understood this only the second time? In what way did the Buddha change her understanding?

Ans. The second time Kisa Gotami wanted a medicine for her dead son and she was sent to the house which had not seen death and then she realises that death is common to all. The first time she was seeing only her own grief, but the second time she saw the grief was there for all.

65. How do you usually understand the idea of 'selfishness'? Do you agree with Kisa Gotami that she was being 'selfish in her grief '?

Ans. Selfishness means thinking about oneself and wanting things for one's own needs. Kisa Gotami was being selfish in her grief because she was only thinking of her own loss and was looking for a way to remove it not realising that death is common to all.

Thinking about Language

66. This text is written in an old-fashioned style, for it reports an incident more than two millennia old. Look for the following words and phrases in the text and try to rephrase them in more current language, based on how you understand them.

   ● give thee medicine for thy child—Give you medicine for your child.
   ● Pray tell me---Please tell me.
   ● Kisa repaired to the Buddha---Kisa went to the Buddha.
   ● there was no house but someone had died in it—There was no house where someone had not died.
   ● kinsmen—Relatives
   ● Mark!—Pay attention, mark my words

67. Here is a sentence from the text that uses semicolons to combine clauses. Break up the sentence into three simple sentences. Can you then say which has a better rhythm when you read it, the single sentence using semicolons, or the three simple sentences?

For there is not any means by which those who have been born can avoid dying; after reaching old age there is death; of such a nature are living beings.

There is no way that those who have been born can avoid dying.

After reaching old age there is death.

Such is the nature of living things.

A single sentence using semicolons has a better rhythm.

Short Answer Type Questions

20-30 Words

68. What was Gautam Buddha's life before he became Buddha?

Ans. Buddha was a prince named Siddhartha Gautama, in northern India. At twelve, he was sent away for schooling in the Hindu sacred scriptures and four years later, he returned home to marry a princess. They had a son and lived for ten years as befitted royalty.

69. Why did the Buddha choose Benares to preach his first sermon?★

Ans. Benares is the most holy dipping spot/destination on the River Ganges, which is usually crowded with pilgrims who come to get a dip, thus, getting rid themselves of their sorrows and sufferings. Buddha's aim was to lessen the suffering of human.

70. How does Kisa compare the city lights to the fate of men?

Ans. Kisa considered the fate of men like the city lights that flicker up in the evening and are extinguished again. Similarly, the lives of men also flicker and then are extinguished.

71. Who, according to Buddha, will obtain peace?

Ans. According to Buddha, he who seeks peace should draw out the arrow of lamentation, complaint and grief. He, who has drawn out the arrow and has become composed, will obtain peace of mind.

Long Answer Type Questions

100-120 words

72. Describe the journey of Sidhartha Gautama becoming the Buddha.★

Ans. Gautama Buddha began his life as a royal prince. He was named Siddhartha Gautama. At twelve, Gautama was sent away for schooling in the Hindu sacred scriptures. At the age of sixteen, he returned home to marry a princess. The prince was deliberately shielded from all sufferings of the world by his family. But this attempt was failed when the prince chanced upon a sick man while he was out hunting. Then, he saw a weak aged man and a funeral procession. Finally, he saw a monk, begging for alms. These sights of suffering, sickness and decay, shocked the prince. He wanted to seek the final solution of all these sorrows and sufferings. He wandered for seven years in search of enlightenment. Finally, he sat down under a fig tree. He meditated there until he was enlightened after seven days. He renamed the tree as the Bodhi Tree or the Tree of Wisdom. He then finally came to be known as the 'Buddha', the 'Awakened' or the Enlightened one. The Buddha gave his first sermon at Benares on the River Ganges.

73. How did the Prince come to be known as Buddha?

Ans. At about the age of twenty-five, the Prince saw human sufferings. He was born into the royal household and hence, he had all the privileges in life. His father had taken care not to expose him to the harshness of the world. But the prince, one night, goes to explore the world outside the palace where he sees the pain of people. These sights so moved him that he went out into the world to seek enlightenment concerning the sorrows he had witnessed. He wandered for seven years and finally sat down under a peepal tree, where he vowed to stay until enlightenment came. Enlightened after seven days, he renamed the tree as the Bodhi Tree (Tree of Wisdom) and began to teach and to share his new understandings. At that point, he became to be known as the Buddha (the Awakened or the Enlightened).

74. What lesson did Kisa Gotami learn the second time that she had failed to learn the first time?★

Ans. Kisa Gotami understood that death is common to all and that she was being selfish in her grief. She understood this only the second time because it was then that she found that there was not a single house where somebody's beloved had not died. At the first time, she was only thinking about her grief and was therefore, asking for a medicine that could bring back her son. At second time, when she met Buddha, he asked her to get a handful of mustard seeds from a house where no one had ever died. He did this purposely to make her realise that there was not a single house where no beloved had ever died, and that death is natural. When she went to all the houses for the second time, she felt dejected that she could not gather the mustard seeds. Then, when she sat and thought about it, she realised that the fate of men is such that they live and die. Death is common to all. This was what Buddha had intended her to understand.

75. What does the Buddha make Gotami understand and how?

Ans. When Kisa Gotami came to him looking for a medicine to bring her dead son back to life, Buddha realised that she did not understand the truth about life and death. If he would have lectured her that time she must have not understood the philosophy of life. So, he wished to practically teach her the truth about life the way he himself had learnt it. He sends her looking for mustard seeds from a house where no one has died. On not finding such a house, Gotami realises what Buddha was trying to make her understand. She understands that death is common to all and in her grief she was being selfish in believing that only she had to face such grief. She understands that to obtain peace, one has to accept death as part of our being.

76. What lesson on death and suffering did the Buddha teach Gotami in the chapter, 'The Sermon at Benares'?★

Ans. In his sermon at Benares, Buddha taught Gotami that the life of mortals is brief, troubled and combined with pain. Death is common for all, it cannot be avoided. He compares human life to ripe fruits that eventually decay or as earthen vessels that will break someday. Neither a father nor his kinsmen can save anyone. Weeping or grieving cannot bring back the dead to life nor bring peace of mind but can only cause pain and suffering to the grieving body. One should accept death without lamentation, complaint and overcome sorrow and grief thus bringing peace of mind, which is a blessing.

77. Through 'The Sermon at Benares', the Buddha preached that death is inevitable and we need to overcome the suffering and pain that follows. Based on your reading of the lesson, write how one should cope with the death of a loved one.★

Ans. Everything we need to achieve has to undergo pain and suffering. We must let go of grief, sorrow and even the fear of death to step out into the world to achieve something. World is afflicted with death and decay, nothing is spared and no one can avoid it. If we fear or grieve over the death of our loved one, it will not lessen our sorrow nor will the person come back to life, in fact, we will end up spoiling our own health and losing our peace of mind. Surrendering selfishness and leading a virtuous life is the safest option.

78. *"The life of mortals in this world is troubled and brief and combined with pain......"* With this statement of the Buddha, find out the moral value that Kisa Gotami learnt after the death of her child.★

Ans. Kisa Gotami learnt that death and suffering are the part and parcel of life. Nothing is everlasting and one has to accept this truth in the hour of grief. In order to detach themselves from the worldly life and the farsightedness to gain peace of mind one must remain calm and composed. Weeping and grieving does not bring peace of mind but only pain, which affects the body. People who are wise, never complain or lament over their loss. They accept the truth and are blessed with it. So, the wisdom lies in the fact that people should not get distressed with pain, suffering or death.

79. Life is full of trials and tribulations. Kisa Gotami also passes through a period of grief in her life. How does she behave in those circumstances ? What lesson does a reader learn from the story of her life ? Give any two points how you would like to act in the midst of adverse circumstances.★

Ans. Kisa Gotami's only son had died. Grief-stricken, she went about asking people for medicine to revive her dead son. At the behest of a man, she went to the Buddha who said he would cure her son only if she could gather some mustard seeds from a house where no death had ever occurred. After knocking several doors and being unsuccessful, she realised that death was common to all and it could not be avoided. No one can save anyone, so, weeping over a dead soul was fruitless. It was wise to stop grieving and accept the truth.

★ **are board exam questions from previous years**

Grieving over what is lost would only cause pain and suffering and doing that too, cannot bring one back to life. Accept life as it comes, be grateful and live it to the fullest with peace of mind and good health.

Reference to Context Questions

Read the extract given below and answer the questions that follow :

80. *At twelve, he was sent away for schooling in the Hindu sacred scriptures and years later he returned home to marry a princess. They had a son and lived for ten years as befitted royalty. At about the age of twenty-five, the prince heretofore shielded from the sufferings of the world, while going out on hunting, chanced upon a sick man, then an aged man, then a funeral procession, and finally a monk begging for alms. These sights so moved him that he at once became a beggar and went out into the world to seek enlightenment concerning the sorrows he had witnessed.*

(a) Who was 'he' in the passage ? When and where was 'he' born ?

(b) Mention the incident which prompted 'him' to become a beggar ?

Ans. (a) 'He' was Gautam Buddha, a Prince who was named Siddhartha Gautam by his parents. He was born in 563 B.C. in North India.

(b) Once Prince Siddhartha had gone for hunting where he came across a sick man, an aged man, a monk asking for alms and also witnessed a funeral procession. Unable to understand those sufferings, he became an ascetic and went in search of spiritual knowledge.

81. *And she thought to herself, "How selfish am I in my grief! Death is common to all; yet in this valley of desolation there is a path that leads him to immortality who has surrendered all selfishness." The Buddha said, "The life of mortals in this world is troubled and brief and combined with pain. For there is not any means by which those that have been born can avoid dying; after reaching old age there is death; of such a nature are living beings.*

(a) Why was Kisa Gotami sad ? What did she do in her hour of grief ?

(b) What did the Buddha want Kisa Gotami to understand ?

Ans. (a) Kisa Gotami was sad because her only son had died. In her hour of grief, she went from house to house in search of a medicine to cure him. She had become selfish in wanting her son back.

(b) Buddha wanted Kisa Gotami to understand that death is common to all and no one could avoid dying. No one can save their relatives. So wise do not grieve after accepting this truth of dead.

82. *Mark! While relatives are looking on and lamenting deeply, one by one mortals are carried off, like an ox that is led to the slaughter. So the world is afflicted with death and decay, therefore the wise do not grieve, knowing the terms of the world.*

(a) What is the fate of mortals?

   (i) They will die.

   (ii) They will come back to life.

   (iii) They will kill others.

   (iv) They will get killed.

(b) Choose the answer that lists the correct option about the meaning of the Buddha's message.

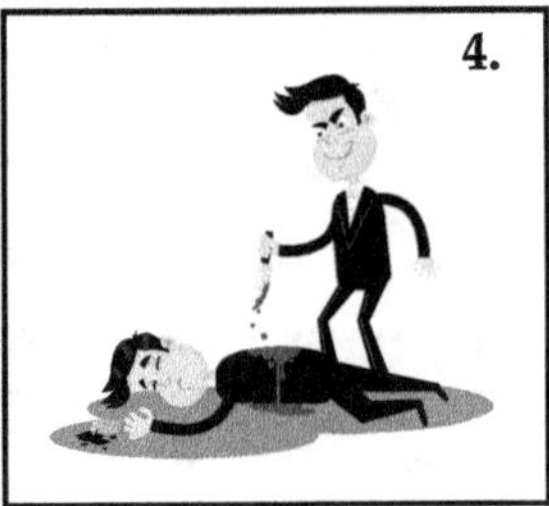

   (i) Option 1   (ii) Option 2

   (iii) Option 3   (iv) Option 4

(c) What do the relatives do when one dies?

   (i) They participate in rituals.

   (ii) They do the rituals.

   (iii) They lament deeply.

   (iv) They make merry.

(d) What do the wise men know?

   (i) Their friends

   (ii) Their relatives

    (iii) Their parents

    (iv) The facts of life

(e) The extract uses the phrase, '… *Knowing the terms of the world.'* Which of the following expressions is incorrect with respect to the word 'terms'?

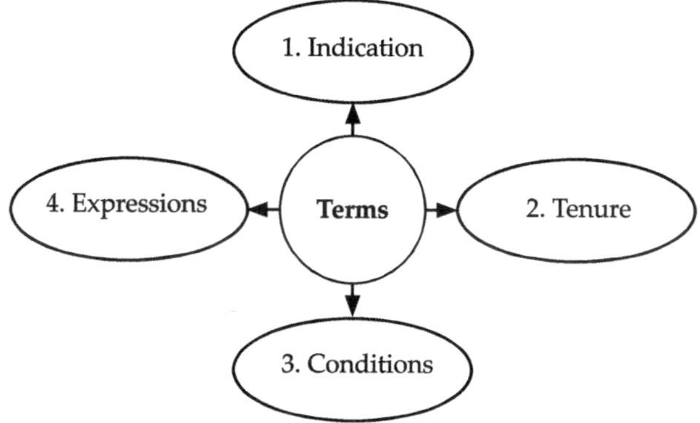

    (i) Option 1

    (ii) Option 2

    (iii) Option 3

    (iv) Option 4

Ans. (a) (i) They will die.

    (b) (iii) Option 3

    (c) (iii) They lament deeply.

    (d) (iv) the facts of life.

    (e) (iv) Option 4.

❑❑

The Proposal (Play)

—By Anton Chekov

Summary :

'The Proposal' is a one-act play, a farce, by the Russian short story writer and dramatist Anton Chekhov. It was written in 1888–89. The play is about the tendency of wealthy families to seek ties with other wealthy families, to increase their estates by encouraging marriages that make good economic sense. Ivan Lomov, a long time wealthy neighbour of Stepan Chubukov, also wealthy, comes to seek the hand of Chubukov's twenty-five-year-old daughter, Natalya. All three are quarrelsome people and they quarrel over petty issues. To begin with, Lomov starts to quarrel with Natalya about a piece of land called Oxen meadows which both claim is theirs. When Lomov has left because of ill health, Chubukov mentions that Lomov had come with a marriage proposal for Natalya. On hearing this, she quickly calls Lomov back so as to accept the proposal. But instead of proposing to her, Lomov starts quarreling with her over their dogs. The proposal is in danger of being forgotten amidst all this quarreling. Chubukov intervenes and gives his daughter's hand for marriage to Lomov, who despite palpitations, accepts and then continues his quarrel with Natalya. So economic good sense ensures that the proposal is made after all—although the quarreling perhaps continues!

Extract Based Questions

I. Read the given extract to attempt the questions that follow:

CHUBUKOV: *My dear fellow, whom do I see! Ivan Vassilevitch! I am extremely glad! [Squeezes his hand] Now this is a surprise, my darling... How are you?*

LOMOV: *Thank you. And how may you be getting on?*

CHUBUKOV: *We just get along somehow, my angel, thanks to your prayers, and so on. Sit down, please do... Now, you know, you shouldn't forget all about your neighbours, my darling. My dear fellow, why are you so formal in your get-up! Evening dress, gloves, and so on. Can you be going anywhere, my treasure?*

LOMOV: *No. I've come only to see you, honoured Stepan Stepanovitch.*

CHUBUKOV: *Then why are you in evening dress, my precious? As if you're paying a New Year's Eve visit!*

LOMOV: *Well, you see, it's like this. [Takes his arm] I've come to you, honoured Stepan Stepanovitch, to trouble you with a request. Not once or twice have I already had the privilege of applying to you for help, and you have always, so to speak... I must ask your pardon, I am getting excited. I shall drink some water, honoured Stepan Stepanovitch.*   **(The Proposal)**

1. **How does Mr Chubukov feel on seeing Lomov?**
   1. Happy   2. Excited
   3. Angry   4. Surprised
   5. Annoying

   Choose the correct option from the following:
   (a) (1), (2) and (4)   (b) (2), (3) and (4)
   (c) (1), (3), and (5)   (d) (2) and (5)

Ans. (a) (1), (2) and (4)

2. **Select the most appropriate option for (1) and (2).**
   (1) How may you be getting on?
   (2) How are you?
   (a) (1) is true and (2) false
   (b) (2) is the opposite of (1).
   (c) (2) further relates to (1).
   (d) Both (1) and (2) cannot be inferred from the extract.

Ans. (c) (2) further relates to (1).

3. **From the options given below, identify the nature of Chubukov by his conversation with Lomov.**
   (a) Loving   (b) Inquisitive
   (c) Jovial   (d) Stubborn

Ans. (b) Inquisitive

4. **Select the option to indicate why Lomov was not able to answer Chubukov properly:**
   (a) confused   (b) frightened
   (c) excited   (d) nervous

Ans. (c) excited

5. Which word in the extract means 'liberty'?

   (a) Excited   (b) Request

   (c) Privilege   (d) Formal

Ans. (c) Privilege

II. CHUBUKOV: *[aside] He's come to borrow money. Shan't give him any!*

[aloud] What is it, my beauty?

LOMOV: *You see, Honoured Stepanitch... I beg pardon Stepan Honouritch... I mean, I'm awfully excited, as you will please notice... In short, you alone can help me, though I don't deserve it, of course... and haven't any right to count on your assistance...*

                              (The Proposal)

1. What is the first thought of Chubukov when he sees Lomov?

   1. Lomov had come with an excuse.

   2. Lomov had come to meet him.

   3. Lomov had come to borrow money.

   4. Lomov had come to fight.

   5. Lomov had come to argue.

Choose the correct option from the following:

   (a) (1), (2) and (4)   (b) (2), and (3)

   (c) (1), (3), and (5)   (d) (2) and (5)

Ans. (b) (2), and (3)

2. Select the option which displays *'awfully'* as in the extract.

   (a) I am awfully glad you are my sister.

   (b) The team played awfully and lost the football match.

   (c) She looked awfully sad in the patched dress.

   (d) I did awfully miserable in the exam.

Ans. (a) I am awfully glad you are my sister

3. From the options given below, Lomov reaches out to Chubukov saying__________

   (a) he is a beauty.

   (b) he is a responsible man.

   (c) he is a good father.

   (d) he alone can help him.

Ans. (d) he alone can help him.

4. Choose the appropriate option for (1) and (2).

   (1) Though I don't deserve it.

   (2) Though I deserve it.

   (a) (1) is true and (2) false.

   (b) (2) is the opposite of (1).

   (c) (2) further relates to (1).

   (d) Both (1) and (2) cannot be inferred from the extract.

Ans. (b) (2) is the opposite of (1).

5. Which word in the extract means *'depend'* ?

   (a) Deserve   (b) Assistance

   (c) Count on   (d) Notice

Ans. (c) Count on

III. CHUBUKOV: *What's that? What did you say?*

NATALYA: *Papa, send the mowers out to the Meadows at once!*

CHUBUKOV: *What did you say, sir?*

NATALYA: *Oxen Meadows are ours, and I shan't give them up, shan't give them up, shan't give them up!*

LOMOV: *We'll see! I'll have the matter taken to court, and then I'll show you!*

CHUBUKOV: *To court? You can take it to court, and all that! You can! I know you; you're just on the look-out for a chance to go to court, and all that. You pettifogger! All your people were like that! All of them!*

LOMOV: *Never mind about my people! The Lomovs have all been honourable people, and not one has ever been tried for embezzlement, like your grandfather!*

                              (The Proposal)

1. What was the tone Chubukov spoke in when he said "What's that? What did you say"?

   1. Questioning   2. Joking

   3. Confused   4. Surprised

   5. Playful.

Choose the correct option from the following:

   (a) (1), (2) and (4)   (b) (2), (3) and (4)

   (c) (1), (3), and (4)   (d) (2) and (5)

Ans. (c) (1), (3), and (4)

2. Select the most appropriate option for (1) and (2).

   (1) Shan't give them up

   (2) Then I'll show you!

   (a) (1) is true and (2) false.

   (b) (2) is the opposite of (1).

   (c) (2) further relates to (1).

   (d) Both (1) and (2) cannot be inferred from the extract.

Ans. (c) (2) further relates to (1).

3. Which word below best matches *'pettifogger'*?

   (a) An honest, underhanded lawyer.

   (b) A sneaky, underhanded lawyer.

   (c) A stealthy lawyer.

   (d) A good straight forward lawyer.

Ans. (b) A sneaky, underhanded lawyer.

4. **Select the option to indicate meaning of** *Embezzlement.*

(a) Compensation

(b) Reimbursement

(c) Returns

(d) Misappropriation of funds

Ans. (d) Misappropriation of funds

5. **From the options given below, identify the person Lomov is accusing of for 'Misappropriation of funds.**

(a) His Grandfather

(b) Chubukov

(c) Natalya

(d) Chubukov's grandfather

Ans. (d) Chubukov's grandfather

IV. *He is old, but I wouldn't take five Squeezers for him. Why, how can you? Guess is a dog; as for Squeezer, well, it's too funny to argue. Anybody you like has a dog as good as Squeezer... you may find them under every bush almost. Twenty-five roubles would be a handsome price to pay for him.* **(The Proposal)**

1. **'He is old, but I wouldn't take five Squeezers for him' who said these words to whom and whom were they referring to?**

1. Lomov to Chubukov referring the dog.

2. Chubukov to Natalya referring the dog.

3. Natalya to Chubukov referring the dog.

4. Chubukov to Lomov referring the dog.

5. Lomov to Natalya referring the dog.

Choose the correct option from the following:

(a) (1), (2) and (4) (b) (2), (3) and (4)

(c) Only (5) (d) (2) and (5)

Ans. (c) Only (5)

3. **Select the most appropriate option for (1) and (2).**

(1) I wouldn't take five Squeezers for him.

(2) As for Squeezer, well, it's too funny to agree.

(a) (1) is true and (2) false .

(b) (2) is the opposite of (1).

(c) (2) further relates to (1).

(d) Both (1) and (2) cannot be inferred from the extract.

Ans. (a) (1) is true and (2) false.

2. **Select the option which displays an example of '- Old' in the context of this extract.**

(a) The actress looked gorgeous dressed in a latest outfit.

(b) The elderly man was sitting in the park.

(c) The little boy dressed in jazzy clothes danced on stage.

(d) The young gymnast did a stunning act.

Ans. (b) The elderly man was sitting in the park.

4. **What are roubles?**

(a) Monetary unit of China.

(b) Monetary unit of Japan.

(c) Monetary unit of Russia.

(d) Monetary unit of Germany.

Ans. (c) Monetary unit of Russia.

5. **From the options given below, what would you understand by the term** *'handsome'* **in the context of this extract?**

(a) Stunning (b) Striking

(c) Moderately large D. Meagre

Ans. (c) Moderately large

Multiple Choice Questions

1. **The introduction to the text talks about the simplicity of Russian weddings. But as we continue with our reading, we find the wedding traditions in Russia includes 'fights'. How will you explain the article in the prelude to the text?**

(a) Sarcastic (b) Hyperbolic

(c) Antithesis (d) Ironical

Ans. (d) Ironical

2. **After reading the passage, the impression you get about Russian weddings, is that their duration from the time of their conjuring to finish is usually__________than a week.**

(a) shorter (b) longer

(c) more (d) less

Ans. (c) more

3. **What do you think the real reason is for Russian couples to have a procession of cars for the marriage?**

(a) Their love for each other.

(b) Draw attention to their stature.

(c) Have fun.

(d) Entertain their friends.

Ans. (b) Draw attention to their stature.

4. **What can be another way of explaining 'toasts'?**

(a) In honour of (b) Baked

(c) Heated (d) Flatter

Ans. (a) In honour of

5. **A very important universally followed marriage custom is found missing in the passage. Which one is it?**

(a) Tying of knot.

(b) A visit to a church or any other religious place.

(c) Swearing oath.

(d) Exchange of rings.

Ans. (b) A visit to a church or any other religious place.

6. What is not possible in a Russian wedding?

(a) Non use of alcohol

(b) Liberal use of cash

(c) Cars

(d) Partying

Ans. (a) Non use of alcohol

7. *Marriage is an occasion in Russia.* **Which word is closest to the word** *'occasion'* **in the passage?**

(a) Gathering   (b) Get -together

(c) Ceremony   (d) Moment

Ans. (c) Ceremony

8. Who is Lomov?

(a) A farmer   (b) A landowner

(c) A factory worker   (d) None of these

Ans. (b) A landowner

9. The word 'proposal' in the text of the play suggests ....

(a) an offer on a project

(b) an offer for a possible plan or action

(c) an offer of marriage

(d) an offer of redevelopment

Ans. (c) an offer of marriage

10. The play is more about wealthy families seeking ties with other wealthy families indicates that:

(a) estates expansion

(b) wealth expansion

(c) economic expansion

(d) marriage alliance

Ans. (d) marriage alliance

11. Chubukov seems______at the visit of his neighbour Lomov.

(a) glad   (b) surprised

(c) worried   (d) confused

Ans. (b) surprised

12. How are the Lomovs and Chubukovs related?

(a) Friends   (b) Cousins

(c) Neighbours   (d) Business associates

Ans. (c) Neighbours

13. Choose the correct option that shows the behaviour of Chubukov when he says *'My dear fellow, why are you so formal in your get-up! Evening dress, gloves, and so on.***

(a) Cautious   (b) Conscientious

(c) Curious   (d) Composed

Ans. (c) Curious

14. When Chubukov said *'Now, you know, you shouldn't forget all about your neighbours.* **This meant that____.**

(a) they had never met

(b) they met after a long time

(c) they often met

(d) None of the above

Ans. (b) they met after a long time

15. Then why are you in *evening dress?* **says Chubukov. What does the underlined words refer to?**

(a) A night suit   (b) A formal dress

(c) An informal dress   (d) A gardeners dress

Ans. (b) A formal dress

16. When Lomov says *'I've come to you, to trouble you with a request. Not once or twice have I already had the privilege of applying to you for help.* **It means that Chubukov was______ in nature.**

(a) a money lender   (b) obliging

(c) stingy   (d) sympathetic

Ans. (b) obliging

17. What request did Chubukov think Lomov would make?

(a) Ask for her daughter's hand in marriage.

(b) Borrow money.

(c) Borrow land.

(d) All of these.

Ans. (b) Borrow money.

18. What purpose has Lomov come for?

(a) To run away with Natalya.

(b) To propose Natalya.

(c) To kill Natalya.

(d) To hide with Natalya.

Ans. (b) To propose Natalya

19. *By Jove! Ivan Vassilevitch! Say it again — I didn't hear it all! Meant that Chubukov was________.*

(a) an expression of awe

(b) an expression of surprise

(c) an expression of relief

(d) an expression of irritation

Ans. (b) an expression of surprise

20. What was Chubukov not expecting from Lomov?

(a) Money

(b) Wealth

(c) Proposal of marriage

(d) Estate

Ans. (c) Proposal of marriage

21. *I've been hoping for it for a long time* indicates that Chubukov.

(a) Waiting in doubt.

(b) Waiting expectantly.

(c) Waiting for some one.

(d) Waiting without hope.

Ans. (b) Waiting expectantly.

22. Who does Chubukov call a "lovesick cat"?

(a) Lomov   (b) Himself

(c) His maid   (d) Natalya

Ans. (d) Natalya

23. *She's in love; egad.* What does the term egad mean hear.

(a) A curse   (b) An abuse

(c) A mild oath   (d) A disapproval

Ans. (c) A mild oath

24. Why was Lomov feeling cold before meeting Natalya?

(a) It was winter.   (b) It was breezy.

(c) He was nervous.   (d) He was confident.

Ans. (c) He was nervous.

25. The phrase 'mind made up' implies _____.

(a) not certain   (b) decided

(c) possible   (d) hesitant

Ans. (b) decided

26. Lomov was all the time________from the time Chubukov left him till the time Natlya entered.

(a) thinking of what to say

(b) introspecting himself

(c) contemplating himself

(d) optimistic

Ans. (c) contemplating himself

27. What are the options playing in Lomov's head that will favour him to get married?

(a) Quick Decisions

(b) Hesitation

(c) Too much talking

(d) Looking for real love

Ans. (a) Quick Decisions

28. What explanation did Lomov give for his shouting?

(a) His frustration

(b) His short temper

(c) His palpitations

(d) He can't stand unfairness

Ans. (c) His palpitations

29. In his anxiety waiting for Natalya, Lomov considers one of his reason to marry is during sleep he finds himself jumping like a________.

(a) Monkey   (b) Clown

(c) Kangaroo   (d) Lunatic

Ans. (d) Lunatic

30. What was the age of Lomov?

(a) 32   (b) 34

(c) 35   (d) 36

Ans. (c) 35

31. What did Natalya offer Lomov?

(a) Tea   (b) Breakfast

(c) Coffee   (d) Lunch

Ans. (d) Lunch

32. What does Natlya mean by asking Lomov *'Why are you got up like that'*? It was since Lomov____.

(a) rose from his seat

(b) was informally dressed

(c) was formally dressed

(d) looked nervous

Ans. (c) was formally dressed

33. Identify the pronoun that starts the conflict between Lomov and Natlya.

(a) His   (b) Her

(c) Our   (d) My

Ans. (d) My

34. Where do Lomov and Natalya get on the wrong foot?

(a) While talking about the weather.

(b) While talking about their land.

(c) While talking about their family relations.

(d) While the proposal.

Ans. (b) While talking about their land.

35. Natalya is surprised by the way Lomov claims_________.

(a) the ownership of Squeezer

(b) the ownership of Oxen Meadows

(c) the ownership of Birchwood

(d) the ownership of Burnt marsh

Ans. (b) the ownership of Oxen Meadows

36. The purpose of the argument, was ________.

(a) to put the other down

(b) argue about ownership

(c) to just confront each other

(d) None of the above

Ans. (b) Argue about ownership

37. Lomov tells Natalya *'I have long, since my childhood, in fact, had the privilege of knowing your family'*.

The term privilege used here in this text is __________.

(a) show authority

(b) show appreciation

(c) show benefit

(d) show advantage

Ans. (b) show appreciation

38. *'I'm speaking of those Oxen Meadows which are wedged in between your birchwoods and the*

Burnt Marsh'. What does wedged mean that the speaker is talking about______.

(a) Wood (b) Squeezer
(c) Crammed (d) Marsh

Ans. (c) Crammed

39. Lomov's remark *'There's nothing to argue about'* clearly indicates that______.

(a) it is all settled (b) waste of time
(c) don't bother (d) it is useless

Ans. (a) it is all settled

40. The Idiom *'I can hardly believe my own ears'* used here by Natalya indicates.

(a) Surprise (b) Shock
(c) Awe (d) Sadness

Ans. (b) Shock

41. Lomov's aunts grandmother wanted in return from Natalya's father's grandfather for use of the meadows.

(a) Fodder (b) Bricks
(c) Milk (d) 300 Roubles

Ans. (a) Fodder

42. Why does Lomov stop short of this sentence, now my aunt's grandmother, wishing to make them a pleasant____.

(a) Lomov was tired
(b) Natalya was intercepting him
(c) Natalya had covered her ears
(d) Lomov was frightened

Ans. (b) Natalya was intercepting him

43. *Hear me out, I implore you*! Why does Lomov have to implore Natalya?

(a) To listen to him.
(b) To understand him.
(c) She was doing all the talking.
(d) None of the above

Ans. (d) None of the above

44. *Can't make head or tail of* is an________.

(a) Phrase (b) Idiom
(c) Proverb (d) Quote

Ans.

45. Identify the appropriate phrase where Lomov tries to prove his decency.

(a) I'll make you a present of them.
(b) But I am acting on principle.
(c) Hear me out, I implore you!
(d) I'll show you the documents.

Ans. (b) But I am acting on principle.

46. Identify the correct word in the lesson 'The Proposal' that means *disrespectful*.

(a) Squeezer (b) Abuse
(c) Malicious (d) Impudent

Ans. (d) Impudent

47. Who is squeezed between Lomov and Natalya emotionally?

(a) Natalya's father (b) Natalya's mother
(c) Natalya's brother (d) Natalya's aunt

Ans. (a) Natalya's father

48. What did Chubukov had to say about the land?

(a) They were his
(b) They were Lomov's
(c) They were still disputed
(d) They belong to none of them

Ans. (a) They were his

49. Lomov has come to ask Chubukov for the hand of his daughter Natalya in marriage. The three of them ______.

(a) resolve the issue of the property amicably
(b) sit to discuss the marriage proposal
(c) lose their temper on silly and trivial issues
(d) decide on the wedding and reception.

Ans. (c) lose their temper on silly and trivial issues

50. What is Lomov's side of justification about the land?

(a) Their land extended till Burnt Marsh.
(b) His grandmother always talked about it.
(c) His grandmother gave it to her great grandfather's peasants.
(d) Both (a) and (b)

Ans. (c) His grandmother gave it to her great grandfather's peasants.

51. Who gave the meadows to Natalya's father?

(a) Aunt's grandmother of Lomov.
(b) Aunt's grandfather of Lomov.
(c) Aunt's sister of Lomov.
(d) Aunt's brother of Lomov

Ans. (a) Aunt's grandmother of Lomov.

52. Who threatened to take the matter to court?

(a) Natalya (b) Lomov
(c) Chubukov (d) None

Ans. (b) Lomov

53. Which option correctly replaces the underlined phrase *'my foot's gone to sleep'*.

(a) My foot aches.
(b) My foot has blisters.
(c) My foot has turned numb.
(d) My foot is swollen.

Ans. (c) My foot has turned numb.

54. Why did Chubukov think it was a curse to be a father of a grown up daughter?

(a) He had to go to call the man they had just shun out.

(b) He had to go to call the man who insulted them.

(c) He had to go call tthe man who shouted at them.

(d) All of the above

Ans. (d) All of the above

55. What is the name of Lomov's dog?

(a) Guess (b) Guard

(c) Squeezer (d) Sweater

Ans. (a) Guess

56. According to Lomov, what defect does Squeezer have?

(a) Lame (b) Old age

(c) Overshot (d) Fat

Ans. (c) Overshot

57. Lomov calls Chubukov an intriguer. Choose the appropriate meaning of the word intriguer.

(a) A person who meddles in others affairs.

(b) A person who devises plots and schemes.

(c) An absentminded person.

(d) A wearied person.

Ans. (b) A person who devises plots and schemes.

58. What do you understand by 'Under the slipper of your house-keeper'? It indicates that Lomov was________.

(a) dominance (b) control over

(c) reign over (d) helpless

Ans. (d) helpless

59. When Natalya screams that Lomov is dead Chubukov reacts _________.

(a) joyfully (b) fearfully

(c) anxiously (d) scornfully

Ans. (c) anxiously

60. When does Natalya accept the proposal?

(a) When Lomov went unconscious.

(b) When they finished arguing.

(c) When he proposed her.

(d) WhenLomov came back in.

Ans. (a) When Lomov went unconscious.

61. Chubukov exclaimed *'What a weight off my shoulders'* this meant that he ______.

(a) was anxious (b) was stressed

(c) was relieved (d) was heavy burdened

Ans. (c) was relieved

62. What is the climax of the play 'The Proposal'?

(a) Lomov wants to fight for his property.

(b) Lomov is timid and yet wants to argue.

(c) Lomov is timid and still cannot bring himself to propose.

(d) Lomov is timid and yet too proud to propose.

Ans. (c) Lomov is timid and still cannot bring himself to propose.

63. Lomov experiences twitching and trembling which also means________.

(a) an upset tummy

(b) a type of tremor

(c) a type of headache

(d) a type of excitement

Ans. (b) a type of tremor.

64. What type of play would you rate 'The Proposal'?

(a) One-act comedy

(b) One-act farce

(c) One-act musical drama

(d) One-act drama

Ans. (b) One-act farce

Text Book Questions

65. Activity

Do you think India and Russian wedding have any customs in common ? Fill in the table below.

Wedding Ceremonies in Russia and India

Customs similar to Indian ones	Customs different from Indian ones
• A Russian wedding lasts for two days.	• Necessary part of the wedding ceremony is a wedding procession of several cars.
• Some weddings last as long as a week and the occasion becomes something to remember for years.	• When the groom arrives to fetch the bride for the registration, he has to fight to get her.
• The couple sits at a specially arranged table with their family, friends and invited guests.	• At each landing he must answer a question to be allowed to go up.
• The bride's friends—they steal the bride-groom's shoes. The groom must pay money for the shoes.	• After some time, the bride gets 'stolen'!

Thinking about the Play

66. What does Chubukov at first suspect that Lomov has come for? Is he sincere when he later says "And I've always loved you, my angel, as if you were my own son"? Find reasons for your answer from the play.

Ans. Chubukov first suspects that Lomov has come to borrow money. He is not at all sincere when he says that he has always loved Lomov. Many times Chubukov has called Lomov with disgraceful names. He wouldn't have done so if he truly loved him as he claimed. He called him 'angel' only because he had come with the proposal to marry his daughter.

67. Chubukov says of Natalya: "... *as if she won't consent! She's in love; egad, she's like a lovesick cat...*" Would you agree? Find reasons for your answer.

Ans. No I wouldn't agree that Natalya was in love. The way she quarrels with Lomov and even kicks him out of the house suggests that what her father says is not true.

68. (i) Find all the words and expressions in the play that the characters use to speak about each other, and the accusations and insults they hurl at each other. (For example, Lomov in the end calls Chubukov an intriguer; but earlier, Chubukov has himself called Lomov a "malicious, double-faced intriguer." Again, Lomov begins by describing Natalya as "an excellent housekeeper, not bad-looking, well-educated.")

(ii) Then think of five adjectives or adjectival expressions of your own to describe each character in the play.

(iii) Can you now imagine what these characters will quarrel about next?

Ans. (i) Landgrabber, grabber, pettifogger, guzzling gambler, backbiters, intriguer, malicious, double-faced intriguer, rascal, monster, The villain! The scarecrow!, stuffed sausage! The wizen-faced frump!, Intriguer! Boy! Pup! Old rat! Jesuit! Boy! Milksop! Fool! blind hen, turnip-ghost

(ii) Lomov—unhealthy, quarrelsome, ambitious, headstrong, nervous

Natalya—young, flighty, ambitious, quarrelsome, headstrong

Chubukov--- quarrelsome, headstrong, hypocrite, pompous, ambitious

(iii) Maybe about who has better horses.

Thinking about Language

69. Read through the play carefully and find expressions that you think are not used in contemporary English and contrast these with idiomatic modern English expressions that also occur in the play.

Ans. Modern English expressions: weight off my shoulders, seems to be coming round, to lose my temper, make head or tail of.

Older English expressions: to the devil with you, to get in with, intriguer, go and lie on the kitchen oven and catch black Beetles, Be hanged to, some demon of contradiction in you, give it to them in the neck, why are you got up like that, how may you be getting on

70. Look up the following phrases in a dictionary to find out their meaning, and then use each in a sentence of your own.

(i) You may take it that
After seeing his performance, you may take it that he will win.

(ii) He seems to be coming round
The heat caused him to faint but now he seems to be coming round.

(iii) My foot's gone to sleep
After attending the three hour long lecture my foot's gone off to sleep.

Reported Speech

71. You must have noticed that when we report someone's exact words, we have to make some changes in the sentence structure. In the following sentences fill in the blanks to list the changes:

1. To report a question, we use the reporting verb '<u>may take</u>' (as in Sentence Set 1).
2. To report a statement, we use the reporting verb <u>said</u> .
3. The adverb of place here changes to <u>there</u> .
4. When the verb in direct speech is in the present tense, the verb in reported speech is in the <u>past</u> tense (as in Sentence Set 3).
5. If the verb in direct speech is in the present continuous tense, the verb in reported speech changes to <u>past continuous</u> tense. For example, '<u>gets</u>' changes to '<u>was getting</u>.'
6. When the sentence in direct speech contains a word denoting respect, we add the adverb <u>respectfully</u> in the reporting clause (as in Sentence Set 1).
7. The pronouns I, me, our and mine, which are used in the first person in direct speech,

change according to the subject or object of the reporting verb such as <u>he, his, she, her, their</u> in reported speech.

72. *Here is an excerpt from an article from the Times of India dated 27 August 2006. Rewrite it, changing the sentences in direct speech into reported speech. Leave the other sentences unchanged.*

"Why do you want to know my age? If people know I am so old, I won't get work!" laughs 90-year-old A. K. Hangal, one of Hindi cinema's most famous character actors. For his age, he is rather energetic. "What's the secret?" we ask. "My intake of everything is in small quantities. And I walk a lot," he replies. "I joined the industry when people retire. I was in my 40s. So I don't miss being called a star. I am still respected and given work, when actors of my age are living in poverty and without work. I don't have any complaints," he says, adding, "but yes, I have always been underpaid." Recipient of the Padma Bhushan, Hangal never hankered after money or materialistic gains. "No doubt I am content today, but money is important. I was a fool not to understand the value of money earlier," he regrets.

Ans. 90-year-old A. K. Hangal asked why we wanted to know his age. He said that if people knew he was so old, he wouldn't get any work. For his age, he is rather energetic. We asked what the secret was. He replied that it was his intake of everything in small quantities. And that he walked a lot. He also said that he joined the industry when people retire. He was in his 40s, so he didn't miss being called a star. He was still respected and given work, when actors of his age were living in poverty and without work. He didn't have any complaints and added that he had always been underpaid. Recipient of the Padma Bhushan, Hangal never hankered after money or materialistic gains. He regretted that though he was content today, money was important. He was a fool not have understood the value of money earlier.

Short Answer Type Questions

20-30 Words

73. Who is Lomov and why does he go to Chubukov's house?

Ans. Lomov is a wealthy land owner. He is thirty five years old and is Chubukov's neighbour. Lomov goes to Chubukov's house to ask for his daughter Natalya's hand in marriage.

★ **are board exam questions from previous years**

74. How is the quarrel over Oxen meadows settled at last?

Ans. When Natalya realises that Lomov had come to propose to her, she agrees that the Oxen Meadows were indeed Lomov's property and that is how the Oxen Meadow's matter is settled.

75. Why does Chubukov go and call Lomov back?

Ans. Natalya quarrels with Lomov and throws him out of the house. But when she learns that he had come to propose her, she sends her father to go and call Lomov back.

Long Answer Type Questions

100-120 words

76. Describe the first quarrel between Lomov and Natalya.

Ans. Lomov has come to Natalya's house to propose to her. When she comes out to speak with him, he starts talking of irrelevant things and then mentions Oxen meadows, a piece of land near Natalya's land. He claims it to be his and Natalya on hearing it, starts asserting that the land was hers. He keeps saying that he has the papers to prove but Natalya is not prepared to hear any argument and they start quarreling on this issue. Natalya was not aware that Lomov had come to her with a proposal for marriage and not for quarrelling about a patch of land, hence she behaved foolishly and argued though Lomov had evidence of his ownership.

77. Write a character sketch of Natalya.

Ans. Natalya is a young girl of twenty five years. She lives in the neighbourhood of Lomov. She is very smart for her age. She has a cunning mind and uses her presence of mind to go with the flow of situations and turn things in her benefits. She is a good house keeper and is not bad looking. She is still unmarried and is thirsting for love. Her father calls her a lovesick cat. She is educated but doesn't seem so. She is very quarrelsome and abusive. She is also very ambitious. When she learns Lomov had come to propose her she back tracks on her stand and agrees to Lomov's argument.

78. Chekov has used humour and exaggeration in the play to comment on courtship in his times. Illustrate with examples from the lesson, 'The Proposal.' Also mention the values, you think, any healthy relationship requires.★

Ans. The Proposal is one of Anton Chekov's famous plays where he uses humour and exaggeration in the play to provide a commentary on courtship in his times. Chekov has used several stereotypes that help play the character's part beautifully in the play. Lomov, Natalya 'the shrew', Chubukov 'the hypocrite father' all help in adding humor to the play. Lomov uses exaggerated actions that, sometimes exceeds the limits of common sense like, Lomov gulping down water, putting his hand to the heart or running to the door and staggering out.

Another interesting aspect of this storytelling is how the story progresses from cordiality to the hurling of insults which is seen when Lomov called Chubukov 'a swindle' and Chubukov promptly called Lomov an 'intriguer'. The elements of exaggeration and absurdity set the tone of ridicule, which mars the elements of love and romance that is intended in the play. The playwright, through this play, ironically emphasizes that courtesy, sincerity, love and mutual understanding are the keys to a healthy relationship.

Reference to Context Questions

Read the extract given below and answer the questions that follow :

79. *I've been hoping for it for a long time. It's been my continual desire (shed a tear) And I've always loved you, my angel, as if you were my own son. May god give you both-His help and His love and so on, and so much hope.*

(a) Who is the speaker here ? Who is he talking to ?

(b) Why does the speaker shed a tear ?

Ans. (a) The above lines are spoken by Stepan Stepanovitch Chubukov in response to the proposal for his daugher, Natalya Stepanovana by Ivan Vassilevitch Lomov.

(b) The tear shed here has no significance. Chubukov is merely feigning emotions because to him, the marriage proposal is simply an opportunity to extend their estates.

80. Don't excite yourself, my precious one. Allow me. Your Guess certainly has his good points. He's purebred, firm on his feet, has well-sprung ribs, and all that. But, my dear man, if you want to know the truth, that dog has two defects: he's old and he's short in the muzzle.

(a) The extract uses the phrase, *'Don't excite yourself, my precious one.'* Which of the following expressions is incorrect with respect to the word 'excite'?

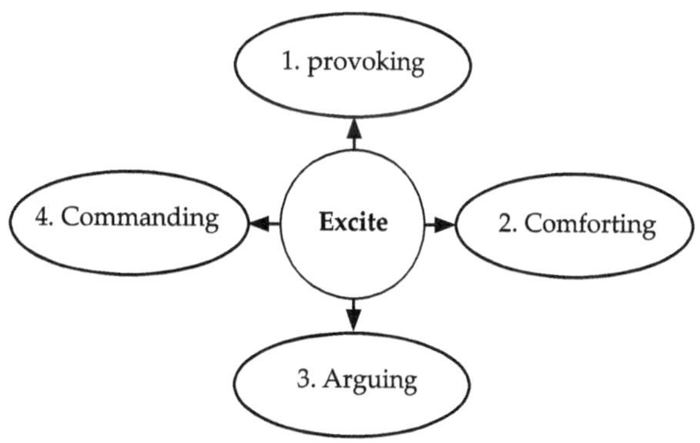

(i) Option 1

(ii) Option 2

(iii) Option 3

(iv) Option 4

(b) Squeezer was different from other dogs because________

(i) he kept sleeping

(ii) he kept barking

(iii) he ran after a sheep

(iv) he kept eating

(c) What happened to Squeezer on the Marusinsky hunt?

(i) He was afraid

(ii) He was attacked

(iii) He was ahead

(iv) He was left far behind

(d) Choose the answer that lists the CORRECT option about the recording of the situation between the couple Ivan and Natalya.

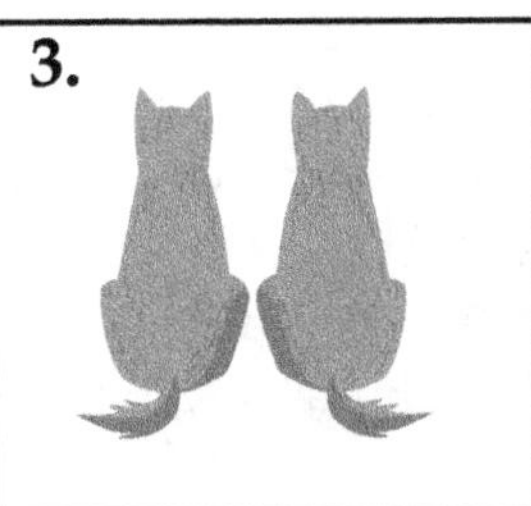
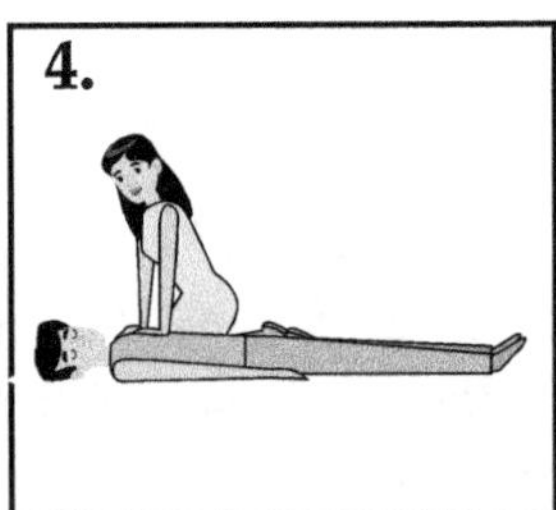

(i) Option 1	(iii) Lethargic
(ii) Option 2	(iv) Slow in running
(iii) Option 3	**Ans.** (a) (ii) Option 2
(iv) Option 4	(b) (iii) He ran after a sheep
(e) The 'truth' about Lomov's dog is that he is?	(c) (iv) He was left far behind
(i) Old and short	(d) (i) Option 1
(ii) Stupid	(e) (i) Old and short

❏❏

LITERATURE

FIRST FLIGHT
[POETRY]

Amanda

—by Robin Kiein

Chapter
6

Summary :

This poem is about a little girl, Amanda, who is constantly instructed about what to do and what not to do. She is told not to hunch her shoulders and to sit up straight. She is told to finish her homework and clean her room. She is forbidden from eating a chocolate that she has. But Amanda keeps dreaming of a life of freedom in the open. She dreams of mermaids in the sea, of roaming barefoot in the dusty street and of the golden-haired Rapunzel who lived alone in a high tower. She takes no note of what is being said to her and is rebuked for being moody and sulking all the time.

Extract Based Questions

I. *(There is a languid, emerald sea,*
where the sole inhabitant is me —
a mermaid, drifting blissfully.)

1. There is a languid, emerald sea....
   Why is the sea called languid?
   (a) To create a relaxed and carefree atmosphere.
   (b) To give a human attribution to the sea.
   (c) To express that Amanda is lazy.
   (d) To express Amanda's yearning for freedom and silence.

Ans. (d) To express Amanda's yearning for freedom and silence.

2. What does the word languid not mean in the extract?
   (a) Relaxed   (b) Active
   (c) Lazy   (d) Slow

Ans. (b) Active

3. How does Amanda describe the sea?
   (a) Purple   (b) Golden
   (c) Blue   (d) Emerald

Ans. (d) Emerald

4. Why does Amanda want to be at sea all alone?
   1. Because she is an introvert.
   2. Because she is angry with her parents.
   3. Because she wants to live freely without anyone's restrictions.
   4. Because she is tired of the constant nagging.
   (a) (1) and (2)   (b) (3) and (4)
   (c) (3) only   (d) (4) only

Ans. (b) (3) and (4)

5. Why does Amanda suddenly thinks about a mermaid?
   (a) Because she wants to be beautiful like a mermaid.
   (b) Because she wants to be a mermaid and be free and away from everyone.
   (c) Because she is depressed and therefore having these thoughts.
   (d) Because she yearns for silence and freedom like a mermaid.

Ans. (d) Because she yearns for silence and freedom like a mermaid.

II. *Did you finish your homework, Amanda?*
Did you tidy your room, Amanda?
I thought I told you to clean your shoes,
Amanda!

1. For what do you think the speaker is constantly nagging Amanda?
   (a) To make Amanda be at her best behaviour.
   (b) To teach Amanda refined manners.
   (c) It is the speaker's nature.
   (d) To deliberately restrict Amanda's freedom.

Ans. (b) To teach Amanda refined manners.

2. Does Amanda listen to the speaker? What does she do?
   (a) Yes, she becomes obedient.
   (b) No, she doesn't care and continues with her work.
   (c) No, she is immersed in her own thoughts.
   (d) No, she doesn't move as she is lazy.

Ans. (c) No, she is immersed in her own thoughts.

3. What are the information that can be inferred from the extract? Choose the correct answer:
   1. The speaker is Amanda's mother.
   2. The speaker is very strict and overprotective towards her child.
   3. The speaker is very dominating.

4. The speaker only wants Amanda to be well mannered and disciplined.

   (a) (1) and (2) (b) (2) and (3)

   (c) (1), (2), (4) (d) (1) and (4)

Ans. (c) (1), (2), (4)

4. Why do you think each stanza ends with an exclamation mark?

   (a) To show the anger of the speaker.

   (b) To show that the speaker is surprised at Amanda's attitude.

   (c) To show the irritation of the speaker.

   (d) To stress on the name, as it is the very title of the poem.

Ans. (c) To show the irritation of the speaker.

5. What instruction was given to Amanda right before this extract?

   (a) Not to eat chocolates.

   (b) To stop sulking.

   (c) To stop slouching and sit straight.

   (d) Not to bite nails.

Ans. (c) To stop slouching and sit straight.

III. *(I am an orphan, roaming the street.*

   I pattern soft dust with my hushed, bare feet.

   The silence is golden, the freedom is sweet.)

1. Why does Amanda want to be an orphan?

   1. Because she is tired of the constant nagging and wants to be left alone.

   2. Because she hates to be around her parents as they are very strict and overprotective.

   3. Because she is brought up by her teacher and she doesn't have parents.

   4. Because she wants to live a carefree life without any binding rules and restrictions.

   (a) (1) and (2) (b) (3) only

   (c) (2) and (4) (d) (1) and (4)

Ans. (d) (1) and (4)

2. What does hushed feet mean in the extract?

   (a) Amanda is standing still with her bare feet.

   (b) Amanda has wounded her bare feet.

   (c) Amanda is making patterns with her soft bare feet.

   (d) Amanda is making patterns in the dust very softly and quietly with her bare feet.

Ans. (d) Amanda is making patterns in the dust very softly and quietly with her bare feet.

3. Which word is the antonym of bare?

   (a) To tolerate (b) Uncover

   (c) Robed (d) Protected

Ans. (c) Robed

4. **Identify the figure of speech used in the line, silence is golden, freedom is sweet.**

   (a) Personification

   (b) Alliteration

   (c) Metaphor

   (d) Transferred Epithet

Ans. (c) Metaphor

5. What does the extract tell about Amanda's state or mind?

   (a) She is depressed

   (b) She is annoyed

   (c) She yearns for freedom

   (d) She is having mood swings

Ans. (c) She yearns for freedom

IV. Read the given extract to attempt the questions that follow:

   Don't eat that chocolate, Amanda!

   Remember your acne, Amanda!

   Will you please look at me when I'm speaking to you, Amanda!

1. Which word is perfectly synonymous to the word eat in the above extract?

   (a) Consume (b) Chew

   (c) Bite (d) Feed

Ans. (a) Consume

2. What does his worrying about Amanda's acne tell us about the speaker?

   1. The speaker is overprotective.

   2. The speaker is a health conscious person.

   3. The speaker gives much importance to the physical beauty.

   4. The speaker is insensitive to the child's emotions.

   (a) (1) and (3) (b) (1), (3), (4)

   (c) (2), (4) (d) (1) and (4)

Ans. (a) (1) and (3)

3. The speaker says, "will you please look at me when I'm talking to you". Why do you think Amanda is not looking at the speaker?

   (a) She does not like the speaker.

   (b) She is arrogant.

   (c) She doesn't care.

   (d) She is lost in her thoughts.

Ans. (d) She is lost in her thoughts.

4. Which word in the above extract is an example of repetition?

   (a) Don't (b) Amanda

   (c) Remember (d) Look

Ans. (b) Amanda

5. Right in the next stanza, after the above extract, Amanda imagines herself as _____.

(a) Rapunzel   (b) Mermaid

(c) A free child   (d) An orphan

Ans. (a) Rapunzel

V. *(I am Rapunzel, I have not a care;*

life in a tower is tranquil and rare;

I'll certainly never let down my bright hair!)

Stop that sulking at once, Amanda!

You're always so moody, Amanda!

Anyone would think that I nagged at you,

Amanda!

1. In the line, life in a tower is tranquil and rare, what does tranquil mean?

(a) Annoyed   (b) Lazy

(c) Peaceful   (d) Monotonous

Ans. (c) Peaceful

2. Who is the speaker of the line, Stop that sulking at once, Amanda!

(a) Her mother   (b) Her grandfather

(c) Her friend   (d) Her teacher

Ans. (a) Her mother

3. What is the meaning of the word sulking in the above extract?

(a) Frowning   (b) Daydreaming

(c) Being Moody   (d) Annoying

Ans. (d) Annoying

4. What does the extract tells about Amanda? Choose from the following:

1. Amanda is an imaginative girl.
2. Amanda yearns for freedom.
3. Amanda is a child and she is docile.
4. Amanda is lost in her thoughts.

(a) (1), (2), (4)   (b) (1), (2), (3)

(c) (2), (3), (4)   (d) (2) only

Ans. (a) (1), (2), (4)

5. Why do you think there is no parenthesis in the last stanza?

(a) Because the constant nagging has made Amanda disobedient.

(b) Because her thoughts are forcefully supressed by the harsh real world.

(c) Because she has realised her mistake.

(d) Because she has given up on her thoughts and wishes due to the constant restrictions, rules and instructions.

Ans. (d) Because she has given up on her thoughts and wishes due to the constant restrictions, rules and instructions.

Multiple Choice Questions

1. Who is the poet of the poem 'Amanda'?

(a) Robert Browning   (b) Robin Klein

(c) Ogden Nash   (d) Robert Frost

Ans. (b) Robin Klein

2. What is Amanda doing with her nails?

(a) She is biting her nails.

(b) She is applying nail polish.

(c) She is cutting her nails.

(d) She is rubbing her nails against each other.

Ans. (a) She is biting her nails.

3. Name the literary device used in the line *"Don't bite your nails, Amanda! Don't hunch your shoulders, Amanda!"*.

(a) Anaphora   (b) Enjambment

(c) Metaphor   (d) Alliteration

Ans. (a) Anaphora

4. What does the speaker ask Amanda not to do to her nails?

(a) Wash it   (b) Bite it

(c) Hurt it   (d) None of these

Ans. (b) Bite it

5. What does the exclamation, *'Don't bite your nails, Amanda!'* meant?

(a) Her parents were concerned about her bad habit.

(b) Her parents were encouraging her bad habit.

(c) Her parents were docile.

(d) Her parents were not concerned.

Ans. (a) Her parents were concerned about her bad habit.

6. Which option correctly explains the phrase in the given line from 'Amanda'

Don't hunch your shoulders.

(a) Stand up straight

(b) Look into my eyes

(c) Don't stare

(d) Don't avoid

Ans. (a) Stand up straight

7. The purpose of warning Amanda 'Don't hunch your shoulders' was to _________.

(a) correct her posture

(b) correct her language

(c) correct her freedom

(d) she was the mother

Ans. (a) correct her posture

8. **In the poem Amanda, which option would fall in line with 'correct posture' slouching:: sit up straight : hunch::______**
   (a) bend down   (b) droop
   (c) straighten   (d) arched

Ans. (c) straighten

9. **What should Amanda not do to her shoulders?**
   (a) Straighten   (b) Slouch
   (c) Hunch   (d) Move

Ans. (c) Hunch

10. **What is the meaning of the word 'slouching'?**
   (a) Sitting in a lazy way
   (b) Bending
   (c) Lying down
   (d) Curling

Ans. (a) Sitting in a lazy way

11. **Name the literary device used in the line, "*Stop that slouching and sit up straight*".**
   (a) Alliteration   (b) Simile
   (c) Metaphor   (d) Assonance

Ans. (a) Alliteration

12. **How should Amanda sit?**
   (a) Long Sit   (b) Side Sit
   (c) Straight   (d) Ring Sit

Ans. (c) Straight

13. **Which word in the poem means the same as relaxed?**
   (a) Hunch   (b) Blissfully
   (c) Languid   (d) Drifting

Ans. (c) Languid

14. **What kind of sea does Amanda imagine?**
   (a) Dark Sea   (b) Turquoise Sea
   (c) Emerald Sea   (d) Black Sea

Ans. (c) Emerald Sea

15. **In the poem Amanda, what does '*languid emerald sea*', indicate?**
   It indicates that the sea is:
   (a) rough blue sea   (b) calm green sea
   (c) calm blue sea   (d) rough green sea

Ans. (b) calm green sea

16. **Which option correctly replaces the following phrase in the given line from Amanda? *Where the sole inhabitant is me.***
   (a) Control   (b) Ownership
   (c) Loneliness   (d) Associates

Ans. (b) Ownership

17. **What does Amanda visualise in the second stanza of the poem?**
   (a) A mermaid   (b) A fish
   (c) Rapunzel   (d) An orphan

Ans. (a) A mermaid

18. **With whom does Amanda want to be in the sea?**
   (a) Mermaid   (b) Friends
   (c) Nobody   (d) Father

Ans. (c) Nobody

19. **What does Amanda wish to do in the sea?**
   (a) Catch the fishes
   (b) Hunt various animals
   (c) Watch soft-moving waves
   (d) None of the above

Ans. (d) None of the above

20. **What could Amanda do if she were a mermaid?**
   (a) Be in the green sea (b) Lead a relaxing life
   (c) Both (a) and (b)   (d) None of these

Ans. (c) Both (a) and (b)

21. **Amanda refers to 'herself as a sole mermaid' because then__________**
   (a) she would be alone in the beautiful sea.
   (b) she would see her nagging parents.
   (c) she would be followed by friendly sea animals.
   (d) she would be taken care of by the sea animals.

Ans. (a) she would be alone in the beautiful sea.

22. **Amanda's thoughts of drifting, meant that she would ________**
   (a) be enjoying with her controlling parents.
   (b) be enjoying herself alone amidst the beautiful sea.
   (c) to overcome her bad habits.
   (d) improve her bad habits.

Ans. (b) be enjoying herself alone amidst the beautiful sea.

23. **Amanda refers to liberty as "mermaid" because:**
   (a) a mermaid is governed.
   (b) a mermaid drifts alone freely in the open sea.
   (c) a mermaid cannot do what she wants.
   (d) a mermaid is not a happy go lucky.

Ans. (b) a mermaid drifts alone freely in the open sea.

24. **Which option correctly replaces the following phrase in the given line from Amanda? *Drifting blissfully.***
   (a) Flowing with the tide.
   (b) Swimming against the tide.
   (c) Splashing with the waves.
   (d) Sinking in the sea.

Ans. (a) Flowing with the tide.

25. How old is Amanda and how do you know?

  (a) Amanda is a teenager. It is evident from her moody nature and acne.

  (b) Amanda is below ten years of age. It is evident from her imaginations.

  (c) Amanda is about nine to ten years old. It is evident from her scolding and the mention of homework.

  (d) Amanda is a young adult. It is evident from her moody nature.

Ans.(c) Amanda is about nine to ten years old. It is evident from her scolding and the mention of homework.

26. What was Amanda about to finish?

  (a) Her homework   (b) Her hair

  (c) Her bath   (d) Catch the fishes

Ans.(a) Her homework

27. She is being instructed to:

  (a) clean her room   (b) clean her uniform

  (c) wash the dress   (d) lit the candle

Ans.(a) clean her room

28. After getting scolded from her mother Amanda imagined herself as a/an.

  (a) Predat   (b) Free bird

  (c) Orphan   (d) Mother herself

Ans.(c) Orphan

29. What is the synonym of the word 'roaming' in the poem Amanda?

  (a) Drifting   (b) Wandering

  (c) Slouching   (d) Meandering

Ans.(b) Wandering

30. In the poem Amanda, what would the girl do as an orphan.

  (a) She would sweep the streets.

  (b) She would roam about in the streets.

  (c) She would sleep on the streets.

  (d) She would beg on the streets.

Ans.(b) She would roam about in the streets.

31. The poem focuses on ________ in relation to the child when Amanda thinks I am an orphan.

  (a) the behaviour of children

  (b) the behaviour of adults

  (c) the struggle the child is facing

  (d) the blissful world of the child

Ans.(c) the struggle the child is facing

32. Which option correctly replaces the underlined phrase in the given line from Amanda?

I am an orphan, roaming the street.

  (a) An urchin   (b) A vagabond

  (c) A thief   (d) A laborer

Ans.(b) A vagabond

33. *I pattern soft dust with my ____, bare feet.* Fill in the blank with appropriate word given in the poem.

  (a) cold   (b) dull

  (c) bruised   (d) hushed

Ans.(d) hushed

34. What does Amanda want to do as an orphan? Choose the correct option.

  1. Roam freely in the street

  2. Pattern dust with her bare feet

  3. Not care

  4. Lead a secluded life

  (a) (1) only   (b) (2) and (4)

  (c) (3) only   (d) (1) and (2)

Ans.(d) (1) and (2)

35. Which amongst the following words is not synonymous to 'hushed'?

  (a) Very quiet   (b) Still

  (c) Tranquil   (d) Chaotic

Ans.(d) Chaotic

36. Which among the following is the correct sentence used in the poem, Amanda?

  (a) The silence is golden, the freedom is bitter.

  (b) The freedom is golden, the silence is bitter.

  (c) The freedom is golden, the silence is sweet.

  (d) The silence is golden, the freedom is sweet.

Ans.(d) The silence is golden, the freedom is sweet.

37. Name the literary device used in the line *"freedom is sweet"*

  (a) Anaphora   (b) Enjambment

  (c) Metaphor   (d) Alliteration

Ans.(c) Metaphor

38. Amanda want to play with ______ being an orphan child.

  (a) stones   (b) dust

  (c) friends   (d) toys

Ans.(b) dust

39. In her imagination silence is ______ in colour.

  (a) golden   (b) black

  (c) green   (d) yellow

Ans.(a) golden

40. What according to the poem will happen to Amanda if she eats chocolate?

  (a) She will become fat.

  (b) She will get allergy.

  (c) She will become moody.

  (d) She will get acne.

Ans.(d) She will get acne.

41. The purpose of the mother asking Amanda to refrain from chocolates was to _______

(a) teach her obedience.

(b) punish her.

(c) prevent her from getting acne.

(d) prevent her from getting improve her diet.

Ans.(c) prevent her from getting acne.

42. *Will you please look at me when I'm speaking to you, Amanda!* **Said the mother since__________.**

(a) Amanda was not listening

(b) Amanda was not making an eye contact

(c) Amanda was grumbling

(d) Amanda was deceptive

Ans.(b) Amanda was not making an eye contact

43. Why do you think Amanda wants to be a Rapunzel?

(a) Because she wants to escape the freedom.

(b) Because she wants to enjoy the freedom away from any restraint.

(c) Because she wants to feel like a princess in the tower.

(d) Because she wants to have a long hair like Rapunzel.

Ans.(b) Because she wants to enjoy the freedom away from any restraint.

44. *"I am Rapunzel, I have not a care..."*
What is the poetic device used in the given line?

(a) Personification   (b) Assonance

(c) Allusion   (d) Simile

Ans.(c) Allusion

45. Why do you think Amanda, being Rapunzel, will never let her hair down the tower?

(a) So that nobody can cut her hair.

(b) So that nobody can enter the tower and she can be in peace.

(c) Because she has now become obedient.

(d) Both (b) and (c)

Ans.(b) So that nobody can enter the tower and she can be in peace.

46. Amanda thinks that she'll never let down her:

(a) white hair   (b) bright hair

(c) yellow hair   (d) bronze hair

Ans.(b) bright hair

47. In the poem Amanda What does *'I am Rapunzel, I have not a care'* **indicate? It indicates that Amanda.**

(a) Wants to be left all to herself.

(b) Wants to be partially free.

(c) Wants to enjoy combing her long hair.

(d) Wants to be a princess

Ans.(a) Wants to be left all to herself.

48. Amanda states *I'll certainly never let down my bright hair!* **Indicates that___________.**

(a) she will never let anyone into her life and dominate her.

(b) she will never let anyone near her parents.

(c) she will take full control of her parents and her life.

(d) she will protect herself and whoever lives with her.

Ans.(a) she will never let anyone into her life and dominate her.

49. Arrange Amanda's imagination in chronological order as appeared in the poem:

1. Orphan   2. Mermaid

3. Rapunzel   4. To be a nobody

(a) (2), (1), and (3)   (b) (1), (2), and (3)

(c) (4) only   (d) (1), (3), (2)

Ans.(a) (2), (1), and (3)

50. Who is asked to stop sulking?

(a) Amanda   (b) Poet

(c) Amanda's mother (d) Poet's friend

Ans.(a) Amanda

51. Why do you think Amanda is sulking?

(a) Because she is being nagged constantly.

(b) Because she is not allowed to eat chocolates.

(c) Because her parents do not love her.

(d) Because she is moody.

Ans.(a) Because she is being nagged constantly.

52. *"Anyone would think that I___at you, Amanda!"*
Fill in the blank with the appropriate answer.

(a) nagged   (b) harassed

(c) shouted   (d) beat

Ans.(a) nagged

53. What is the meaning of the word 'nagged'?

(a) Harassed   (b) Shouted

(c) Beat   (d) Tortured

Ans.(a) Harassed

54. In the poem Amanda, what does excessive nagging lead to? It indicates that the child.

(a) Will listen to her parents.

(b) Will ignore her parents.

(c) Will enter into the world of dreams and imagination.

(d) Will make them aggressive.

Ans.(c) Will enter into the world of dreams and imagination.

55. According to your view excessive nagging would lead a child to ___________.

(a) obedience   (b) snobbishness

(c) defiance   (d) sympathetic

Ans.(c) defiance

56. Why does the poet use brackets:
(a) reveal the nagging thoughts of the child.
(b) visual contrast between Amanda's thoughts and mothers instructions.
(c) confusing contrast between Amanda's thoughts and mothers instructions.
(d) reveal the imagination of Amanda's mother

Ans.(b) visual contrast between Amanda's thoughts and mothers instructions.

57. What does she picture herself as in the last stanza?
(a) Mermaid
(b) Orphan
(c) Rapunzel
(d) None of these

Ans.(d) None of these

58. Whenever Amanda was told 'not to' she felt __________.
(a) she was loved
(b) she was overlooked
(c) she was ignored
(d) she had no choice

Ans.(d) she had no choice

59. In the poem Amanda, which words have been used to create an imaginative Effect on her?
(a) Don't bite; don't cry
(b) Don't bite; slouch
(c) hunch; Sit up straight
(d) Don't do this; Do that

Ans.(d) Don't do this; Do that

60. What is the theme of the poem Amanda?
(a) Parents should not make their children feel imprisoned.
(b) Children are moody.
(c) Children must be handled with care.
(d) Children must be guided all the time.

Ans.(a) Parents should not make their children feel imprisoned.

61. From whose perspective do you think the poem is written?
(a) Amanda's perspective
(b) Poet's perspective
(c) Amanda's mother's perspective
(d) Omniscient narrator's perspective

Ans.(a) Amanda's perspective

62. Armanda always felt ____________ when she was corrected by her parents.
(a) controlled and instructed
(b) controlled and ignored
(c) ignored and unloved
(d) both curtailed and free

Ans.(a) controlled and instructed

63. Choose the correct option related to the poem 'Amanda':
1. Amanda does not desire for freedom.
2. Amanda's mother is too harsh on her.
3. Amanda's mother loves her child.
4. Amanda's mother wants to instil good values at the cost of her daughter's happiness.
(a) (1) and (2)
(b) (2) and (3)
(c) (2), and (4)
(d) (1), (2), (3), (4)

Ans.(c) (2), and (4)

64. What is the tone of Amanda's mother in the poem?
(a) Dominating
(b) Tired
(c) Angry
(d) Authoritative

Ans.(d) Authoritative

65. In the poem Amanda, do you feel it is wrong for the parent to correct a child if wrong?
(a) Yes- child should be given a choice.
(b) Yes-A child should be provoked.
(c) Yes- A child should be corrected by explaining the consequences.
(d) No-A child should be ignored.

Ans.(c) Yes- A child should be corrected by explaining the consequences.

66. Identify the option that aptly describes Amanda' parents according to you.
(a) Proud, controlling
(b) Concerned and correcting
(c) Considerate and selfish
(d) Dominant and strict

Ans.(b) Concerned and correcting

67. The strictness of Amanda's parents made Amanda feel ____________.
(a) free
(b) controlled
(c) happy
(d) comfortable

Ans.(b) controlled

68. What does, *"Did you"*, mean in the poem Amanda?
(a) Commanding question.
(b) Commanding order.
(c) Exclamation of joy.
(d) Disgustful exclamation.

Ans.(a) Commanding question.

69. The poem focuses on ____________ when she is asked, "if she has finished her homework."
(a) responsibility of a parent on a child
(b) responsibility of a child on her parent
(c) responsibility of a teacher on a child
(d) responsibility of a friend on his peer

Ans.(a) responsibility of a parent on a child

70. According to the poem, Amanda is an ____ girl.

(a) arrogant   (b) moody

(c) sincere   (d) imaginative

Ans. (d) imaginative

71. Who was Amanda?

(a) A college going girl

(b) A school going girl

(c) A factory worker

(d) None of these

Ans. (b) A school going girl

72. The Poet feels for the child but at the same time thinks that the parents are responsible for the ___________.

(a) behaviour of the teacher

(b) environment of the child

(c) performance of the child at school

(d) upbringing of the child

Ans. (d) upbringing of the child

73. In the poem 'Amanda', Amanda is a ___________

(a) mermaid   (b) rapunzel

(c) girl   (d) mother

Ans. (c) girl

74. Reading through the imagination of a child the poem conveys the message that________.

(a) children should be overlooked.

(b) children's behaviour should be overlooked.

(c) children need to be allowed more liberty.

(d) children should be corrected.

Ans. (c) children need to be allowed more liberty.

75. Identify the option that aptly describes Amanda.

(a) haughty   (b) moody

(c) careless   (d) proud

Ans. (b) moody

76. Identify the option that best describes what the parents are trying to inculcate in Amanda in the poem.

(a) Holiness and good manners.

(b) Good manners and habits.

(c) Good manners and egotism.

(d) Egotism and selflessness.

Ans. (b) Good manners and habits.

77. According to Amanda the mannerism of her parents were ___________ for her.

(a) happy   (b) sad

(c) nagging   (d) loving

Ans. (c) nagging

78. How does the poet design the inner thoughts of Amanda in the poem Amanda?

(a) by putting it within brackets.

(b) by highlighting.

(c) by always using metaphors.

(d) by personification.

Ans. (a) by putting it within brackets.

79. According to the poet what does every child feel in connection with the poem 'Amanda'.

(a) Free   (b) Not controlled

(c) Well instructed   (d) Dominated

Ans. (d) Dominated

80. In the poem Amanda, what do you feel about Amanda?

(a) Mature and innocent.

(b) Immature and innocent.

(c) Jaded and mature.

(d) Naughty and haughty.

Ans. (b) Immature and innocent.

81. What do you think Amanda feels missing in her words all through the poem.

(a) Parents guidance   (b) Parents dominance

(c) Parents love   (d) Parents brutality

Ans. (c) Parents love

82. What according to you in the poem, 'Amanda' is she at fault to be corrected? If yes or no why?

(a) Yes, she is disobedient to her parents.

(b) Yes, she does not like to be corrected by her parents.

(c) No, she is too immature to understand why she is corrected.

(d) No, She is mature enough to understand to be corrected.

Ans. (c) No, she is too immature to understand why she is corrected.

Text Book Questions

Thinking about the Poem

83. What could Amanda do if she were a mermaid?

Ans. She would drift blissfully on a calm sea where she would be all alone.

84. Is Amanda an orphan? Why does she say so?

Ans. No, Amanda is not an orphan but she wishes she was as she wants to be alone with lack of instructions and freedom to roam the streets.

85. How old do you think Amanda is? How do you know this?

Ans. Amanda is probably a school going girl entering her teens. The reference to homework and acne suggests this.

86. Do you know the story of Rapunzel? Why does she want to be Rapunzel?

Ans. She wants to be Rapunzel so that she can live far above in a tower alone with no one instructing or saying anything to her.

87. Who do you think is speaking to her?

Ans. A parent, most probably her mother, is speaking to her.

88. Why are Stanzas 2, 4 and 6 given in parentheses?

Ans. The parentheses enclose the thoughts of Amanda while her parent is talking to her.

89. Who is the speaker in Stanzas 2, 4 and 6? Do you think this speaker is listening to the speaker in Stanzas 1, 3, 5, and 7?

Ans. Amanda is the speaker in Stanzas 2, 4 and 6. No, Amanda is not listening to the speaker of the other stanzas.

90. What does the girl yearn for? What does this poem tell you about Amanda?

Ans. The girl yearns for freedom from the rules and instructions which she is bombarded with continuously. She loves freedom.

91. Read the last stanza. Do you think Amanda is sulking and is moody?

Ans. No, Amanda is not moody or sulking. She is just lost in her own world and dreams of a free life.

Short Answer Type Questions

20-30 Words

92. What impression of Amanda do you get from the poem 'Amanda'?

Ans. Amanda is a little school going girl. She is constantly nagged by her parent. It is probably the mother. She keeps asking Amanda to do this or that but poor Amanda longs to be free and live life in her own way.

93. What is Amanda asked to do or not to do?

Ans. Amanda is asked not to bite her nails, not to hunch her shoulders and not to eat chocolate. She is asked to sit up straight, to finish her homework, to clean her room and to clean her shoes. In fact, she is constantly asked to do or not to do that.

94. What all does Amanda dream to do?

Ans. Amanda dreams of being a mermaid drifting on the sea all alone. She dreams of being an orphan walking in the streets with no care. She dreams of being Rapunzel living in a high tower away from everybody.

Reference to Context Questions

Read the extract given below and answer the questions that follow :

95. *Don't bite your nails, Amanda!*
Don't hunch your shoulders, Amanda!
Stop that slouching and sit up straight, Amanda!
(There is a languid, emerald sea,
where the sole inhabitant is me —
a mermaid, drifting blissfully.)

(a) Why are there lines given within brackets?

(b) Amanda is getting instructions for what purpose?

Ans. (a) There are lines given within brackets because they reveal the inner thoughts of Amanda. Brackets are used for visual contrast between what Amanda is saying and what her mother is instructing.

(b) Amanda is getting instructions as a part of her upbringing by her parents. Her conduct and manners are getting refined for future purposes.

96. *I am an orphan, roaming the street.*
I pattern soft dust with my hushed, bare feet.
The silence is golden, the freedom is sweet.

(a) Who is the speaker here?
    (i) An orphan   (ii) Amanda
    (iii) The poet   (iv) Amanda's parents

(b) Who is being described in the above lines?
    (i) A tree   (ii) Amanda
    (iii) An orphan   (iv) A small boy

(c) How does the speaker make designs?
    (i) With bare feet   (ii) With hands
    (iii) With a brush   (iv) With colours

(d) Where is the speaker making designs?
    (i) On a paper   (ii) On soft dust
    (iii) On the wall   (iv) On a notebook

(e) How does the speaker look at freedom?
    (i) With anxiety   (ii) With anger
    (iii) With love   (iv) With surprise

Ans. (a) (ii) Amanda
(b) (ii) Amanda
(c) (i) With bare feet
(d) (ii) On soft dust
(e) (iii) With love

❏❏

Animals

Chapter

7

—byWalt Whitman

Summary :

The poet tells us that he feels more at home with animals than humans, whom he finds complicated and false. He feels that humans are always whining and crying for something. Man is very materialistic and selfish. Among the animals, he says, there is no hero worshiping and all the creatures love each other unconditionally. He says that he shares the simplicity and innocence with the animals.

Extract Based Questions

I. *I think I could turn and live with animals, they are*
So placid and self-contain'd ,
I stand and look at them long and long.
They do not sweat and whine about their condition

1. What does the poet mean by referring the line "I think I could turn and live with animals"?

(a) The poet wants to change into an animal and live with them.

(b) The poet doesn't want to live with the humans but animals.

(c) The poet does not want to turn away from humans and live with animals.

(d) The poet wants to turn to the side of the animals and live with them in the animal world.

Ans. (b) The poet doesn't want to live with the humans but animals.

2. Why does the poet feel the animals are better than humans?

1. Because animals are always self-satisfied and treat each other equally.

2. Because animals do not have lust of owning things.

3. Because the poet hates the human world.

4. Because humans neglect their values and virtues.

(a) (1) and (2)   (b) (3) and (4)

(c) (1), (2), (4)   (d) (1), (2), (3), (4)

Ans. (c) (1), (2), (4)

3. Why do you think has the poet used the word 'long' twice in the above extract?

(a) To emphasise the word long.

(b) To rhyme the word.

(c) To signify the duration of time.

(d) To use it as a poetic device.

Ans. (c) To signify the duration of time.

4. The phrase "sweat and whine" means____. Choose the most appropriate option.

(a) to sweat and cry

(b) to feel frustrated and helpless

(c) to cry and complain

(d) to feel uneasy and therefore cry

Ans. (c) to cry and complain

5. The animals do not weep for their ___.

(a) failures   (b) sins

(c) condition   (d) ancestors

Ans. (c) condition

II. *"They do not lie awake in the dark and weep for their sins,*
They do not make me sick discussing their duty to God".

1. Why do you think they are always happy?

(a) Because they do not have the desire to possess worldly things.

(b) Because they are insane.

(c) Because they do not have emotions.

(d) Because they cannot weep.

Ans. (a) Because they do not have the desire to possess worldly things.

2. What does "discussing their duty to God" mean in this context?

(a) To show off the duties to God.

(b) Meaningless rituals.

(c) To ask God to fulfil their desires in return of their duties.

(d) To serve God honestly

Ans. (c) To ask God to fulfil their desires in return of their duties.

3. Do animals discuss their duty to God? Why? Choose the correct option:

1. No, because they live a simple and peaceful life.

2. No, because animals do not have human gods.

3. No, because they live with equality, without worrying.

4. No, because they never commit a sin.

(a) (1), (3), (4) (b) (2) only

(c) (1) and (3) (d) (2) and (4)

Ans. (a) (1), (3), (4)

4. For whom does 'they' refer to?

(a) Humans

(b) Animals

(c) Children

(d) Humans and animals

Ans. (b) Animals

5. What does the above extract tell about animals nature?

(a) They are rational

(b) They are more intelligent

(c) They are self satisfied

(d) Both (A) and (C)

Ans. (d) Both (A) and (C)

III. *Not one is dissatisfied, not one is demented with the mania of owning things*

Not one kneels to another, nor to his kind that lived thousands of years ago.

1. What things do humans own?

(a) Materialistic things

(b) Moral virtues

(c) Car

(d) Money

Ans. (a) Materialistic things

2. What do *mania of owning things* indicate?

(a) Maddening desire of possessing materialistic things.

(b) Maddening desire of collecting things.

(c) Excessive desire of giving things.

(d) Lust.

Ans. (a) Maddening desire of possessing materialistic things.

3. Which among the following is the antonym of the word demented?

(a) Insane (b) Balanced

(c) Crazy (d) Maniac

Ans. (b) Balanced

4. What according to you should humans possess?

(a) Materialistic things

(b) Worldly possessions

(c) Equality

(d) Honesty

Ans. (c) Equality

5. What does the poet laments for?

(a) Loss of human values.

(b) Negligently dropping of human values.

(c) Degeneration of the society.

(d) Non-cooperation with the animal world.

Ans. (b) Negligently dropping of human values.

IV. *Not one kneels to another, nor to his kind that lived thousands of years ago,*

Not one is respectable or unhappy over the whole earth

So they show their relations to me and I accept them,

They bring me tokens of myself, they evince them plainly in their possession

1. What is the attitude of the animals towards their sins?

(a) Confused and peaceful

(b) Calm, peaceful and self confident

(c) Confused and sad

(d) Complaining

Ans. (b) Calm, peaceful and self confident

2. What relations is the poet talking about?

(a) The animals show the poet their relation with him.

(b) The animals show the human virtues to the poet and he could relate to them.

(c) The animals show their relation with other animals to the poet.

(d) The animals show how well they are related to the poet.

Ans. (b) The animals show the human virtues to the poet and he could relate to them.

3. *"So they show their relations to me and I accept them"*. What does accepting the relations mean here?

1. It means that the poet agrees that animals have all the noble virtues that should be present in humans.

2. It means that the poet has accepted that he and the animals have similar values.

3. It means that the poet has accepted the animal and human relation.

4. It means that the poet has accepted that animals are more rational than humans.

(a) (1) and (2) (b) (1) only

(c) (2) and (3) (d) (4) only

Ans. (a) (1) and (2)

4. For whom does the phrase 'not one' refer to in the extract?

(a) Animals

(b) Human beings

(c) Animals and Human beings

(d) Nobody

Ans. (a) Animals

5. What is the tone and nature of the poem?

(a) Tone is critical and the nature is satirical.

(b) Tone is critical and the nature is didactic.

(c) Tone is soft and the nature is love.

(d) Tone is critical, nature is religious.

Ans. (b) Tone is critical and the nature is didactic.

V. Read the given extract to attempt the questions that follow:

Not one is respectable or unhappy over the whole earth.

So they show their relations to me and I accept them,
They bring me tokens of myself, they evince
them plainly in their possession
I wonder where they get those tokens,
Did I pass that way huge times ago and negligently drop them?

1. The poet says, "They bring me tokens of myself..." What does tokens mean here?
  (a) Symbols   (b) Souvenir
  (c) Values   (d) Gifts
Ans. (c) Values

2. By the line, *Not one is respectable or unhappy,* **the poet means ____**
  (a) all of them are equal, hence all are happy.
  (b) they are always disrespectful and insulting.
  (c) they lack good values.
  (d) unlike humans, they are always happy.
Ans. (a) all of them are equal, hence all are happy.

3. What does the poet negligently drops?
  (a) Truthfulness   (b) Equality
  (c) Self Confidence   (d) All of these
Ans. (d) All of these

4. Which word in the above extract means 'reveal'?
  (a) Wonder   (b) Tokens
  (c) Evince   (d) Possession
Ans. (c) Evince

5. What does the poem convey according to the extract?
  1. The poet is an animal lover.
  2. Humans are disrespectful and complicated.
  3. The poem shows a contrast between animals and humans.
  4. Animals are wiser and happier than humans.
  (a) (1) and (2)   (b) (2) only
  (c) (3) and (4)   (d) (3) only
Ans. (c) (3) and (4)

Multiple Choice Questions

1. "I think I could turn and live with animals..." Whom is the poet turning from?
  (a) Himself   (b) Society
  (c) Humans   (d) God
Ans. (c) Humans

2. Who, according to the poet, is better?
  (a) Human beings   (b) Animals
  (c) Both are equal   (d) None of these
Ans. (b) Animals

3. The poet is ___________ when he says, "I think I could turn and live with animals."
  (a) doubtful   (b) worried
  (c) considering   (d) liable
Ans. (c) considering

4. Which option correctly replaces the following phrase in the given line from 'Animals'? 'they are so placid and self-contain'd'.
  (a) Calm, thoughtless and dependent.
  (b) Calm, serene and independent.
  (c) Calm, selfish and dependent.
  (d) Calm, selfless and dependent.
Ans. (b) Calm, serene and independent.

5. The purpose of the poet thinking of turning and living with animals is that he is________
  (a) fed up of himself.
  (b) he is filled with anger.
  (c) he is lonely.
  (d) impressed by their calmness.
Ans. (d) impressed by their calmness.

6. Name the literary device used in the line "I think I could turn and live with animals".
  (a) Simile   (b) Metaphor
  (c) Assonance   (d) Personification
Ans. (c) Assonance

7. What is the meaning of the word 'placid' in the poem Animals?
  (a) Confused   (b) Greedy
  (c) Clumsy   (d) Peaceful
Ans. (d) Peaceful

8. In the poem Animals, the poet addresses to stand and look at them long and long? It indicates that the poet is:
  (a) envied   (b) impressed
  (c) grieved   (d) opposed
Ans. (b) impressed

9. What shows that the poet loves animals?
  (a) He looks at the animals for short time.
  (b) He stands and looks at the animals long and long.
  (c) He feed the animals.
  (d) None of the Above
Ans. (b) He stands and looks at the animals long and long.

10. What is the meaning of the word 'whine' in the poem Animals?
  (a) Relaxed   (b) Sulk
  (c) Cry   (d) Beverage
Ans. (c) Cry

11. **The animals do not whine about:**
    - (a) their place
    - (b) their feeding
    - (c) their appetite
    - (d) their condition

Ans. (d) their condition

12. **The poet refers to a figure of speech in *'they do not sweat and whine about their condition'* identify the 'figure of speech'.**
    - (a) Alliteration
    - (b) Hyperbole
    - (c) Tautology
    - (d) Metaphor

Ans. (c) Tautology

13. **Choose the appropriate word for the meaning of *'They do not sweat and whine about their condition'*.**
    - (a) Excited
    - (b) Happy
    - (c) Mourn
    - (d) Rejoice

Ans. (c) Mourn

14. **The poet is ___________ when he says, *'They do not sweat and whine about their condition'*.**
    - (a) perplexed
    - (b) sorry
    - (c) relentless
    - (d) remorseless

Ans. (a) perplexed

15. **The poet refers 'complaint' to____in the context.**
    - (a) whine
    - (b) sweat
    - (c) dissatisfied
    - (d) placid

Ans. (b) sweat

16. **In the poem Animals what is the attitude the poet indicates of the animals towards their sins.**
    - (a) They do not mourn
    - (b) They feel sad
    - (c) They keep calm
    - (d) They repent

Ans. (a) they do not mourn

17. **What is the attitude of animals towards their sins?**
    - (a) Calm and self-confident
    - (b) Confused and stressful
    - (c) Sad and regretful
    - (d) They do not care

Ans. (a) Calm and self-confident

18. **Why do humans lie awake in the dark?**
    - (a) They pray to God.
    - (b) They do not feel sleepy.
    - (c) They weep for their sins.
    - (d) They feel lonely.

Ans. (c) They weep for their sins.

19. **What is the attitude of the animals toward their sins?**
    - (a) They do not weep.
    - (b) They feel sad.
    - (c) They keep calm.
    - (d) None of these

Ans. (a) They do not weep

20. **Which option correctly replaces the following phrase in the given line from Animals?**
    'They do not lie awake in the dark and weep for their sins'.
    - (a) Animals are seldom remorse like humans.
    - (b) Animals do not stay awake and repent like humans.
    - (c) Animals and humans have the same pattern.
    - (d) Humans can sleep without worrying.

Ans. (b) Animals do not stay awake and repent like humans.

21. **To whom do the animals not talk about their duty according to the poem?**
    - (a) Poet
    - (b) Humans
    - (c) Society
    - (d) God

Ans. (d) God

22. **In the poem Animals, what makes the poet sick?**
    - (a) humans whining about their condition.
    - (b) humans discussing their duty to God.
    - (c) humans weeping for their sins.
    - (d) human's mania of possessing things.

Ans. (b) humans discussing their duty to God.

23. **The purpose of the poet expressing his opinion *'They do not make me sick discussing their duty to God'* in Animals is to highlight that______.**
    - (a) humans sing their praises for the work they do.
    - (b) animals follow the religion of nature.
    - (c) animals do not account for their sins.
    - (d) animals and humans are self-contained.

Ans. (a) humans sing their praises for the work they do.

24. **What mania does human beings possess according to the poem?**
    - (a) Weeping over their sins
    - (b) Praying to God
    - (c) Owning things
    - (d) Killing animals

Ans. (c) Owning things

25. **Find the word from poem Animals which means the same as insane.**
    - (a) Sick
    - (b) Dissatisfied
    - (c) Mania
    - (d) Demented

Ans. (d) Demented

26. **Who is not dissatisfied always?**
    - (a) Humans
    - (b) Animals
    - (c) Poet
    - (d) All of these

Ans. (b) Animals

27. **What do humans do that animal don't?**
    - (a) Greed
    - (b) Jealous
    - (c) Restless
    - (d) All of these

Ans. (d) All of these

28. **The poet prefers animals to humans because __________.**

    (a) humans are selfish and animals are less selfish.
    (b) humans are always fighting and animals fight less.
    (c) humans are greedy and never satisfied while animals are self-reliant.
    (d) humans and animals are self-reliant.

Ans. (c) humans are greedy and never satisfied while animals are self-reliant.

29. **Identify one negative attitude that humans have and animals don't that keep them happy.**

    (a) happiness   (b) greatness
    (c) dissatisfied   (d) satisfaction

Ans. (c) dissatisfied

30. **In the poem Animals, which word indicates 'the desire to own things has been called madness' by the poet.**

    (a) Dissatisfied   (b) Placid
    (c) Mania   (d) Contained

Ans. (c) Mania

31. **In the poem Animals, what does 'Not one is dissatisfied, indicate?**

    (a) Suppression   (b) Aggression
    (c) Satisfaction   (d) Opposition

Ans. (c) Satisfaction

32. **What are the qualities that makes the poet opt for animals over humans?**

    (a) They whine about their condition.
    (b) They are satisfied and happy.
    (c) They fight over wealth.
    (d) They are never happy.

Ans. (b) They are satisfied and happy.

33. **Whom does the phrase that lived thousand years ago refer to in the poem Animals?**

    (a) Primitive Men   (b) Human Ancestors
    (c) Extinct Animals   (d) Hunter Gatherers

Ans. (b) Human Ancestors

34. **What is the attitude of humans about those who lived thousands of years ago?**

    (a) They kneel   (b) They stand
    (c) They fly   (d) None of these

Ans. (a) They kneel

35. **According to the poem, Animals, the animals are never ____.**

    (a) unhappy   (b) overconfident
    (c) independent   (d) immoral

Ans. (a) unhappy

36. **The poet finds the humans ___. Which option best fits the blank?**

    (a) complicated and false
    (b) negligent
    (c) unhappy and materialistic
    (d) fraud

Ans. (c) unhappy and materialistic

37. **Whatsoever happen on the earth, none of the animals is:**

    (a) unhappy   (b) delighted
    (c) crazy   (d) crack

Ans. (a) unhappy

38. **The poet in the poem Animals admires the fact that whatever be the condition the animals are _______.**

    (a) never unhappy   (b) never delighted
    (c) always greedy   (d) never happy

Ans. (a) never unhappy

39. **"So they show their relations to me and I accept them". Who is the speaker of this line?**

    (a) Robert Frost
    (b) W.B Yeats
    (c) Robert Browning
    (d) Walt Whitman

Ans. (d) Walt Whitman

40. **The poet feels that animals show:**

    (a) waving tail   (b) teeth to him
    (c) pictures to him   (d) relation to him

Ans. (d) relation to him

41. **In the poem Animals, which positive attitude does the poet admire in animals and are missing in humans?**

    (a) Greed   (b) Vibrant nature
    (c) Selfishness   (d) Discontentment

Ans. (b) Vibrant nature

42. **"They bring me tokens of myself" - What does this line mean?**

    (a) Animals show qualities of love and affection of to the poet.
    (b) Animals show human love and affection to other animals.
    (c) Animals reflect human qualities as the poet possess.
    (d) Humans reflect animal qualities.

Ans. (c) Animals reflect human qualities as the poet possess.

43. **What does the word 'tokens' mean in the poem Animals?**

    (a) Coupons   (b) Material
    (c) Human virtues   (d) Souvenir

Ans. (c) Human virtues

44. What is the difference in the possession of the animals and that of the humans according to the poem *Animals*?

(a) Animals possess human virtues, whereas humans are dropping them.

(b) Humans possess animal qualities, whereas, animals run after food.

(c) Animals do not possess any quality, whereas humans possess all the moral virtues.

(d) There is hardly any difference between the possession of animals and humans.

Ans. (a) Animals possess human virtues, whereas humans are dropping them.

45. Which word in the poem is the antonym of conceal?

(a) Evince   (b) Demented

(c) Sins   (d) Placid

Ans. (a) Evince

46. Name the literary device used in *"They bring me tokens of myself"*.

(a) Anaphora   (b) Assonance

(c) Metaphor   (d) Alliteration

Ans. (c) Metaphor

47. The animals evidently show that the tokens were:

(a) near the others   (b) away from them

(c) in their possession (d) in the pockets

Ans. (c) in their possession

48. They evince them is what the poet says in the poem Animals, the synonym of evince here is:

(a) discern   (b) distract

(c) demonstrate   (d) deteriorate

Ans. (c) demonstrate

49. In the poem Animals 'tokens' indicate:

(a) virtues   (b) difficulty

(c) morals   (d) contentment

Ans. (a) virtues

50. *I wonder where they get those tokens.* Identify the poem and "they" in this line.

(a) The poem is Animals, "they" refers to the humans.

(b) The poem is The Tale of Custard the Dragon, "they" refers to Belinda's pet animals.

(c) The poem is Animals, "they" refers to the animals.

(d) The poem is Animals, "they" refers to both humans and animals.

Ans. (c) The poem is Animals, "they" refers to the animals.

51. "Did I pass that way ____ and negligently drop them?" Fill in the blank with the correct option as given in the poem.

(a) huge times ago   (b) once upon a time

(c) long time ago   (d) many years ago

Ans. (a) huge times ago

52. What qualities have the humans given up?

(a) Innocence   (b) Kindness

(c) Truthfulness   (d) All of these

Ans. (d) All of these

53. identify the word in the poem that means the same as carelessly?

(a) Placid   (b) Demented

(c) Negligently   (d) Evince

Ans. (c) Negligently

54. How can you say that the poet loves animals?

(a) He hates humans, therefore loves animals.

(b) He stands and looks at the animals for long.

(c) He is an animal lover.

(d) Animals love poet the same way as he loves them.

Ans. (b) He stands and looks at the animals for long.

55. From which work of the poet is the poem Animals taken from?

(a) 'Song of Myself' in Leaves of Grass.

(b) 'Going Somewhere' in Leaves of Grass.

(c) 'A Farm Picture' in Leaves of Grass.

(d) 'A Song of Joy' in Leaves of Grass.

Ans. (a) 'Song of Myself' in Leaves of Grass.

56. What type of poem is Animals?

(a) Dramatic Monologue

(b) Free Verse

(c) Ballad

(d) Sonnet

Ans. (b) Free Verse

57. Walt Whitman is a/an ___ author.

(a) Danish   (b) Irish

(c) American   (d) British

Ans. (c) American

58. Identify the option that aptly describes the animals.

(a) Envious and placid

(b) Placid and jealous

(c) Calm and undisturbed

(d) Never satisfied

Ans. (c) Calm and undisturbed

59. Human's behaviour as compared with the animals makes the poet ____________.

(a) irritated   (b) happy

(c) elevated   (d) proud

Ans. (a) irritated

60. In the poem Animals the poet praises the animals for possessing______that humans lack.

(a) interest in material things

(b) qualities

(c) dominance

(d) worldly things

Ans. (b) qualities

61. The poet in the poem Animals desires to compare humans with animals highlight the ______of their nature.

(a) strength   (b) shortcomings

(c) advantages   (d) upcoming

Ans. (b) shortcomings

62. Identify the option that aptly does not describe human quality.

(a) Greedy   (b) Innocent

(c) Whine   (d) Sinful

Ans. (b) Innocent

63. What do the animals show and the poet accepts as told in the poem Animals?

(a) Understanding   (b) Relationship

(c) Friendship   (d) Respect

Ans. (b) Relationship

64. The poet keeps repeating the words 'Not one' several times in the poem Animals. It signifies the poet's______.

(a) anger and vengeance

(b) try to enhance a sense of continuity

(c) disappointment and frustration

(d) attempt to write it with a rhythm

Ans. (c) disappointment and frustration

65. The qualities attributed to animals in the given poem Animals are ______________.

(a) happy, egocentric, possessive

(b) bold, materialistic, reputable

(c) discontented, furious, respectful

(d) contented, identical, possessive

Ans. (d) contented, identical, possessive

66. Choose the option which 'Cannot' be finally concluded from the poem Animals.

(a) Man is curious

(b) Man complaints about his misery

(c) Man is materialistic

(d) Man loves to exaggerate

Ans. (a) Man is curious

Text Book Questions

Thinking about the Poem

67. Notice the use of the word 'turn' in the first line, *"I think I could turn and live with animals..."*. What is the poet turning from?

Ans. The poet wants to turn away from humans. He wishes to live with the animals and nature. It may also be a reference to humans' evolution from animals.

68. Mention three things that humans do and animals don't.

Ans. Animals don't sweat and whine about their condition, they do not lie awake in the dark and weep for their sins and they do not discuss their duty to God.

69. Do humans kneel to other humans who lived thousands of years ago?

Ans. Yes, humans do kneel to other humans who lived thousands of years ago. They treat them as their gods.

70. What are the 'tokens' that the poet says he may have dropped long ago, and which the animals have kept for him? Discuss this in class. (Hint: Whitman belongs to the Romantic tradition that includes Rousseau and Wordsworth, which holds that civilisation has made humans false to their own true nature. What could be the basic aspects of our nature as living beings that humans choose to ignore or deny?

Ans. The tokens are the qualities of innocence, simplicity and contentment which man has dropped and forgotten but the animals have kept them intact.

Short Answer Type Questions

20-30 Words

71. Why don't the animals lie awake at night?

Ans. Animals don't commit any sins and are not involved in wrong doings. Hence, they don't lose sleep over any of their actions and so do not lie awake at night.

72. What makes the poet sick?

Ans. The poet is sick of people who keep discussing their duty towards God. He does not like people who talk of their duties towards God but do nothing for God's men.

73. What are the tokens that the animals give him?

Ans. The tokens that the animals give him are the qualities of innocence, simplicity and contentment. These are the qualities that man had but now has left them on his journey towards a materialistic world.

Long Answer Type Questions

100-120 Words

74. Which qualities of animals has the poet lost and now wants to regain? Answer with reference to the poem, 'Animals'. ★

Ans. The poet wants to regain the qualities of animals as in, animals are natural and do not adapt to material goods like human beings do. This natural aspect of animals has helped them maintain their values. Humans, in order to possess more and more, have forgotten their kindness and innocence.

Animals do not complain about their situation, they are considered to be happier than humans. Animals live in natural surroundings, they accept their natural lives. Humans, on the other hand, have never accepted nature, *i.e.*, they complain about it and try to change it, leading to an unhappy life.

Animals are free from any possession and are also free from sins, worries and complaints. The poet desires to imbibe these selfless and natural qualities of animals.

Reference to Context Questions

Read the extract given below and answer the questions that follow :

75. *I think I could turn and live with animals, they are so placid and self-contain'd,*

I stand and look at them long and long.

They do not sweat and whine about their condition,

They do not lie awake in the dark and weep for their sins,

They do not make me sick discussing their duty to God,

(a) Which qualities of animals attract the poet?

(b) What do humans do according to the poet?

Ans. (a) The poet is attracted to the calmness and poise of the animals, they don't make him sick, they don't lie, and they also don't whine about their condition.

(b) Humans lie awake in the dark weeping for their sins. They also sweat and whine about their condition.

76. *Not one is dissatisfied, not one is demented with the mania of owning things,*

Not one kneels to another, nor to his kind that lived thousands of years ago,

Not one is respectable or unhappy over the whole earth.

(a) How are the animals not dissatisfied?

(b) Who is the poet referring to that lived thousands of years ago?

Ans. (a) Since animals do not have the desire to own anything, therefore they are never dissatisfied.

(b) Here, the poet is referring to the ancestors of human beings who used to live thousands of years ago.

77. *Not one is respectable or unhappy over the whole earth.*

So they show their relations to me and I accept them,

They bring me tokens of myself, they evince them plainly in their possession

(a) The poet of the poem from which the above lines are taken is:

    (i) Carolyn Well   (ii) Robin Klein

    (iii) Walt Whitman   (iv) Robert Frost

(b) Through this poem, the poet proves that:

    (i) he wants to live with the animals.

    (ii) animals are better than man.

    (iii) animals have left their traits in human beings.

    (iv) he loves animals more than human beings.

(c) By 'tokens of myself, the poet means _____ that the animals possess but humans don't.

    (i) tokens of sincerity

    (ii) symbols of love

    (iii) tokens of familiarity

    (iv) tokens of love and affection

(d) The animals neither respect nor _____ another.

    (i) attack   (ii) love

    (iii) demean   (iv) affect

(e) What is the theme of the poem?

    (i) Animals are violent.

    (ii) Animals are loving.

    (iii) Animals attack humans.

    (iv) Animals live with humans.

Ans. (a) (iii) Walt Whitman

    (b) (ii) animals are better than man.

    (c) (iv) tokens of love and affection.

    (d) (iii) demean

    (e) (ii) Animals are loving.

★ are board exam questions from previous years

The Tale of Custard the Dragon

—by Ogden Nash

Chapter 10

Summary :

This poem is written in the style of a ballad—a song or a poem that tells a story. The story here is of Belinda, who lives in a little white house with her pets. The pets are a mouse, kitten, dog and a dragon. All her pets claim to be brave except for the dragon, so they name him Custard. One day, when a pirate comes to loot, the kitten, mouse and the dog hide in fear but Custard the dragon fights and eats the pirate. When there is no danger anymore, the other pets come and claim they too would have done the same thing and that they were very brave. The dragon still says that he is not brave and just wants a safe cage.

Extract Based Questions

I. *Custard the dragon had big sharp teeth,*
And spikes on top of him and scales underneath,
Mouth like a fireplace, chimney for a nose,
And realio, trulio daggers on his toes.

1. "Mouth like a fireplace, chimney for a nose". What does this line suggest?

1. The poet wants to show how funny the dragon looks.
2. The poet wants to show how contrasting the dragon is in his appearance and in nature.
3. The poet wants to show that in spite of being the most powerful in the house, he is mocked and hence it is very ironic.
4. The poet wants to show that dragons are ugly creatures.

   (a) (1) and (4)   (b) (2) and (3)
   (c) (2) only   (d) (3) only

Ans. (b) (2) and (3)

2. Which among the following means the same as dagger?

   (a) Spoon   (b) Hammer
   (c) Sword   (d) Knife

Ans. (d) Knife

3. Why did the timid dragon suddenly become ferocious?

   (a) He wanted to prove himself in front of everyone.
   (b) He wanted to be like the hero of a story.
   (c) He loved Belinda and all the pets, therefore, wanted to protect them.
   (d) Due to the fight or flight response in him.

Ans. (c) He loved Belinda and all the pets, therefore, wanted to protect them.

4. Why does the poet devote one whole stanza to describe the dragon and only one line each to describe Belinda and her pets? Choose an appropriate option.

   (a) Because the poem is based on the dragon.
   (b) To show that the dragon is the most powerful among all.
   (c) To show that the dragon has power but he does not realise it.
   (d) Because the dragon is a big creature and it needs a bigger description.

Ans. (c) To show that the dragon has power but he does not realise it.

5. Why is Custard teased in spite of his ferocious appearance?

   (a) Because they are not afraid of Custard.
   (b) Because Custard is bold and confident.
   (c) Because Custard always cries for a nice and safe cage.
   (d) Because they love teasing Custard.

Ans. (c) Because Custard always cries for a nice and safe cage.

II. Read the given extract to attempt the questions that follow:

Belinda was as brave as a barrel full of bears,
And Ink and Blink chased lions down the stairs,
Mustard was as brave as a tiger in a rage,
But Custard cried for a nice safe cage.

1. Is everyone really as brave as they claim?

   (a) No, they are only boastful.
   (b) No, they are jealous of Custard.
   (c) Yes, they are braver than Custard.
   (d) No, they are actually fools.

Ans. (a) No, they are only boastful.

2. The figure of speech used in the line—'Mustard was as brave as a tiger' is:

   (a) Metaphor   (b) Simile
   (c) Oxymoron   (d) Alliteration

Ans. (b) Simile

3. Identify the figures of speech used in the above extract.

(a) Alliteration, Imagery

(b) Simile, Irony

(c) Alliteration, Simile

(d) Oxymoron, Metaphor

Ans. (c) Alliteration, Simile

4. How does Custard's physical appearance contrasts his nature?

(a) Custard looks ferocious. His nature is innocent and timid.

(b) Custard looks ugly. He pretends to be innocent.

(c) Custard looks violent. He is actually a coward.

(d) Custard looks very ferocious. He is also very courageous.

Ans. (a) Custard looks ferocious. His nature is innocent and timid.

5. The above extract is a ____ .

(a) Hyperbole   (b) Enjambment

(c) Refrain   (d) Satire

Ans. (c) Refrain

III. *Belinda giggled till she shook the house,*
And Blink said Weeck! which is giggling for a mouse,
Ink and Mustard rudely asked his age,
When Custard cried for a nice safe cage.

1. Why did Belinda giggle?

(a) Because Custard ticked her.

(b) Because she was laughing at Custard.

(c) Because she was making fun of her pets.

(d) Because she was playing with her pets.

Ans. (b) Because she was laughing at Custard.

2. "Belinda giggled till she shook the house". Which poetic device do you think has been used in this line?

(a) Onomatopoeia   (b) Alliteration

(c) Hyperbole   (d) Irony

Ans. (c) Hyperbole

3. Ink and Mustard rudely ask whose age?

(a) Blink   (b) Pirate

(c) Custard   (d) Belinda

Ans. (c) Custard

4. Why is it rude of Blink and Mustard to ask his age? It is rude:

1. because they spoke to him with arrogance.

2. because they were making fun of his appearance and character.

3. because they wanted to hurt him.

4. because they were very disrespectful.

(a) (2) and (4)   (b) (1) and (4)

(c) (2), (3), (4)   (d) (2) only

Ans. (a) (2) and (4)

5. Identify a word in the given extract which means the same as the word quake.

(a) Giggled   (b) Cried

(c) Shook   (d) Weeck

Ans. (c) Shook

IV. *Belinda paled, and she cried Help! Help!*
But Mustard fled with a terrified yelp,
Ink trickled down to the bottom of the household,
And little mouse Blink strategically mouseholed.
But up jumped Custard, snorting like an engine,
Clashed his tail like irons in a dungeon,
With a clatter and a clank and a jangling squirm,
He went at the pirate like a robin at a worm

1. From the given extract, find a word which means the same as prison.

(a) Yelp   (b) Trickled

(c) Dungeon   (d) Mousehold

Ans. (c) Dungeon

2. Identify the figure of speech in the lines, 'But up jumped Custard, snorting like an engine, Clashed his tail like irons in a dungeon'.

(a) Alliteration   (b) Personification

(c) Simile   (d) Metaphor

Ans. (c) Simile

3. What is the rhyme scheme of the above extract?

(a) ABCD ABCD   (b) ABBA ABBA

(c) AABB AABB   (d) ABAB ABAB

Ans. (c) AABB AABB

4. What message do you think the poet conveys through this extract?

1. One should never underestimate anyone.

2. Custard is actually a coward.

3. Custard proved his bravery and courage in times of adversity, so he is the bravest of all.

4. Belinda is overconfident and a proud woman.

(a) (2) and (4)   (b) (1) and (3)

(c) (2) and (3)   (d) (2) only

Ans. (b) (1) and (3)

5. The pirate attacked the dragon by firing ____ bullets.

(a) two   (b) four

(c) one   (d) three

Ans. (a) two

V. *But presently up spoke little dog Mustard,*
I'd have been twice as brave if I hadn't been flustered.
And up spoke Ink and up spoke Blink,
We'd have been three times as brave, we think,...

1. **"I'd be twice as brave if I hadn't been flustered".**
Flustered here means ____.

(a) scared   (b) confused

(c) angered   (d) fainted

Ans. (b) confused

2. **What does Custard say in reply?**

(a) Custard agrees to them and says that Belinda is the bravest.

(b) Custard agrees and says that everybody is braver than him.

(c) Custard argues to this and says that Ink and Blink have been three times as brave as him.

(d) Custard agrees and says that all are equally brave.

Ans. (b) Custard agrees and says that everybody is braver than him.

3. **What is the rhyme scheme of this extract?**

(a) abab   (b) aabb

(c) baba   (d) bbaa

Ans. (b) aabb

4. **Where were Mustard, Ink and Blink when the pirate attacked?**

1. They ran away as fast as they could
2. They stood and watched Custard fight
3. They ran here and there
4. They all were shouting for help

(a) (1) and (3)   (b) (3) and (4)

(c) (1) only   (d) (2) only

Ans. (a) (1) and (3)

5. **Who was the first one to run away?**

(a) Belinda   (b) Ink

(c) Mustard   (d) Blink

Ans. (c) Mustard

Multiple Choice Questions

1. **Where does Belinda live?**

(a) In a cottage

(b) In a cabin

(c) In a bungalow

(d) In a little white house

Ans. (d) In a little white house

2. **What does 'realio', trulio' mean in the poem?**

(a) True reality

(b) Really and Truly

(c) Gibberish

(d) Just two rhyming words without meaning

Ans. (b) Really and Truly

3. **Name the poetic device used in the line, "And the little yellow dog was sharp as mustard".**

(a) Metaphor   (b) Personification

(c) Hyperbole   (d) Simile

Ans. (d) Simile

4. **In the poem The Tale of Custard the Dragon, what is the name of the grey mouse?**

(a) Link   (b) Blink

(c) Mustard   (d) Ink

Ans. (b) Blink

5. **What was the name of Belinda's little black kitten?**

(a) Blink   (b) Custard

(c) Ink   (d) Rither

Ans. (c) Ink

6. **Name the poetic device used in the line "And the little yellow dog was sharp as mustard".**

(a) Oxymoron   (b) Metaphor

(c) Assonance   (d) Simile

Ans. (d) Simile

7. **Who was Blink?**

(a) Belinda's little grey rat.

(b) Belinda's little grey mouse.

(c) Belinda's little grey dog.

(d) Belinda's little grey dragon.

Ans. (b) Belinda's little grey mouse.

8. **What name was given to the dragon?**

(a) Blink   (b) Custard

(c) Shrake   (d) Rither

Ans. (b) Custard

9. **Belinda named her yellow dog mustard in the poem 'The Tale of Custard the Dragon' why does she compare him to as sharp as Mustard.**

(a) The dog had sharp teeth

(b) The dog was energetic

(c) The dog was dirty

(d) The dog was lazy

Ans. (b) The dog was energetic

10. **Who was Mustard?**

(a) Belinda's little yellow rat.

(b) Belinda's little yellow mouse.

(c) Belinda's little yellow dog.

(d) Belinda's little grey dragon.

Ans. (c) Belinda's little yellow dog.

11. **In the poem 'The Tale of Custard the Dragon', identify the odd one out.**

(a) black kitten   (b) grey mouse

(c) red wagon   (d) yellow dog

Ans. (c) red wagon

12. Why was the dragon named Custard?
  (a) Because he looked like Custard.
  (b) Because he was weak.
  (c) Because he was a coward.
  (d) Because he was not as brave as the other animals.
Ans. (c) Because he was a coward.

13. The characters in the poem are:
  (a) little black kitten
  (b) little grey mouse
  (c) little yellow dog
  (d) all of these
Ans. (d) all of these

14. The poet used figure of speech in his poem 'The Tale of Custard the Dragon'. Identify the Alliteration.
  (a) Chimney for a nose.
  (b) The dragon was a coward, and she called him Custard.
  (c) Daggers on his toes.
  (d) as brave as a barrel full of bears.
Ans. (b) the dragon was a coward, and she called him Custard.

15. What does the dragon possess?
  (a) Big sharp teeth
  (b) Spikes on top of him
  (c) Sharp toes
  (d) All of these
Ans. (d) All of these

16. How does the poet describe the dragon's mouth and nose?
  (a) His mouth is like a chimney and nose is like a fireplace.
  (b) His mouth is like a house on fire and nose is like an engine of a train.
  (c) His mouth is like a fireplace and nose is like a chimney.
  (d) His mouth is like a dagger and nose is like a fireplace.
Ans. (c) His mouth is like a fireplace and nose is like a chimney.

17. What was on top of the dragon's body?
  (a) Spikes
  (b) Daggers
  (c) Scales
  (d) Scars
Ans. (a) Spikes

18. Name the poetic device used in the line *"mouth like a fireplace"*.
  (a) Oxymoron
  (b) Metaphor
  (c) Assonance
  (d) Simile
Ans. (d) Simile

19. The poet describes the dragon's mouth to a fireplace in the poem 'The Tale of Custard the Dragon', why?
  (a) Dragon's mouth is round.
  (b) Dragons mouth spits fire.
  (c) Dragon's mouth is square in shape.
  (d) Dragon's mouth spits smoke.
Ans. (b) Dragons mouth spits fire.

20. The physical appearance of Custard has the features of a ___________.
  (a) Fireplace
  (b) Chimney
  (c) Dagger
  (d) Dragon
Ans. (d) Dragon

21. What does Custard's fireplace like mouth indicate?
  (a) Power
  (b) Might
  (c) Cowardice
  (d) Built
Ans. (a) Power

22. Which option correctly replaces the following phrase in the given line from 'The Tale of Custard the Dragon'? *'Daggers on his toes'*.
  (a) Knives on his feet
  (b) Pointed and sharp toes
  (c) Toes fixed with daggers
  (d) Blunt knives on toes
Ans. (b) Pointed and sharp toes

23. In the poem The Tale of Custard the Dragon, custard has something similar to the fish and reptiles can you identify it?
  (a) Spikes
  (b) Daggers
  (c) Scales
  (d) Fins
Ans. (c) Scales

24. The poet compares bravery with____.
  (a) Lions
  (b) Wolves
  (c) Tigers
  (d) Bears
Ans. (d) Bears

25. The poet states *'is as brave as a barrel full of bears'* this combined bravery is compared to that of_____.
  (a) the dragon
  (b) the dog
  (c) Belinda
  (d) kitten
Ans. (c) Belinda

26. All the characters in 'The Tale of Custard the Dragon 'pride themselves on.......... Identify the appropriate option.
  (a) cowardice and beauty
  (b) fearlessness and bravery
  (c) fearlessness and beauty
  (d) energetic and brave
Ans. (b) fearlessness and bravery

27. What did the dragon cry for?
  (a) Because he was hurt.
  (b) For a new mouse.
  (c) For a nice safe cage.
  (d) None of the above
Ans. (c) For a nice safe cage.

28. Why did Belinda tickle Custard mercilessly? Choose the correct option:
  1. Because Custard was always scared.
  2. Because she wanted to tease him for his cowardice.
  3. Because she wanted to hurt him

(a) (1) only (b) (2) only

(c) (1) and (2) only (d) (1), (2) and (3)

Ans. (b) (2) only

29. Who did Belinda used to tease?

(a) Kitten (b) Mouse

(c) Dragon (d) Dog

Ans. (c) Dragon

30. Identify the option that aptly describes Belinda's behaviour with Custard before being attacked by the pirate in the poem 'The Tale of Custard the Dragon '.

(a) Partial (b) Unmerciful

(c) Loving (d) Proud

Ans. (b) Unmerciful

31. Identify the word in the poem 'The Tale of Custard the Dragon 'that means the same as unkind________.

(a) rudely (b) cowardly

(c) unmerciful (d) percival

Ans. (c) unmerciful

32. By what name was the dragon rudely called by the other animals?

(a) Coward (b) Percival

(c) Robin (d) Custard

Ans. (b) Percival

33. Choose the correct option that best describes a hyperbole. (A hyperbole is an exaggeration of anything)

(a) Custard cried for a nice safe cage.

(b) Clashed his tail like irons in a dungeon.

(c) Belinda giggled till she shook the house.

(d) Custard gobbled him, every bit.

Ans. (c) Belinda giggled till she shook the house.

34. In the poem The Tale of Custard the Dragon the poet used a homophone, identify it.

(a) Meowch (b) Weeck

(c) Gyrate (d) Gulped

Ans. (b) Weeck

35. What kind of a giggling sound did the mouse make?

(a) Squeak (b) Meowch

(c) Weeck (d) Growl

Ans. (c) Weeck

36. Why do you think that Belinda and the other animals always teased the dragon?

(a) Because he was weak.

(b) Because he wasn't ferocious.

(c) Because he was really a coward.

(d) Because he always cried for a safe cage.

Ans. (d) Because he always cried for a safe cage.

37. Custard's sulkiness caused his friends to __________in The Tale of Custard the Dragon.

(a) praise him (b) applaud him

(c) mock him (d) commend him

Ans. (c) mock him

38. The purpose of Belinda and the animals giggling was to_____

(a) make Custard cry.

(b) cheer Custard up.

(c) lower Custards esteem.

(d) force him to leave.

Ans. (b) cheer Custard up.

39. The animals and Belinda heard a:

(a) jingle voice (b) twinkling sound

(c) pleasant noise (d) threatening sound

Ans. (d) threatening sound

40. Which option correctly replaces the underlined phrase in the given line from 'The Tale of Custard the Dragon '? *Heard a nasty sound.*

(a) Snorting sound (b) Giggling sound

(c) Horrendous sound (d) Jangling squirm

Ans. (c) Horrendous sound

41. From where did the pirate enter?

(a) Back door (b) Chimney

(c) Window (d) Stairs

Ans. (c) Window

42. Winda' here stands for:

(a) wind (b) window

(c) winner (d) winning

Ans. (b) window

43. Who asked the dragon his age?

(a) Mustard and Blink (b) Ink and Blink

(c) Belinda (d) Ink and Mustard

Ans. (d) Ink and Mustard

44. In the poem The Tale of Custard the Dragon, The pirate was equipped with weapons. They were ____.

(a) spikes and pistols

(b) daggers and a cutlass

(c) cutlass and pistols

(d) barrels and pistols

Ans. (c) cutlass and pistols

45. In the poem 'The Tale of Custard the Dragon' identify the handicap of the pirate.

(a) He had a black beard

(b) He had a cutlass

(c) He had pistols

(d) He had a wooden leg

Ans. (d) He had a wooden leg

46. **How did Belinda's pets react at the sight of the pirates?**
    (a) They were scared.
    (b) They ran away to hide themselves.
    (c) They cried for help.
    (d) They ran behind Belinda.
Ans. (b) They ran away to hide themselves

47. ***"Ink trickled down to the bottom of the household"*. What does the phrase trickled down mean?**
    (a) Ran down   (b) Reduced down
    (c) Wither away   (d) Jumped down
Ans. (a) Ran down

48. **Identify the option that aptly describes Mustard's reaction when he saw the pirate in The Tale of Custard the Dragon.**
    (a) Paled   (b) Growled
    (c) Mouse holed   (d) Fled
Ans. (d) Fled

49. **In the poem The Tale of Custard the Dragon, what does trickled down indicate in this scenario?**
    (a) Spilling over   (b) Entering in
    (c) Retreating   (d) Advancing
Ans. (c) Retreating

50. **Coward Custard rushed to the rescue of Belinda and the other pets making explosive sounds referred to as_____.**
    (a) jangling   (b) snorting
    (c) clattering   (d) clanking
Ans. (b) snorting

51. **Which figure of speech is used in the phrase "clatter and clank"?**
    (a) Alliteration   (b) Onomatopoeia
    (c) Personification   (d) Both (a) and (b)
Ans. (d) Both (a) and (b)

52. **Identify the poetic device used here Clashed his tail like irons in a dungeon?**
    (a) Metaphor   (b) Hyperbole
    (c) Simile   (d) Personification
Ans. (c) Simile

53. **Coward Custard cried for a safe cage then why is this he clashed his tail like irons in a dungeon. It was a reaction as if he was:**
    (a) set free from an underground prison.
    (b) he was afraid of the dungeon.
    (c) set in an underground prison and wanted freedom.
    (d) he was comfortable in the underground cell.
Ans. (c) set in an underground prison and wanted freedom

54. **In the poem The Tale of Custard the Dragon, what feature of Custard made the pirate gape at Belinda.**
    (a) Physical appearance
    (b) His paling appearance
    (c) His frightful appearance
    (d) His provoking appearance
Ans. (b) His paling appearance

55. **How did Custard attack the pirate?**
    (a) Like an engine snorting
    (b) Ferociously
    (c) Like a robin falling on a worm
    (d) Like an eagle attacking a worm
Ans. (c) Like a robin falling on a worm

56. **What was the reaction of the pirate on seeing Belinda's dragon?**
    (a) He was scared.
    (b) He stared at him with his mouth wide open.
    (c) He pounced at him.
    (d) He stood there blankly.
Ans. (b) He stared at him with his mouth wide open

57. **Indicate why the pirate do this "gulped some grog from his pocket flagon." in The Tale of Custard the Dragon.**
    (a) To overcome his fear
    (b) For happiness
    (c) For enjoyment
    (d) He was habitual
Ans. (a) To overcome his fear

58. **The word pocket flagon in The Tale of Custard the Dragon refers to.**
    (a) a barrel   (b) an earthen vessel
    (c) a pint   (d) a wineskin
Ans. (c) a pint

59. **What did Custard do to the pirate?**
    (a) Gobbled him   (b) Burnt him
    (c) Threw him away   (d) Tore him apart
Ans. (a) Gobbled him

60. **What happened to the pirate?**
    (a) He got hurt by dragon.
    (b) He got a new ship.
    (c) He got a new workers.
    (d) He was killed by the dragon.
Ans. (d) He was killed by the dragon.

61. **What is the meaning of the word 'gobbled'?**
    (a) Chewed   (b) Swallowed
    (c) Nibbled   (d) Ate in a hurry
Ans. (d) Ate in a hurry

62. **What is the poet trying to indicate in the underlined word "And gulped some grog from his pocket flagon." in The Tale of Custard the Dragon.**

(a) Sipped   (b) Swallowed

(c) Puked   (d) Spewed

Ans. (b) Swallowed

63. **In the poem The Tale of Custard the Dragon the pirate gaped at Custard In__________.**

(a) surprise   (b) disgust

(c) composure   (d) happiness

Ans. (a) surprise

64. **Identify the option that aptly describes how Custard sheds his cowardice in the poem The Tale of Custard the Dragon.**

(a) He asks for a cage.

(b) He gobbled the pirate.

(c) He paled and cried.

(d) He fled away leaving every one.

Ans. (b) He gobbled the pirate.

65. **After Custard killed the dragon, what was the reaction of everyone?**

(a) Belinda embraced him and Mustard licked him.

(b) Belinda embraced him and all the other animals surrounded him in glee.

(c) Belinda embraced him and all the other animals were jealous of him.

(d) Ink and Blink were not happy.

Ans. (a) Belinda embraced him and Mustard licked him.

66. **What was the immediate reaction of Belinda when Custard gobbled the pirate in The Tale of Custard the Dragon.**

(a) Belinda danced around Custard.

(b) Belinda mourned for the pirate.

(c) Belinda embraced Custard.

(d) Belinda licked Custard all over.

Ans. (c) Belinda embraced Custard.

67. **In the poem The Tale of Custard the Dragon, the response of Custard's friends when Custard braved the pirate was ___________.**

(a) disgusted   (b) truly commendable

(c) jeering   (d) mocking

Ans. (b) truly commendable

68. **Who faced the pirate bravely?**

(a) Blink   (b) Custard

(c) Ink   (d) Rither

Ans. (b) Custard

69. **Which quality did Custard display when he said, 'I quite agree That everybody is braver than me'. This meant that Custard was___________.**

(a) proud   (b) humble

(c) arrogant   (d) overbearing

Ans. (b) humble

70. **Identify the refrain in the poem.**

1. Realio, Trulio, little pet dragon.

2. Realio, Trulio, cowardly dragon.

3. Custard cried for a nice safe cage.

4. And a little yellow dog and the little red wagon.

(a) (1), (2), (3)   (b) (1), (2), (3), (4)

(c) (1) and (3)   (d) (1), (3), (4)

Ans. (c) (1) and (3)

71. **What kind of a poem is The Tale of Custard the Dragon?**

(a) Sonnet   (b) Dramatic Monologue

(c) Free Verse   (d) Ballad

Ans. (d) Ballad

72. **Who is the poet of the poem "The tale of Custard the Dragon"?**

(a) Carl Sandburg   (b) Ogden Nash

(c) Carolyn Wells   (d) Walt Whitman

Ans. (b) Ogden Nash

73. **The Tale of Custard the Dragon is written in a ___________ form.**

(a) Limerick   (b) Verse

(c) Ballad   (d) Ode

Ans. (c) Ballad

74. **Identify the correct option that describes the sequence of the poem The Tale of Custard the Dragon?**

(a) Summary   (b) Theme

(c) Message   (d) Introduction

Ans. (d) introduction

75. **In the poem The Tale of Custard the Dragon the poet tries to convey the message that ________.**

(a) every human has his/own capabilities and way of living.

(b) every human is brave but always wants help.

(c) every human gives up when he does not succeed.

(d) every human does what he does not want to do.

Ans. (a) every human has his/own capabilities and way of living.

76. **What moral does the poet convey via the poem The Tale of Custard the Dragon. Choose the appropriate option.**

(a) never underestimate a person by his words or what others say.

(b) never underestimate a person by his looks or what others say.

(c) never underestimate a person by his status or what others say.

(d) never underestimate a person by his looks and what others say

Ans. (b) never underestimate a person by his looks or what others say.

77. What is the main theme of the poem The Tale of Custard the Dragon?

(a) Hypocrisy vs. courage.

(b) Love vs. jealousy.

(c) Appearance vs. reality.

(d) Reality vs. courage.

Ans. (c) Appearance vs. reality.

Text Book Questions

Thinking about the Poem

78. Who are the characters in this poem? List them with their pet names.

Ans. The characters in the poem are as follows: Belinda; Ink, the black kitten, Blink, the grey mouse; Mustard, the yellow dog; Custard, the cowardly dragon and a firate.

79. Read stanza three again to know how the poet describes the appearance of the dragon.

Ans. Custard, the dragon, had big sharp teeth, spikes on top of him and scales underneath. His mouth was like a fireplace, he had a chimney for a nose and daggers on his toes.

80. Why did Custard cry for a nice safe cage? Why is the dragon called "cowardly dragon"?

Ans. Custard, despite having a large scary appearance, believed that he was not brave and so all he wanted was a cage to be safe in. That is why he was called a cowardly dragon.

81. "Belinda tickled him, she tickled him unmerciful..." Why?

Ans. Belinda tickled the dragon to have fun and to tease him for his cowardliness.

82. The poet has employed many poetic devices in the poem. For example: "Clashed his tail like iron in a dungeon" — the poetic device here is a simile. Can you, with your partner, list some more such poetic devices used in the poem?

Ans. He went at the pirate like a robin at a worm--simile

as brave as a barrel full of bears,--simile

as brave as a tiger in a rage,--simile

snorting like an engine—simile

Mouth like a fireplace--simile

83. Can you find out the rhyme scheme of two or three stanzas of the poem?

Ans. The rhyme scheme is a,a,b,b

84. Writers use words to give us a picture or image without actually saying what they mean. Can you trace some images used in the poem?

Ans. Mouth like a fireplace, daggers on his toes, chimney for a nose etc.

85. Do you find 'The Tale of Custard the Dragon' to be a serious or a light-hearted poem? Give reasons to support your answer.

Ans. The tale of Custard the dragon is a light hearted ballad. How a dragon, being a coward, is made fun of by a kitten, a mouse and a dog, it is all told in a humorous way.

Short Answer Type Questions

20-30 Words

86. Describe the pirate who comes through the window?

Ans. The pirate had a wooden leg and his beard was black. He had a pistol in both his left and right hand and he held a cutlass in his teeth.

87. What do all of them do when the pirate comes?

Ans. When they see the pirate, Belinda cries for help, Ink, the cat, hides under the house, the mouse runs to his hole, the dog yelps and runs but the dragon attacks the pirate.

88. How do they celebrate Custard getting rid of the pirate?

Ans. Belinda embraces him, Mustard, the dog licks him. Ink, the cat and Blink, the mouse dance around him in circles in celebration of Custard eating up the pirate.

Reference to Context Questions

Read the extract given below and answer the questions that follow :

89. *Custard the dragon had big sharp teeth,*
And spikes on top of him and scales underneath,
Mouth like a fireplace, chimney for a nose,
And realio, trulio daggers on his toes.
Belinda was as brave as a barrel full of bears,
And Ink and Blink chased lions down the stairs,
Mustard was as brave as a tiger in a rage,
But Custard cried for a nice safe cage.

(a) What did the dragon look like?

(b) Why is the dragon's mouth called a fireplace?

Ans. (a) The dragon had spikes on top and scales underneath. His mouth was like a fireplace and nose was like a chimney. He looked dangerous as his toes looked like daggers.

(b) Dragon's nose is called a chimney because he can spit fire, therefore Custard's mouth has been called a fireplace.

90. *"Belinda tickled him, she tickled him unmerciful,*
Ink, Blink and Mustard, they rudely called him Percival,
They all sat laughing in the little red wagon
At the realio, trulio, cowardly dragon."

(a) What does realio and trulio mean?

(b) What did the other three pet call the dragon?

Ans. (a) Realio and trulio actually mean 'really' and 'truly'. The words have been changed by the poet so as to give rhythm to the poem.

(b) The other three pets namely Ink, Blink, and Mustard, they rudely called Custard, the dragon as Percival.

91. *Suddenly, suddenly they heard a nasty sound,*
And Mustard growled, and they all looked around.
Meowch! cried Ink, and ooh! cried Belinda,
For there was a pirate, climbing in the winda.
Pistol in his left hand, pistol in his right,
And he held in his teeth a cutlass bright,
His beard was black, one leg was wood;
It was clear that the pirate meant no good.

(a) Describe the physical appearance of the pirate.

(b) How many weapons was the pirate carrying?

Ans. (a) The pirate's beard was black and he had one wooded leg. He also looked very frightening.

(b) The pirate was carrying two pistols in both his hands and a bright cutlass in his teeth.

92. *But presently up spoke little dog Mustard,*
I'd have been twice as brave if I hadn't been flustered.

And up spoke Ink and up spoke Blink,
We'd have been three times as brave, we think,

(a) The above lines are taken from the poem:
   (i) Animals
   (ii) The Tale of Custard the Dragon
   (iii) A Tiger in the Zoo
   (iv) Dust of Snow

(b) Little dog Mustard spoke to
   (i) show his bravery
   (ii) impress Belinda
   (iii) make fun of Custard
   (iv) explain why he had not fought the pirate

(c) Ink and Blink ______
   because the pirate was killed.
   (i) gyrated in happiness
   (ii) acted stupid
   (iii) acted angrily
   (iv) acted superior

(d) The irony of the poem is that Custard killed the pirate but ____.
   (i) he was caught by the police
   (ii) he was injured
   (iii) he was annoyed with Belinda
   (iv) he agreed everyone else was brave

(e) Which of the following words means the opposite of 'confident'?
   (i) Presently
   (ii) Brave
   (iii) Flustered
   (iv) Spoke

Ans. (a) (ii) The Tale of Custard the Dragon
   (b) (iv) explain why he had not fought the pirate
   (c) (i) gyrated in happiness
   (d) (iv) he agreed everyone else was brave
   (e) (iii) Flustered

❑❑

LITERATURE
FOOTPRINTS WITHOUT FEET

The Making of a Scientist

—by Robert W. Peterson

Chapter 6

Summary :

'The Making of a Scientist' is a fascinating story of Richard Ebright, an only child who is curious and has a love for collecting things. With encouragement from his mother, he collects all the species of butterflies in the vicinity, learns to tag them and track their journey with the help of Dr. Urquhart. All through his high school, he participates in Science Fairs with increasing level of confidence and research and wins laurels. Along with his roommate, Richard then starts investigating the relevance of the gold spots on a pupa. They isolate the hormone present in these spots and win permission to work in prestigious laboratories. Then they use this information to try and decipher the form and function of a cell. His high school research on the purpose of the spots on a monarch pupa eventually leads him to his theory about cell life. Richard has the right attitude to be a great scientist. He not only spends time on his research but also becomes a great debater, public speaker and a canoeist.

Extract Based Questions

I. Read the given extract to attempt the questions that follow:

It was the first time this important scientific journal had ever published the work of college students. In sports, that would be like making the big leagues at the age of fifteen and hitting a home run your first time at bat. For Richard Ebright, it was the first in a long string of achievements in science and other fields. And it all started with butterflies.

1. "It was the first time this important scientific journal had ever published the work of college students.' This statement implies that ________

(a) The scientific journal had published such work earlier.

(b) The work of college students was so important that it was given space in this scientific journal.

(c) It was a very common thing for the scientific journal.

(d) A large number of college students were engaged in research.

Ans. (b) The work of college students was so important that it was given space in this scientific journal.

2. 'Making the big leagues and hitting a home run at first time' has been compared to Richard Ebright's ________

(a) batting skills in a baseball game.

(b) making great achievements in life.

(c) research paper getting published at a young age.

(d) achievements in the college.

Ans. (c) research paper getting published at a young age.

3. Select the option listing Ebright's characteristics, as revealed in the extract:

1. naïve   2. brilliant

3. prodigy   4. a great scientist

5. kind

(a) (2) and (3)   (b) Only (5)

(c) (2), (3) and (4)   (d) Only (2)

Ans. (c) (2), (3) and (4)

4. Select the most appropriate option based on (1) and (2).

(1) Ebright's had started the research work at a young age.

(2) His research started with the butterflies.

(a) (2) is true and (1) is false.

(b) (1) is the cause for (2).

(c) (2) is the result for (1).

(d) (2) is false and (1) is true.

Ans. (b) (1) is the cause for (2).

5. The phrase hitting the home run suggests that Ebright ....

(a) hit the ball for the first time.

(b) made run in first ball

(c) got success at the first attempt.

(d) hit the target to get the run.

Ans. (c) got success at the first attempt.

II. *Then in the seventh grade he got a hint of what real science is when he entered a county science fair —*

and lost. "It was really a sad feeling to sit there and not get anything while everybody else had won something," Ebright said. His entry was slides of frog tissues, which he showed under a microscope. He realised the winners had tried to do real experiments, not simply make a neat display.

1. **' ...... he entered a county science fair – and lost' here being lost means _____**

(a) lost in the fair

(b) lost his mind

(c) lost the concept of science

(d) understood the real meaning of science.

Ans. (d) understood the real meaning of science.

2. **What do we get to know about Ebright when he says the following?**

It was really a sad feeling to sit there and not get anything while everybody else had won something."

Choose one from the following to answer:

(a) He is proud of his experiment.

(b) He is struggling to do an experiment..

(c) He is unsure of other's work.

(d) He was dissatisfied with his presentation.

Ans. (d) He was dissatisfied with his presentation.

3. **Select the most appropriate option for (1) and (2).**

(1) Participating in the county science fair had open the world of science for Ebright .

(2) Doing real experiments was required to win the prize.

(a) (1) is true and (2) is false.

(b) (2) is the opposite of (1).

(c) (2) furthers the meaning of (1).

(d) Both (1) and (2) are not inferred in the extract.

Ans. (c) (2) furthers the meaning of (1).

4. **Select the suitable word from the extract to complete the following:**

triumph: victory: : clue : _______

(a) real   (b) hint

(c) lost   (d) neat

Ans. (b) hint

5. **Choose the option listing Ebright's qualities as depicted by the above extract.**

1. quick learner   2. naive

3. competitive   4. liberal

5. conceited

(a) 1, 3   (b) 3, 5

(c) 1, 2   (d) 4, 5

Ans. (a) 1, 3

III. *When he saw those photos, Ebright didn't shout, 'Eureka!' or even, 'I've got it!' But he believed that, along with his findings about insect hormones,*

the photos gave him the answer to one of biology's puzzles: how the cell can 'read' the blueprint of its DNA. DNA is the substance in the nucleus of a cell that controls heredity. It determines the form and function of the cell. Thus, DNA is the blueprint for life. Ebright and his college room-mate, James R. Wong, worked all that night drawing pictures and constructing plastic models of molecules to show how it could happen. Together they later wrote the 97 paper that explained the theory.

1. **Ebright was expected to shout 'Eureka!' because he had:**

(a) realised that he needed a partner to work with to finalise his findings.

(b) discovered something new and 'Eureka!' was a cry to announce it.

(c) worked hard and was relieved at nearing the end of his project.

(d) given shape to the teachings of his teachers by choosing this field of science.

Ans. (b) discovered something new and 'Eureka!' was a cry to announce it.

2. **"DNA is the blueprint for life", means that the DNA contains a genetic __________.**

(a) experiment   (b) ultimatum

(c) takeaway   (d) plan or outline

Ans. (d) plan or outline

3. **Select the most appropriate option based on (1) and (2).**

(1) Ebright was working on the function of insect hormones.

(2) He got the idea for his new theory about cell life.

(a) (2) is true and (1) is false.

(b) (2) is the result for (1).

(c) (2) is the cause for (1).

(d) (2) is false and (1) is true.

Ans. (b) (2) is the result for (1).

4. **Choose the suitable news headline that could describe the research work of Ebright and Wong in the most appropriate way:**

1. Wong Denies Contributing To Ebright's Theory.

2. Ebright Collaborates With Room-Mate Wong.

3. Wong And Ebright Exaggerate Their Theory- Defy Logic.

4. Ebright And Wong's Theory Proved Wrong.

(a) Headline 1   (b) Headline 2

(c) headline 3   (d) Headline 4

Ans. (b) Headline 2

5. Choose the option that lists the compound words from the above extract.

   1. puzzles   2. blueprint
   3. hormone   4. heredity
   5. room-mate

   (a) 1, 3   (b) 2, 4
   (c) 1, 4   (d) 2, 5

Ans. (d) 2, 5

IV. *"Richard would always give that extra effort," Mr Weiherer said. "What pleased me was, here was this person who put in three or four hours at night doing debate research besides doing all his research with butterflies and his other interests.*

"Richard was competitive," Mr Weiherer continued, "but not in a bad sense." He explained, "Richard wasn't interested in winning for winning's sake or winning to get a prize. Rather, he was winning because he wanted to do the best job he could. For the right reasons, he wants to be the best."

1. ' ….. *give that extra efforts*' refers to Ebright's quality of being________

   (a) disciplined   (b) perseverant
   (c) casual   (d) systematic

Ans. (b) perseverant

2. When Mr. Weilhere called Ebright 'competitive' but not in bad sense', he meant that Ebright ________

   (a) wanted to compete fairly.
   (b) always wanted to win.
   (c) felt bad at not winning.
   (d) discouraged to participate.

Ans. (a) wanted to compete fairly.

3. Select the most appropriate option for (1) and (2).

   (1) Ebright worked equally hard to prepare a debate as he did for his research.
   (2) He did his research to prove himself the best.

   (a) (1) is true and (2) is false.
   (b) (2) is the opposite of (1).
   (c) (1) furthers the meaning of (2).
   (d) Both (1) and (2) cannot be inferred from the extract.

Ans. (a) (1) is true and (2) is false.

4. Select the option which displays an example of '*winning for winning's sake*'.

   (a) Radhika scored the highest marks by using unfair means in the exams.
   (b) Manu worked hard to get the highest marks.
   (c) Ravi studied as usual during examination.
   (d) Lata was less worried about her performance in the exams.

Ans. (a) Radhika scored the highest marks by using unfair means in the exams.

5. From the options given below, identify Mr. Weiherer's tone in the extract:

   1. proud   2. admiring
   3. hurt   4. pleased
   5. unsure

   (a) 2 and 3   (b) 3 and 5
   (c) 1, 2, and 4   (d) 1 and 4

Ans. (c) 1, 2, and 4

Multiple Choice Questions

1. Who is the writer of the story "The Making of a Scientist"?

   (a) HG Wells   (b) Robert W. Peterson
   (c) Ruskin Bond   (d) Guy De Maupassant

Ans. (b) Robert W. Peterson

2. What was Ebright fond of in his childhood?

   (a) basketball   (b) collecting things
   (c) baseball   (d) none of these

Ans. (b) collecting things

3. How did his mother help him?

   (a) Took him on trips
   (b) Bought him telescopes and microscopes
   (c) Encouraged him to learn
   (d) All of the above

Ans. (d) All of the above

4. "It was his fascination for _____ that opened the world of science to him."

   (a) cats   (b) dogs
   (c) birds   (d) butterflies

Ans. (d) butterflies

5. How many species of butterflies had he collected till second grade?

   (a) 20   (b) 21
   (c) 24   (d) 25

Ans. (d) 25

6. What did he collect during his childhood?

   (a) Coins   (b) Rocks
   (c) Butterflies   (d) All of these

Ans. (d) All of these

7. Where did Ebright come from?

   (a) Reading   (b) Oxford
   (c) London   (d) None of these

Ans. (a) Reading

8. At what age did Ebright invent the theory on how cells work?

(a) twenty   (b) twenty one

(c) twenty two   (d) twenty four

Ans. (c) twenty two

9. When did he get a hint of real science?

(a) In the 7th grade

(b) When he entered a county science fair

(c) When he lost

(d) All of the above

Ans. (d) All of the above

10. When did he find the cause of a viral disease common among caterpillars?

(a) In the 7th grade   (b) In the 8th grade

(c) In college   (d) None of these

Ans. (b) In the 8th grade

11. "__________is the blueprint for life".

(a) Cells   (b) DNA

(c) Both of these   (d) None of these

Ans. (b) DNA

12. He tried to grow____in the presence of betties.

(a) butterflies   (b) catterpillar

(c) rats   (d) snakes

Ans. (b) catterpillar

13. Which butterlies were not eaten by birds?

(a) Viceroy   (b) Monarch

(c) General   (d) None of these

Ans. (b) Monarch

14. What did he realise was necessary for winning a prize at the fair?

(a) Display   (b) Experiment

(c) All of these   (d) Creativity

Ans. (b) Experiment

15. Where did Ebright graduate from?

(a) Oxford   (b) Yale

(c) Harvard   (d) none of the above

Ans. (c) Harvard

16. Who did he write to get an idea for a real science experiment?

(a) His mother

(b) His friend

(c) Dr Frederick A. Urquhart

(d) None of the above

Ans. (c) Dr Frederick A. Urquhart

17. Which book did his mother give him?

(a) Travels of Monarch X

(b) Travels of Viceroy X

(c) Travels of Viceroy Y

(d) Travels of Monarch X

Ans. (a) Travels of Monarch X

18. Ebright was an excellent _____.

(a) debater   (b) scientist

(c) photographer   (d) all of these

Ans. (b) scientist

19. What ground breaking research did Ebright do?

(a) Working of body   (b) Working of DNA

(c) Working of heart   (d) None of these

Ans. (b) Working of DNA

20. The publishing of Ebright's article in the Proceedings of the National Academy of Science was so special because:

(a) it was a new theory on the working of cells

(b) for the first time , it had published the work of college students.

(c) Ebright worked hard to get it published.

(d) Ebright and his friend had worked hard for this research.

Ans. (b) for the first time , it had published the work of college students.

21. Select the qualities which were possessed by the child Ebright:

1. inquisitive
2. clever
3. bright mind
4. naïve
5. interest in learning

(a) Option 1 and 2   (b) Option 3 and 4

(c) Option 3, 4 and 5   (d) Option 1, 3 and 5

Ans. (d) Option 1, 3 and 5

22. "That probably would have been the end of my butterfly collecting," what could have possibly ended his butterfly collecting?

(a) his disinterest in collecting butterflies

(b) No butterfly was found in his area

(c) His mother did not like it.

(d) He had collected all species of butterflies of his area.

Ans. (d) He had collected all species of butterflies of his area.

23. Ebright decided to raise butterflies instead of catching them because:

(a) monarch butterflies were not found there.

(b) he wanted to study the life cycle of the butterflies

(c) monarch butterflies were found only for a limited time.

(d) he enjoyed raising the butterflies than catching them

Ans. (c) monarch butterflies were found only for a limited time

24. Choose the correct reason for Ebright to choose insect work for his research.

(a) he had been working on it for many years

(b) he was forced to do work in this field.

(c) he wanted win the prize in the county fair

(d) Dr. Urquhart suggested him to choose this field.

Ans. (a) he had been working on it for many years

25. What was the theory about viceroy butterflies?

(a) Viceroy butterflies resembles Monarch butterflies.

(b) Viceroy butterflies copy monarchs to escape being eaten by birds.

(c) Birds do feed on Viceroys.

(d) Monarchs are liked by the birds.

Ans. (b) Viceroy butterflies copy monarchs to escape being eaten by birds.

26. 'It also led to his new theory on the life of cells.' What could have led him to his new theory on the life of cells?

(a) his discovery of unknown insect hormone.

(b) the cause of viral disease among monarch caterpillars

(c) his study on viceroy butterflies

(d) his showing slides of frog tissues under microscope

Ans. (a) his discovery of unknown insect hormone.

27. What was the real purpose of the twelve tiny gold spot on a monarch pupa?

(a) they were only ornamental

(b) they were very essential for the butterfly's wings.

(c) they produced hormones needed for the growth of the butterfly.

(d) they formed the wing of the butterfly.

Ans. (c) they produced hormones needed for the growth of the butterfly

28. 'he got a hint of what real science is' means Ebright got an idea that real science is ____.

(a) doing real experiment

(b) displaying of models

(c) showing slides under the microscope

(d) displaying any experiment

Ans. (a) doing real experiment

29. Ebright was perhaps expected to shout 'Eureka!' because he had:

(a) realised that he needed a partner to work with to finalise his findings.

(b) discovered something new and 'Eureka!' was a cry to announce it.

(c) worked hard and was relieved at nearing the end of his project.

(d) given shape to the teachings of his teachers by choosing this field of science

Ans. (b) discovered something new and 'Eureka!' was a cry to announce it.

30. DNA is called the blueprint of life because it.

1. helps in the respiration of living beings.

2. controls heredity

3. determines the form and function of the cell.

4. Helps in the life cycle of butterflies.

5. is a substance in the nucleus of a cell.

(a) Option 1 only

(b) Option 2 and 5 only

(c) Option 2 and 3 only

(d) Option 2, 3 and 5

Ans. (c) Option 2 and 3 only

31. When Mr. Weiherer said, "Richard would always give that extra effort," he highlighted that Richard was a/an________ boy.

(a) brilliant   (b) inquisitive

(c) diligent   (d) careful

Ans. (c) diligent

32. Select the most appropriate option for (1) and (2)

(1) Richard Ebright has been interested in science since his childhood.

(2) He hasn't time for other interests and activities.

(a) (1) is true and (2) is false.

(b) (2) is true and (1) is false.

(c) (2) is the result of (1).

(d) Both (1) and (2) cannot be understood from the story.

Ans. (a) (1) is true and (2) is false.

33. Choose the correct word to describe Ebright's mother.

(a) dutiful   (b) concerned

(c) strange   (d) manipulative

Ans. (b) concerned

34. "There wasn't much I could do there," state the reason for it.

(a) Ebright did not want to do any work.

(b) The house was too small to get any work there.

(c) Ebright did not have much company in Reading.

(d) His mother did not allow him to do any work.

Ans. (c) Ebright did not have much company in Reading

35. What made Ebright win first prize in county fair and an entry into International Science and Engineering fair?

(a) tagging of Monarch butterfly

(b) cause of viral disease among the Monarch caterpillars

(c) Viceroys do copy monarchs

    (d) hormones produced by the golden spots helped in the growth of butterfly.

Ans. (d) hormones produced by the golden spots helped in the growth of butterfly.

36. Select the qualities that go into making of a scientist like Richard Ebright:

1. first-rate mind
2. curiosity
3. stubborn
4. will to win for the right reason
5. clever

    (a) 1, 2, and 4   (b) 2, 3 and 4

    (c) 1,2 and 3   (d) 3, 4, and 5

Ans. (a) 1, 2, and 4

37. How can one become a scientist, an economist, and historian…..?

    (a) by reading many books

    (b) by being observant and curious

    (c) only by doing experiments

    (d) only by learning the facts

Ans. (b) by being observant and curious

38. Who did Ebright write to get an idea for a real science experiment?

    (a) his mother

    (b) James R. Wong

    (c) Dr Frederick A. Urquhart

    (d) Mr. Weiherer

Ans. (c) Dr. Frederick A. Urquhart

39. Richard Ebright is a leading scientist who has contributed significantly to the ___________ branch/branches of science.

    (a) Biochemistry   (b) Molecular Biology

    (c) Zoology   (d) Both (a) and (b)

Ans. (d) Both (a) and (b)

40. Select the most appropriate option for (1) and (2)

1. Starling feeds on viceroys.
2. Starling does not eat seeds and insects.

    (a) Both (1) and (2) are clearly mentioned in the text.

    (b) (1) cannot be clearly inferred from the text but (2) is true.

    (c) (1) is false and (2) cannot be clearly inferred from the extract.

    (d) Both (1) and (2) are false.

Ans. (c) (1) is false and (2) cannot be clearly inferred from the extract.

41. When he invented the theory on how cells work, his age was _______.

    (a) Twenty   (b) twenty one

    (c) twenty two   (d) twenty four

Ans. (c) twenty two

42. The book The Travels of Monarch X is about:

    (a) migration of Monarch butterflies to Central America

    (b) Life cycle of Monarch butterflies

    (c) the characteristics of Monarch

    (d) Species X of monarch butterflies

Ans. (a) migration of Monarch butterflies to Central America

43. The foundation of Ebright's scientific temperament lay in his hobby of_________.

    (a) studying science

    (b) collecting things

    (c) reading books

    (d) writing in science journals

Ans. (b) collecting things

44. Ebright's eighth grade project was to _______.

    (a) find the cause of the death of monarch caterpillars

    (b) show the slide of frog tissues under the microscope

    (c) find the purpose of gold spot on a monarch pupa

    (d) show the chemical structure of DNA

Ans. (a) find the cause of the death of monarch caterpillars

Text Book Questions

Read and Find Out :

45. How did a book become a turning point in Richard Ebright's life?

Ans. When in the second grade, Richard had collected all the species of butterflies found around his hometown due to which there was a possibility of him losing interest in science. However, that is when his mother brought him the book 'Travels of Monarch X' which opened up a whole new world of science for him and was a turning point is his life.

46. How did his mother help him?

Ans. His mother encouraged him for his interest in learning. She took him on trips, bought him telescopes, microscopes, cameras, mounting materials and other equipments, and helped him in many other ways. If he didn't have things to do, his mother found work for him — not physical work but learning things.

47. What lesson does Ebright learn when he does not win anything at a science fair?

Ans. When Ebright does not win anything at the Science Fair, he realises the winners had tried to do real experiments, not simply make a neat display. Then he knows that for the next year's fair he would have to do a real experiment.

48. What experiments and projects does he then undertake?

Ans. For his eighth grade project, Ebright tries to find the cause of a viral disease that kills nearly all monarch caterpillars every few years. Then for his science fair project, he tests the theory viceroy butterflies copy monarchs. In his high school, he tries to find the purpose of the twelve tiny gold spots on a monarch pupa. Later, he researches further on the Monarch butterflies.

49. What are the qualities that go into the making of a scientist?

Ans. The three most important qualities of a scientist are a first-rate mind, curiosity, and the will to win for the right reasons. A scientist has to be competitive but not with others ---with himself.

Think About It :

50. How can one become a scientist, an economist, a historian... ? Does it simply involve reading many books on the subject? Does it involve observing, thinking and doing experiments?

Ans. To be good in any field, be it science, economics, history etc., one has to have some basic qualities. Along with reading a lot, one has to observe, think and experiment. One has to have a first rate mind, curiosity to learn more and also the will to win.

Short Answer Type Questions

20-30 Words

51. What other interests, besides Science, did Richard Ebright pursue? What did Mr. Kleiherer, his Social Studies teacher, tell us about Ebright?★

Ans. Richard Ebright was interested in science since childhood but he also had many other interests. He was a passionate public speaker and was an important part of Debating Society and Model United Nations Club. He was an enthusiastic photographer, especially interested in nature and scientific exhibits. He was also a canoeist and enjoyed the outdoors.

Mr. Kleiherer said that Ebright would always put extra effort. Not only did he put in three or four hours at night engaging himself in debate research but would also do all his research with butterflies and deal with his other areas of interest. Mr. Kleiherer was of the opinion that

Ebright was competitive in a true sense. He didn't want to win just for the sake of winning but to accomplish his ambition and contribute the best that he could in this field. In fact, Mr. Kleiherer always said, "For the right reasons, he wants to be the best."

52. Why did Ebright raise a bunch of butterflies?

Ans. Ebright wanted to catch butterflies to tag them in order to follow their migration. He realised that it was easier to raise them in his basement rather than try and catch them one by one. So he would catch a female Monarch, take her eggs and help them grow into butterflies which he would tag.

53. Why did Richard begin to lose interest in tagging butterflies?

Ans. Tagging butterflies was a tedious process with not much feedback. In all the time that he tagged butterflies only two were reported caught and that too from near his home.

54. Apart from science research what else was Richard interested in?

Ans. Apart from being a scientist, Richard was also a champion debater, public speaker, a good canoeist and an all-around outdoor-person. He was also an expert photographer, particularly of nature and scientific exhibits.

55. Which book did Ebright's mother get for him? How did it change his life?

Ans. Ebright's mother got him a children's book titled 'The Travels of Monarch X'. The book described how Monarch butterflies migrate to Central America. This opened the world of science to the young and enthused collector, Ebright.

56. How did Richard Ebright's mother help him?

Ans. Richard Ebright was curious as well as bright. His mother played a pivotal role in encouraging his interest to learn. She took him on trips. She also brought him telescopes, microscopes, cameras, mounting materials as well as other equipment. She pushed him to learn more and explore the environment around him.

57. What lesson did Ebright learn when he did not win anything at a science fair ?

Ans. In the seventh grade, Ebright entered a county science fair. For the fair, he entered with slides of frog tissues, which he showed under the microscope. He had simply made a neat display. At the end of the fair, he realized that unlike his display the winners had tried to do real experiments. This was where he failed.

★ **are board exam questions from previous years**

Long Answer Type Questions

100-120 words

58. Give a brief character sketch of Ebright's mother.★

Ans. Richard H. Ebright's mother was an important driving force behind him who laid the foundation of his success . Ebright was her only child whom she affectionately called 'Richie'. After her husband's death, her son who was in third grade, was her whole life. She would encourage his interest in learning and would take him to trips, buy him telescopes, microscopes, cameras, mounting materials, and other equipments. She was his only companion until he started school. After that, she would bring home his friends for him and at night be with him to do things together. She would spend almost every evening at the dining room table with her son 'Richie', When he did not have things to do, she would find work for him that would help him learn things. This support, guidance, care and concern of Ebright's mother, helped the growth of a curious child into an accomplished scientist.

59. Without the encouragement of his mother, Ebright would not have been the scientist he became. Discuss.

Ans. The support of parents has been one of the greatest strength in the lives of people who have achieved greatness in their fields of work. In the case of Ebright too, his mother contributed hugely to him becoming a great scientist. Ebright's mother encouraged his interest in learning. She took him on trips, bought him telescopes, microscopes, cameras, mounting materials and other equipments and helped him in many other ways. She would sit with him every night and help him learn new things by creating relevant work for him. She allowed his curiosity to learn to flourish. When his interest was beginning to wane, his mother got him a book called "The Travels of Monarch X." That book opened the world of science to Ebright. Thus, without the encouragement of his mother, Ebright would not have reached the heights that he did.

60. Richard Ebright had all the ingredients for the making of a scientist. Discuss.

Ans. Richard Ebright was bright and intelligent from childhood. Beginning in kindergarten, Ebright collected butterflies with the same determination

that has marked all his activities. It is necessary for a scientist to be curious about the things around him, so that it may ignite a quest for further research and finding satisfactory answers to unanswered questions. He had a driving curiosity along with a bright mind. His competitive spirit led him to win many laurels at Science Fairs. The three most important qualities of a scientist are a first-rate mind, curiosity, and the will to win for the right reasons. A scientist has to be competitive but not in the bad way. All these qualities were there in Richard Ebright and so he was a great scientist.

Reference to Context Questions

Read the extract given below and answer the questions that follow :

61. From the first he had a driving curiosity along with a bright mind. He also had a mother who encouraged his interest in learning.

(a) Choose the answer that lists the correct statements about Ebright.

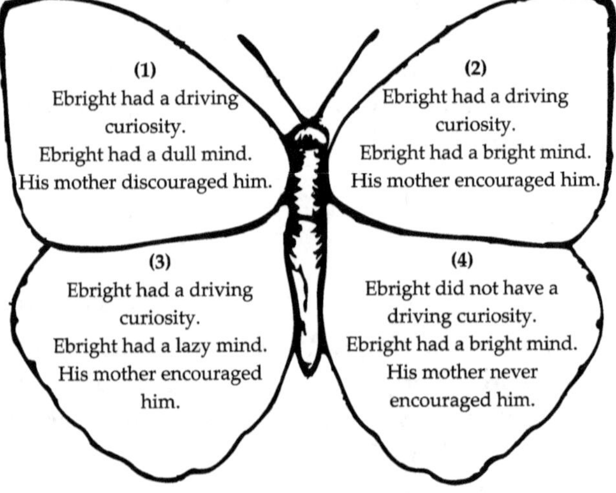

  (i) Option 1   (ii) Option 2
 (iii) Option 3   (iv) Option 4

(b) Which of the following qualities did he possess?

  (i) Lazy mind   (ii) Bright mind
 (iii) Foolish mind   (iv) Anxious mind

(c) How did his mother encourage his interest in learning?

  (i) By getting scientific instruments
  (ii) By getting movie tickets
 (iii) By taking him to parks
 (iv) By giving him practical tasks

(d) In which of the following was he most interested in?

   (i) Animals   (ii) Birds

   (iii) Butterflies   (iv) Ants

(e) Which of the following is a synonym for the word 'curiosity'?

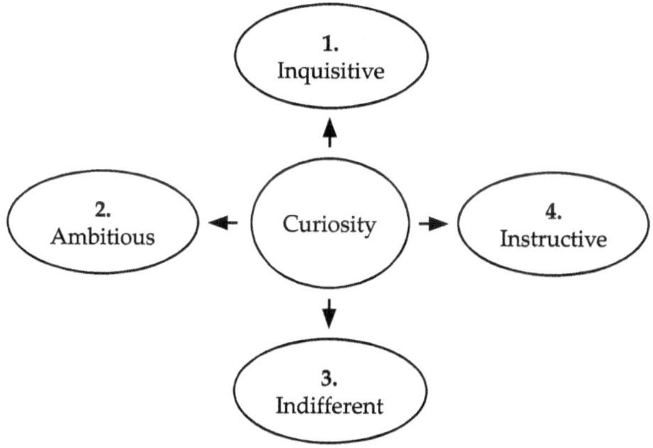

   (i) Option 1   (ii) Option 2

   (iii) Option 3   (iv) Option 4

Ans. (a) (ii) Option 2

   (b) (ii) Bright mind

   (c) (i) by getting scientific instruments

   (d) (iii) Butterflies

   (e) (i) Option 1

62. To find the answer, Ebright and another excellent science student first had to build a device that showed that the spots were producing a hormone necessary for the butterfly's full development. This project won Ebright first place in the county fair and entry into the International Science and Engineering Fair. There he won third place for zoology. He also got a chance to work during the summer at the entomology laboratory of the Walter Reed Army Institute of Research.

(a) Which project was Ebright working on?

(b) How did Ebright win the third prize for Zoology?

Ans. (a) Ebright was building a device to show that the tiny spots on a monarch pupa produce hormones necessary for a butterfly's development and are not just ornamental.

   (b) Ebright's project of building a device to show tiny spots on pupa produce necessary hormones, led him to win the first place in county fair and an entry in International Science and Engineering Fair, where he won the third place for Zoology.

63. And that is one of the ingredients in the making of a scientist. Start with a first-rate mind, add curiosity, and mix in the will to win for the right reasons. Ebright has these qualities. From the time the book, The Travels of Monarch X, opened the world of science to him, Richard Ebright has never lost his scientific curiosity.

(a) What qualities did Ebright have?

(b) How did the book become a turning point in Ebright's life?

Ans. (a) Ebright was competitive in a good sense. He wished to be the best for all the right reasons. He had a first-rate mind, added with curiosity and not just the will to win for a prize, but to do a good job.

   (b) The book, 'The Travels of Monarch X' was the reason he was able to communicate with Dr. Urquhart, who guided and motivated him to initiate scientific research on butterflies.

❑❑

The Necklace

—by Guy de Maupassant

Summary :

Guy de Maupassant wrote this wonderful short story about how running after superficial things and luxuries could ruin you. The story is about Matilda, a young lady who has to marry a clerk as she herself comes from a similar family. She is very unhappy as she believes she deserves a life full of luxuries and extravagances.

Once they get an invitation to attend a dinner at a senior official's house but instead of being happy, Matilda is depressed as she does not have a dress worthy of the event. Her husband foregoes his plans for the money he has saved and buys her a dress. For the jewellery to go with the dress, Matilda borrows a diamond necklace from her friend. On reaching home after a successful party, Matilda realises she has lost the necklace. Both husband and wife borrow money, use up all their savings and work hard for the next ten years to repay the loans they take in order to buy a replacement of the friend's necklace.

Years later, a haggard–looking Matilda meets her friend in a park. Here she comes to know that the necklace she had borrowed was fake and that she had broken her back trying to repay the money for the real necklace which went all in vain.

Extract Based Questions

I. Read the given extract to attempt the questions that follow:

When she seated herself for dinner opposite her husband who uncovered the tureen with a delighted air, saying, "Oh! the good potpie! I know nothing better than that...," she would think of elegant dinners, of shining silver; she thought of the exquisite food served in marvelous dishes. She had neither frocks nor jewels, nothing. And she loved only those things.

She had a rich friend, a schoolmate at the convent, who she did not like to visit — she suffered so much when she returned. She wept for whole days from despair and disappointment.

1. Choose the option that list the set of statements that are NOT TRUE according to the given extract.

1. Matilda was contented with her life.
2. Matilda felt troubled, because she desired a luxurious life.
3. M Loisel didn't appreciate what Matilda cooked.
4. Matilda despised the fact that she lived a life of poverty.
5. Matilda always had grand dinners and silverware at her dinner table.

(a) 1, 2, 3   (b) 1, 3, 5
(c) 2, 3, 4   (d) 1, 3, 4

Ans. (b) 1, 3, 5

2. "She suffered so much when she returned ' The reason for Matilda's suffering was that _______

(a) she was badly treated by her friend.
(b) she remembered her old school days after meeting her friend.
(c) She envied her friend for being well off and felt depressed after visiting her.
(d) She felt bad to see her friend's poverty-stricken condition.

Ans. (c) She envied her friend for being well off and felt depressed after visiting her.

3. Select the most appropriate option for (1) and (2).

(1) Matilda longed for a luxurious life.
(2) She was a very honest and reliable friend.

(a) (1) is true and (2) is false.
(b) (2) is the opposite of (1).
(c) (1) furthers the meaning of (2).
(d) Both (1) and (2) cannot be inferred from the extract.

Ans. (a) (1) is true and (2) is false.

4. Select the option listing Matilda's characteristics, as revealed in the extract.

(1) conceited   (2) depressed
(3) appeased   (4) envious
(5) contented

(a) (2) and (4)   (b) Only (5)
(c) (1), (2) and (4)   (d) Only (2)

Ans. (a) (2) and (4)

5. **Select the suitable word from the extract to complete the following:**

   elegant: clumsy : : hope : :

   (a) delighted   (b) exquisite

   (c) marvelous   (d) despair

Ans. (d) despair

II. *He was grieved, but answered, "Let us see, Matilda. How much would a suitable costume cost, something that would serve for other occasions, something very simple?"*

She reflected for some seconds thinking of a sum that she could ask for without bringing with it an immediate refusal and a frightened exclamation from the economical clerk. Finally she said, in a hesitating voice, "I cannot tell exactly, but it seems to me that four hundred francs ought to cover it."

1. **What could have brought 'an immediate refusal' and 'a frightened exclamation' from M Loisel?**

   (a) His disbelief at the refusal of invitation.

   (b) His surprise for his wife's reaction.

   (c) His inability to provide a new dress.

   (d) The unreasonable amount demanded by his wife.

Ans. (d) The unreasonable amount demanded by his wife.

2. **M Loisel was astonished seeing his wife's reaction. He writes a diary entry that night. Complete the entry by choosing the correct option.**

   11 January,Monday

   9.00 pm

   I thought Matilda would be (i)_____seeing the invitation in my hand.However, her reaction has left me (ii)________. I don't know how I would be able to (iii)______a new dress for her.

   (a) (i) vexed (ii) disturbed (iii) bring

   (b) (i) elated (ii) surprised (iii) afford

   (c) (i) keen (ii) depressed (iii) bring

   (d) (i) elated (ii) distressed (iii) afford

Ans. (d) (i) elated ii) distressed iii) afford

3. **Given below are the different opinions of M Loisel's friends about the relationship of M Loisel and his wife, Matilda. Choose the most suitable opinion about them.**

   (a) I think Matilda was being reasonable and realistic.

   (b) I feel that M Loisel loved Matilda and wanted her to be happy.

   (c) In my opinion M Loisel was being too harsh with Matilda.

   (d) I feel that M Loisel should not have brought the invitation home.

Ans. (b) I feel that M Loisel loved Matilda and wanted her to be happy.

4. **M Loisel was an 'economical clerk'. It means that he was __________**

   (a) spendthrift even though he earned a lot.

   (b) thrifty as he had a meagre income.

   (c) calculating money all the time as he was a clerk.

   (d) stingy about money and didn't spend it.

Ans. (b) thrifty as he had a meagre income.

5. **'He was grieved', here the word 'grieved' can be replaced by:**

   (a) disappointed   (b) disturbed

   (c) distressed   (d) perplexed

Ans. (c) distressed

III. *Mme Loisel now knew the horrible life of necessity. She did her part, however, completely, heroically. It was necessary to pay this frightful debt. She would pay it. They sent away the maid, they changed their lodgings; they rented some rooms in an attic.*

1. **Why did Mme Loisel lead a horrible life of necessity?**

   (a) to save money for her future.

   (b) to pay the debt that she had taken to buy the diamond necklace.

   (c) to buy the diamond necklace for herself.

   (d) to buy a house for her family.

Ans. (b) to pay the debt that she had taken to buy the diamond necklace.

2. **'She did her part, completely, heroically'. Here, the word 'heroically' implies that she:**

   (a) boldly accepted the hardship of life.

   (b) fought with her husband.

   (c) sadly performed her duties.

   (d) played her part in a drama.

Ans. (a) boldly accepted the hardship of life.

3. **Select the option listing Mme Loisel's characteristics, as revealed in the extract.**

   1. adjusting   2. stingy

   3. courageous   4. hard- working

   5. manipulative

   (a) (2) and (3)   (b) Only (5)

   (c) (1), (3) and (4)   (d) Only (2)

Ans. (c) (1), (3) and (4)

4. Select the most appropriate option based on (1) and (2).

1. The debt had made Mme Loisel's life miserable.

2. Mme Loisel did not want to pay the debt.

(a) (2) is true and (1) is false.

(b) (2) is the result for (1).

(c) (2) is the cause for (1).

(d) (2) is false and (1) is true.

Ans. (d) (2) is false and (1) is true.

5. The literary device used in the phrase 'the frightful debt' is ________

(a) alliteration   (b) transferred epithet

(c) personification   (d) hyperbole

Ans. (b) transferred Epithet

IV. *Her friend did not recognise her and was astonished to be so familiarly addressed by this common personage. She stammered, "But, Madame — I do not know — you must be mistaken—"*

"No, I am Matilda Loisel."

Her friend uttered a cry of astonishment, "Oh! my poor Matilda! How you have changed!"

"Yes, I have had some hard days since I saw you; and some miserable ones — and all because of you ..."

1. 'Her friend' did not recognize Matilda Loisel because Matilda _____

(a) was looking young and beautiful.

(b) was changed and looking older than her age.

(c) met her for the first time.

(d) behaved strangely to her.

Ans. (b) was changed and looking older than her age.

2. Who was being blamed for the hard and the miserable days of the speaker?

(a) Mme Loisel   (b) M Loisel

(c) Mme Forestier   (d) the jeweler

Ans. (c) Mme Forestier

3. Select the option listing the reactions of Mme Loisel's friend after meeting her, as revealed in the extract:

1. surprised   2. unsure

3. unfriendly   4. confused

5. indifferent

(a) (1) and (2)   (b) (3) and (4)

(c) (3) and (5)   (d) (1), (2) and (4)

Ans. (d) (1), (2) and (4)

4. Select the most appropriate option based on (1) and (2)

1. Mme Loisel had had hard days.

2. Mme Forestier was the cause of Matilda's miserable life.

(a) (2) is true and (1) is false.

(b) Both (1) and (2) are true

(c) (2) is the cause for (1).

(d) Both (1) and (2) are false.

Ans. (b) Both (1) and (2) are true

5. Select the option which displays an example of 'a cry of astonishment'.

(a) While he was walking on the street, he saw a snake.

(b) He was watching a movie when he heard a weird noise.

(c) As she opened the door, she saw her long lost friend in front of her.

(d) A barking dog chased him on the road.

Ans. (c) As she opened the door, she saw her long lost friend in front of her.

Multiple Choice Questions

1. Who is the author of the story "The Necklace"?

(a) HG Wells

(b) Robert W. Peterson

(c) Guy De Maupassant

(d) None of these

Ans. (c) Guy De Maupassant

2. Matilda always remained ________________ .

(a) Happy   (b) Unhappy

(c) Fulfilled   (d) Grateful

Ans. (b) Unhappy

3. What is the actual state of Matilda's family?

(a) Rich   (b) Middle-class

(c) Poor   (d) Wealthy

Ans. (c) Poor

4. What did Matilda dream of while having dinner?

(a) Elegant dinner   (b) Exquisite food

(c) Marvellous dishes   (d) All of these

Ans. (d) All of these

5. From whom did M. Loisel receive an invitation?

(a) The Minister of Public Instruction

(b) The Minister of Public Health

(c) The Minister of Public Safety

(d) The Minister of Public Education

Ans. (a) The Minister of Public Instruction

6. What was he planning to do with the money he had saved?

(a) Buy her a dress

(b) Buy a gun for himself

(c) Invest somewhere

(d) All of these

Ans. (b) Buy a gun for himself

7. What seemed as the next problem to her lafter arranging the dress?

(a) Not finding a dress good enough

(b) Having no jewels

(c) There was no problem

(d) None of these

Ans. (b) Having no jewels

8. What solution did they come up to?

(a) Wearing natural flowers in they name of jewels

(b) Asking her friend to lend some of her jewels

(c) Buy some new jewellery

(d) None of these

Ans. (b) Asking her friend to lend some of her jewels

9. What all did Matilda do in the party?

(a) Danced with enthusiasm

(b) Intoxicated with pleasure

(c) Thought of all the admiration

(d) All of these

Ans. (d) All of these

10. When did Mr and Mrs Loisel return home from the ball?

(a) At 2 a.m.

(b) At 3 a.m.

(c) At 4 a.m.

(d) At 5 a.m.

Ans. (c) At 4 a.m.

11. What do you mean by the word "stupefied?

(a) Make someone unable to think

(b) Make someone able to think

(c) To think

(d) None of the above

Ans. (a) Make someone unable to think

12. What all did they do as an attempt to find the necklace?

(a) He went looking for it.

(b) Went to the police.

(c) Posted an advertisement for ir offering a reward.

(d) All of the above

Ans. (d) All of the above

13. How much time did they take to repay the loan?

(a) Two years

(b) Five years

(c) Ten years

(d) Twenty years

Ans. (c) Ten years

14. Did Mrs Loisel come to know the real cost of the necklace?

(a) Yes

(b) No

(c) May be

(d) May not be

Ans. (a) Yes

15. What change came in the life of Loisels after raising a big loan?

(a) They sent away the maid.

(b) They changed their lodgings.

(c) They rented some rooms in an attic.

(d) All of the above

Ans. (d) All of the above

16. Did they find the lost necklace?

(a) Yes

(b) No

(c) May be

(d) Not known

Ans. (b) No

17. How did they pay for the new jewels?

(a) Using the money given by his father

(b) By borrowing

(c) By stealing

(d) Both (a) and (b)

Ans. (d) Both (a) and (b)

18. What did Matilda's friend say when she was told the entire story?

(a) She was angry.

(b) She hated her for that.

(c) She cursed her.

(d) She told that her necklace was not original

Ans. (d) She told that her necklace was not original

19. What do you mean by the word "dismay"?

(a) Shock

(b) Surprise

(c) Concern

(d) All of these

Ans. (d) All of these

Text Book Questions

Read and Find Out :

20. What kind of a person is Mme Loisel — why is she always unhappy?

Ans. Mme Loisel is unhappy because she believes she is born to enjoy luxuries and a rich life. She cannot stand their poverty and is enamoured by the glamour of money.

21. What kind of a person is her husband?

Ans. Her husband is a petty and economical clerk who believes in saving money and not spending it on luxuries.

22. What fresh problem now disturbs Mme Loisel?

Ans. Mme Loisel is now worried because although, she has a dress to wear to the party, she doesn't have any appropriate jewel to wear with it.

23. How is the problem solved?

Ans. Her husband advises her to borrow some jewellery from her rich friend and that is how they solve the problem.

24. What do M and Mme Loisel do next?

Ans. When M and Mme Loisel realise that they have lost the necklace, M Loisel goes in search of it. He looks for it at the minister's house, tells the police, puts an advertisement for a reward but fails to find it.

25. How do they replace the necklace?

Ans. In a shop of the Palais-Royal, they find a chaplet of diamonds which seems to them exactly like the one they had lost. They buy that after taking huge loans and return that instead of the one they took.

Think About It :

26. The course of the Loisels' life changed due to the necklace. Comment.

Ans. When she wears the necklace at the party, Mme Loisel enjoys the attention she gets. However, on losing it, she and her husband have to buy a replacement for necklace. The necklace costs a lot and they have to borrow a lot of money for it. The next ten years they both have to live a life of poverty all because of the necklace they have lost. If she had not borrowed the necklace, they would have lived a better life without the hardships of the poverty.

27. What was the cause of Matilda's ruin? How could she have avoided it?

Ans. Matilda belonged to a poor family, but she craved for all the riches and luxuries. This greed and craving led to her ruin. She could have avoided it by not giving into her craving for things of superficial beauty like the necklace.

28. What would have happened to Matilda if she had confessed to her friend that she had lost her necklace?

Ans. If Matilda had confessed to her friend that she had lost the necklace, she would have come to know that the necklace was fake and then she need not have worked so hard to repay the loans they took to buy the original necklace.

29. If you were caught in a situation like this, how would you have dealt with it?

Ans. I would have told the truth in the first place itself. Lies never beget any good hence, telling

the truth is always the best bet.

Talk About It :

30. The characters in this story speak in English. Do you think this is their language? What clues are there in the story about the language its characters must be speaking in?

Ans. Though the characters are speaking in English, the story is set in France. The titles of the lady and her husband, the name of the shop, all suggest that the language they must be using is French.

31. Honesty is the best policy.

Ans. If Matilda had been honest with her friend and had told her that she had lost the necklace, her friend would have told her the real cost of the necklace which Matilda and her husband could have easily repaid. However, Matilda hides the truth, believes that the necklace had real diamonds, buys a replacement for necklace to return to her friend at a very high cost and ruins her life in the bargain. Hence, Honesty is the best policy.

32. We should be content with what life gives us.

Ans. Matilda had a decent life, a house to call her own, some money a husband who earned reasonable money but she craved for all the luxuries and riches she saw some people had. She felt she deserved a life full of extravagances. This greed led her to their ruin. Therefore, we should be happy and contented with whatever we have and make the most of it.

Short Answer Type Questions

20-30 Words

33. Why was Matilda unhappy in her early married life?★

Ans. Matilda was unhappy in her early married life because she was married to a clerk working at the Ministry of Public Instruction, who could not satisfy Matilda's all desires for an elegant and luxurious life-style.

34. What did Matilda's husband bring home one evening? Why was he so elated?

Ans. One evening Matilda's husband brought home an invitation for both of them to attend a party at a minister's house. He was elated because he was one of the few clerks to get an invitation and also because he thought Matilda would be thrilled.

35. Why did Matilda not like to visit her rich friend?

Ans. Whenever Matilda visited her rich friend, she remained sad for many days thereafter. The contrast between her life and her friend's in terms of the luxuries, pained her very much.

36. Why did Jeanne, Matilda's friend not recognize her?

Ans. Over ten years, Matilda let go of all the little pleasures of her life, worked extremely hard in order to save money so as to repay the loan they had taken to buy the replacement for necklace. All the hardships had given her a haggard look and that is why Jeanne could not recognize her.

37. Why did Matilda (Mme Loisel) leave the ball in a hurry? What does it show about her character?★

Ans. Since no one noticed her shabby shawl, Matilda (Mme Loisel) left the ball in a hurry. Her character depicts her false pride and vanity in material things.

38. How did M. Loisel try to make his wife happy?★

Ans. M. Loisel had saved four hundred francs to buy a gun to join some hunting parties the next summer. The gun was to be used when he and his friends went to shoot larks. However, he tried to make his wife happy by offering to give her the saved four hundred francs to buy a suitable costume.

39. Why was Matilda always unhappy after her marriage?★

Ans. Matilda was a discontented woman. She was born into a family of clerks. She had received no dowry and had no hopes of becoming famous. Mathilda was married to a clerk but she wanted to enjoy a life of luxury just like her rich friends who had money and power.

40. Why was Matilda in a hurry to go to her house after the ball?★

Ans. Mr. and Mrs. Loisel had gone to a ball that was attended only by the most famous people of the society. Unlike the other rich ladies drapped in their elegant wrap, Mr. Loisel covered Matilda with a modest wrap which was not befitting those belonging to the upper class society and that clashed severely with her elegant costume. Matilda wished to hurry in order to go unnoticed by the other women who wrapped themselves in rich furs.

41. Why did Matilda not want to see her rich friends?★

Ans. Matilda had an inferiority complex and considered herself unlucky to be born in a lower-class family. Unlike her, her friends were extremely rich and full of power. Matilda also felt inferior because she was married to a simple clerk, whereas her rich friends were married to high-class men.

Long Answer Type Questions

100-120 words

42. What is the twist at the end of the story 'The Necklace'?

Ans. Matilda and her husband incur big debts in order to buy a replacement for necklace for her friend. They cut down on all expenses, she works hard at the household chores, he does extra jobs etc. in order to earn more money. All this for a necklace they thought was of real diamonds. However at the end of the story, Matilda meets her friend who tells her after ten years that the necklace they had lost was a fake, worth not even one tenth of the price they thought it had. They worked so hard to repay the loan because they felt they had lost the real necklace. It they knew the truth and had worked so hard for their own benefit, it must have tremendously upgraded their standard of living. This was the twist at the end of the tale.

43. Compare Matilda's life before and after the fateful dinner party.

Ans. Before the dinner: Matilda led a frugal life as they did not have too much money and hence had no luxuries. However, they did have a maid and other basic facilities. She dreamt of all the extravagances of life and was unhappy as she did not lead a luxurious life.

After the dinner: Matilda and her husband had to borrow large amounts of money to repay the loans they had taken. This meant letting go of the maid, doing all chores herself and having no savings to fall back on. She then, led a hard and harsh life that made her look much older than she was.

44. What was the cause of Matilda's ruin ? How could she have avoided it ?★

Ans. Matilda hailed from a poor background but, was very proud. She wanted to live an extravagant and a royal life but pitied herself since her family did not accept it. She was not ready to live her normal life with what she had and despised her wealthy friend Mme Forestier.

She could have avoided her ruin by learning to accept the reality and her present situation. She could have sought employment or start some small business using her talents. She could have put her thoughts into use, worked hard and profited thus, realising a dream instead of just dreaming in the idle time.

Reference to Context Questions

Read the extract given below and answer the questions that follow :

45. Instead of being delighted, as her husband had hoped, she threw the invitation spitefully upon the table murmuring, "What do you suppose I want with that?"

(a) What did the husband hope for?

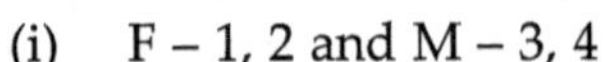

    (i)   F – 1, 2 and M – 3, 4

    (ii) F – 1, 3 and M – 2, 4

    (iii) F –1, 4 and M – 2, 3

    (iv) F – 4 and M – 1

(d) What do you understand by the wife's behaviour?

    (i)   Wife was unhappy

    (ii) Wife was surprised

    (iii) Wife was joking

    (iv) Wife was busy

(e) Which of the following words means 'speaking in a low voice'?

    (i)   That his wife will be happy

    (ii) That his wife will be angry

    (iii) That his wife will be surprised

    (iv) That his wife will be crying

(b) Choose the option that lists the set of statements that are NOT TRUE according to the given extract.

    1.   Matilda was happy at the invitation.

    2.   Her husband hoped to see her happy at the invitation.

    3.   Matilda threw the invitation.

    4.   Matilda happily sang after seeing the invitation.

    5.   Matilda asked her husband what she supposed to do with the invitation.

    6.   Matilda threw the invitation out of the window.

    7.   Matilda didn't know what to do with the invitation.

    (i) 1, 2, 3   (ii) 1, 3, 5

    (iii) 1, 4, 6   (iv) 1, 6, 7

(c) Pick the option that correctly classifies fact/s (F) and myths (M) of the students below.

    (i)   Delighted   (ii) Murmuring

    (iii) Spiteful   (iv) Suppose

Ans. (a) (i)   that his wife will be happy

     (b) (iii) 1, 4, 6

     (c) (ii) F –1, 3 and M – 2, 4

     (d) (i)   Wife was unhappy

     (e) (ii) Murmuring

46. She was the prettiest of all — elegant, gracious, smiling and full of joy. All the men noticed her, asked her name, and wanted to be presented. She danced with enthusiasm, intoxicated with pleasure, thinking of nothing but all this admiration, this victory so complete

and sweet to her heart. She went home towards four o'clock in the morning. Her husband had been half asleep in one of the little salons since midnight, with three other gentlemen whose wives were enjoying themselves very much. He threw around her shoulders the modest wraps they had carried whose poverty clashed with the elegance of the ball costume. She wished to hurry away in order not to be noticed by the other women who were wrapping themselves in rich furs.

(a) What was the cause of her inferiority complex?

(b) How would you prove that M. Loisel was a loving husband?

Ans. (a) Matilda thought that they are poor and all the other guests of the party belong to the upper class. This was the cause for her inferiority complex.

(b) M. Loisel was a loving husband as when his wife was enjoying the dance and gratifying her vanity through the admiration of the men-folk, he waited on her patiently.

47. **And she responded, "I am vexed not to have a jewel, nothing to adorn myself with. I shall have such a poverty-stricken look. I would prefer not to go to this party."**

He replied, "You can wear some natural flowers. In this season they look very chic."

She was not convinced. "No", she replied, "there is nothing more humiliating than to have a shabby air in the midst of rich women."

(a) Which party is she referring to?

(b) Why did she not want to go to the party?

Ans. (a) Matilda is referring to the party hosted by the Minister of Public Instruction for which her husband got an invitation to go to, alone with her.

(b) She was grieved for her poverty-stricken look. She felt that she did not have an appropriate party dress and a jewel for the party.

❑❑

The Hack Driver

—by Sinclair Lewis

Chapter 8

Summary :

'The Hack Driver' is the story of a young lawyer who is sent to New Mullion to serve summons on a man named Oliver Lutkins. When the lawyer reaches the village, he meets a hack driver who promises to take him around town in order to find Lutkins. As they move around the village, to all the spots Lutkins is likely to be in, they always manage to just miss him. The hack driver takes him to the shops, the barber shop, the poolroom and even to Lutkin's mother's house but he still manages to elude them. Even though the narrator is unsuccessful in his job, he enjoys the day with the hack driver because he has been a good company. He talks about all the people living in the village and paints a pretty picture of the otherwise drab looking village.

The lawyer goes back to the city and to his office where he faces a lot of flak for failing to serve the summons. The next day, the narrator is sent back to New Mullion with a colleague who had worked with Lutkins. As soon as they arrive, the colleague confirms the hack driver to be Oliver Lutkins. All those present there have a good laugh at the gullibility of the narrator. The hack driver and his mother ask him to go to a neighbour's house for coffee as they are the only ones in town to have missed meeting him the previous day.

Extract Based Questions

I. Read the given extract to attempt the questions that follow:

I was sent, not to prepare legal briefs, but to serve summons, like a cheap private detective. I had to go to dirty and shadowy corners of the city to seek out my victims. Some of the larger and more self confident ones even beat me up. I hated this unpleasant work, and the side of city life it revealed to me. I even considered fleeing to my hometown......

1. 'Like a cheap private detective' is a reference to the fact that the speaker____________.

(a) was drawing as good a salary as a detective.

(b) was upset about working in the private sector.

(c) wasn't trying to be an established detective.

(d) was disappointed with his allotted work.

Ans. (d) was disappointed with his allotted work.

2. Which work did the narrator find as 'unpleasant'?

(a) To work as a private detective

(b) To prepare legal briefs

(c) To serve summons to people

(d) To be a city dweller

Ans. (c) To serve summons to people

3. Select the options which were a part of this unpleasant work?

1. Seeking victims

2. serving summons

3. getting beaten up

4. preparing legal documents

(a) 1 only   (b) 2 and 3

(c) 4 only   (d) 1,2 and 3

Ans. (d) 1,2 and 3

4. Select the most appropriate option for (1) and (2).

1. The speaker found this side of the city life unpleasant.

2. The city people had robbed others of their belongings.

(a) (1) is true and (2) is false.

(b) (2) is true and (1) is false.

(c) (2) is the cause of (1).

(d) Both (1) and (2) cannot be inferred from the extract.

Ans. (a) (1) is true and (2) is false.

5. The phrase 'the shadowy corners of the city' conjure up images of places.

(a) with many trees to provide shade.

(b) where crime is not uncommon.

(c) which receive absolutely no sunlight.

(d) with tall buildings and their shadows.

Ans. (b) where crime is not uncommon.

II. *Fritz looked at me, hiding behind Bill. He hesitated, and then admitted, "Yes, he was in here a little while ago. Guess he's gone over to Gustaff's to get a shave."*

"Well, if he comes in, tell him I'm looking for him."
We drove to Gustaff's barber shop. Again, Bill went in first, and I lingered at the door.

1. **'Fritz's hesitation' indicates that he wanted to:**
   - (a) take a moment to comprehend and fall in with the prank.
   - (b) understand what was being asked and answer accordingly.
   - (c) pretend ignorance at the question asked to waste time.
   - (d) confirm that it was him being addressed, before replying.

   Ans. (a) take a moment to comprehend and fall in with the prank.

2. **The narrator was hiding behind Bill because he:**
   - (a) wanted to eavesdrop on the conversation.
   - (b) didn't trust Bill to enquire sternly.
   - (c) was instructed by Bill to do so.
   - (d) found the interior too stuffy.

   Ans. (c) was instructed by Bill to do so.

3. **'I lingered at the door……..'. Pick up the option that does not correctly use the word 'linger' in the sentence:**
   - (a) It's best if you can linger in the lobby while I get my luggage.
   - (b) I blurted out the final question that had been lingering in my mind.
   - (c) If a customer lingers over a product, the cameras zoom in to record facial expressions.
   - (d) Mom reminded us that household business cannot be lingered hastily.

   Ans. (a) It's best if you can linger in the lobby while I get my luggage.

4. **"Well, if he comes in, tell him I'm looking for him." The tone of the speaker is________.**
   - (a) informal
   - (b) threatening
   - (c) casual
   - (d) authoritative

   Ans. (d) authoritative

5. **The extract is an example of writing in the style of a:**
   - (a) personal narrative
   - (b) biography
   - (c) historical fiction
   - (d) research article

   Ans. (a) personal narrative

III. *I considered returning to New Mullion to practice law. If I had found Bill so deep and richly human, might I not grow to love Fritz and Gustaff and a hundred other slow-spoken, simple, wise neighbours? I pictured an honest and happy life beyond the strict limits of universities and law firms. I was excited. I had found a treasure. I had discovered a new way of life.*

1. **Select the reason/s that inspired the narrator to picture a 'new way of life'.**
   1. The deep and richly human hack driver.
   2. Slow- spoken, simple and wise people of the town.
   3. Better job opportunities.
   4. The scenic beauty of the place.
   - (a) 1 only
   - (b) 2 and 4
   - (c) 1, 2 and 4
   - (d) 3 only

   Ans. (c) 1, 2 and 4

2. **What was the 'treasure' found by the narrator?**
   - (a) practicing law in the town
   - (b) to lead a simple and contented country life
   - (c) summon was finally served to Lutkins
   - (d) got a new job of lawyer

   Ans. (b) to lead a simple and contented country life

3. **Select the most appropriate option for (1) and (2).**
   - (1) 'I considered returning to New Mullion.'
   - (2) I found the people of New Mullion simple and honest.
   - (a) (1) is true and (2) is false.
   - (b) (2) is true and (1) is false.
   - (c) (2) is cause of (1).
   - (d) Both (1) and (2) cannot be inferred from the extract.

   Ans. (c) (2) is cause of (1).

4. **The extract reveals the narrator's longing for ____________.**
   - (a) a contented life
   - (b) an affluent life
   - (c) a successful life
   - (d) a prosperous life

   Ans. (a) contented life

5. **Here, the phrase 'the strict limits of universities and law firms' refers to:**
   - (a) the limitation of educational institutions
   - (b) dualact training regime of laws firms
   - (c) strict rules of colleges and law firms
   - (d) restrictions for being educated and cultured

   Ans. (c) strict rules of colleges and law firms

IV. *What really hurt me was that when I served the summons, Lutkins and his mother laughed at me as though I were a bright boy of seven. With loving kindness they begged me to go with them to a neighbour's house for a cup of coffee.*

"I told them about you and they're anxious to look at you," said Lutkins joyfully. "They're about the only folks in the town that missed seeing you yesterday."

1. **Select the reasons that hurt the narrator when he served the summons to Lutkins.**
   1. The purpose of serving the summons proved fake.
   2. His trust was broken.
   3. He had been laughed at by Lutkins and his mother.
   4. He was befooled by Lutkins.
   (a) 1 only
   (b) 2 and 4
   (c) 2 only
   (d) 2, 3 and 4

Ans. (d) 2, 3 and 4

2. **'….as though I were a boy of seven', implies that the narrator was ________**
   (a) a boy of seven years old
   (b) a school boy
   (c) an innocent boy
   (d) a foolish boy

Ans. (d) a foolish boy

3. **Select the most appropriate option based on (1) and (2).**
   (1) The narrator was welcomed by Lutkins and his mother.
   (2) The neighbours wanted to see the narrator.
   (a) (2) is true and (1) is false.
   (b) (2) is the result for (1).
   (c) (2) is the cause for (1).
   (d) (2) is false and (1) is true.

Ans. (a) (2) is true and (1) is false.

4. **What could have been possible reason for the neighbours to be 'anxious 'to meet the lawyer?**
   (a) They wanted to offer him a cup of coffee.
   (b) They had not seen a lawyer before.
   (c) The lawyer was educated but befooled easily.
   (d) He had come to serve summons to Lutkins.

Ans. (c) the lawyer was educated but befooled easily.

5. **Select the option which displays an example of being 'anxious'.**
   (a) She saw beautiful bouquet in the shop.
   (b) The batsman hit the ball to the boundary.
   (c) All the voters were waiting to hear the election results.
   (d) The crowd saw a celebrity at the airport.

Ans. (c) All the voters were waiting to hear the election results.

Multiple Choice Questions

1. **What are 'summons'?**
   (a) An official notice from the police
   (b) Ordered to be present before a government authority.
   (c) A written order to a person asking him to be present before a Judge in the court of law.
   (d) Called by the Mayor to be present before him on any particular day and time.

Ans. (c) A written order to a person asking him to be present before a Judge in the court of law.

2. **What do you think are legal briefs?**
   (a) Legal diaries carried by lawyers
   (b) Notes pertaining to laws and constitutional acts
   (c) Notes prepared by lawyers to argue in court of law
   (d) Notes as requested for by Judges to be presented by lawyers.

Ans. (c) Notes prepared by lawyers to, to argue in court of law

3. **What was the young lawyer's impression about his profession?**
   (a) Very negative.
   (b) Very Positive
   (c) Good ,but too many challenges
   (d) Mixed feelings

Ans. (c) Good ,but too many challenges

4. **What exactly does the author mean by,' his wife could not make him put on a collar and a tie on the same day'?**
   (a) The lawyer was not good.
   (b) The lawyer hated wearing ties.
   (c) The lawyer either wore a collar or a tie
   (d) The lawyer didn't like listening to his wife.

Ans. (a) The lawyer was not good.

5. **Which of the following sentences suits the narrator's expectations of New Mullion?**
   (a) An airtight compartment that fits in a limited number of people
   (b) The object is like a feast for the eyes
   (c) I love country sides for the beauties of nature that surrounds it.
   (d) Every profession must confirm to the professional and ethical standards

Ans. (c) I love country sides for the beauties of nature that surrounds it.

6. **How did the town New Mullion turn out to be a disappointment?**
   (a) The town was undeveloped and over crowded.
   (b) The town had a shabby look much against his expectations.

  (c) The appearance of the town seemed to blend with the shady character of Oliver Lutkins.

  (d) Both B and C

Ans. (d) Both B and C

7. **What does the writer want us to infer about the delivery man from his first appearance?**

  (a) He was extremely familiar about New Mullion and its residents.

  (b) He was a friend of Oliver Lutkins.

  (c) He had a hack carriage.

  (d) He was keeping a pet horse.

Ans. (a) He was extremely familiar about New Mullion and also the town's residents.

8. **The phrase "glowed with warmth of his affection" can be attributed to which figure of speech?**

  (a) Metaphor   (b) Simile

  (c) Hyperbole   (d) Personification

Ans. (c) Hyperbole

9. **From the first few paragraphs of the story, what can you judge about the attitude of the lawyer?**

  (a) He was a confident man.

  (b) He was easily prone to lean on others to get his job completed.

  (c) He was an inquisitive man.

  (D) He was impatient and would get his job done anyhow

Ans. (b) He was easily prone to lean on others to get his job completed.

10. **If the name Gustaff is of Swedish origin then what is Fritz?**

  (a) English   (b) Dane

  (c) Russian   (d) German

Ans. (d) German

11. **The Phrase' greasy meal 'can complement with:**

  (a) The beautiful flower

  (b) Village

  (c) Dust on furniture

  (d) Oil and spices

Ans. (d) Oil and spices

12. **Why were Lutkins' neighbours anxious to meet the lawyer?**

  (a) The lawyer was a comedian by nature

  (b) The lawyer was a gullible man

  (c) The Lawyer had dared to summon a man like Lutkins

  (d) The lawyer had been taken on a ride by Lutkins

Ans. (d) The lawyer had been taken on a ride by Lutkins

13. **Which of the following characteristics suits the narrator?**

  (a) A grave and disciplined person

  (b) A fun-loving ,romantic personality

  (c) A. man well suited to fit in 'The survival of the fittest'

  (d) A man bubbling with confidence

Ans. (b) A fun-loving ,romantic personality

14. **Which word comes nearest in meaning for witness in the passage?**

  (a) Observer   (b) Spectator

  (c) Testimony   (d) Deponent

Ans. (d) Deponent

15. **The narrator and Bill's search for Lutkins can be described as_____**

  (a) Snake and Ladder game

  (b) Wild goose chase

  (c) Cat and Mouse game

  (d) Marathon

Ans. (b) Wild goose chase

16. **The lawyer's trip with Bill can be described as a _____.**

  (a) catch   (b) peruse

  (c) chase   (d) pursue

Ans. (c) chase

17. **After carefully reading the story, which of the following sentences tells us that the young lawyer was losing sight of his objective of visiting New Mullion?**

  (a) The young lawyer was easily befriended by Magnuson.

  (b) The young lawyer's trips around the town increased in the company of Bill.

  (c) The young lawyer seemed to forget his woes in the company of the jovial Bill.

  (d) The Young lawyer gave too much importance to the gossips of his companion.

Ans. (d) The Young lawyer gave too much importance to the gossips of his companion.

18. **What makes this story interesting?**

  (a) It is humorous, witty and unpredictable

  (b) It is full of suspense

  (c) It is satirical and panoramic

  (d) Both B and C

Ans. (a) It is humorous, witty and unpredictable

19. **The phrase 'old tigress Lutkins mother' can be attributed to the figure of speech,______.**

  (a) Metaphor   (b) Simile

  (c) Personification   (d) Alliteration

Ans. (a) Metaphor

20. The last sentence of the story can be said to be loaded with:

    (a) Laughter   (b) Pity

    (c) Intelligence   (d) Sarcasm

Ans. (d) Sarcasm

Text Book Questions

Read and Find Out :

21. Why is the lawyer sent to New Mullion? What does he first think about the place?

Ans. The lawyer is sent to New Mullion to serve summons on Oliver Lutkins who is a witness in a law case. When he reaches there, he is disappointed because the streets are rivers of mud, with rows of wooden shops, either painted sour brown or bare of any paint at all and he had expected a pretty countryside village.

22. Who befriends him? Where does he take him?

Ans. The delivery man at the station befriends him. He takes the lawyer around the village in his hack in search for Oliver Lutkins.

23. What does he say about Lutkins?

Ans. He says that Lutkins is a hard man to catch and that he is always up to something.

24. What more does Bill say about Lutkins and his family?

Ans. Bill talks about Lutkins's talent for dishonesty and also his knack of deceiving people. The fact that he always owes people money is also told by Bill. Bill calls Lutkins's mother a terror who everybody is scared of.

25. Does the narrator serve the summons that day?

Ans. No, the narrator is unable to find Oliver to serve him the summons that day.

26. Who is Lutkins?

Ans. Lutkins is actually the hack driver who takes the narrator around on a wild goose chase.

Think About It :

27. When the lawyer reached New Mullion, did 'Bill' know that he was looking for Lutkins? When do you think Bill came up with his plan for fooling the lawyer?

Ans. When the lawyer reached New Mullion, 'Bill' did not know that he was looking for Lutkins. However, as soon as the lawyer asked for Lutkins, Bill came up with the plan to fool the lawyer by taking him around on a wild goose chase.

28. Lutkins openly takes the lawyer all over the village. How is it that no one lets out the secret? (*Hint: Notice that the hack driver asks the lawyer to keep out of sight behind him when they go into Fritz's.) Can you find other such subtle ways in which Lutkins manipulates the tour?*

Ans. Lutkins openly takes the lawyer all over the village. No one in the village lets out the secret because everywhere the hack driver goes in, he first announces his name as Bill and then asks for Lutkins. He also asks the narrator to keep out of sight. The village people knowing his nature play along with Lutkins in fooling the narrator.

29. Why do you think Lutkins' neighbours were anxious to meet the lawyer?

Ans. The neighbours were the only people to whom Bill didn't take the lawyer when they were looking for Lutkins. They were the only people who had not seen the person Lutkins had made fool on the previous day.

30. After his first day's experience with the hack driver the lawyer thinks of returning to New Mullion to practise law. Do you think he would have reconsidered this idea after his second visit?

Ans. After the first day the lawyer is so enamoured with the simple life of the village that he considers returning to New Mullion to practice law. On realising the next day that he has been made a fool by the very villagers he thought were simple, I am sure he would have reconsidered this idea.

31. Do you think the lawyer was gullible? How could he have avoided being taken for a ride?

Ans. Yes, I think the lawyer was gullible. He could have avoided being taken for a ride if he had at least used a photograph of Lutkins to identify him or if he had taken someone along who recognised Lutkins along with him the first day itself.

Talk About It :

32. Who is a 'con man', or a confidence trickster?

Ans. A con man is a man who cheats or tricks someone by means of a confidence trick. He/She first earns the victim's confidence by talking sweet or helping them out and then tricks or cheats them.

Short Answer Type Questions

20-30 Words

33. Why did the narrator think of fleeing to his hometown to practice law?

Ans. The narrator was a junior assistant clerk in a law firm where he had the job of serving summons. He hated this work as it took him to the wrong side of the city and he had been beaten up too.

This is why he had considered fleeing to his hometown and practicing law there.

34. What happened at Lutkins's mother's farm?

Ans. When the lawyer and Bill reached the farmyard looking for Lutkins, his mother shouted at them and charged at them with an iron off the stove. However, they did manage to search the house by peering through the windows.

35. Why did the narrator think that in finding New Mullion he had found a treasure?

Ans. The narrator had found Bill, a deep and richly human, he thought he would grow to love Fritz and Gustaff and a hundred other slow-spoken, simple, wise neighbours. He pictured an honest and happy life beyond the strict limits of universities and law firms. He had discovered a new way of life and so thought that he had found a treasure.

36. Who befriended the narrator when he went to New Mullion ? Where did he take him ?★

Ans. The hack driver befriended the lawyer when he went to New Mullion to serve summons on a man called Oliver Lutkins. The hack driver took him to all the places that Lutkins hanged out at. They went to Fritz's to see if Oliver was playing a game of poker, then to so many other places and finally to Lutkin's mother's farm. But all this was in vain.

Long Answer Type Questions

100-120 words

37. Write a character sketch of the hack driver.★

Ans. The hack driver seemed to be a simple countryman at his first appearance who was ready to help the narrator. The lawyer was in search of Lutkins and hence, the hack driver took him to various places where he might find Lutkins. The next day, the case came up in court. As he was unable to find Lutkins, the lawyer was asked to go back to New Mullion with a man who had worked with Lutkins. The lawyer was shocked to find that the hack driver himself was Lutkins. He felt humiliated and learned not to be hasty in judging a person.

Bill told the lawyer that Lutkins was a hard fellow to catch. He was always up to something or the other. He owed money to many people, including Bill, and had never even paid anybody a cent. He also said that Lutkins played a lot of poker and was good at deceiving people.

38. Lutkins was really a 'hard fellow to catch'. Explain on the basis of the story 'The Hack Driver'?

Ans. The lawyer from the city who comes to serve summons on Lutkins does not recognize him. He had never seen Lutkins or did he have any image or photograph of him. This absence of identity proof helped Lutkins in fooling the lawyer and pretending to be someone else named Bill. Lutkins uses this to his advantage and takes the lawyer on a merry ride around the village pretending to be someone else and helping him catch himself. This craftiness makes him a very hard fellow to catch. He not only avoids being served summons by the lawyer but he also earns money off him for looking for himself. He befriends the lawyer and earns his confidence easily and then proceeds to befool him throughout the day. Lutkins really is a hard fellow to catch.

39. What did the hack driver tell the narrator about Lutkin's mother? How did she treat the narrator?★

Ans. The hack driver told the narrator that Lutkins' mother was a terror. He also told him that she was about nine feet tall and four feet thick. He also told him that once he had taken a trunk for her at her farmhouse. She almost had taken his skin off because he had not treated the trunk like a box of eggs. The narrator and Bill went to Lutkins' farmyard and found an enormous and cheerful old woman. Bill asked Lutkins' mother to inform him about her son. The lady said she did not know about him. Bill then told that the narrator was a lawyer and came to search her property. Lutkins, mother invited them both in the kitchen and then took out an iron rod from the stove and threatened them to burn them with it. She chased them out and laughed at them.

40. Appearances can be deceptive. Discuss on the basis of the story 'The Hack Driver'?

Ans. When the lawyer arrives at the station of New Mullion, he doesn't like the look of the village. The only thing he finds agreeable is the delivery man at the entrance who looks very cheerful and helpful. He starts liking the village and its villagers after spending the day with the hack driver. However, it is only the next day that he realises that the very same hack driver and the seemingly simple people of the village have made a fool of him. The village that seemed boring and uninteresting to him, suddenly became a place he wanted to move to leaving his city life. Also, the cheerful and helpful hack driver turned out to be a very cunning and troublesome man. Hence, it can be said with surety that appearances can be deceptive.

41. In life, people who easily trust others are sometimes made to look foolish. One should not be too trusting. Describe how Oliver Lutkins made a fool of the young lawyer.★

Ans. Lutkins impressed the young lawyer with his friendly manner, thus leading the lawyer to think that the people of the town were trustworthy. He claimed to know most of the places where Lutkins could be found. Lutkins charged the young lawyer a high price for the hack and food. He alerted Fritz, his friends and mother not to reveal his identity to the lawyer. He even went to the railway station to see the young lawyer, off. The young lawyer, on his second visit, learnt that the hack driver himself was Lutkins. The young lawyer thus learned a lesson that no one should be too trustworthy and one must be alert at all times.

Reference to Context Questions

Read the extract given below and answer the questions that follow :

42. So I rejoiced one day when they sent me out forty miles in the country, to a town called New Mullion, to serve summons on a man called Oliver Lutkins.

(a) Pick the option that correctly classifies fact/s (F) and myths (M) of the reasons given below.

   (i)   F – 2, 3 and M – 1, 4

   (ii) F – 1, 4 and M – 2, 3

   (iii) F – 4, 2 and M – 1, 3

   (iv) F – 4, 3 and M – 1, 2

(b) What was the profession of the narrator?

   (i)   He was a lawyer of the High Court

   (ii) He was a junior clerk in a law firm

   (iii) He was a private detective

   (iv) He was an informer

(c) Why had the narrator been asked to serve summons on Oliver Lutkins?

   (i)   Oliver Lutkins was a criminal

   (ii) Oliver Lutkins was a fugitive

   (iii) Oliver Lutkins was a witness in a law case

   (iv) Oliver Lutkins had cheated someone

(d) Identify a word from the above lines which means the same as 'exulted'.

   (i)   Rejoiced

   (ii) Serve

   (iii) Summons

   (iv) Sent

(e) From the phrase 'rejoiced one day' what can be thought of the narrator's mindset?

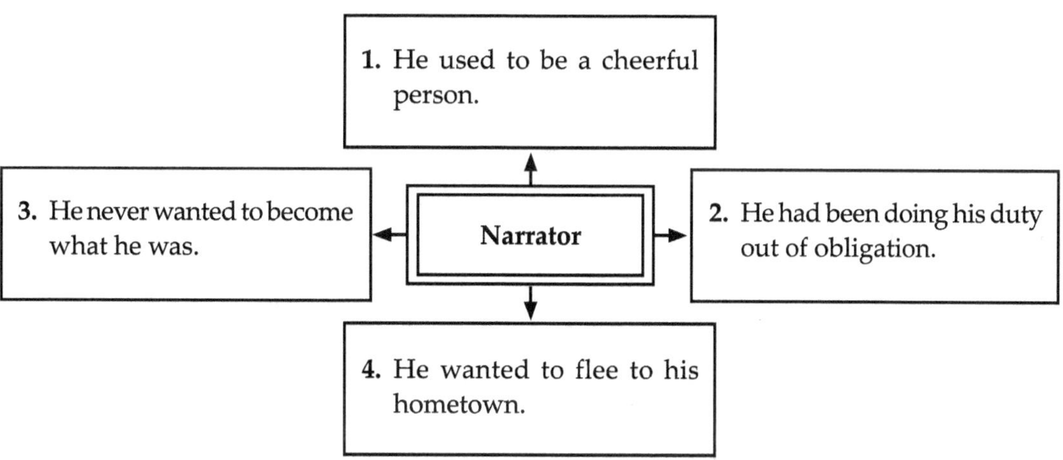

(i) Option 1   (ii) Option 2

(iii) Option 3   (iv) Option 4

Ans. (a) (ii) F – 1, 4 and M – 2, 3

(b) (ii) He was a junior clerk in a law firm

(c) (iii) Oliver Lutkins was a witness in a law case

(d) (i) Rejoiced

(e) (ii) Option 2

43. "Now, look here. We've had just about enough nonsense. This young man represents the court in the city, and we have a legal right to search all properties for this Oliver Lutkins."

(a) Pick the option that correctly classifies fact/s (F) and myths (M) in the options given below.

(i) F – 2, 4 and M – 1, 3

(ii) F – 2, 3 and M – 1, 4

(iii) F – 1, 4 and M – 2, 3

(iv) F – 2, 1 and M – 3, 4

(b) What did Bill tell about Lutkin's mother?

(i) She was a cheerful lady

(ii) She was an amicable woman

(iii) She was a terror

(iv) She was a humorous woman

(c) What information did the driver give lawyer about Lutkins?

(i) Lutkins was an offensive person who had borrowed money from many people.

(ii) Lutkins was a successful man.

(iii) Lutkins was a rich man of the community.

(iv) Lutkins was an influential personality.

(d) Identify a word from the above lines which means the same as 'be hired to act on behalf of someone'.

(i) Enough

(ii) Represents

(iii) Legal

(iv) Search

(e) Hack driver's introducing lawyer as 'This young man represents the court in the city' made lawyer feel……

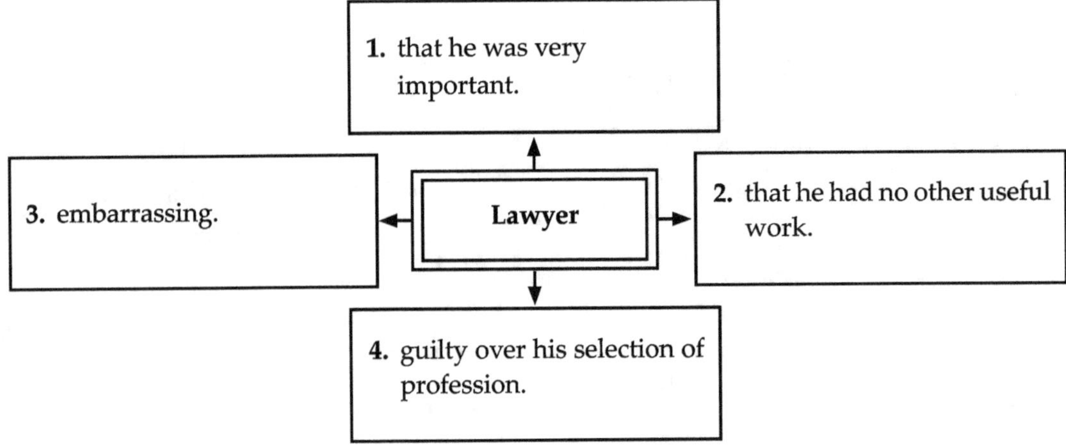

    (i)   Option 1   (ii) Option 2

    (iii) Option 3   (iv) Option 4

Ans. (a) (ii) F – 2, 3 and M – 1, 4

     (b) (ii) She was a terror

     (c) (i) Lutkins was an offensive person who had borrowed money from many people.

     (d) (ii) Represents

     (e) (i) Option 1

44. When I got to New Mullion, my eager expectations of a sweet and simple country village were severely disappointed. Its streets were rivers of mud, with rows of wooden shops, either painted a sour brown, or bare of any paint at all. The only agreeable sight about the place was the delivery man at the station. He was about forty, red-faced, cheerful, and thick about the middle. His working clothes were dirty and well-worn, and he had a friendly manner. You felt at once that he liked people.

(a) Why was the narrator's spirit dampened when he reached the New Mullion?

(b) How has the delivery man been described here?

Ans. (a) The narrator was disappointed as he thought of visiting a sweet and simple country village but instead he found it out to be dull, when he saw the muddy streets and unpainted looks of the shops around.

     (b) The narrator describes the delivery man as a red-faced man in his forties, he looked cheerful, thick in the middle. His clothes seemed dirty yet well-worn and he looked pleasant.

45. His cheerful country wisdom was very refreshing to a country boy like myself who was sick of the city. As we sat on the hilltop, looking over the pastures and creek which slipped among the trees, he talked of New Mullion, and painted a picture in words of all the people in it. He noticed everything, but no matter how much he might laugh at people, he also understood and forgave their foolishness.

(a) What did narrator think of city life?

(b) How did the hack driver explain the country life?

Ans. (a) The narrator considered himself to be a city boy. He felt refreshed as the delivery man talked of the country as the narrator was sick and tired of the city life.

     (b) The hack driver talked of New Mullion as they sat on the hilltop, looking over the pastures and creeks, painting a picture in words of all the people in it. He was very descriptive as he noticed everything.

❑❑

Bholi

—by K. A. Abbas

Summary :

Bholi is the name given to Sulekha, the fourth daughter of Numberdar Ramlal. She is called so because she is a simpleton. Owing to a fall and a bout of small pox, Bholi is neither intelligent nor pretty. Everyone makes fun of her and calls her a 'dumb cow'. She is sent to the newly opened primary school in the village where the teacher encourages her to come out of her shell and learn to read and write. The teacher's attitude and encouragement changes Bholi and gives her a lot of confidence. However, her parents believing her to be the stammering fool arrange her marriage to a rich grocer from the neighbouring village who is old and has a limp. During the marriage ceremony, the groom looks at Bholi's pock marked face and refuses to marry her unless her father gives him five thousand rupees. The helpless father starts to do so but Bholi takes a stand and refuses to marry a man who is greedy and old. She declares this with the confidence education had given her and vows to look after her parents and work in the same school she has studied.

Extract Based Questions

I. *"I am only taking you to school." Then he told his wife, "Let her wear some decent clothes today or else what will the teachers and the other schoolgirls think of us when they see her? New clothes had never been made for Bholi. The old dresses of her sisters were passed on to her. No one cared to mend or wash her clothes. But today she was lucky to receive a clean dress which had shrunk after many washings and no longer fitted Champa. She was even bathed and oil was rubbed into her dry and matted hair. Only then did she believe that she was being taken to a place better than her home! When they reached the school, the children were already in their classrooms."*

1. **When Bholi was told about being taken to school, ____________**

   (a) she thought she was going to be neglected by her parents.

   (b) she thought her parents were going to get rid of her.

   (c) she felt that she would be thrown out of the house and sold.

   (d) she thought her parents were thinking of ways to throw her out.

   Ans. (c) She felt that she would be thrown out of the house and sold.

2. **Choose the correct statements based on the given extract.**

   1. Bholi was not treated on a par with her siblings.
   2. Bholi received new clothes on every occasion.
   3. Bholi was excited and anxious to go to school.
   4. Bholi was dressed in decent clothes because her father was conscious of his status.

   (a) 1 and 2   (b) 2 and 4

   (c) 2 and 3   (d) 1 and 4

   Ans. (d) 1 and 4

3. **What does the phrase 'Bholi's hair matted', suggests?**

   (a) It was entangled and oiled.

   (b) It was never oiled or combed.

   (c) It was not combed regularly.

   (d) It was unkempt and oiled.

   Ans. (b) It was never oiled or combed.

4. **Select the reason which made Bholi think that school would be a better place than home.**

   (a) She had been given a good description of the school.

   (b) She would make many friends there.

   (c) She was given a bath and clean dress.

   (d) She was taken to the school by her father.

   Ans. (c) She was given a bath and clean dress.

5. **Pick the sentence that brings out the meaning of 'decent' as used in the extract.**

   (a) He gets a decent amount of salary.

   (b) One must be decent when having a conversation with strangers.

   (c) She was dressed in a decent manner for the interview.

   (d) It was very decent of him to lend me some money.

   Ans. (c) She was dressed in a decent manner for the interview.

II. *"In one month you will be able to read this book. Then I will give you a bigger book, then a still bigger one. In time you will be more learned than anyone else in the village. Then no one will ever be able to laugh at you. People will listen to you with respect and you will be able to speak without the slightest stammer. Understand? Now go home, and come back early tomorrow morning."*

Bholi felt as if suddenly all the bells in the village temple were ringing and the trees in front of the school-house had blossomed into big red flowers. Her heart was throbbing with a new hope and a new life.

1. "Then I will give you a bigger book, then a still bigger one.'. Here the speaker's intention is to ______

(a) encourage the child to pursue studies regularly.

(b) lure the child to see the book only.

(c) tempt the child to get a big book.

(d) make the child realise the value of books.

Ans. (a) encourage the child to pursue studies regularly.

2. Which among the following is the correct reason for the teacher insisting Bholi to become learned.

(a) People will become sensitive.

(b) Bholi would become confident and respected by the people.

(c) Bholi could speak with stammer.

(d) Villagers may realize their mistake.

Ans. (b) Bholi would become confident and respected by the people.

3. Select the most appropriate option for (1) and (2).

1. When Bholi will be learned then no one will ever be able to laugh at her.

2. Everyone makes fun of Bholi .

(a) (1) is true and (2) is false.

(b) (2) is true and (1) is false.

(c) (2) furthers the meaning of (1).

(d) Both (1) and (2) cannot be inferred from the extract.

Ans. (c) (2) furthers the meaning of (1).

4. From the options given below, identify the teacher's character traits in the extract.

1. soft-spoken 2. indifferent

3. considerate 4. rude

5. caring

(a) (1), (2) and (3) (b) (2), (3) and (4)

(c) (2) (4) and (5) (d) (1), (3) and (5)

Ans. (d) (1), (3) and (5)

5. Select the suitable word from the extract to complete the following:

Hope: despair:: ______: wither

(a) respect (b) throb

(c) blossom (d) life

Ans. (c) blossom

III. *"Pitaji! Take back your money. I am not going to marry this man."*

Ramlal was thunderstruck. The guests began to whisper, "So shameless! So ugly and so shameless!"

"Bholi, are you crazy?" shouted Ramlal. "You want to disgrace your family? Have some regard for our izzat!"

"For the sake of your izzat," said Bholi, "I was willing to marry this lame old man. But I will not have such a mean, greedy and contemptible coward as my husband. I won't, I won't, I won't."

"What a shameless girl! We all thought she was a harmless dumb cow."

Bholi turned violently on the old woman, "Yes, Aunty, you are right. You all thought I was a dumb–driven cow. That's why you wanted to hand me over to this heartless creature. But now the dumb cow, the stammering fool, is speaking. Do you want to hear more?"

1. When Bholi declared , "……….. I am not going to marry this man." Her decision portrays her as______ girl.

(a) rude and shameless

(b) bold and assertive

(c) tongue-tied and mild

(d) sharp and sarcastic

Ans. (b) bold and assertive

2. Choose the statements which are true according to the given extract:

1. Bholi had become self-reliant and was able to take decisions at the end of the story.

2. Bholi's parents considered Bishambhar as an unworthy bridegroom.

3. Bishambhar had demanded extra money from her father.

4. Bholi refused to marry Bishambhar and she demanded money from him.

5. Bholi know that Bishabhar was a greedy man of ill-intent.

6. Villagers appreciated Bholi's step of refusing to marry Bishambhar.

(a) 1, 2 and 4 (b) 2, 4 and 6

(c) 4, 5 and 6 (d) 1, 3 and 5

Ans. (d) 1, 3 and 5

3. **Bholi had refused to get married because:**
   - (a) her father couldn't afford the dowry that was demanded.
   - (b) the bridegroom had been greedy.
   - (c) the bridegroom had insulted her father.
   - (d) her father was getting her married to a man older to her.

Ans. (c) the bridegroom had insulted her father

4. **From the options given below, identify villagers' character traits in the extract.**
   1. orthodox
   2. helpful
   3. understanding
   4. conservative
   5. gossip monger

   - (a) 1, 4 and 5
   - (b) 2, 3, and 4
   - (c) 1, 3 and 5
   - (d) 3, 4 and 5

Ans. (a) 1, 4 and 5

5. **Which word does 'contemptible' not correspond to?**
   - (a) worthless
   - (b) shameful
   - (c) praiseworthy
   - (d) despicable

Ans. (c) praiseworthy

Multiple Choice Questions

1. **Who is the author of the story "Bholi"?**
   - (a) KA Abbas
   - (b) Mark Twain
   - (c) Guy De Maupassant
   - (d) Sinclair Lewis

Ans. (a) KA Abbas

2. **What was Bholi's real name?**
   - (a) Sulekha
   - (b) Sudekha
   - (c) Champa
   - (d) Chamla

Ans. (a) Sulekha

3. **Who was Bholi's father?**
   - (a) Village Numberdar
   - (b) Village Sarpanch
   - (c) Village Tehsildar
   - (d) None of these

Ans. (a) Village Numberdar

4. **What happened when Bholi was two years old?**
   - (a) Falling off a cot
   - (b) Falling off the stairs
   - (c) Falling off a verandah
   - (d) Small-pox

Ans. (d) Small-pox

5. **Who was Lakshmi?**
   - (a) Bholi's friend
   - (b) Bholi's classmate
   - (c) Bholi's sister
   - (d) Bholi's cow

Ans. (d) Bholi's cow

6. **What was the purpose of the Tehsildar's village visit?**
   - (a) To inaugurate a girl's school
   - (b) To address complaints of the village
   - (c) To meet the people of the village
   - (d) None of the above

Ans. (a) To inaugurate a girl's school

7. **What was Bholi's first reaction on hearing that she was going to school?**
   - (a) She cried with tears of joy
   - (b) She cried with fear
   - (c) She screamed
   - (d) She was excited

Ans. (b) She cried with fear

8. **Why did the girls laugh at Bholi?**
   - (a) At her dress
   - (b) At her looks
   - (c) At her stammering
   - (d) All of these

Ans. (c) At her stammering

9. **Why did Bholi talk very little in school?**
   - (a) She stammered
   - (b) Other kids mimicked her and made fun of her
   - (c) She was an introvert
   - (d) None of these

Ans. (b) Other kids mimicked her and made fun of her.

10. **Whose paintings did she see in the classroom wall?**
    - (a) Cow
    - (b) Goat
    - (c) Parrot
    - (d) All of these

Ans. (d) All of these

11. **Who is referred to as the "artist" in the lesson?**
    - (a) Bholi's friend
    - (b) Bholi
    - (c) Bholi's cow
    - (d) Bholi's teacher

Ans. (d) Bholi's teacher

12. **What according to you, was wrong in Bishamber's marrying Bholi?**
    - (a) His age
    - (b) His limbs
    - (c) Another village
    - (d) All of these

Ans. (a) His age

13. **How did Bholi's prospective husband react on seeing Bholi's face?**
    - (a) Asked for compensation
    - (b) Got frightened
    - (c) Both of the above
    - (d) None of the above

Ans. (a) Asked for compensation

14. How does Bholi describe her prospective husband?

(a) Mean   (b) Greedy

(c) Coward   (d) All of these

Ans. (d) All of these

Text Book Questions

Read and Find Out :

15. Why is Bholi's father worried about her?

Ans. Bholi is neither intelligent nor pretty. She also stammers. All this means that no one would be ready to marry her. This is why Bholi's father is worried about her.

16. For what unusual reasons is Bholi sent to school?

Ans. When a new girls' primary school is opened in the village, the tehsildar asks Ramlal to send his daughters and set an example. So, despite having the view that education makes girls unsuitable for marriage, Bholi's parents sent her to school. They think that with her lack of looks and intelligence, nobody would marry her.

17. Does Bholi enjoy her first day at school?

Ans. When Bholi enters school, she is very nervous but by the end of the day the teacher's encouraging attitude helps her to like school and enjoy her first day at school.

18. Does she find her teacher different from the people at home?

Ans. Bholi was always being made fun of by the people at home. They called her a 'dumb cow'. Bholi hardly ever spoke to anyone as she stammered. However, her teacher was different. She encouraged Bholi to speak and did not make fun of her. She was very kind to her.

19. Why do Bholi's parents accept Bishamber's marriage proposal?

Ans. Bholi's lack of looks and intelligence and her stammering meant that no one would marry her. So Bholi's parents accepted Bishamber's proposal, even though, he was too old for her, had grown up children and was limped.

20. Why does the marriage not take place?

Ans. The groom, on seeing the bride's pock-marked face, refuses to marry her unless the father of the bride gives him five thousand rupees. Even though the father was ready to give the money, the bride refuses to marry an old greedy man and the marriage does not take place.

Think About It :

21. Bholi had many apprehensions about going to school. What made her feel that she was going to a better place than her home?

Ans. Bholi had no idea what a school would be like. She thought it was a bad place. However, when she had a bath, dressed in fresh clothes, got her hair oiled and braided then she started thinking that maybe she was being taken to a place better than home.

22. How did Bholi's teacher play an important role in changing the course of her life?

Ans. Bholi's teacher was very encouraging. Instead of making fun of her or scolding her like the people at home, the teacher listened to her patiently, taught her to read and write and above all, gave her the self confidence that made her a strong person. This confidence helped Bholi in rejecting the marriage to an old greedy man. She decided to stand on her own feet. Thus, the teacher played an important role in changing Bholi's life.

23. Why did Bholi at first agree to an unequal match? Why did she later reject the marriage? What does this tell us about her?

Ans. Bholi had been made to believe, since childhood, that she was a 'dumb cow' and that no one would want to marry her. This is why, she agrees to the match for the reputation of her father. However, when she sees that the man despite, being, too old and limping, asks for five thousand rupees to marry her, she rejects the marriage calling him greedy and callous. This shows how she uses her education and confidence to lead a better life and not give in to social pressures.

24. Bholi's real name is Sulekha. We are told this right at the beginning. But only in the last but one paragraph of the story is Bholi called Sulekha again. Why do you think she is called Sulekha at that point in the story?

Ans. Sulekha is named Bholi since childhood as she is a simpleton with little intelligence. Everybody calls her Bholi. By the end of the story, she is an educated and confident girl who can go against the social pressures and lead a life she wants. This shows that she is no longer the simpleton everyone would laugh at and so she is called Sulekha.

Talk About It :

25. Bholi's teacher helped her overcome social barriers by encouraging and motivating her. How do you think you can contribute towards changing the social attitudes illustrated in this story?

Ans. Creating awareness among the rural population about the benefits of educating the girl child and increasing tolerance towards special needs people is the way we can contribute towards changing social attitudes.

26. Should girls be aware of their rights and assert them? Should girls and boys have the same rights, duties and privileges? What are some of the ways in which society treats them differently? When we speak of 'human rights', do we differentiate between girls' rights and boys' rights?

Ans. Girls should be aware of their rights and assert them. Girls and boys both should have the same rights. Female infanticide and not sending girls to school are some of the ways that society treats them differently. Human rights do not differentiate between girls and boys.

27. Do you think the characters in the story were speaking to each other in English? If not, in which language were they speaking? (You can get clues from the names of the persons and the non-English words used in the story.)

Ans. No, the characters in the story were not speaking in English. They were speaking in Hindi.

Short Answer Type Questions

20-30 Words

28. Why was Sulekha called Bholi by every one?

Ans. When she was ten months old, Bholi had fallen off the cot on her head and perhaps it had damaged some part of her brain. That was why she remained a dull witted child and came to be known as Bholi, the simpleton.

29. Why did other children make fun of Bholi and mimic her?

Ans. Bholi's entire body was permanently disfigured by deep black pockmarks. Little Bholi could not speak till she was five and when at last she learnt to speak, she stammered. This is why other children often made fun of her and mimicked her.

30. Why do the teacher's eyes depict satisfaction when Bholi rejects the marriage?

Ans. The teacher has taught Bholi to be confident and has educated her. She feels satisfied that her education has given Bholi the strength to defy the social pressures and decide to lead her life on her own terms.

★ **are board exam questions from previous years**

31. What filled Bholi, a dumb cow, with a new hope?★

Ans. As a child, Bholi was always shunned and ignored because of her looks. She faced a tough childhood and was extremely anxious and timid. Bholi's teacher's soft and soothing voice coupled with her encouraging words filled Bholi with new hope. The teacher's faith in Bholi helped her grow.

Long Answer Type Questions

100-120 words

32. What do you know about Bishamber Nath? Why did Bholi refuse to marry him?★

Ans. Bishamber was a middle-aged man. He was nearly as old as Bholi's father. He limped while walking. He also had children from his first wife. He had a big house and a shop and also a lot of money in the bank. He agreed to marry Bholi without demanding dowry. But when he came to marry her on the day of wedding, he asked for ₹5000 to marry Bholi after seeing the pock scars on her face. Bholi's father Ramlal begged him to not demand for dowry but Bishamber stuck to his demand. Ramlal placed his turban at his feet but Bishamber was not moved. At last, Ramlal went in and opened his locker and came out with ₹5000 and placed the money at Bishamber's feet. But Bholi refused to marry such a mean and greedy person and decided to remain unmarried to take care of her parents.

33. How did education change Bholi's personality?★

Ans. Bholi used to be a meek girl. She had pockmarks on her entire body. Her brain got damaged when she was just ten months old. She was also a slow learner. She could not speak till she was five. Later on, she suffered from stammering while speaking. She was sent to school just for a formality. Her parents were not serious about her studies. But her teacher changed her life. She encouraged her to speak properly and to become independent. She taught Bholi what is good and what is bad? and how to differentiate between right and wrong? Education totally changed her personality. Even then she behaved like an obedient★ girl and agreed to marry Bishamber who was fifty years old. She could not stand his demand of dowry hence, she refused to fulfill Bishamber's demand of five thousand rupees and denied marrying him. Thus, education changed her attitude towards her life.

34. Education is the passport to a better life. Discuss on the basis of the story 'Bholi'.

Ans. Bholi is the neglected, ostracized child in a family in a village. She lacks looks and intelligence and hence, is often made fun of and called a 'dumb cow'. Then she gets the opportunity to attend school and learns to read and write. She is educated and this increases her self confidence and makes her a stronger person. She is an example of how education changes the way one thinks and how then one has the confidence to fight against the social barriers in order to lead a happier life. Education helps one recognize his rights and duties. Understanding one's duties make, one responsible, while the knowledge of one's rights equips a person with courage and confidence. Education, for Bholi, has been the passport to a better life.

35. What social injustices does the story 'Bholi' highlight? Discuss them with Bholi as the one effected.

Ans. The story highlights some of our society's injustices. One of them is gender bias. Bholi, being a girl, is treated differently. When her parents have to send a girl to school, they feel that educating a girl will be a barrier to her marriage. The other injustice is towards special needs children. There is zero tolerance towards special-needs children in our society. Here, Bholi is often made fun of because she is less intelligent. Another major injustice is for 'looks' and stammering. When it comes to her marriage, she is being made to get married off at a very young age and that too with an old and limping man. Had she been beautiful and normal like others, her parents would have never thought of marrying her to such a person. The curse of dowry is an element in the story. Bholi has a pockmarked face due to small pox and also stammers as a child. All this leads to her being treated cruelly by her own family.

36. School education turned Bholi from a dumb cow into a bold girl. How did she save her father from a huge expense and become his support in his old age?★

Ans. Bholi, despite her pet name, slowly gained her confidence and a good education with the help of her teacher. She understood how society worked and was brave enough to stand up against the evils present in the society. She saved her father from huge expenses and became his support in his old age by refusing to marry Bishamber who was an old and lame man. She also refused to pay the dowry of five thousand rupees. She stood up with courage and acted boldly in spite of being aware that she might not get married. Bholi decided to serve her parents in their old age and work in the same school in which she studied.

37. Education is always a great asset in the life of a woman. How did Bholi, an educated girl, face the challenge posed by Bishambar's greed?★

Ans. Education is always a great asset especially in the life of a woman. Education brings about a change in the quality of life of a woman. Education also helps change the outlook of a woman, the way she perceives things and how she responds to situations. Bholi was a simple girl. She had pockmarks on her face as a result of which, she was shunned for her looks. Her parents as well as the villagers neglected her. She was sent to school where she received great encouragement from her teacher. Despite her education, she did not get any marriage prospects mainly due to her looks. Bishambar, her prospective husband, was a lame, old man who was greedy for Bholi's money. Bholi, however, took a bold step and rejected Bishambar's marriage proposal. She promised to serve her parents in their old age and went back to teach in the school where she had studied.

38. *"Don't you worry, Pitaji! In your old age I will serve you and mother"*. Through this statement the narrator wants to highlight the moral values Bholi was imbued with. Based on the reading of the lesson, what made Bholi aware of her rights and how did she use them?★

Ans. Bholi, as a child, was mostly ignored and made fun of. Her peers made fun of her looks while her parents gave up on her, finding a good groom to marry. In the end, they found a greedy and an old-widowed man for her to marry. Bholi, despite the treatment meted out by her parents, displayed utmost respect and concern for them. She showed love and affection towards her parents and rarely disobeyed their words. This attitude is noticed when despite knowing the attitude of her to-be husband, she willingly

---

agrees to get married to him for the sake of her parents.

Bholi, while being submissive, was also a determined and confident girl who gained her self-respect through her education. Her teacher during the course of Bholi's education, made her aware of self-esteem rights. She wasn't ready to demean herself so she stood up confidently against the proposal of the greedy man and told her parents that she would take care of them life long, instead of getting married.

39. What social attitudes are presented in the story, 'Bholi' ? How does Bholi's teacher help her overcome these barriers ?★

Ans. Bholi stammered so, everyone used to laugh and make fun of her. In the beginning, when she first started attending school, she was afraid to even look up when questioned as she was just a bundle of nerves.

Her teacher treated her kindly and affectionately. She encouraged her to have confidence in herself and to be bold, confirming that she would be able to break the barrier of stammering and be like the other girls. The teacher taught her to read and write and made her an independent girl who was aware of her rights. This changed her life.

Reference to Context Questions

Read the extract given below and answer the questions that follow :

40. But Ramlal had not the courage to disobey the Tehsildar. At last his wife said, "I will tell you what to do."

(a) Pick the option that correctly classifies fact/s (F) and myths (M) in the options given below.

   (i) F – 2, 3 and M – 1, 4

  (ii) F – 2, 4 and M – 1, 3

 (iii) F – 3, 4 and M – 1, 2

 (iv) F – 4, 1 and M – 2, 3

(b) What was Tehsildar's instruction which Ramlal couldn't disobey?

   (i) Tehsildar wanted Ramlal to send his daughters to school.

  (ii) Tehsildar wanted Ramlal to leave the village.

 (iii) Tehsildar wanted Ramlal to marry his daughter with his son.

 (iv) Tehsildar wanted Ramlal to send his son to city.

(c) For which occasion did Tehsildar perform the opening ceremony in the village?

   (i) Opening of the hospital

  (ii) Opening of the primary school

 (iii) Opening of the college

 (iv) Opening of the community center

(d) Identify a word from the above lines which means the same as 'audacity'.

   (i) Courage

  (ii) Disobey

 (iii) Last

 (iv) Said

(e) With which intention did Ramlal's wife said to him "I will tell you what to do?"

____

★ **are board exam questions from previous years**

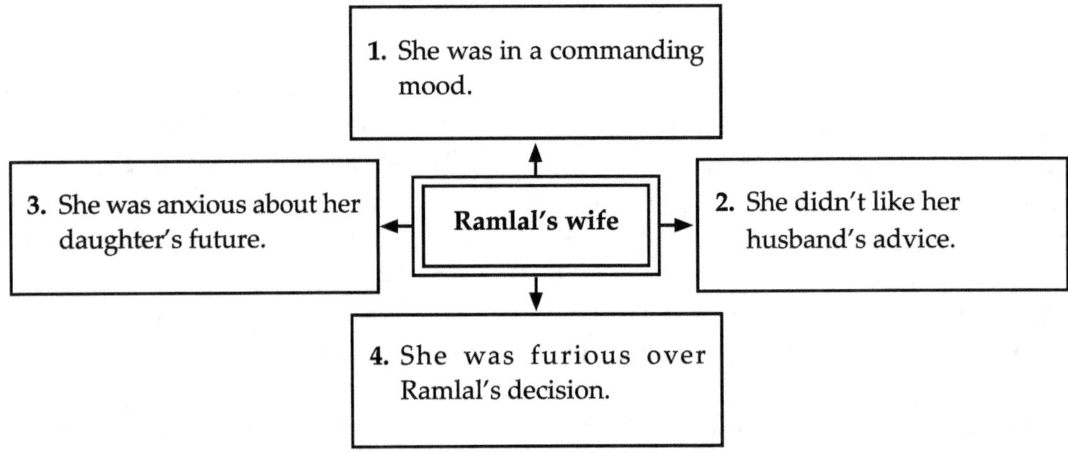

(i) Option 1   (ii) Option 2

(iii) Option 3   (iv) Option 4

Ans. (a) (ii) F – 2, 4 and M – 1, 3

(b) (i) Tehsildar wanted Ramlal to send his daughters to school.

(c) (ii) Opening of the primary school

(d) (i) Audacity

(e) (iii) Option 3

41. **Sweat broke out over her whole body. Would her stammering tongue again disgrace her? For the sake of this kind woman, however, she decided to make an effort. She had such a soothing voice; she would not laugh at her.**

(a) Pick the option that correctly classifies fact/s (F) and myths (M) in the options given below.

(i) F – 4, 1 and M – 2, 3

(ii) F – 1, 2 and M – 3, 4

(iii) F – 1, 3 and M – 2, 4

(iv) F – 2, 4 and M – 1, 3

(b) How did Bholi's stammering tongue disgrace her earlier?

(i) She wasn't able to sing properly.

(ii) She wasn't able to tell her name.

(iii) She wasn't able to spell her father's name friends.

(iv) She wasn't able to converse with her.

(c) Why was Bholi glad to go to school?

(i) She had the eagerness to learn many things.

(ii) She found her teacher friendly.

(iii) There she found many girls of her age.

(iv) She wanted to escape from household work.

(d) Identify a word from the above lines which means the same as 'Ignominy'.

(i) Disgrace

(ii) Stammering

(iii) Effort

(iv) Soothing

(e) 'She would not laugh at her', what does this tell about the nature of the teacher?

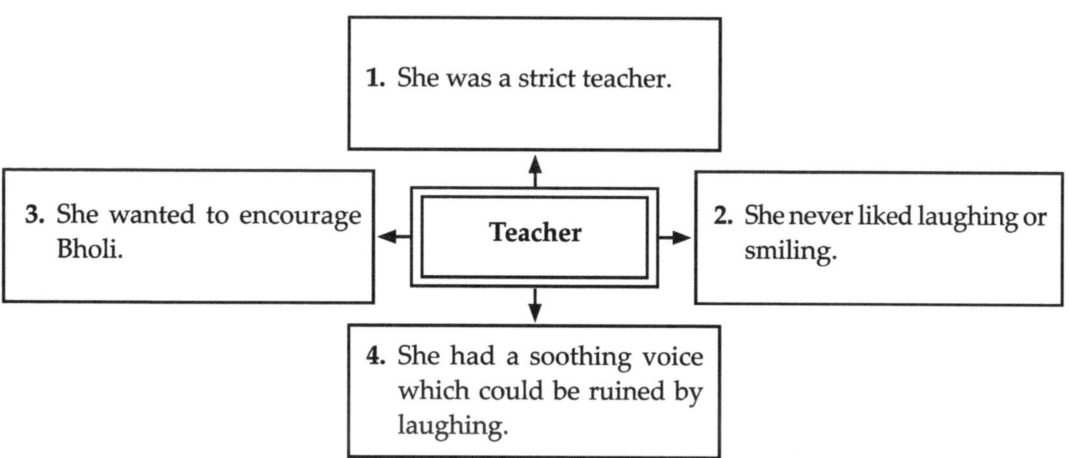

   (i) Option 1   (ii) Option 2

   (iii) Option 3   (iv) Option 4

Ans. (a) (iii) F – 1, 3 and M – 2, 4

   (b) (ii) She wasn't able to tell her name.

   (c) (iii) There she found many girls of her age.

   (d) (i) Disgrace

   (e) (iii) Option 3

42. "What's the matter with you, you fool?" shouted Ramlal. "I am only taking you to school." Then he told his wife, "Let her wear some decent clothes today, or else what will the teachers and the other schoolgirls think of us when they see her?"

New clothes had never been made for Bholi. The old dresses of her sisters were passed on to her.

(a) What did Ramlal want his wife to do?

(b) Why was Bholi scared of school?

Ans. (a) Ramlal asked his wife to get Bholi ready into some decent clothes than what she wears usually, so the teachers and other schoolgirls don't think poorly of Bholi's family.

   (b) Bholi was scared to go to school as she didn't know what a school was like, what happens there, actually, she had no idea of a school altogether.

43. **Bishamber Nath was a well-to-do grocer. He came with a big party of friends and relations with him for the wedding. A brass-band playing a popular tune from an Indian film headed the procession, with the bridegroom riding a decorated horse. Ramlal was overjoyed to see such pomp and splendour. He had never dreamt that his fourth daughter would have such a grand wedding. Bholi's elder sisters who had come for the occasion were envious of her luck.**

(a) What was Ramlal's reaction to the wedding decor?

(b) Why were Bholi's elder sisters envious of her luck?

Ans. (a) Ramlal had almost no hopes for his fourth daughter, Bholi. He never dreamt of her to have such a grand wedding. He was delighted with the pomp and splendour of the event.

   (b) Seeing the pomp and show of Bholi's ceremony, her elder sisters felt jealous as they were envious of her grand wedding as they never expected it for her.

❏❏